# 1989  Tahoe  Sierra  update

**p. 18**: Lake Tahoe Basin Management Unit. Their new address is P.O. Box 731002, South Lake Tahoe, CA 95731-7302.

**p. 19, col. 1, line 2**: topographic map should be topographic maps.

**p. 124-136**: New trailhead for Hikes 35-38, 41. To reach this lot by vehicle, take the Interstate 80 exit signed for Castle Peak and Boreal Ridge. This is the first exit west of the interstate's two safety roadside rest areas, and it is the first exit east of the Soda Springs exit. Immediately south of the eastbound lanes' onramp and offramp, you'll reach an obvious road which you follow 0.3 mile east to its end at the trailhead parking lot. From the lot, you hike 300 yards eastward to a nature trail (first paragraph of route description in Hike 41), go $^1/_4$ mile up along it, then leave it at a junction. There, just above a shallow, murky lakelet, you make a 200-yard traverse east to a junction with the PCT, this spot being $^1/_4$ mile south of Interstate 80.

**p. 132, col. 1, par. 2, line 5**: Views north and northwest should be views north and north*east*.

**p. 134**: Map 17. Along the top edge of the map should be the label "see Map 5" and along its right edge should be the label "see Map 16."

**p. 173 and 225**: Fallen Leaf Lodge site. The lodge is now back in operation. For more information, write to Fallen Leaf Lake Lodge, P.O. Box 8879, South Lake Tahoe, CA 95731, or phone (916) 541-6330.

**p.297-301**: Tahoe Rim Trail. More miles of the trail continue to be built. Here's where the route stood in late summer, 1988.

## Highway 89 to Highway 207

The trail goes to Armstrong Pass and beyond. Hopefully you'll be able to hike to Star Lake in 1989.

## Highway 207 to Highway 50

South from Highway 50, a completely waterless stretch goes about 8 miles to a saddle (center of Section 31) that is about one mile south-southwest of Genoa Peak. You should hike about 5 miles south up to the northwest edge of South Camp Peak, which is more of a plateau than a peak. The views from the northwest edge rival those of Mt. Tallac and Snow Valley Peak.

## Highway 50 to Highway 431

North from Highway 50, a completely waterless stretch goes about 4 miles north to a saddle at the south end of Snow Valley Peak's long, south ridge. From the saddle a flagged side trail descends about 1.3 miles to North Canyon's backcountry campground (p. 290, col. 1). Hopefully, this trail will be hikeable in 1989, and hopefully the TRT north from the saddle also will be built a mile north to the saddle with Snow Valley Peak's jeep road. You'll then be able to do two loop routes, using the TRT and the North Canyon road. From the jeep road saddle, about 3 miles of TRT are completed, the route dying out near a broad saddle southeast of Marlette Peak.

## Highway 431 to Highway 267

Unbuilt and unchanged.

## Highway 267 to Highway 89

About 7 miles of essentially waterless trail have been built from Tahoe City north to Painted Rock and beyond toward Mt. Watson.

## Highway 89 to Luther Pass

Unchanged.

# The Tahoe Sierra

A Natural History Guide to 106 Hikes

in the Northern Sierra

Jeffrey P. Schaffer

First edition 1975
Second printing 1977
Third printing 1978
Revised fourth printing 1979
Second edition 1984
THIRD EDITION 1987

Photographs, maps and design by the author
Topographic maps revised and updated by the author,
  based on U.S. Geological Survey maps

Library of Congress Card Catalog Number 87-6198
International Standard Book Number 0-89997-082-6

Manufactured in the United States of America

Published by Wilderness Press
          2440 Bancroft Way
          Berkeley, CA 94704

          (415) 843-8080

          Write for free catalog

**Dedication**
This book is affectionately dedicated to
Francis and Lorraine Schaffer,
my parents,
who let me as a boy roam the hills
and
encouraged me to study nature.

*Front cover:* Fannette Island in Lake Tahoe's Emerald Bay
*Title page:* Cascade Lake, Emerald Bay, Lake Tahoe
  and the Carson Range, as seen from Mt. Tallac

Library of Congress Cataloging-in-Publication Data

Schaffer, Jeffrey P.
   The Tahoe Sierra.

   Bibliography: p.
   Includes index.
   1. Hiking--Sierra Nevada Mountains (Calif. and Nev.)
--Guide-books.  2. Rock climbing--Sierra Nevada
Mountains (Calif. and Nev.)--Guide-books.  3. Natural
history--Sierra Nevada Mountains (Calif. and Nev.)
4. Sierra Nevada Mountains (Calif. and Nev.--
Description and travel--Guide-books.  I. Title.
GV199.42.S55S3  1987        917.94'4        87-6198
ISBN 0-89997-082-6

# Contents

# Acknowledgments

In the first edition and its three subsequent printings, I acknowledged four professors at my alma mater, the University of California, Berkeley. Garniss Curtis (Geology Department) gave me a better understanding of the area's volcanic history. Mitchell Reynolds (also of the Geology Department, but later with the U.S. Geological Survey) was unrelenting in pushing me to my limits of field-mapping ability—hence my obsession with producing accurate maps. Theodore Oberlander (Geography Department) also helped my field mapping by sharpening my interpretation of topographic maps. Finally, Robert Stebbins (retired from the Zoology Department) verified my conclusions about certain reptiles.

For the second edition one or more of the manuscript's chapters were sent to various government employees for review—a procedure which proved to be necessary. Those people reviewing a substantial part of the manuscript were: Keith Thurlkill and Glenn Hampton (USFS Lake Tahoe Basin Management Unit), Robert K. Henley (Eldorado N.F.) and Doug Hatch and Ann Westling (Tahoe N.F.). Checking smaller portions of the manuscript were: Karl Stein and Harlow Scott (Eldorado N.F.), Edwin Gregg, Andrea Holland and Robert G. Lancaster (Tahoe N.F.), R.W. Jessen (Plumas N.F.), Dale R. Gerry (Toiyabe N.F.), Woody Banks and Dave Harris (B.L.M., Folsom District Office), Brenda Boswell (Cal. Dept. Parks & Rec.), Mike Callen (Malakoff Diggins S.H.P.), K.R. Fetherston (Sugar Pine Point S.P.) and James H. Ryan (Cal. Dept. Fish & Game).

The geology chapter was reviewed in its original form by Scott A. Mathieson (U.S. Geological Survey). This was later greatly shortened and simplified, resulting in the current chapter. For the botany chapter I was very fortunate to have the Tahoe area's foremost botanist, Gladys L. Smith, review it—and review some of my wildflower photos to verify their identities.

George Cardinet, Jr., a past president of the California State Horsemen's Association, is one of the driving forces for the construction of the Tahoe Rim Trail, and he reviewed my material on that subject. As members of the Tahoe Rim Trail Association, both of us plan to see this project through to completion.

Working in the mountains can be a lonely task, so it is good when you can get someone to share your hiking and camping activities, plus shuttle you around the terrain. For all of my nine guidebooks, Ken Ng has helped me in my field work for at least a week or more—sometimes for as much as two months. For the second edition my wife, Bonnie Myhre, accompanied me on two trips. However, for most of the summer she patiently endured the time alone, and in the fall, winter and spring gave me moral support to help bring this project to its completion. She also provided support, both in the field and at home, during the summers of '84, '85 and '86, when I was working on the latest edition. Finally, I would like to thank "Mac" Magary (USFS Lake Tahoe Basin Management Unit) and Vicki Raucci (Tahoe Rim Trail's Executive Director), who both provided me with last-minute updates on the state of the Tahoe Rim Trail.

—Jeffrey P. Schaffer
Hercules, California
January 1987

# Part One    Introductory Chapters

Lake Tahoe, viewed from the Rubicon Trail in D.L. Bliss State Park

**Waterfall at union of Umpa Lake and Twin Lakes creeks**

# Ch. 1                 Introduction

**The Tahoe Sierra**   Due to its unique mode of origin Lake Tahoe greatly surpasses all other Sierra Nevada lakes in area and depth. Indeed, the lake ranks as one of the world's great lakes; few mountain lakes are larger, and few lakes at any elevation are deeper. Each summer, multitudes of bathers and boaters flock to its shores, while thousands of hikers explore its rim of snow-capped mountains.

This book is mainly about the trails in and around the Lake Tahoe Basin. However, the area defined by the author as the Tahoe Sierra is considerably larger. The northern limit is fairly easy to define: Plumas-Eureka State Park. Beyond this park you enter prime Feather River country, and both the quantity and quality of natural lakes decrease dramatically. In that country the best recreation lakes are man-made: Little Grass Valley Reservoir, Bucks Lake and Lake Almanor.

The south boundary of the Tahoe Sierra is harder to define. Carson Pass is only a mile south of the Lake Tahoe Basin rim, so it had to be included. After all, the quickest way into the basin's southern lakes is from the Carson Pass environs. But the best trails from the Carson Pass area lead south, away from the basin, climbing up to lakes below the ruins of an old volcano, Round Top peak. These lakes, which are within the northern part of Mokelumne Wilderness, are too alluring to be omitted. Here, along an east-west ridge dominated by Round Top, the Tahoe Sierra's southern boundary was drawn. Mokelumne Wilderness, like the Tahoe Sierra's Desolation Wilderness, is blessed with lakes, though except for the northern ones, most are quite small, typically one to several acres in size. An exception is 16-acre Fourth of July Lake, which is about a mile southwest of Round Top, and it is included in this book. Southeast of Round Top the West Fork Carson River drainage gives way to the East Fork drainage, and one enters the Blue Lakes area, which is popular among car campers, who have come mostly to fish. Hikers and equestrians are certainly in the minority.

The Tahoe Sierra's east boundary lies along the Sierra Nevada's east edge, where its mountain vegetation gives way to Great Basin vegetation. In the Lake Tahoe area proper, this edge is along the east base of the Carson Range, which is a subsidiary range of the Sierra Nevada. If it stood isolated, the Carson Range would be fairly impressive, for in stature it equals southern California's highest range, the San Bernardino Mountains.

The western boundary is poorly defined. The author would have liked to cover all the trails down through the lower montane forest to its western edge, which lies at roughly 1000-2000 feet elevation. Unfortunately, few good trails exist in this land of tall pines and firs. The land has been extensively utilized, first by miners, then by loggers, and presently by Californians enlarging their cities. This latest commercial episode presents grave danger to the forest and its associated plants and animals. At present only one sizable park exists—Malakoff Diggins. Much more parkland is needed if we are to preserve the native plants and animals. Deer in particular are going to be hampered as their migratory routes get blocked by suburban condos, residential subdivisions and recreation communities.

**Scope and purpose of this book**  This guide-book has four purposes. First, it is primarily a guide to virtually all the trails in the Tahoe Sierra that are, in the author's opinion, worth hiking. While most of the area's trails above 6000 feet are worth hiking, most of them below this elevation are not. In fact, if you were to rely on USGS 15′ topographic maps to locate these lower trails, you'd be in for many disappointments. Over half of the trails shown on these maps no longer exist and many others have been substantially altered. Above 6000 feet the situation is reversed. New trails have been built, and they aren't shown on the popular USGS 15′ maps. The longest new trail is the Pacific Crest Trail, which runs for about 143 miles through the Tahoe Sierra. However, an even longer Tahoe Sierra route, the Tahoe Rim Trail (Chapter 17), is being constructed, and when it is completed it will undoubtedly be one of California's most scenic and most used trails. While this guidebook is aimed primarily at hikers, who will compose the great majority of its users, it is also intended for equestrians.

Second, this book is a natural history of the Tahoe Sierra. As a matter of opinion, the author considers the book more of a natural-history guide than a trail guide. If the natural history were omitted, the book would be only half as heavy as it now is (which, for some hikers, is not a bad idea). The geology chapter is extensive so that you can appreciate all the major changes in the Tahoe landscape over its entire existence. The botany chapter introduces you to the area's major plant communities, to all its conifers, and to over 70 of its common wildflowers. The zoology chapter completes the natural-history triad. Hopefully, each will be thought-provoking. In addition to these chapters I've mentioned the common rocks and vegetation seen along virtually every hike. In many hikes I've elaborated on the local natural history, particularly on summits from which you see much of the landscape. Up high the assemblage of plants is quite different from that in mid-elevation lands, so I've included additional wildflower plates. In all, over 150 wildflowers are illustrated.

Third, this is a fishing guide. In Chapter 4 virtually all the named lakes that you can reach by trail, plus ones near the trailheads, have been included in a chart, which shows the kind of trout you can expect to catch at each lake. However, because this book is more of a trail guide than a fishing guide, it does omit the lower-elevation

lakes which are frequented by car campers. The following Table of Activities indicates the hikes along which you can do some fishing.

Last, this book is a climbing guide. Since the late 1960s the vertical walls of Yosemite Valley have been overpopulated with climbers. Looking for new, less crowded routes, climbers have often turned to the high country of the central Sierra, but not until the early 1970s did they actively pursue possibilities near and around the Tahoe Basin. (Lovers Leap and Sugarloaf, both above Highway 50 near Strawberry, are two exceptions, having been popular even back in the 1960s.) For climbers in search of isolated climbing areas in the northern Sierra, this guide identifies almost all the faces that can be reached by trail. The Table of Activities identifies the appropriate hikes.

**Selecting your hike**  If you are familiar with the Tahoe region, you may already know which of this book's 100+ hikes will interest you. If you are only vaguely familiar or unfamiliar with the region, then you can make an acquaintance with it by reading each hiking chapter's introduction, which tells you what you can expect in that particular area. Alternatively, you can get a brief idea of what to expect by referring to the two following tables, which list some general characteristics of every hike in the book. Once you select a hike, read its description and see if it still sounds appealing.

The first table lists each hike's classification plus activities you can do while on it. The classification ranges from an easy 1A to a hard 5E. The numbers refer to each hike's mileage, the letters to the net elevation gain:

| | | | |
|---|---|---|---|
| 1 = | 0.0– 4.9 miles | A = | 0– 499 feet |
| 2 = | 5.0– 9.9 miles | B = | 500– 999 feet |
| 3 = | 10.0–14.9 miles | C = | 1000–1999 feet |
| 4 = | 15.0–19.9 miles | D = | 2000–2999 feet |
| 5 = | 20.0+ miles | E = | 3000+ feet |

"Net gain" is the difference between the hike's highest and lowest elevations. In reality, you may do a lot more gaining, particularly on the longer hikes, along which you may climb and descend a number of ridges and hills. Nevertheless, net gain does give you a rough estimate of the climbing involved. The distance given for each hike is for the destination most people are likely to visit, which is usually, though not always, the farthest point. The distance, in most cases, is the total distance to and from the main destination, not just a one-way hike.

In the first table a plus (+) indicates that a certain activity can be found along a hike; a minus (−) indicates it can't be found. Four straight minuses don't mean a hike is completely unrewarding. Hike 30, for example, has four straight minuses, yet it stands out because it is the *only* hike that goes to giant sequoias. If a hike were indeed unrewarding, it wouldn't be in this book.

Where there is water there are usually, but not always, fishing and swimming opportunities. In like manner the presence of a lake doesn't always mean these two activities are available. No one, for instance, would knowingly swim in leech-infested Bloodsucker Lake (Hike 70), nor can you swim in some shallow lakes and creeks. The Independence Trail (Hike 1) does take you to some large potholes, which are adequate for frolicking but are certainly too small for swimming laps. If you're more interested in fishing than in swimming, you'll want to consult Chapter 4, which is devoted to this subject.

Most hikes give you views, some give you good views. Summit views, as used in the table, are those obtained from a distinctive summit—views which alone make the hike worth the effort.

Rock climbing can be done in many places in the Tahoe Sierra, but much of it wouldn't be worth your effort. In this table rock climbing is limited to hikes that pass cliffs worth climbing, and these hikes specifically identify these good cliffs. (In some cases two or more hikes may go along a certain stretch of trail. In such instances the climbing potential is usually mentioned only in the first of these hikes.)

The second table lists sights, which should help photographers and nature lovers plan their hikes. *Lake* is taken to mean any large body of water, natural or man-made. A hike with only ponds along it would be classified as minus (−) for lakes.

Rocks are divided into three groups: granitic, metamorphic and volcanic. Granitic rocks are the most common rock type. Volcanic rocks are the least common of the three, but where they occur, they are usually very conspicuous and are often the dominant rock type. Sedimentary rocks, which are rare in the entire Sierra Nevada, are not included. The largest exposures of these rocks are found in Hike 5, which explores the Malakoff Diggins.

Vegetation, too, is divided into three groups: lower montane, upper montane and subalpine. The first is a low-elevation forest whose dominant species include ponderosa pine, white fir, sugar pine, incense-cedar, Douglas-fir and black oak. The second is a mid-elevation forest that includes Jeffrey pine, red fir, western white pine and western juniper. The third is a high-elevation *sparse* forest that includes whitebark pine, some mountain hemlock, and occasionally some marginally alpine shrubs and herbs.

Finally, historical places are mentioned for the sake of history buffs. Each hike with a plus (+) is one that contains an elaboration of the history of that hike's nearby area and/or related areas, or that visits historic structures, such as the Vikingsholm (Hike 54).

**Interpreting each hike's basic data**   Certain data are given at the beginning of each hike. The first two are *distance(s)* and *low/high elevations,* which are quite obvious. The third category, *classification,* is a bit subjective. Hikes range from "very easy" to "very strenuous," though most of them fit in the "moderate" range. Four parameters were used in determining the classification rating: length, elevation gain, steepness of trail and altitude of trail (at high elevations, you tire more easily).

*Season* is the period of the year you should be able to drive to a trailhead and then hike an essentially snow-free trail. Weather varies considerably from year to year, so that the hiking season may be shorter or longer, depending largely on whether the winter-spring precipitation (most of it as snow) has been above or below normal.

Tahoe Sierra summer days are usually ideal at higher elevations, warming up to the 70s during the day and cooling down to the 40s by sunrise. Rain is in the form of sporadic thunderstorms, which may occur daily for a whole week or more, or, more likely, may not occur for weeks at a time. Generally, the morning is cloudless, but clouds build up in the afternoon, only to dissipate around dusk. At lower elevations, such as at Malakoff Diggins, daytime temperatures soar into the 90s, and such an area is best visited during cooler months unless you specifically intend to go sunbathing and/or swimming.

Those who like to go swimming will generally find lakes warmer than nearby streams. Most lakes warm up to the 60s—a few even topping 70°F—and almost all are at their maximum in late July through mid-August. Rivers and streams, continuously being fed by cold ground water, rarely get above the low 50s.

# Table of Activities

| Hike | Classification | Fishing | Swimming | Summit views | Rock climbing | Hike | Classification | Fishing | Swimming | Summit views | Rock climbing |
|---|---|---|---|---|---|---|---|---|---|---|---|
| 1 | 1A | − | − | − | − | 55 | 1A | − | − | − | − |
| 2 | 3A | + | + | − | − | 56 | 1A | − | − | − | − |
| 3 | 2B | + | + | − | − | 57 | 1A | + | + | − | − |
| 4 | 1C | + | + | − | − | 58 | 1C | + | + | − | − |
| 5 | 1A | − | − | − | − | 59 | 3B | + | + | + | − |
| 6 | 1A | + | + | − | − | 60 | 5B | + | + | − | − |
| 7 | 2A | − | − | − | − | 61 | 1A | + | + | − | − |
| 8 | 1A | + | − | − | − | 62 | 2A | + | + | − | − |
| 9 | 2C | − | − | − | − | 63 | 3C | + | + | − | − |
| 10 | 3D | + | − | − | − | 64 | 4C | + | + | − | + |
| 11 | 1A | + | − | − | − | 65 | 5C | + | + | − | + |
| 12 | 4E | − | − | + | − | 66 | 5D | + | + | − | + |
| 13 | 2E | − | − | + | − | 67 | 2C | + | + | − | − |
| 14 | 2C | + | + | − | − | 68 | 2C | + | + | − | − |
| 15 | 1B | + | + | − | − | 69 | 2C | + | + | − | + |
| 16 | 2C | − | − | + | − | 70 | 1B | − | − | − | − |
| 17 | 2B | + | + | − | − | 71 | 3E | + | + | + | + |
| 18 | 1B | + | + | − | − | 72 | 3E | + | + | + | − |
| 19 | 1B | + | + | − | − | 73 | 2D | − | − | + | − |
| 20 | 1A | + | + | − | − | 74 | 3D | + | + | + | − |
| 21 | 1A | + | + | − | − | 75 | 5C | + | + | − | − |
| 22 | 1A | + | + | − | + | 76 | 5D | + | + | − | + |
| 23 | 2B | + | + | − | + | 77 | 2C | + | + | − | + |
| 24 | 3C | + | + | + | + | 78 | 2C | + | + | + | − |
| 25 | 1A | + | − | − | − | 79 | 2E | + | + | + | − |
| 26 | 1A | + | − | − | − | 80 | 1B | + | + | − | − |
| 27 | 4D | + | + | + | + | 81 | 3E | + | + | + | − |
| 28 | 1C | + | + | + | + | 82 | 3C | + | + | − | − |
| 29 | 1A | + | − | − | − | 83 | 3C | + | + | − | − |
| 30 | 1A | − | − | − | − | 84 | 2D | + | + | + | − |
| 31 | 1A | + | + | − | − | 85 | 2C | + | + | + | + |
| 32 | 2B | + | + | − | − | 86 | 3C | − | − | + | + |
| 33 | 2B | + | + | + | + | 87 | 3C | + | + | − | + |
| 34 | 2C | + | + | − | + | 88 | 3C | + | − | − | − |
| 35 | 4C | + | + | − | − | 89 | 4C | + | + | − | − |
| 36 | 4C | + | + | − | + | 90 | 1B | − | − | − | − |
| 37 | 1A | + | + | − | + | 91 | 2C | + | + | − | + |
| 38 | 4B | + | + | − | − | 92 | 2B | + | + | − | + |
| 39 | 1B | − | − | + | − | 93 | 3A | + | + | − | − |
| 40 | 2A | − | − | − | − | 94 | 2B | + | + | + | − |
| 41 | 2A | − | + | − | + | 95 | 1A | + | + | − | + |
| 42 | 4D | + | + | − | + | 96 | 2B | + | + | − | − |
| 43 | 3C | − | − | + | + | 97 | 2D | + | + | + | − |
| 44 | 4D | − | − | + | + | 98 | 2C | + | + | − | − |
| 45 | 4D | + | + | + | + | 99 | 2B | + | + | − | − |
| 46 | 1C | + | + | − | − | 100 | 3C | − | − | − | + |
| 47 | 2C | + | − | − | + | 101 | 1B | − | − | − | − |
| 48 | 4C | + | − | − | + | 102 | 2E | − | − | + | + |
| 49 | 2C | − | − | + | + | 103 | 4E | + | + | + | + |
| 50 | 3D | + | + | + | − | 104 | 3D | − | + | + | − |
| 51 | 3D | − | − | + | + | 105 | 3C | − | − | + | − |
| 52 | 4C | + | + | − | − | 106 | 5E | + | + | + | + |
| 53 | 2A | + | + | − | + | | | | | | |
| 54 | 1A | + | + | − | − | | | | | | |

# Table of Sights

| Hike | Lakes | Granitic | Metamorphic | Volcanic | Lower Montane | Upper Montane | Subalpine | History |
|---|---|---|---|---|---|---|---|---|
| 1 | − | + | + | − | + | − | − | − |
| 2 | − | − | + | − | + | − | − | − |
| 3 | − | − | + | − | + | − | − | − |
| 4 | − | − | + | − | + | − | − | − |
| 5 | − | − | + | − | + | − | − | + |
| 6 | + | − | + | − | + | − | − | + |
| 7 | − | − | + | + | + | − | − | − |
| 8 | − | − | + | − | + | − | − | − |
| 9 | − | − | + | + | + | + | − | − |
| 10 | − | + | + | − | + | + | − | − |
| 11 | − | − | + | − | + | − | − | − |
| 12 | − | − | + | − | + | + | + | − |
| 13 | − | − | + | − | + | + | + | + |
| 14 | + | − | + | − | − | + | − | + |
| 15 | + | − | + | − | − | + | − | − |
| 16 | + | − | + | − | − | + | + | − |
| 17 | + | − | + | − | − | + | − | − |
| 18 | + | − | + | − | − | + | − | − |
| 19 | + | − | + | − | − | + | − | − |
| 20 | + | − | + | − | − | + | − | − |
| 21 | + | − | + | − | − | + | − | − |
| 22 | + | − | + | − | − | + | − | − |
| 23 | + | − | + | − | − | + | − | − |
| 24 | + | − | + | − | − | + | − | − |
| 25 | + | − | + | − | + | + | − | − |
| 26 | + | − | + | − | + | + | − | − |
| 27 | + | − | + | + | + | + | − | + |
| 28 | + | − | + | − | − | + | − | + |
| 29 | − | − | + | − | + | + | − | − |
| 30 | − | − | + | − | + | − | − | − |
| 31 | + | + | + | − | − | + | − | − |
| 32 | + | + | + | − | − | + | − | − |
| 33 | + | + | + | + | − | + | − | − |
| 34 | + | − | + | − | − | + | − | − |
| 35 | + | + | − | + | − | + | − | − |
| 36 | + | + | − | + | − | + | + | − |
| 37 | + | + | − | − | − | + | − | − |
| 38 | + | + | + | + | − | + | − | − |
| 39 | − | + | + | + | − | + | − | − |
| 40 | − | + | + | + | − | + | − | − |
| 41 | + | + | − | − | − | + | − | − |
| 42 | + | + | + | + | − | + | − | − |
| 43 | − | + | − | + | − | + | + | − |
| 44 | − | + | + | + | − | + | + | − |
| 45 | + | + | − | + | − | + | − | − |
| 46 | + | + | − | + | − | + | − | − |
| 47 | − | + | + | + | + | + | − | − |
| 48 | − | + | + | + | + | + | − | − |
| 49 | − | + | + | + | + | + | + | − |
| 50 | + | + | + | + | − | + | + | − |
| 51 | − | + | − | + | − | + | + | − |
| 52 | + | + | − | − | + | + | − | − |
| 53 | + | + | − | − | + | + | − | − |
| 54 | + | + | − | − | + | + | − | + |
| 55 | − | + | − | − | − | + | − | − |
| 56 | − | + | − | − | + | + | − | + |
| 57 | + | + | − | − | − | + | − | − |
| 58 | + | + | − | − | − | + | − | − |
| 59 | + | + | + | + | − | + | − | − |
| 60 | + | + | − | + | − | + | − | − |
| 61 | + | + | − | − | − | + | − | − |
| 62 | + | + | − | − | − | + | − | − |
| 63 | + | + | − | − | − | + | − | − |
| 64 | + | + | + | − | − | + | − | − |
| 65 | + | + | + | − | − | + | − | − |
| 66 | + | + | + | − | − | + | + | − |
| 67 | + | + | − | − | − | + | − | − |
| 68 | + | + | − | − | − | + | − | − |
| 69 | + | + | − | − | − | + | − | − |
| 70 | + | + | − | − | − | + | − | − |
| 71 | + | + | − | − | − | + | + | − |
| 72 | + | + | − | − | − | + | + | − |
| 73 | − | + | − | − | − | + | + | − |
| 74 | + | + | − | − | − | + | + | − |
| 75 | + | + | − | + | − | + | − | − |
| 76 | + | + | − | − | − | + | − | − |
| 77 | + | + | − | − | − | + | − | − |
| 78 | + | + | − | − | − | + | − | − |
| 79 | + | + | + | − | − | + | + | − |
| 80 | + | + | + | − | − | + | − | − |
| 81 | + | + | + | − | − | + | + | − |
| 82 | + | + | + | − | − | + | − | − |
| 83 | + | + | + | − | − | + | − | − |
| 84 | + | + | + | − | − | + | + | − |
| 85 | + | + | − | − | − | + | + | − |
| 86 | − | + | − | − | − | + | + | − |
| 87 | + | + | − | − | − | + | − | − |
| 88 | + | + | − | − | − | + | − | − |
| 89 | + | + | − | + | − | + | + | − |
| 90 | − | + | − | − | − | + | − | + |
| 91 | + | + | + | + | − | + | − | − |
| 92 | + | + | − | + | − | + | − | − |
| 93 | + | + | − | + | − | + | + | − |
| 94 | + | + | − | + | − | + | + | − |
| 95 | + | + | − | + | − | + | − | − |
| 96 | + | + | − | + | − | + | + | − |
| 97 | + | + | − | + | − | + | + | − |
| 98 | + | + | − | + | − | + | + | − |
| 99 | + | + | − | + | − | + | + | − |
| 100 | − | + | − | + | − | + | + | − |
| 101 | − | + | − | − | − | + | − | + |
| 102 | − | + | − | − | − | + | + | − |
| 103 | + | + | − | − | − | + | + | − |
| 104 | + | + | + | − | − | + | − | − |
| 105 | − | + | − | + | − | + | + | − |
| 106 | + | + | + | + | + | + | + | + |

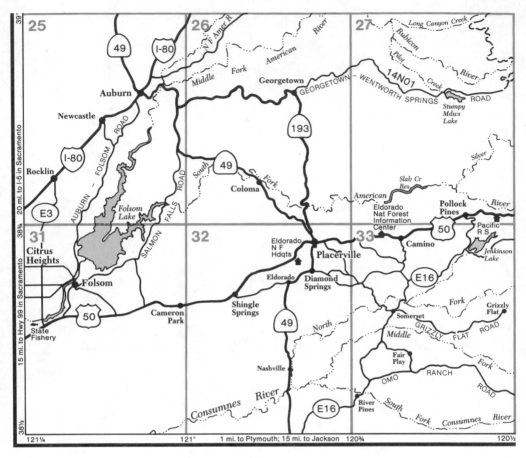

# A General Map of the TAHOE SIERRA

### Index to *Tahoe Sierra* Topographic Maps

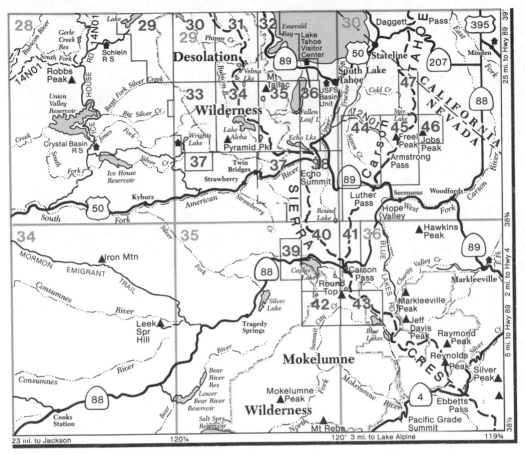

# and Vicinity

## U.S. Geological Survey 15' Topographic Maps
### (Numbers 1–36 of the light grid)

| | | | |
|---|---|---|---|
| 1 | Bucks Lake | 19 | Grass Valley |
| 2 | Quincy | 20 | Colfax |
| 3 | Blairsden | 21 | Duncan Peak |
| 4 | Portola | 22 | Granite Chief |
| 5 | Chilcoot | 23 | Tahoe |
| 6 | Dogskin Mountain | 24 | Carson City |
| 7 | Mooreville Ridge | 25 | Auburn |
| 8 | Downieville | 26 | Georgetown |
| 9 | Sierra City | 27 | Saddle Mountain |
| 10 | Sierraville | 28 | Robbs Peak |
| 11 | Loyalton | 29 | Fallen Leaf Lake |
| 12 | Reno | 30 | Freel Peak |
| 13 | Nevada City | 31 | Folsom |
| 14 | Alleghany | 32 | Placerville |
| 15 | Emigrant Gap | 33 | Camino |
| 16 | Donner Pass | 34 | Leek Spring Hill |
| 17 | Truckee | 35 | Silver Lake |
| 18 | Mt. Rose | 36 | Markleeville |

### Legend

U.S. Geological Survey
15-minute topographic
map

*Tahoe Sierra* topographic map.
Index to these maps
on the opposite page.

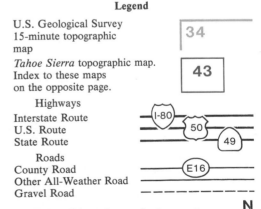

Highways
Interstate Route
U.S. Route
State Route

Roads
County Road
Other All-Weather Road
Gravel Road

U.S.F.S. Office or Ranger Station

0        5        10 mi

N

Declination averages 16½°e

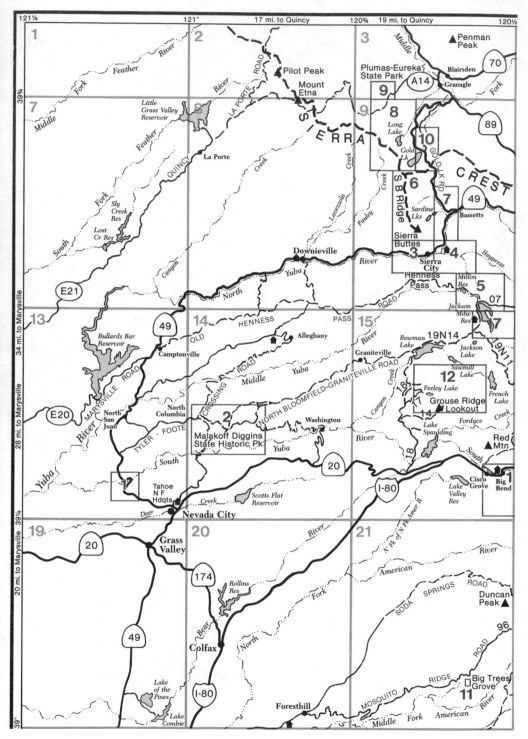

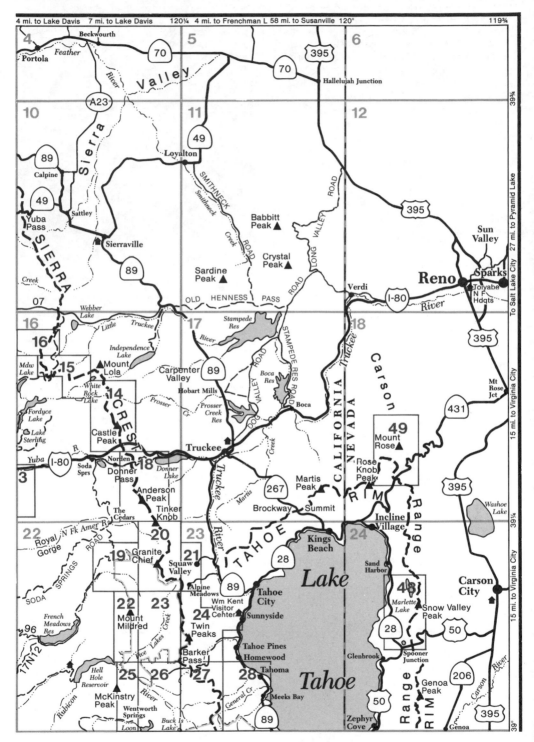

4

Beckwourth

Portola  *Feather*

70

Valley

5

395

70

Hallelujah Junction

39¾

10

A23

Sierra

11

49

Loyalton

12

SMITHNECK

ROAD

LONG VALLEY ROAD

395

To Salt Lake City  27 mi. to Pyramid Lake

89

Calpine

49

Yuba Pass

Sattley

Sierraville

89

*Creek*

SIERRA

Babbitt Peak ▲

Crystal Peak ▲

Sardine Peak ▲

Sun Valley

Reno  Sparks

Verdi  Tolyabe N F Hdqts

I-80  *River*

07

Webber Lake  *Little Truckee*

OLD  HENNESS  PASS

STAMPEDE RES ROAD

395

15 mi. to Virginia City

16

16

15

Mdw Lake

Independence Lake

Mount Lola ▲

White Rock Lake

Fordyce Lake

Lake Sterling

Yuba  I-80

Soda Sprs

3

17

Stampede Res

89

*River*

Carpenter Valley

Hobart Mills

Prosser Cr.

Prosser Creek Res

Truckee

Boca Res

DOG VALLEY ROAD

Boca

*Truckee*

18

CALIFORNIA

NEVADA

Carson

49

Mount Rose ▲

Mt Rose Jct

431

15 mi. to Virginia City

14 CREST

Castle Peak

Norden  18

Donner Pass  Donner Lake

Anderson Peak

Tinker Knob

*Truckee River*

*Martis Creek*

267

Martis Peak ▲

Brockway  Summit

Rose Knob Peak ▲

Incline Village

RIM

Range

395

22

Royal Gorge  N Fk Amer R.

SPRINGS ROAD

The Cedars

20

19

Granite Chief

21

Squaw Valley

89

23

Alpine Meadows

Wm Kent Visitor Center

TAHOE

28

Kings Beach

Lake

24

Sand Harbor

Carson City

48

Marlette Lake

Snow Valley Peak ▲

SODA

French Meadows Res

96

22

Mount Mildred ▲

*Tahoe Lakes Creek*

23

24

Twin Peaks

Tahoe City

Sunnyside

Tahoe Pines

Homewood

Tahoma

28

Glenbrook

Spooner Junction

50

17N12

Hell Hole Reservoir

*Rubicon*

25

26

McKinstry Peak ▲

Wentworth Springs

Loon

27

Barker Pass

*General Cr.*

28

Meeks Bay

89

Zephyr Cove

Tahoe

50

Range

RIM

Genoa Peak ▲

*Carson River*

206

395

Genoa

39¼

39

The *map* refers to the appropriate topographic map (or maps) that show the hike.
Where several maps are required, they are listed
in the order you will need them. On this chapter's four-page general map of the Tahoe Sierra,
all of the topographic maps are shown as well as
what page each appears on. Most of the maps
are at the same scale and are aligned so that the
map's north edge is along the top of the page.
Where a map is at a different scale, a scale bar is
given, and where the map is turned sideways, a
north-arrow is given. For all but Map 11, the
scale is about 1:42,100, which is about 1½
inches per mile (conversely, one mile equals ⅔
inch). A mileage scale bar is provided below.
Also, for all these topographic maps, the following legend applies.

### Legend

| | |
|---|---|
| Heavy-duty paved road | ─────────── |
| Medium-duty paved road | ─ ─ ─ ─ ─ ─ |
| Light-duty paved road | ═══════════ |
| Gravel road | ================= |
| Described trail | ─────────── |
| Other trail or jeep road | ─────────── |
| Permanent stream | ～～～～～～ |
| Seasonal stream | ─ ‥ ─ ‥ ─ ‥ ─ |
| Lake | ⬭ |

The *trailhead* mentions directions to the start
of each hike and usually mentions the amount of
parking space you can expect to find. In most
cases this space is adequate, but for some routes,
such as Hikes 4 and 58, it is virtually nonexistent. Finally, the *introduction* tells you what
you can expect. It is useful in your decision of
what trail to hike.

**Studying the map at the Pacific Crest/Tahoe-
Yosemite trail junction (Hikes 98-99)**

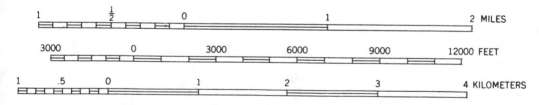

1     ½     0                    1                    2 MILES

3000        0        3000        6000        9000        12000 FEET

1   .5   0              1              2              3              4 KILOMETERS

# Ch. 2 Towns, Resorts, Lodges and Campgrounds

**Introduction** For camping and lodging, the Tahoe Sierra can be divided into two areas: lands within the Lake Tahoe Basin and lands outside it. Outside the basin the milieu is generally relaxed and tranquil. On the other hand, within the basin the setting is somewhat urban along the lake's north shore, and very urban along its south shore. To list all the basin's visitor-related facilities could in itself create a small guidebook, and hence will not be attempted. Despite an abundance of most services, the basin nevertheless has an insufficient number of campgrounds, at least during the summer. Particularly on summer weekends, a search for a campsite can be an exercise in futility, so think twice before dropping into the basin for a campsite. However, most of the basin's campgrounds, like its hotels, motels, resorts and lodges, do take reservations, and you can eliminate a lot of frustration by making them. Outside the basin you generally cannot make reservations for campsites, although you can (and should) make them for motels and resorts.

## Towns

The Tahoe Sierra's towns can be grouped according to the services they provide the visitor. The first category is the full-service town, which has everything—car dealerships, hospitals, government administrative offices, shopping centers—plus a broad assortment of gas stations, restaurants and motels. Auburn, Grass Valley-Nevada City, Placerville and South Lake Tahoe-Stateline certainly fit into this category, as does the swath of Tahoe's north-shore settlements, which extends from Tahoe City east to Incline Village. To a lesser extent the Donner Lake-Truckee settlements also qualify.

The second category is towns with one to several of each of the following: gas station, restaurant or coffee shop, motel or lodge, and general store or food market. Only the towns convenient for this book's users are considered. These are Downieville, Sierra City and Graeagle, all in the Chapter 9 area and most of Lake Tahoe's west-shore towns.

Finally, there are smaller settlements which offer gas or food or lodging, but not all three. Along Highway 49 there are North San Juan, which is not far past Nevada City, and Sierraville, which lies in a beautiful east-side agricultural valley. Neither is particularly tourist-oriented. Along Interstate 80 and Highway 50 there are a number of settlements—too many to mention. Most are merely a gas station and attendant cafe.

## Resorts and Lodges

In the author's opinion the best resorts and lodges are situated in the Highway 49 country. Some exist close to Downieville, but these aren't considered, since this book deals only with Highway 49 trails that are above Sierra City. Above that Gold Rush town, all the resorts occur in one area: along side roads branching west from the Gold Lake Road. Driving north on this broad, well-graded highway, you pass roads to Sardine Lake Resort (Map 7), Packer Lake Lodge and Salmon Lake Resort (both Map 6), and Gold Lake, Elwell and Gray Eagle lodges (all Map 8). The first three lie along lakeshores, while the last three lie closer to the Gold Lake Road but are nevertheless within a short walking distance of two or more lakes. When the snowpack begins to break up in June, the resorts usually open for business, and they generally stay open at least through the start of deer-hunting season, which is the last weekend in September.

Along Interstate 80 and its feeder roads there are no resorts which would cater to hikers other than at Donner Lake. Highway 50 is equally deficient in acceptable resorts, having only two candidates. The first is Camp Sacramento (Map 37), which is primarily for Sacramento's residents, although, if space is available, it does take nonresidents. The second is at the gateway to Desolation Wilderness: Echo Lake Resort (Map 36). Although each has its good points, neither can offer the solitude found at the Gold Lake Road resorts.

The Tahoe Sierra, as defined in this book, extends south to Highway 88. In this area you'll find popular, fishermen-oriented Caples Lake Resort (Map 40), which lies just across from a USFS campground. Silver Lake is just west of and outside the book's area, but it offers you several more resorts. In the opposite direction from Caples is Sorensen's Resort, which lies just east of the Highways 88/89 junction. Being on a busy road and not being within walking distance of any lake, it is the least desirable of the Highway 88 resorts.

Then there are three resorts in the southwest part of the Tahoe Basin that deserve mention. From south to north these are Angora Lakes Resort (Map 35), Camp Richardson (Map 32 inset), and Meeks Bay Resort (Map 28). Angora Lakes Resort is tiny and isolated, and perhaps because of its pleasant ambience it is always booked. For this summer-only resort you may have to make reservations a year in advance—if you can get any at all. The other two are readily accessible and have a longer season. Both Meeks Bay Resort and Camp Richardson lie along Lake Tahoe. Each has a small marina, and each is strongly oriented toward water sports. In addition, Camp Richardson has horse stables, with miles of horse trails awaiting the equestrian. There are also stables adjacent to Meeks Bay Resort.

# Campgrounds

Most of this book's users will stay at campgrounds rather than at lodges, resorts or motels. Consequently, the author has attempted to list all the appropriate Tahoe Sierra campgrounds. Out-of-the-way campgrounds, such as those in the lower parts of the Tahoe and Eldorado national forests, are omitted. If a campground appears on one of the book's topographic maps, that is indicated below. If you can make reservations at a campground, this too is indicated. Seasons are approximate, for they vary from year to year.

Some of the larger, more popular Forest Service campgrounds are now maintained by private corporations, and the result is that their camp fees are higher. Fallen Leaf Campground is one of the more expensive ones, because like all Tahoe Basin sites that produce sewage, its sewage must now be pumped out of the basin, which is quite expensive. Before 1985, when the Forest Service maintained all its campgrounds, the taxpayers picked up part of the bill.

## ELDORADO NATIONAL FOREST
**Caples Lake C.G.**   35 sites. 7840'. At Caples Lake. Open early July through mid-Oct. Map 40.

**Gerle Creek C.G.**   50 sites. 6300'. Entrance road is 2¾ mi. n. of Loon Lake Rd. jct. Open early June through mid-Oct.

**Ice House C.G.**   83 sites. 5450'. At Ice House Reservoir, e. of the Loon Lake Road. Open early June through mid-Oct.

**Kirkwood C.G.**   12 sites. 7680'. At Kirkwood Lake, which is between Silver and Caples lakes. Open early July through mid-Oct. Map 39.

**Loon Lake C.G.**   34 sites. 6430'. At Loon Lake. Open mid-June through mid-Sept. Map 29.

**Schneider Camping Area**   Primitive c.g. with several sites. 8300'. About 1¼ mi. n.w. of Caples Lake Maintenance Station, via rough rd. Open mid-July through mid-Oct. Map 40.

**Silver Creek C.G.**   11 sites. 5200'. About 9 mi. up Ice House Rd. Open early June through mid-Oct.

**Silver Lake C.G.**   97 sites. 7250'. Along Hwy. 88 near lake's n. shore. Open early July through mid-Oct.

**South Fork C.G.**   17 sites. 5160'. From a jct. 0.2 mi. n. of the Loon Lake Rd. jct., drive 1.2 mi. s.w. Open early June through mid-Oct.

**Sunset C.G.**   131 sites. 4850'. At Union Valley Reservoir. Open early June through mid-Oct.

**Wench Creek C.G.**   100 sites plus 2 group sites. 4900'. At Union Valley Reservoir. Open early June through mid-Oct.

**Wentworth Springs C.G.**   10 sites. 6160'. From the Loon Lake Rd. jct., drive n. 5½ mi. to Wentworth Springs Rd. and follow it 5 mi. e. Open mid-June through mid-Oct. Map 25.

**Woods Lake C.G.**   14 sites. 8240'. At Woods Lake. Open early July through mid-Oct. Map 40.

**Wrights Lake C.G.**   71 sites. 6940'. At Wrights Lake. Open mid-June through mid-Oct. Ticketron reservations from mid-July through early Sept. Map 33.

**Yellowjacket C.G.** 40 sites. 4900'. At Union Valley Reservoir. Open early June through mid-Oct.

## LAKE TAHOE BASIN MANAGEMENT UNIT (USFS)
**Bayview C.G.** 16 sites. 6850'. On Hwy. 89, above Emerald Bay. Open late May through mid-Oct. One-day limit; no drinking water. Map 32.
**Fallen Leaf C.G.** 206 sites. 6340'. Between Hwy. 89 and n. shore of Fallen Leaf Lake. Open mid-May through mid-Oct. Map 32.
**Meeks Bay C.G.** 40 sites. 6230'. At Meeks Bay. Open mid-June through mid-Sept. Map 28.
**William Kent C.G.** 95 sites. 6250'. Along Hwy. 89, 2¼ mi. s. of Tahoe City. Open May through Sept.

## PLUMAS NATIONAL FOREST
**Gold Lake Camping Area** Primitive c.g. with about 10 sites. 6420'. Along Gold Lake, just off Gold Lake Rd. Very poor rd. to c.g. Open July through mid-Oct. Map 10.
**Lakes Basin C.G.** 24 sites plus 1 group site. 6300'. About midway along Gold Lake Rd. Poor rd. through c.g. Open late June through Sept. Map 8.

## TAHOE NATIONAL FOREST
**Ahart C.G.** 17 sites. 5340'. About 1½ mi. above French Mdws. Res. See Hike 43 trailhead. Open early June through mid-Oct.
**Aspen C.G.** 15 sites plus 1 group site. 6100'. Jackson Mdw. Res. Open June through Oct. Map 5.
**Berger C.G.** Primitive c.g. with about 10 sites. 5940'. Along For. Rte. 93, about 2⅓ mi. above the Gold Lake Rd. jct. Open late June through mid-Oct. Map 6.
**Big Bend C.G.** 12 sites. 5730'. Behind Big Bend Ranger Station. Open late May through early Sept. Map 13.
**Bowman C.G.** Primitive c.g. with 15 sites. 5650'. Along Bowman Rd. 18, by e. shore of Bowman Lake. Open late June through mid-Oct. Map 12.
**Canyon Creek C.G.** 20 sites. 6000'. Midway between Sawmill and Faucherie lakes. Open late June through mid-Oct. Map 12.
**Carr Lake C.G.** 4 sites. 6700'. Primitive c.g. near end of F.S. Rd. 17. Open early July through mid-Oct. Map 12.
**Chapman Creek C.G.** 29 sites. 5840'. Along Hwy. 49, about 3¼ mi. above the Gold Lake Rd. jct. Open June to mid-Oct.

**Coyote Group C.G.** 4 sites. 5300'. Above n.e. corner of French Mdws. Res. See Hike 43 trailhead. Open June through Oct.
**Diablo Camping Area** Primitive c.g. with about 20 sites. 5900'. Along For. Rte. 93, about 2 mi. above the Gold Lake Rd. jct. Open late June through mid-Oct. Map 6.
**East Meadow C.G.** 46 sites. 6100'. Jackson Mdw. Res. Open June through Oct. Map 5.
**Faucherie Group C.G.** 1 site. 6100'. At Faucherie Lake. Open June through mid-Oct. Map 12.
**Findley C.G.** 15 sites. 6200'. Jackson Mdw. Res. Open June through Oct. Map 17.
**Fir Top C.G.** 12 sites. 6200'. Jackson Mdw. Res. Open June through Oct. Map 17.
**French Meadows C.G.** 75 sites. 5300'. Above s.e. shore of French Mdws. Res. See Hike 43 trailhead. Open early June through mid-Oct.
**Fuller Lake C.G.** 11 sites. 5350'. At lake, 4⅓ mi. n. of Hwy. 20 on Bowman Rd. 18. Open May through Oct. Map 12.
**Gates Group Camp** 3 sites. 5330'. About 1 mi. above French Mdws. Res. See Hike 43 trailhead. Open mid-June through mid-Oct.
**Goose Meadow C.G.** 30 sites. 5980'. Along Hwy. 89, about 5 mi. s. of I-80 (west Truckee exit). Open May through mid-Sept.
**Granite Flat C.G.** 75 sites. 5880'. Along Hwy. 89, about 2 mi. s. of I-80 (west Truckee exit). Open May through mid-Sept.
**Grouse Ridge C.G.** 9 sites. 7440'. Near end of rough F.S. Rd. 14. Open mid-July through mid-Oct. Map 12.
**Hampshire Rocks C.G.** 31 sites. 5890'. One mi. e. of Big Bend Ranger Station. Open early June through early Sept. Map 13.
**Indian Springs C.G.** 36 sites. 5500'. About 2 mi. n.w. of Cisco Grove. Open late May through mid-Oct.
**Jackson Creek C.G.** 14 sites. 5650'. Along Bowman Rd. 18, about ½ mi. e. of Bowman Lake. Open late June through mid-Oct.
**Lakeside C.G.** Primitive c.g. with about 30 sites. 5760'. Along Prosser Creek Res. Leave Hwy. 89 about 3⅔ mi. n. of I-80. Open late Apr. through late Oct.
**Lewis C.G.** 40 sites. 5350'. Above n.e. shore of French Mdws. Res. See Hike 43 trailhead. Open late May through late Oct.
**Lower Little Truckee C.G.** 15 sites. 6120'. Along Hwy. 89, 11¼ mi. n. of I-80. Open late May through early Nov.
**Packsaddle Camping Area** Primitive c.g. with about 20 sites. 6140'. Along For. Rte. 93, about 2¾ mi. above the Gold Lake Rd. jct. Open late June through mid-Oct. Map 6.

**Pass Creek C.G.**   30 sites. 6100'. Jackson Mdw. Res. Open June through Oct. Map 5.

**Poppy C.G.**   12 sites. 5300'. Above n. shore of French Mdws. Res. See Hike 43 trailhead. Open early June through mid-Oct.

**Prosser C.G.**   29 sites. 5770'. Near Prosser Creek Res. Leave Hwy. 89 about 3⅔ mi. n. of I-80. Open late May through mid-Oct.

**Salmon Creek C.G.**   33 sites. 5700'. Along s. part of Gold Lake Rd. Open mid-June through mid-Oct. Map 7.

**Sardine Lake C.G.**   29 sites. 5740'. Near s. part of Gold Lake Rd. Open mid-June through mid-Oct. Map 7.

**Sierra C.G.**   15 sites. 5670'. Along Hwy. 49, about 2 mi. above the Gold Lake Rd. jct. Open June through Oct.

**Silver Creek C.G.**   30 sites. 6060'. Along Hwy. 89, 1⅓ mi. n. of the Squaw Valley jct. Open mid-May through mid-Oct.

**Silver Tip Group C.G.**   2 sites. 6050'. Jackson Mdw. Res. Open June through Oct. Map 17.

**Snag Lake C.G.**   Primitive c.g. with about 16 sites. 6670'. Along Gold Lake Rd., 1½ mi. s.e. of Gold Lake. Open July through mid-Oct. Map 10.

**Sterling Lake C.G.**   5 sites. 7000'. At the lake, about 3 mi. above Woodchuck C.G. Open early July through early Sept.

**Talbot C.G.**   Primitive c.g. with 5 sites. 5600'. Near the Hike 43 trailhead. Open mid-June through mid-Oct. Map 19.

**Union Flat C.G.**   18 sites. 3380'. Along Hwy. 49, about 6½ mi. below Sierra City. Open May through Oct.

**Upper Little Truckee C.G.**   19 sites. 6170'. Along Hwy. 89, 11¾ mi. n. of I-80. Open late May through early Nov.

**Wild Plum C.G.**   47 sites. 4400'. E. of Sierra City, at end of Wild Plum Rd. Open May through Oct. Map 4.

**Woodcamp C.G.**   20 sites. 6080'. Jackson Mdw. Res. Open June through Oct. Map 17.

**Woodchuck C.G.**   8 sites. 6260'. About 2½ mi. up Fordyce Rd., which begins ½ mi. n.w. of Cisco Grove. Open late June through early Sept.

**Yuba Pass C.G.**   11 sites. 6710'. Along Hwy. 49 at Yuba Pass. Open July through mid-Oct.

**TOIYABE NATIONAL FOREST**

**Hope Valley C.G.**   26 sites. 7140'. 1.7 mi. s. on Blue Lakes Rd., whose jct. with Hwy. 88 is 6.3 mi. n.e. of Carson Pass and 2.4 mi. s.w. of Hwys. 88/89 jct. Open late May through mid-Oct.

**Kit Carson C.G.**   12 sites. 6880'. Along Hwy 88, 1½ mi. e. of Hwy. 89 jct. Open late May through mid-Oct.

**Mt. Rose C.G.**   24 sites. 8920'. Near Mt. Rose Summit, at top of Nev. Hwy. 431. Open late June through mid-Sept. Map 49.

**Nevada Beach C.G.**   63 sites. 6240'. Along Lake Tahoe. Leave Hwy. 50 about 2 mi. n. of the Calif.-Nev. border. Open late May through late Sept.

**Snowshoe Springs C.G.**   13 sites. 6670'. Along Hwy. 88, about 2 mi. e. of Hwy. 89 jct. Open late May through mid-Oct.

**BUREAU OF LAND MANAGEMENT**

**South Yuba River C.G.**   17 sites. 2500'. Just off the North Bloomfield-Graniteville Rd., opposite the Hike 2 trailhead. Open all year except when snowbound. Map 2.

**STATE PARKS AND RECREATION AREAS**

**D.L. Bliss S.P.**   168 sites in 5 camping areas. 6230'-6650'. North of Emerald Bay. Open mid-June through early Sept. Ticketron reservations for same period. Map 32.

**Donner Memorial S.P.**   154 sites. 5950'. E. shore of Donner Lake. Open late May through late Sept. Ticketron reservations from about late May through early Sept.

**Emerald Bay S.P.**   100 sites in 2 camping areas. Above Emerald Bay. Open mid-June through early Sept. Ticketron reservations for same period. Map 32.

**Breakfast at Fallen Leaf Campground**

**Malakoff Diggins S.H.P.** 30 sites plus 1 group site plus 2 cabins. 3650'. N.e. of Nevada City. See Hike 3 trailhead. Open all year except when snowbound. Ticketron reservations from about early April through early Sept. Map 2.

**Plumas-Eureka S.P.** 70 sites. 5250'. West of Graeagle, via Co. Rd. A14. Open late May through late Oct. Ticketron reservations from about early June through early Sept. Map 8.

**Sugar Pine Point S.P. (General Creek C.G.)** 175 sites. 6340'. Along Hwy. 89 between Meeks and Emerald bays. Open all year. Ticketron reservations from early June through early Sept. Map 28.

**Tahoe S.R.A.** 39 sites. 6240'. At n.e. edge of Tahoe City. Open all year. Ticketron reservations from late May through early Sept.

## CITY PARKS

**Lake Forest C.G.** 21 sites. 6240'. Along Hwy. 28, 2 mi. n.e. of Tahoe City. Open mid-May through early Sept.

**South Lake Tahoe-Eldorado Recreation Area C.G.** 160 sites. 6230'. In n.e. South Lake Tahoe city. Open Apr. through Oct.

## PACIFIC GAS AND ELECTRIC COMPANY

These four campgrounds are along the Blue Lakes Rd., whose jct. with Hwy. 88 is 6.3 mi. n.e. of Carson Pass and 2.4 mi. s.w. of the Hwys. 88/89 jct. Blue Lakes Rd. goes 10.7 mi. s. to a jct. with Indian Valley rd., 1.2 mi. w. to a jct. with Twin Lakes rd., then turns north. The following mileages are from this last jct. All c.g.s are open from about mid-July through mid-Sept.

**Lower Blue Lake C.G.** 15 sites. 8080'. Immediately past last jct.

**Middle Creek C.G.** 8 sites. 8120'. 1.4 mi. past last jct.

**Upper Blue Lake C.G.** 32 sites. 8200'. 3.0 mi. past last jct. Map 43.

**Upper Blue Lake Damsite C.G.** 10 sites. 8180'. 1.8 mi. past last jct. Map 43.

## PRIVATE

**Camp Richardson C.G.** 335 sites. 6240'. Along Hwy. 89, about 2½ mi. n.w. of S. Lake Tahoe **Y.** Open early May through mid-Oct. Reservations: (916) 541-1801. Map 32 inset.

**Feather River KOA** 55 sites. 4700'. Along Hwy. 70, about 5 mi. e. of Blairsden. Open Apr. 1 through Nov. 1. Res.: (916) 836-2688.

**Lake Tahoe KOA, South Shore** 68 sites. 6370'. Along Hwy. 50, immediately s.w. of Upper Truckee Rd. jct., about 5½ mi. s. of S. Lake Tahoe **Y.** Open all year. Res.: (916) 577-3693.

**Little Bear C.G. and R.V. Park** 57 sites. 4300'. Along Hwy. 70/89, about 1 mi. n.w. of Blairsden. Open May 1 through Nov. 1. Res.: (916) 836-2774.

**Meeks Bay Resort.** 28 sites. 6240'. Along Hwy. 89 at Meeks Bay. Open mid-June through mid-Sept. Res.: (916) 525-7242. Map 28.

**Movin' West Trailer Ranch** 36 sites. 4360'. Near Graeagle, 0.3 mi. w. on Co. Rd. A14. Open all year. Res.: (916) 836-2614.

**Sierra Skies R.V. Park** 30 sites. 4170'. In Sierra City. Open mid-Apr. through Oct. Res.: (916) 862-1166. Map 3.

**Sierra Springs Trailer Resort** 30 sites. 4900'. Along Hwy. 70, about 3½ mi. e. of Blairsden. Open all year. Res.: (916) 836-2747.

**Tahoe Pines C.G.** 80 sites. 6320'. Along Hwy. 50, immediately n.e. of Upper Truckee Rd., about 5¼ mi. s. of S. Lake Tahoe **Y.** Open all year. Res.: (916) 577-1653.

**Tahoe Valley C.G.** 300 sites. 6280'. Just e. of Hwy. 50, about 0.4 mi. s. of S. Lake Tahoe **Y.** Open all year. Res.: (916) 541-2222.

**Zephyr Cove Resort C.G.** 180 sites. 6240'. Along Hwy. 50, about 4 mi. n. of Calif.-Nev. border. Open mid-Apr. through Nov. 1. Res.: (702) 588-6644.

**Hikers approaching Mt. Tallac's summit**

# Ch. 3 Exploring the Tahoe Sierra on Foot, Horseback or Skis

**Introduction** Most of this book is devoted to trails—where they go, what they are like, what lakes, peaks or views you'll see, and what significant plants, animals or geologic formations you're likely to encounter along the trails. Although this book is aimed mainly at hikers, it should be equally useful for equestrians. Cross-country skiers certainly will find it less useful, since during their sport's season the trails are under snow. Still, the author hopes they will find some merit in the text and its accompanying maps. This chapter covers the rules and beneficial practices that apply to all outdoor users, regardless of their mode of travel or time of year. The first thing you must know is that if you enter Desolation Wilderness (Hikes 60, 63–69, 71–87) or Mokelumne Wilderness (Hikes 96–99), you may need a wilderness permit.

## Wilderness Permits

**Introduction** During the decade from 1960 to 1969, backpacking, with its new, lightweight technology, came of age, and hikers proliferated through the Sierra Nevada. By the time Desolation Wilderness was officially created in late 1969, it was already crowded, and a guidebook printed a few months later added to its popularity. It looked like this infant wilderness was about to be trampled to death. Concerned, the Forest Service began a permit system in 1971, in part to determine just how many people were flooding the wilderness, what spots they visited, and how long they stayed. In 1975, the year that the first edition of *The Tahoe Sierra* appeared, about 3400 visitors could be found in the wilderness on a typical summer day, and about 90% of the wilderness' recreational activity took place in about 10% of its area. The Forest Service judged this human impact too great and, after a detailed study, determined the wilderness' optimum capacity to be about 2100 persons at one time. Since this number was less than the number of persons actually using the wilderness, the Forest Service began limiting—from 1978 onward—the number of persons entering the wilderness. *Today, anyone contacted by a ranger within the wilderness without a permit will be issued a violation notice.*

In addition to Desolation Wilderness, the Tahoe Sierra also includes Granite Chief Wilderness and the north part of Mokelumne Wilderness. Permits are not required for the former, but are required for the latter if you camp overnight during the period May 25 through September 30. Neither wilderness has a quota system.

**When** In Desolation Wilderness, permits are necessary every day of the year, even in the dead of winter, when no one may be present but you. Actually, the six-month period from December through May is perhaps the best time for those *experienced in mountain ways* to visit the wilderness, for then it is truly wild, traces of man being buried beneath the snow and solitude reigning supreme.

**How many** The Forest Service gives out a maximum of 700 permits per day to backpackers entering Desolation Wilderness. At present they don't limit the number of day hikers. Regardless of whether you spend just an hour or the legal maximum of two weeks in the wilderness, your party, which is limited to 25 persons, will need a permit. (The Forest Service hopes the size of your party will be much smaller.) Before the Fourth of July and after Labor Day, backpackers usually can get a permit easily; however, during the height of the hiking season, particularly on weekends, they may find wilderness permits extremely scarce. Of the 700 permits issued daily to backpackers, up to 350 can be reserved, and knowledgeable backpackers do just that.

**Where** To reserve a permit for Desolation Wilderness, write the Forest Service *within 90 days* of the start of your proposed excursion. You can phone them for information, but they prefer to take a permit application in writing, not over the phone. If you plan to enter from a west-side trailhead (Chapter 13), contact:

Eldorado National Forest Information
  Center
3070 Camino Heights Drive
Camino, CA 95709
(916) 644-6048.

If you plan to enter from an east-side trailhead (Meeks Bay through Echo Lake), contact:

Lake Tahoe Basin Management Unit
P.O. Box 8465
South Lake Tahoe, CA 95731
(916) 573-2600.

Be sure to mention your trip dates, size of party, number of stock (if any), and proposed hiking itinerary (for example: 8/11, Wrights Lake trailhead to Lake Schmidell; 8/12, Lake Schmidell to Middle Velma Lake; 8/13, Middle Velma Lake to Lake Aloha; 8/14, Lake Aloha to Lake Doris; 8/15, Lake Doris to Wrights Lake trailhead). If you plan to day-hike in Desolation Wilderness, you don't have to worry about quotas, and can pick up a permit at a USFS office on your way to the trailhead.

Although some folks may want to reserve a permit well in advance, which is a good idea for overnighters planning to visit the area on a busy summer weekend, the Forest Service would prefer that you not reserve and just pick up a permit in person. It is much easier this way for both the Forest Service and the user (if he or she can visit during business hours). For Desolation Wilderness there are four USFS offices you can drop by to get a permit.

1. The Lake Tahoe Basin Management Unit is located in the *Plaza 89* center at 870 Emerald Bay Road in South Lake Tahoe. (Emerald Bay Road is none other than Highway 89.) You'll find Plaza 89 on the west side of the highway, just 0.3 mile northwest of the South Lake Tahoe **Y,** at which Highway 50 branches east.

2. If you're entering the wilderness on its east side, you may find the Lake Tahoe Visitor Center a handy place to get a permit. It is located on the east side of Highway 89, about 3.2 miles northwest of the South Lake Tahoe **Y.** The entrance is just 150 yards west of Fallen Leaf Road.

3. If you're driving south toward the wilderness along Highway 89, you can stop at the William Kent Visitor Center, which dispenses permits from about July 4 through the Labor Day weekend. This center, at the entrance to the William Kent Campground, is located 2¼ miles south of Tahoe City. Some folks phone them in advance (916-583-3642), then stop by after hours (say, on a Friday evening) and pick up the permit, which is left outside the office. (Most USFS offices dispensing permits offer this service).

4. Finally, if you're driving east up Highway 50, stop at the Eldorado National Forest Information Center, about 5 miles east of Placerville. Located on Camino Heights Drive, this office is conveniently open seven days a week, year-round, except for certain holidays.

For Mokelumne Wilderness you should stop at the Amador Ranger Station, which is at 26820 Silver Drive in Pioneer [ZIP: 95666; phone: (209) 295-4251]. This Highway 88 town lies about 18 miles east of Jackson. The staff prefers that you pick up your permit in person. They are open 8 A.M. to 4:30 P.M. off season, and also on Saturdays from about mid-May through October. This office is out of the way for those not driving east up Highway 88. To counteract this inconvenience, the Forest Service operates, seven days a week during the summer, a tiny station at the south end of the Carson Pass parking lot.

## Backpacking and Day Hiking

**General** Most of the hikes in this book can be done as day hikes rather than as overnight hikes—although you may want to take more than one day to do many of them. Generally, however, very little planning and preparation for each is required. Novices to backpacking can learn the art by reading a copy of Thomas Winnett's *Backpacking Basics*—aimed directly at them.

Because accurate, up-to-date maps are included in this guide, mileage figures within the text are kept at a minimum. There are, however, numerous instances where vertical distance in feet and horizontal distance in yards are given. The first is given to tell you how much you will have to climb, thereby informing those who like easy hikes what they're in for. The second has a more practical reason: some trail junctions are easily missed, particularly in early season when snow lingers on. Therefore, potentially hard-to-find junctions are identified by their distance from the nearest identifiable feature—often a creek crossing. Yards are given because they approximately equal long strides—the hiker can pace off the distance when he is in doubt.

Your progress along a trail is often measured with respect to a prominent feature in the landscape, such as a mountain or hill above you. On this guide's topographic map, many unnamed high points are identified by an **X**, which marks the point, and a number, which gives its elevation. This guide refers to these high points as peaks—for example, peak 9224.

Some trails in this guide are potentially hard to follow in a few spots. Others may have early-season snow patches hiding them. For both, your route can usually be found by watching for blazes or ducks that mark the trail. A *blaze* is a place on a tree trunk where someone has carved away a patch or two of bark to leave a conspicuous scar. A *duck* is one or several small rocks placed on a larger rock in such a way that the placement is obviously unnatural.

**Minimal-impact hiking**   If thousands of hikers walk through a mountain landscape, with its fragile soils, they are almost bound to degrade it. The following suggestions are offered in the hope they will reduce man's imprint on the landscape, thus keeping it attractive for those who might follow.

First, if you're healthy enough to make an outdoor trip into a wilderness area, you're in good enough condition to do so on foot. Leave horses behind. (However, most hunters who enter Desolation Wilderness and other mountain areas in late September and early October will certainly object to carrying a deer out on their shoulders.) One horse can do more damage than a dozen backpackers. It will contribute at least as much excrement as all of them, but moreover, it will do so indiscriminately, sometimes in creeks or at lake shores. Another problem with horses is that they can trample meadow trails into a string of muddy ruts, particularly in

early season. And they selectively graze the meadows, causing a change in the native flora. For example, only 30 years after Yosemite Valley was set aside as a park, its luxuriant native grasses and wildflowers were reduced to about one-fourth their original number, largely replaced by hardier, less showy alien species. However, cattle more than horses keep many of Tahoe's mountain meadows in a nearly flowerless state. Compare heavily grazed Big Meadow (Hike 92) with lightly grazed Haypress Meadow (Hike 87). Unfortunately, sometimes it's the riders rather than the horses that are the main problem. It's so easy to pack in food for a feast and leave garbage, cans and bottles littering the campsite. If you do bring stock animals into Desolation Wilderness, you are required to provide them with supplemental feed, and you're not allowed to tie or picket them in any meadow or within 100 feet of water. Rules and advice for equestrians, including first aid for horses, are found in Schmidt and Cardinet's book, which is cited in "Recommended Reading and Source Materials."

If at all possible, day-hike rather than overnight-hike. You can, for example, make easy-to-moderate day hikes to over half of the Desolation Wilderness lakes, and the same applies to the lakes outside the wilderness. Actually, if you're *really* in shape, there's no reason you can't day-hike to *any* lake under 8½ miles away and *enjoy* it. Such a lengthy hike should take only 6 hours or less, round trip, if you're truly in shape. Of course fishermen will object, since the best times for fishing are early morning and in the evening. And who wants to get up at three in the morning to fish a lake at dawn? For them, backpacking is a must. Still, trout-stocked

**Llamas, for better or for worse, have become increasingly popular pack animals**

mountain lakes are an unnatural phenomenon, and some naturalists question continuance of the stocking program (some national parks have largely abandoned it).

Why do day-hikers have less impact on the environment? For one thing, they usually use toilets near trailheads rather than soil near lakes. Seven-hundred backpackers in Desolation Wilderness contribute about a ton of human waste per week, and the bulk of this is within 100 yards of a lake, stream or trail. Whereas horse and cattle excrement, lying on the ground, decomposes rapidly, buried human excrement takes longer, for in mountain soils subsurface decomposers such as bacteria and fungi are not abundant. Around a popular lake excrement can lead to deterioration of its water quality. Always defecate *at least 50 yards away* from any lake or stream, and the Forest Service recommends you bury feces 6-8 inches deep. Apparently, the spread of *Giardia,* which is discussed at the end of this chapter, has become a real problem in Sierra Nevada lakes and streams largely because of human feces contaminated with this intestinal parasite.

If, in order to have a satisfactory wilderness experience, you decide to backpack, you might consider the following advice, which is specifically aimed at those visiting Desolation Wilderness, but is applicable to all backpackers (and equestrians).

1. Pack out toilet paper. Popular lakes can receive over a thousand visitors during summer, and there's a limit to how much paper can be buried. You could burn the toilet paper, but this requires a campfire.

2. Don't build a campfire unless you absolutely have to do so, as in an emergency. They aren't prohibited, but downed wood is already too scarce, and cutting or defacing standing vegetation, whether living or dead, is strictly prohibited. *Use a stove instead.* Stoves cook meals faster, leave pots and pans cleaner, and save downed wood for the soil's organisms, which are necessary food for larger animals. Campfires can leave an unsightly mess and, as winter's snowpack melts, campfire ashes can be carried into lakes, reducing their water quality. If you are backpacking *outside* Desolation Wilderness, you will need a *campfire permit* if you intend to build a fire. These can be obtained at ranger stations or at the Forest Service headquarters. A campfire permit requires a group to carry a shovel. If you don't build any fires but use only gas stoves, then you can leave the shovel behind, but you'll still need the permit.

3. Don't pollute lakes and streams by washing clothes or dishes in them or throwing fish guts into them. And don't lather up in them, even with biodegradable soap. *All* soaps pollute. Do your washing and pot scrubbing well away from lakes and streams, and bury fish entrails ashore rather than throw them back into the water.

4. Set up camp at least 100 feet from streams, trails and lakeshores. At some lakes this may be practically impossible, and then you must be extremely careful not to degrade the environment. Always camp on mineral soil (or perhaps even on bedrock, if you've brought sufficient padding), but never in meadows or other soft, vegetated areas. It's best to use a site already in existence rather than to brush out a new campsite. That would result in one more human mark upon the landscape.

5. Leave your campsite clean. Don't leave scraps of food behind, for this only attracts mice, bears and other camp marauders. If you can carry it in, you can carry it out. After all, your pack is lighter on the way out and the trail is probably downhill.

6. Don't build structures. Rock walls, large fireplaces and bough beds were fine in the last century, but not today. There are just too many humans on this planet, and one goes up into the wilderness for a bit of solitude away from them. The hiker shouldn't have to be confronted with continual reminders of man's presence. Leave the wilderness at least as pure as you found it.

7. Noise and loud conversations, like motor vehicles, are inappropriate. Have some consideration for other campers in the vicinity. Also, camp far enough away from others to assure privacy to both them and you.

Regardless of whether you are day-hiking or overnighting, you should observe the following advice.

1. The smaller your party, the better. In Desolation Wilderness hiking parties are limited to 25, though at the more popular trailheads the size is as small as six. Granite Chief Wilderness also has a limit of 25, but Mokelumne Wilderness has a limit of 15. If your party is six or more, you should avoid the more popular trails in any of these wildernesses. This is also good advice to follow outside the wildernesses. For example, a large troop of Boy Scouts at Five Lakes Basin (Hike 46) would have too much impact. You can lessen your group's impact on others by avoiding the main hiking season, which lasts from late July through the Labor Day weekend, when lakes are fairly warm and mosquitoes are minimal.

2. If you're 16 or older, you'll need a California fishing license if you plan to fish (see Chapter 4). The limit is usually 10 trout per day. You also need a license to hunt. Observe all fishing and hunting regulations.

3. Destruction, injury, defacement, removal or disturbance in any manner of any natural feature or public property is prohibited. This includes molesting any animal, picking flowers or other plants; cutting, blazing, marking, driving nails in, or otherwise damaging growing trees or standing snags; writing, carving or painting of name or other inscription anywhere; destruction, defacement or moving of signs.

4. Smoking is not allowed while traveling through vegetated areas. You may stop and smoke in a safe place.

5. Pack and saddle animals have the right of way on trails. Hikers should get completely off the trail, on the downhill side if possible, and remain quiet until the stock has passed.

6. When traveling on a trail, stay on the trail. Don't cut switchbacks, since this destroys trails. When going cross-country, don't mark your route in any way. Let the next person find his way as you did. Use a compass and map.

7. Be prepared for sudden, adverse weather. It's good to carry a poncho even on a sunny day hike. It can also double as a ground cloth or emergency tent. A space blanket (2 oz. light) is also useful. Some day hikes accidentally turn into overnight trips, due to injury, getting lost or bad weather. Early-season and late-season hikers may encounter snow flurries and, rarely, full-fledged storms; and if they plan to camp out overnight, they should have a tent or at least a tube tent. Before you drive off to your trailhead, find out what the weather is supposed to be like, but be prepared—Sierra weather has been known to go from clear blue sky to all-out thunderstorm in only an hour. Never climb to a mountaintop if clouds are building above it, particularly if you hear thunder in the cloudy distance. And if you see lightning, turn back.

8. The farther you are from your trailhead, the greater is the problem if you are injured. Rock climbers and mountaineers, who are in a higher-risk category, should bear this in mind. You shouldn't hike alone, since then you may have no one but yourself to rescue in an emergency. In particular, crossing large streams in early season can be potentially dangerous. However, in the area covered by this book, most of the trails are popular and you are likely to meet other hikers, should you need help.

# Giardiasis

Our clear mountain lakes and streams unfortunately sometimes contain disease-producing organisms. One hidden hazard you should particularly know about is a disease called *giardiasis* (jee-ar-dye-a-sis). It can cause severe intestinal discomfort. The disease is caused by a microscopic organism, *Giardia lamblia*. The cystic form of giardia can be found in mountain streams and lakes. These natural waters may be clear, cold and free-running; they may look, smell and taste fine; still Giardia may be present.

Although giardiasis can be incapacitating, it is not usually life-threatening. After ingestion by humans, giardia organisms normally attach themselves to the small intestine. Disease symptoms usually include diarrhea, gas, loss of appetite, abdominal cramps and bloating. Weight loss may occur from nausea and loss of appetite. These discomforts may last up to six weeks. Most people are unaware that they have been infected, and often return home from vacation before the onset of symptoms. If not treated, the symptoms may disappear on their own, only to recur intermittently over a period of many months. Other diseases can have similar symptoms, but if you drank untreated water, you should suspect giardiasis and so inform your doctor. If properly diagnosed, the disease is curable with medication prescribed by a physician.

There are several ways for you to treat raw water to make it relatively safe to drink. The treatment most certain to destroy giardia is to boil the water, preferably for 3-5 minutes. Chemical disinfectants, such as iodine or chlorine, are not as reliable as boiling unless you use them for a *long* time, such as an hour. This, obviously, is a long time to wait for a drink, so carry two water bottles. While you're drinking from one, the second can be sitting in your pack, with the disinfectant working in it. The recommended dosages, *per quart,* for these substances are: 5 tablets of chlorine or 4 drops of household bleach or 2 tablets of iodine or 10 drops of 2% tincture of iodine. To avoid the nuisance of boiling or the bad taste of chemicals, you can instead carry a water microfiltration system. These cost about $25 and up. Finally, you can avoid drinking untreated water altogether by day-hiking and carrying your own safe supply of water.

**Trout swim past you at the Stream Profile Chamber (Hike 56)**

# Ch. 4  Lakes and Fish of the Tahoe Sierra

**Introduction**  No guide to the Tahoe Sierra could be complete without a chapter on the area's trout and trout lakes. In general, the larger lakes produce the larger fish. Lake Tahoe, being easily the area's largest lake, has produced some whoppers—up to about 32 pounds—for lake trout. The average fish, however, is considerably less, only a couple of pounds. Still, this is a lot larger than most Desolation Wilderness trout, which are typically less than a pound. This wilderness has been touted as a fisherman's paradise, for virtually every lake is stocked. Even so, less than 10% of the wilderness visitors are serious anglers, although many visitors do carry a rod "just in case." Most of the serious anglers in the Tahoe Sierra visit its rivers and major streams plus its larger lakes, which include Loon, Fallen Leaf, Donner, Spaulding and Bowman lakes and Union Valley, Hell Hole, French Meadows, Prosser Creek, Boca, Stampede and Jackson Meadow reservoirs. In the table that follows, most of the larger lakes, which typically lie below 6000 feet, are omitted. Only lakes that are shown on this book's topographic maps are included.

**General fishing regulations**  Everyone 16 years or older needs a fishing license. These are short-term or annual, resident or nonresident—take your pick. The license plus detailed regulations is available at most sporting-goods stores. If none are nearby, you can contact the Department of Fish and Game (Box 944209, Sacramento, CA 94244–2090). Most of the Tahoe Sierra lies within the Sierra Fishing District. In this district the late April through mid-November daily limit is typically 10 fish per day, but is five per day in the following lakes or reservoirs: Boca, Donner, Echo, Jenkinson, Prosser, Rollins, Stampede, Tahoe and Webber. For Milton Reservoir the limit is two. Lake Tahoe lies partly in Nevada, and anywhere on this lake either a California or a Nevada fishing license will do.

**Principal trout and salmon**  There are only two trout species native to the Tahoe Sierra, rainbow and cutthroat. All other species have been introduced. Originally, rainbow trout occurred in western Sierra streams, usually below the lakes, since they much prefer to spawn on stream beds rather than on lake bottoms. Consequently, to maintain their populations in mountain lakes, the Department of Fish and Game must continually plant rainbows, often annually in many lakes. There are about a half dozen subspecies of rainbow trout in California, and they all can be cross-bred (even with cutthroat trout). One such hybrid is a cross of the Shasta rainbow with the British Columbian Kamloops rainbow. This hybrid of two nonna-tive subspecies has been popular in the Tahoe area since 1978.

The Lahontan cutthroat trout is native to the Truckee, Carson and Walker river drainages. It occurred in Lake Tahoe until the 1940s, when it apparently disappeared. The introduction of the aggressive lake trout (mackinaw), from Michigan, is cited as the prime cause for its demise. The brown trout, of European descent, is another introduction, and is found in a few lakes. The arctic grayling, the most recent introduction, has not caught on.

The most successful introduction, from the northeastern United States, is the brook trout, or "brookie." Unlike the rainbow, it spawns in mountain lakes and therefore can maintain its population. Many mountain fishermen consider it the tastiest of the Sierra's trout. Another successful introduction, from the southern end of the High Sierra, is the golden trout. It prefers high mountain lakes, and in the Tahoe Sierra that is where it has been planted. These lakes typically are also the most remote, so to catch a golden trout is a rewarding experience.

The only common salmon in our area is the kokanee, which is a landlocked version of the oceangoing sockeye salmon. Most trout its size eat insects or small fish, but the kokanee prefers to eat plankton. It does well only in the cool, larger lakes, such as Donner and Tahoe. Tahoe has one more native species that is closely related to trout—the mountain whitefish. This edible fish does not occur in any other Tahoe Sierra lake.

# Lakes and Fish of the Tahoe Sierra

| Lake's name | Seen on hike(s) | Shown on map(s) | Elevation (feet) | Size (acres) | Depth (if known) | Trout or salmon |
|---|---|---|---|---|---|---|
| Aloha, Lake | 66, 72, 83, 87 | 34 | 8116 | 630 | 15 | BK, RT |
| Alta Morris Lake | 82 | 34 | 8150 | 5 | 18 | BK, GT |
| American Lake | 72 | 34 | 8100 | 11 | 40 | BK |
| Angora Lake, Lower | 58 | 35 | 7390 | 8 | 32 | CT |
| Angora Lake, Upper | 58 | 35 | 7460 | 14 | 48 | CT |
| Audrain, Lake | — | 38 | 7140 | 11 | 10 | BK, RT |
| Avalanche Lake | 72 | 35, 37 | 7490 | 2 | 10 | RT |
| Azure Lake | — | 31, 32 | 7700 | 27 | 103 | BK, BN, RT |
| Barrett Lake | 63 | 33 | 7635 | 6 | 30 | BK, RT |
| Bear Lake | 75 | 27 | 7530 | 6 | — | BK |
| Bear Lake, Big | 21, 22 | 8 | 6485 | 24 | 69 | RT |
| Bear Lake, Little | 21, 22 | 8 | 6489 | 4 | 15 | RT |
| Berts Lake | — | 29 | 6730 | 1½ | 10 | BK, RT |
| Beyers Lake, Lower | 33 | 12 | 6870 | 18 | 30 | CT |
| Beyers Lake, Upper | 33 | 12 | 6875 | 6 | 8 | BK |
| Blue Lake | — | 12 | 5964 | 47 | 160 | RT |
| Blue Lake, Upper | — | 43 | 8136 | 298 | 177 | CT, RT |
| Boomerang Lake | 68 | 33 | 8060 | 1 | — | BK |
| Bowman Lake | — | 12 | 5565 | 825 | 160 | RT |
| Buck Island Lake | 60 | 26, 27, 29 | 6430 | 45 | 40 | BK, BN, RT |
| Bugle Lake | 59 | 25 | 6900 | 8 | 7 | BK |
| Cagwin Lake | 85 | 35 | 7750 | 2½ | 12 | RT |
| Caples Lake | 96 | 39, 40 | 7798 | 623 | 70 | BN, LT, RT |
| Carr Lake | 31 | 12 | 6700 | 15 | 22 | BK, RT |
| Cathedral Lake | 79 | 35 | 7630 | 1½ | 25 | BK, GT |
| Channel Lake | 72 | 34 | 8090 | 4 | 16 | BK, RT |
| Cliff Lake | 76 | 31 | 8390 | 4 | — | BK |
| Clyde Lake | 66 | 34 | 8060 | 21 | 30 | BK, GT, RT |
| Crag Lake | 76 | 31 | 7470 | 21 | — | BK, BN, LT, RT |
| Cub Lake | 21, 22 | 8 | 6580 | 2 | 10 | BK |
| Cup Lake | — | 37 | 8500 | 2½ | — | BK, GT |
| Dardanelles Lake | 91, 92 | 38 | 7750 | 16 | 23 | BK |
| Dark Lake | 61 | 33 | 6900 | 14 | 11 | BN, RT |
| Deer Lake | 17, 18, 19 | 6 | 7100 | 28 | 40 | RT |
| Desolation Lake | 72 | 34 | 7980 | 3½ | 13 | BK |
| Devils Oven Lake | 36 | 14 | 7874 | 4 | — | BK, GT |
| Dicks Lake | 66, 77, 78 | 34 | 8425 | 58 | 75 | BK, RT |
| Dipper Pond | — | 31 | 7475 | 1½ | — | BK, RT |
| Donner Lake | — | 18 | 5933 | 840 | — | KOK, LT, MW, RT |
| Doris, Lake | 64-66 | 33 | 8350 | 2½ | — | GT |
| Downey Lake | 33 | 12 | 6870 | 12 | 40 | RT |
| Eagle Lake | 77 | 32 | 6990 | 19 | 25 | BK, RT |
| Echo Lake, Lower | 85-87 | 35 | 7414 | 250 | 180 | BK, KOK, RT |
| Echo Lake, Upper | 85-87 | 35, 36 | 7414 | 80 | — | BK, KOK, RT |
| Elbert Lake | — | 38 | 7550 | 4 | 10 | BK, RT |
| Emigrant Lake | 96 | 42 | 8590 | 21 | 80 | BK |
| Eureka Lake | 28 | 9 | 6180 | 33 | 30 | BK, RT |
| Fallen Leaf Lake | 56 | 32, 35, 36 | 6377 | 1410 | 365 | BN, KOK, LT, RT |
| Faucherie Reservoir | 33 | 12 | 6220 | 140 | 120 | BN, RT |
| Fawn Lake | — | 26, 27 | 6350 | 6 | 12 | RT |
| Feeley Lake | 31, 32 | 12 | 6728 | 51 | 64 | RT |
| Fisher Lake | 34 | 13 | 7035 | 3 | 50 | BK |
| Five Lakes, southern | 46 | 21 | 7520 | 3 | 19 | BK |
| Five Lakes, western | 46 | 20 | 7520 | 5 | 14 | RT |
| Floating Island Lake | 79 | 35 | 7220 | 2 | 15 | BK |
| Fontanillis Lake | 66, 77, 78 | 31 | 8300 | 22 | 76 | BK |
| Forni Lake | — | 29 | 7930 | 6 | — | CT, GT |
| 4-Q Lake, lower | 65 | 30 | 7470 | 2½ | 16 | BK |
| 4-Q Lake, middle | 65 | 30 | 7475 | 3 | 19 | BK |
| 4-Q Lake, upper | 65 | 30 | 7480 | 6 | — | BK |
| Fourth of July Lake | 98 | 42 | 8164 | 16 | 60 | BK, RT |
| Fox Lake | 60 | 30 | 6550 | 4 | 15 | BK |
| Frata Lake | — | 35 | 8065 | 2 | 9 | BK |
| Frog Lake | 97-99 | 41 | 8850 | 7 | 27 | CT, RT |
| Fuller Lake | — | 12 | 5343 | 64 | 31 | BN |

**Fish**   AG: arctic grayling   BK: brook trout   BN: brown trout   CT: cutthroat trout   GT: golden trout
KOK: kokanee salmon   LT: lake trout (mackinaw)   MW: mountain whitefish   RT: rainbow trout (mostly hybrids)

| Lake's name | Seen on hike(s) | Shown on map(s) | Elevation (feet) | Size (acres) | Depth (if known) | Trout or salmon |
|---|---|---|---|---|---|---|
| Gefo Lake | 72 | 34 | 7870 | 3½ | — | BK |
| Genevieve, Lake | 76 | 31 | 7420 | 7 | 12 | BK |
| Gertrude Lake | 67 | 33 | 7995 | 2½ | 11 | BK, GT |
| Gilmore Lake | 81 | 35 | 8310 | 78 | 160 | BK, LT, RT |
| Glacier Lake | 33 | 12 | 7540 | 3 | — | GT |
| Gold Lake | — | 8, 10 | 6407 | 480 | 80 | BN, RT |
| Gold Lake, Little | — | 6, 8 | 6435 | 6 | 13 | BK |
| Granite Lake | 78 | 32 | 7660 | 7 | — | BK |
| Grass Lake | 80 | 35 | 7235 | 17 | 25 | RT |
| Grass Lake | 100, 109 | 44 | 7690 | 10 | 5 | BK |
| Grouse Lake | 69 | 33 | 8140 | 4 | 15 | RT |
| Grouse Lake, Lower | 76 | 31 | 8030 | 1 | — | BK |
| Grouse Lake, Upper | 76 | 31 | 8195 | 2 | — | BK |
| Half Moon Lake | 82 | 34 | 8140 | 21 | 35 | BK, GT, RT |
| Heather Lake | 66, 83 | 34 | 7900 | 31 | 50 | BK, BN, RT |
| Hemlock Lake | 69 | 33 | 8390 | 1½ | 14 | BK |
| Hidden Lake | 76 | 31 | 7575 | 5 | — | RT |
| Highland Lake | 65 | 30 | 7810 | 14 | 88 | RT |
| Horseshoe Lake | 65 | 30 | 7540 | 8 | 10 | BK |
| Island Lake | 31, 32 | 12 | 6820 | 35 | 80 | RT |
| Island Lake | 68 | 33, 34 | 8140 | 21 | — | BK, GT |
| Jabu Lake | — | 35 | 8460 | 1½ | — | GT |
| Jackson Lake | — | 12 | 6598 | 50 | 60 | RT |
| Jackson Meadow Reservoir | 39, 40 | 5, 17 | 6036 | 960 | 125 | RT |
| Jamison Lake | 27 | 8 | 6275 | 23 | 28 | BK, RT |
| Kalmia Lake | — | 34 | 8590 | 4 | 15 | GT |
| Kirkwood Lake | — | 39 | 7670 | 18 | 30 | RT |
| Lake of the Woods | 74, 87 | 35 | 8050 | 70 | 50 | BK |
| Lawrence Lake | 63 | 33 | 7820 | 8 | — | BK, RT |
| LeConte, Lake | 87 | 34 | 8180 | 6 | 35 | BK, RT |
| Leland Lake, Lower | 65 | 30 | 8125 | 5 | 32 | GT |
| Leland Lake, Upper | 65 | 30 | 8190 | 4 | 13 | GT |
| Lily Lake | 25 | 8 | 5918 | 3 | 21 | BK |
| Lindsey Lake, Lower | — | 12 | 6220 | 25 | 44 | RT |
| Lindsey Lake, Upper | — | 12 | 6450 | 20 | 40 | CT |
| Loch Leven Lake, High | 34 | 13 | 6870 | 6 | 9 | BK |
| Loch Leven Lake, Lower | 34 | 13 | 6780 | 11 | 25 | RT |
| Loch Leven Lake, Upper | 34 | 13 | 6790 | 5 | 26 | RT |
| Lois, Lake | 64-66 | 30, 33 | 8290 | 21 | 71 | BK |
| Long Lake | 22-24, 27 | 8 | 6555 | 147 | 191 | RT |
| Long Lake | 31, 32 | 12 | 6870 | 4 | 17 | RT |
| Loon Lake | 59, 60 | 26, 29 | 6378 | 1450 | — | RT |
| Lost Lake | 52 | 28 | 7700 | 10 | — | RT |
| Lost Lake | 63 | 33 | 7790 | 3½ | 15 | BK |
| Lost Lake | — | 35 | 8110 | 2 | — | BK, GT |
| Lost Lake, lower | — | 43 | 8630 | 13 | 25 | BK |
| Lost Lake, upper | — | 43 | 8670 | 17 | 37 | BK |
| Lucille, Lake | 87 | 35 | 8170 | 8 | 20 | BK |
| Lyons Lake | 71 | 34 | 8380 | 7 | 50 | BK, RT |
| Margaret Lake | 95 | 39 | 7530 | 5½ | 20 | BK |
| Margery, Lake | 87 | 35 | 8225 | 4 | 10 | BK |
| Marlette Lake | 104 | 48 | 7823 | 350 | — | CT (no fishing) |
| Maud Lake | 64-66 | 33 | 7660 | 6 | 20 | RT |
| McKinstry Lake | 59 | 25 | 6920 | 9 | — | BK |
| Meiss Lake | 92-94 | 40 | 8314 | 10 | 6 | BK |
| Mildred Lake, middle | 42 | 22 | 7950 | 2 | — | GT |
| Milk Lake | 31 | 12 | 7000 | 13 | — | RT |
| Miller Lake | — | 27 | 7115 | 23 | 8 | BK |
| Milton Reservoir | — | 5 | 5690 | 23 | 8 | BN, CT, RT |
| Needle Lake | 45 | 20 | 8510 | 1½ | — | GT |
| Needle Lake, Little | 45 | 20 | 8070 | 2 | — | GT |
| Number 3, Lake | 63 | 30 | 8230 | 7 | 25 | GT |
| Number 5, Lake | 63 | 33 | 7940 | 3 | 8 | BK |
| Packer Lake | 15 | 6 | 6224 | 11 | 27 | RT |
| Paradise Lake | 35, 38 | 14 | 7728 | 19 | — | RT |
| Pearl Lake | 62 | 33 | 7350 | 4 | 34 | RT |
| Penner Lake | 32 | 12 | 6920 | 20 | — | BK |
| Phipps Lake | 75, 76 | 31 | 8550 | 10 | — | GT |
| Pyramid Lake | 72 | 34 | 8030 | 9 | 20 | BK |
| Ralston Lake | 85 | 35 | 7790 | 12 | 35 | RT |

**Fish**   AG: arctic grayling   BK: brook trout   BN: brown trout   CT: cutthroat trout   GT: golden trout
KOK: kokanee salmon   LT: lake trout (mackinaw)   MW: mountain whitefish   RT: rainbow trout (mostly hybrids)

| Lake's name | Seen on hike(s) | Shown on map(s) | Elevation (feet) | Size (acres) | Depth (if known) | Trout or salmon |
|---|---|---|---|---|---|---|
| Red Lake | — | 41 | 7860 | 85 | 30 | BK |
| Richardson Lake | 75 | 27 | 7395 | 11 | 31 | BK, RT |
| Rock Lake | 27 | 8 | 6315 | 15 | — | BK |
| Rock Lake | 32 | 12 | 6700 | 20 | — | BK |
| Rock Lake, Lower | 32 | 12 | 6620 | 9 | — | BK |
| Rockbound Lake | 60 | 27, 30 | 6529 | 114 | 95 | RT |
| Ropi Lake | 72, 74 | 34 | 7625 | 17 | 50 | BK |
| Round Lake | 21 | 8 | 6716 | 14 | 40 | BK, CT |
| Round Lake | 91, 92 | 38, 40 | 8037 | 40 | 46 | BK, CT |
| Round Top Lake | 96-98 | 40 | 9340 | 9 | 40 | GT |
| Rubicon Lake | 76 | 31 | 8305 | 7 | — | RT |
| Rubicon Reservoir | 60 | 30 | 6548 | 75 | — | RT |
| Rucker Lake | — | 12 | 5462 | 54 | — | RT |
| Salmon Lake | 34 | 13 | 6700 | 3 | 15 | BK |
| Salmon Lake, Lower | — | 6 | 6380 | 25 | 11 | RT |
| Salmon Lake, Upper | 19 | 6 | 6501 | 37 | 46 | BK, RT |
| Sand Ridge Lake | 35 | 14 | 7798 | 4 | 10 | RT |
| Sanford Lake | 33 | 12 | 7050 | 6 | 22 | RT |
| Sardine Lake, Lower | — | 6, 7 | 5762 | 35 | 81 | BK, RT |
| Sardine Lake, Upper | — | 6 | 5995 | 54 | 159 | RT |
| Saucer Lake | — | 35, 37 | 8590 | 1½ | 20 | GT |
| Sawmill Lake | 32 | 12 | 5863 | 120 | 20 | RT |
| Saxonia Lake | — | 6 | 6496 | 10 | 40 | RT |
| Schmidell, Lake | 64-66 | 30 | 7870 | 34 | 100 | BK |
| Secret Lake | — | 33 | 8300 | 1 | — | BK |
| Shadow Lake | — | 29 | 7260 | 6 | 10 | RT |
| Shadow Lake | 76 | 31 | 7660 | 5 | — | BK |
| Shotgun Lake | 32 | 12 | 6520 | 22 | — | RT |
| Showers Lake | 89, 93, 94 | 40 | 8647 | 6 | 20 | BK |
| Silver Lake | 21 | 8 | 6670 | 10 | 16 | BK |
| Smith Lake | 26, 27 | 8 | 6079 | 21 | — | BK |
| Smith Lake | 69 | 33, 34 | 8700 | 9 | 60 | BK |
| Snag Lake | — | 10 | 6670 | 20 | 9 | RT |
| Snake Lake | 20 | 8 | 6730 | 6 | — | RT |
| Snow Lake | — | 32, 35 | 7390 | 14 | 20 | BK |
| Spider Lake | 60 | 26 | 6710 | 42 | 45 | RT |
| Spooner Lake | 104 | 48 | 6980 | 84 | 10 | BK, RT (catch & release only) |
| Squaw Lake | — | 10 | 6670 | 5 | 25 | BK |
| Star Lake | 103 | 45, 47 | 9110 | 20 | — | BK |
| Stony Ridge Lake | 76 | 31 | 7820 | 52 | 84 | BK, LT, RT |
| Summit Lake | 37 | 14 | 7398 | 7 | 15 | BK |
| Susie Lake | 66, 83 | 34 | 7795 | 36 | 68 | RT |
| Sylvia Lake | 71 | 34 | 8060 | 3 | 20 | GT |
| Tahoe, Lake | 53, 54 | 28, 32, 48 | 6229 | 122,000 | 1645 | BN, KOK, LT, MW, RT |
| Tallac Lake | — | 35 | 7900 | 1 | — | GT |
| Tamarack Lake | 85 | 35 | 7830 | 22 | 31 | BK |
| Tamarack Lake, Lower | 15 | 6 | 6715 | 2½ | 9 | BK |
| Tamarack Lake, Upper | 15 | 6 | 6754 | 3 | 14 | BK |
| Toem Lake | 72 | 34 | 7635 | 9 | — | RT |
| Top Lake | 63 | 33 | 8260 | 5 | — | RT |
| Triangle Lake | 84, 85 | 35 | 8010 | 1½ | 20 | RT |
| Twin Lake, Lower | 68 | 33 | 7980 | 9 | — | RT |
| Twin Lake, Upper | 68 | 33 | 7982 | 13 | — | RT |
| Tyler Lake | 67 | 33 | 8220 | 2 | 20 | BK |
| Velma Lake, Lower | 77 | 31 | 7700 | 32 | 61 | RT |
| Velma Lake, Middle | 66, 75-78 | 31 | 7890 | 40 | 44 | RT |
| Velma Lake, Upper | 77, 78 | 31 | 7950 | 13 | 29 | RT |
| Volcano Lake | — | 7 | 6355 | 5 | 29 | BK |
| Waca Lake | 72 | 34 | 8190 | 5 | 20 | BK |
| Wades Lake | 20, 27 | 8 | 6549 | 10 | 36 | BK |
| Warren Lake | 35, 36 | 14 | 7210 | 31 | — | CT |
| West Lake, lower | 41 | 14 | 7180 | 3 | 5 | BK |
| West Lake, upper | 35-37 | 14 | 7240 | 2½ | 15 | BK |
| White Rock Lake | 38 | 14, 15 | 7817 | 89 | — | RT |
| Winnemucca Lake | 97, 98 | 41 | 8980 | 52 | 100 | RT |
| Woods Lake | 97 | 40 | 8220 | 13 | 51 | AG, RT |
| Wrights Lake | 61-70 | 33 | 6941 | 65 | 7 | BK, RT |
| Young America Lake | — | 6 | 7250 | 6 | 48 | GT |
| Zitella, Lake | 65 | 30 | 7660 | 8 | 15 | BK |

**Fish**    AG: arctic grayling    BK: brook trout    BN: brown trout    CT: cutthroat trout    GT: golden trout
KOK: kokanee salmon    LT: lake trout (mackinaw)    MW: mountain whitefish    RT: rainbow trout (mostly hybrids)

# Ch. 5         Geology

**Introduction**   In very general terms we can divide the geologic history of the Tahoe Sierra into three major periods of time, known to geologists as eras. The Paleozoic era, the first era that concerns us, began about 570 million years ago and lasted until about 240 million years ago. It was during this era that the Tahoe Sierra accumulated a lot of volcanic rocks. Before then, the area had been ocean floor. The Mesozoic era, which lasted from about 240 to 65 million years ago, was dominated—in the Sierra—by the formation of granitic rocks, this process occurring several miles underground. The Cenozoic era began about 65 million years ago and we're still in this era today. During the Mesozoic and the Cenozoic, much of the Paleozoic-era rocks were eroded away, exposing the underlying granitic rocks. Then the Tahoe Sierra was largely covered by outpourings of lava and volcanic ash, was subsequently uplifted, and was finally glaciated. That, in a nutshell, is the area's geologic history. In detail, the story is far more complex.

**The earliest rocks**   During much of the Paleozoic era the western shoreline of North America lay in what is now western Nevada, and that meant that the Tahoe Sierra, rather than being a mountainous area, was under water, submerged beneath the Pacific Ocean. Far to the west or southwest lay a chain of islands, perhaps not unlike today's Philippine Islands. And like today's Pacific Ocean islands, this ancient chain was composed of volcanoes, a few of them active. But the ocean floor (and the oceanic crust it rested upon) was moving—much as it does today—and the island chain drifted ever closer to North America, until they collided. What a crunch! This "big crunch," the first of three, occurred "about" 350 million years ago. Another big crunch, involving a much later island chain, occurred about 240 million years ago, and a final crunch, involving a still later island chain, occurred about 155 million years ago. With each crunch a considerable amount of volcanic terrain was added to western North America.

In our book's area the oldest island chain is the most extensive, its remnants forming a north-south band that occupies much of the western Tahoe Sierra. The Melones Fault Zone, shown in the western part of this chapter's glacier map, is the western edge of this band. The eastern edge is more irregular, but basically it runs south from Eureka Peak (Hike 28) to Sierra City (Hike 13) to the Grouse Ridge Recreation Area (Hikes 31-33) and then to Union Valley Reservoir (along the road to Hikes 59-60). The Sierra Buttes are part of this band, and it is interesting to note that early miners called them "the volcano." Rising high above the surrounding landscape, this dark mass does resemble an eroded volcano, but that is mostly coincidental.

The intermediate-age volcanic-rock band has been largely eroded away, but a sizable hunk of it remains east of the Eureka Peak-Sierra Buttes crest. When you go tromping through most of the Lakes Basin Recreation Area (Hikes 18-19, 21-27, 29), you are walking on this assemblage of volcanic rocks. A bit south, in the Sardine Lakes area, this assemblage abruptly gives way to the youngest one. On Hike 14, the Sardine Lakes moraine, you cross the contact between these two assemblages, which you should be able to discern, since there is a distinct change in the color of the rocks.

The remains of the youngest volcanic-rock assemblage exist in large hunks along or close to the Sierra crest. You'll see them along parts of the Pacific Crest Trail (Hikes 10-11, 38-40), in much of the Granite Chief area (Hikes 42-51), and especially in the central part of Desolation Wilderness (Hikes 64-66, 80-83). However, the greatest amount of this assemblage lies west of the Melones Fault Zone, beyond the scope of this book.

While I've called these three assemblages "volcanic," that is what they originally were, not what they are today. Each time any of these volcanic rocks experienced a "big crunch," they were subjected to extreme pressure and considerable heat. The result of extreme pressure and high heat is always what we call *metamorphic rocks*. Because they were originally volcanic, we call these *metavolcanic rocks*. But there were also some sedimentary rocks present among them, which were eroded from the volcanic rocks, and these too were metamorphosed, becoming *metasedimentary rocks*. Just to complicate the picture (at least from a layman's point of view), geologists have further subdivided these classifications. Thus the volcanic rocks called basalt, andesite and rhyolite became under great heat and pressure, metabasalt, meta-andesite and metarhyolite. The metamorphosed sediments have a complex nomenclature, which fortunately we can ignore.

**Granitic intrusions**  The three big crunches were due to movement of the oceanic crust with respect to western North America. When oceanic crust interacts with continental crust in an appropriate manner, granitic rocks result. When oceanic crust dives deeper and deeper beneath continental crust, encountering increasing temperatures and pressures, it begins to melt, and some of this melted material known as *magma*, works its way upward through the continental crust. If the magma solidifies before reaching the earth's surface, it becomes granitic rocks. If it reaches the surface as eruptions of ash or lava, it becomes volcanic rocks.

In the Sierra Nevada magma solidified as discrete bodies called *plutons,* which range in cross section from about ¼ square mile to almost 600 square miles. In the Tahoe Sierra the plutons average about 10 square miles. The composition of these *plutonic* rocks, like that of the other Sierra plutons, is typically of grano-diorite, although a whole spectrum of compositions exists, from gabbro to granite (see the following table of igneous rocks; note that igneous rocks include both plutonic and volcanic rocks). All of them formed during the Mesozoic era, and in the Tahoe Sierra the plutons fall mostly into two age groups: 186-155 and 125-88 million years ago.

Today granitic rocks are exposed over much of the Tahoe Sierra, though they are not the overwhelmingly dominating rock that they are in the High Sierra of Yosemite, Sequoia and Kings Canyon national parks. These generally light gray rocks and the gravelly soils produced from them by weathering are locally prevalant in our area, comprising most of Desolation Wilderness (Chapters 13 and 14) and most of the Carson Range (Chapter 16).

Of course, back at the time of their formation, granitic rocks in the form of plutons lay beneath the Tahoe landscape—as much as 10-15 miles beneath it. It was not until about 50 million years ago, after erosive processes had stripped away much of the overlying rock, that our area was becoming distinctly granitic in character.

Back then the landscape was lower. In the western lands, as around Grass Valley and Nevada City (Hike 1), major ridges stood 1000-1500 feet above the rivers, which in turn were very close to sea level. Eastward, in what is now

## IGNEOUS ROCKS

| generally increasing oxides of silicon, sodium and potassium ↑ | Volcanic Rocks | | Plutonic Rocks | generally increasing oxides of magnesium, iron and calcium; also, increasing melting point and increasing density ↓ |
|---|---|---|---|---|
| | **rhyolite** | approximately equals | **granite** | |
| | **rhyodacite** | approximately equals | **quartz monzonite** | |
| | **dacite** | approximately equals | **granodiorite** | |
| | **andesite** | approximately equals | **diorite** | |
| | **basaltic andesite** | approximately equals | | |
| | **basalt** | approximately equals | **gabbro** | |

the Lake Tahoe area, the major ridges stood perhaps 2000-2500 feet above the rivers. Pyramid Peak and the Freel Peak massif, both considerably bulkier than they are today, stood as much as 3000 feet above the American River, which at Echo Summit, like the South Yuba River at Donner Pass, stood at about 4000 feet elevation (both passes had yet to form).

By this time, 50 million years ago, granitic plutons were exposed over much of the eastern Tahoe Sierra and over adjacent lands in western Nevada. Rivers carried the debris created by weathering of the granite westward toward an inland sea, whose swampy east edge lay around the east edge of today's Central Valley. The rivers' gradients decreased almost to zero as they approached this sea, and as their flow slowed, they had to drop their heavier sediments. The Yuba River in particular deposited a tremendous amount of gravel, which accumulated to a thickness as much as 600 feet in the area of Malakoff Diggins State Historic Park (Hikes 3-7). This gravel was nearly pure quartz because this quartz is very abundant in most granitic rocks and because it is the mineral in granite that is most resistant to intense weathering. This gravel also contained minute pieces of gold scattered throughout it, particularly in the lower strata of sediments. Hike 5 describes the geology of this area plus its interesting "gold fever" history.

**Hiker on an autobrecciated-lava boulder**

**Tahoe Sierra volcanism** Later, about 33 million years ago, the slowly eroding Tahoe Sierra was given new bulk by a series of volcanic eruptions. In the first phase they were infrequent, though very explosive, eruptions of rhyolite, and these continued sporadically until about 19 million years ago. During most of this time the landscape was tranquil and well forested, for the eruptions were occurring at a rate similar to that found in today's Cascades. Although infrequent, these eruptions nevertheless were able to bury local parts of the terrain under as much as 1000 feet of rhyolite. This undoubtedly changed the courses of some streams and rivers, and it certainly buried much of the earlier gold-bearing gravels.

Even larger drainage changes took place in a second phase, with the eruption of basalt and andesite. These eruptions began about 26 million years ago, and were particularly intense from about 10 to 5 million years ago. Most of the Tahoe Sierra's volcanic flows and deposits you see today are from this later phase. Collectively, all the flows and deposits of this second phase are called the Mehrten Formation.

The eruptions that gave rise to this formation were mostly of andesite lava, which flowed from a string of volcanoes that more or less ran north-south along what is today's crest—probably resembling the string of peaks that one sees in today's Oregon Cascades. But although most of the eruptions occurred as lava flows (very little was ash), the Mehrten Formation doesn't contain very many large lava flows. Why? Because most of the flows, as they were being erupted and were slowly descending a volcano's slopes, began to break apart. Each flow typically broke into millions of pieces, in a process called *autobrecciation*. Then the lava flows, being so broken up, were readily eroded and the pieces carried to lower sites, to be deposited as volcanic rubble. This extensive rubble—that is, the Mehrten Formation—thinned to the west, but it nevertheless was thick enough to bury the old river systems. Erosion by new streams led to the creation of today's rivers, which in the intervening 20 or so million years since their birth have cut some impressively deep canyons. This canyon cutting was aided to a great extent by renewed uplift of the range, which may have begun in earnest about 3 million years ago around Desolation Wilderness, but only about 1½ million years ago around the Sierra Buttes (uplift began in the southern Sierra Nevada and worked northward).

**The horizontally layered Mehrten Formation stands above Caples Lake (Hike 96)**

During the last 10 million years, as repeated volcanism constructed an increasingly higher landscape and then as the Sierra began to rise, giant sequoias and other species of plants "migrated" westward down Tahoe Sierra canyons. Of course, it wasn't each tree that was migrating, but rather the population. As elevation increased the trees in the upper part of a canyon were exposed to increasingly colder conditions, and they died. The trees in the lower part survived. Perhaps due to extensive volcanism, most migrating sequoia groves were exterminated. However, at least one specimen—and more likely a grove—survived to give rise to what is now the Placer County Big Trees grove (Hike 30).

**Origin of the Sierra crest** By about 5 million years ago, the Tahoe Sierra landscape may have resembled Oregon's Cascades; it was certainly quite different from today's landscape. There was no Sierra crest, no Tahoe basin and few, if any, lakes. But somewhere around 3–4 million years ago the land to the east began to sink, and as it did, the sinking left a fault scarp whose apex was a Sierra crest.

Streams and rivers which earlier had flowed west from the land that was sinking, could no longer do so, since these eastern lands now lay below the recently formed crest. Today we see evidence that former streams and rivers once flowed out to the Pacific Ocean, for they left deep gaps in what is now the Sierra crest. One of the most notable gaps is immediately above Paradise Lake (Hike 38, Map 14), which is a few miles north of an even larger, though amorphous, gap, Donner Pass. Between 4 and 2 million years ago, one particularly large basin, which was the precursor of the Lake Tahoe Basin, formed as land sank between the Sierra crest and the Carson Range.

**The birth of Lake Tahoe** While faulting created a basin between the Sierra Nevada and Carson Range crests, it didn't create a lake. Streams flowed unimpeded northeastward, beyond the basin. But starting about 2¼ million years ago, lava flows began to erupt in the northern half of the basin, and eventually they impounded water south of them, thus giving birth to Lake Tahoe. Between 2¼ and 1¼ million years ago there were at least seven major eruptions of lava, which caused the lake's surface to rise as much as 800 feet above its current 6229-foot level. Had there been more flows to raise the lake another 200 or 300 feet, the lake might have created a new outlet, spilling north over Brockway Summit, east over Spooner Summit or west through the McKinney Creek-Miller Creek gap in the Sierra crest.

**Glaciation** The rising of the land in the Tahoe Sierra coupled with a worldwide cooling trend may have brought on glaciation as much as 3 million years ago. Nevertheless, the early glaciers were probably small and ineffective, and perhaps not until about one million years ago did major glaciers fill the canyons of our area. Contrary to local folk tales, these glaciers, even at their maximum extent, never filled the Tahoe basin. At most, they advanced about a mile or so beyond the lake's west and south shores, spewing icebergs into the frigid water. Because the mountains above the lake's west shore collected most of the precipitation from Pacific storms, the mountains above its east shore lacked sufficient snow and ice to develop any sizable glaciers (see glacier map on page 32).

Glaciers not only discharged into Lake Tahoe, a few large ones even managed to dam it. These huge glaciers descended east to the north-flowing Truckee River—Tahoe's outlet stream—and they blocked its flow. The glacier dams were immense at the peak of the Tahoe-stage glaciation, which lasted on and off from about 215,000-140,000 years ago. A glacier blocking the lake's outlet was thick enough to raise the lake's level by 600 feet above its present level (as shown on the map). When water pressure became great enough to break the ice dams, inconceivably large walls of water roared down the Truckee River canyon. During the last major period of glaciation, Tahoe's glaciers were smaller, though still impressive. During this last period's Tenaya stage, one or more glacier dams raised the lake by 90 feet. During its more recent Tioga stage, the area's glaciers were a bit smaller and shorter, and apparently no ice dam formed in the Truckee River canyon.

When the last glaciers finally retreated about 12,000 to 10,000 years ago, they left behind the rock and rubble they had been carrying, leaving it in the form of moraines. In much of the High Sierra this rock and rubble is simply strewn across the landscape, and these deposits are called *ground moraines*. Along Lake Tahoe's west shore, another type of moraine is dramatically seen, the *lateral moraine*. Lateral moraines usually occur in pairs, where a glacier flowing down-canyon dropped debris along both its sides. The Tahoe Sierra's most photographed set of lateral moraines is the pair that border Emerald Bay. Where glaciers from two canyons meet and advance side by side, they form between them a special kind of lateral moraine called a *medial moraine*. The Tahoe basin's most prominent one is the long ridge separating Fallen Leaf Lake from the Upper Truckee River canyon. Another kind of moraine is the *end (terminal) moraine*, which is just the continuation of the lateral moraines around the snout of the glacier. No prominent end moraines remain in the lake's basin; they have been carried away by the lake's currents. Indeed, the bouldery debris dropped from the glaciers' snouts probably was carried away as fast as it was deposited. A last kind of moraine is the *recessional moraine*. It forms as a glacier retreats, stagnates for

a while, and then resumes its retreat. The glacier drops some debris as it retreats, but where it stagnates, the debris can form a sizeable ridge, such as the one damming Wrights Lake.

Lake Tahoe was not the only sizeable lake in our area. During part of the Ice Age two other large lakes existed, both lying just outside the scope of this book's coverage. The one closest to Lake Tahoe was Washoe Lake, which at its maximum was about 25 square miles, or roughly five times its present size. The lake's basin was created, like Tahoe's, by subsidence of a land mass between faults. This basin, however, was not dammed by lava flows, so the lake remained quite shallow. At its maximum, it was no more than 80 feet deep. Only one glacier, which was a rather minor one, approached it. This Ophir Creek glacier descended to within 3 miles of the shoreline. During interglacial times, the lake shrunk dramatically, existing more or less as it does in today's interglacial period.

The other lake, situated at the north end of the Tahoe Sierra, was the Mohawk-Sierra lake. In area it rivaled Tahoe, both hovering around 200 square miles. However, in beauty it placed a poor second, for from no spot could you have viewed most of the lake. As you can see on the map, this lake had a very irregular shoreline, its waters flooding three fault-bounded valleys. The largest of these was Sierra Valley, but this lobe was, like the middle Humbug Valley section, quite shallow. At its highest level the shoreline stood at about 5050 feet elevation, giving both sections a maximum depth of about 200 feet. Only the western Mohawk Valley section was deep—up to 800 feet. And it was the most impressive section, for like Tahoe it had glaciers entering it, which calved icebergs into its chilly water. Also like Tahoe it had a lava dam, which held for perhaps 3 million years. The lake in its highest stages overflowed west into Poplar Creek, which drained north to the Middle Fork Feather River. The dam finally gave way about 130,000 years ago, during an interglacial time.

Before that interglacial time, when the Tahoe-stage glaciation was at its maximum, our landscape, wrapped in an ermine robe of ice, must have been a gorgeous sight from the air. The accompanying map shows the possible distribution of glaciers during this time. (The Tenaya and Tioga stages were significantly smaller.) Note on the map that much of the Sierra crest lay under ice. Usually the ice accumulated on the gaps in this crest and flowed away from them,

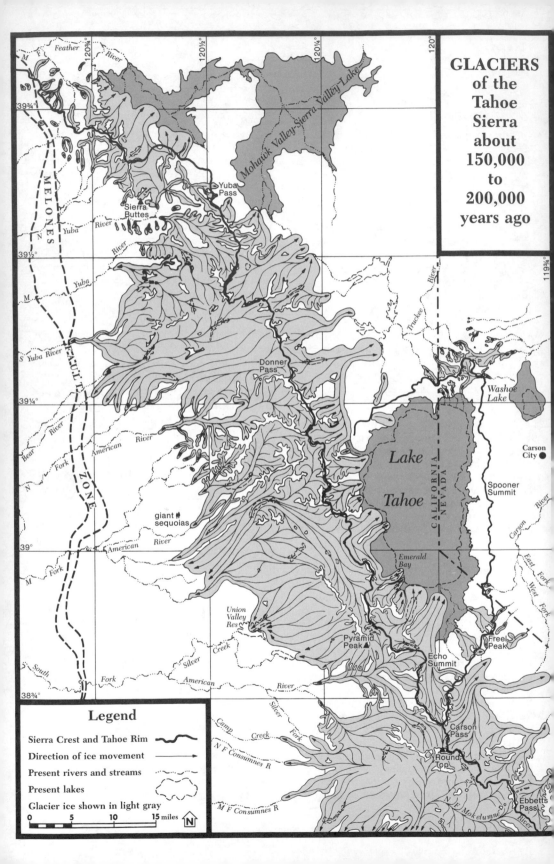

GLACIERS
of the
Tahoe
Sierra
about
150,000
to
200,000
years ago

Feather River

Mohawk Valley-Sierra Valley Lake

MELONES

M F

120¾°

120½°

120¼°

120°

119¾°

39¾°

39½°

39¼°

39°

38¾°

FAULT ZONE

N

M

N

M

Yuba Pass

Sierra Buttes

Yuba River

Yuba River

River

Yuba

S Yuba River

Bear River

N Fork

American River

M Fork

American River

giant sequoias

American River

Donner Pass

Truckee River

Washoe Lake

Lake Tahoe

CALIFORNIA NEVADA

Carson City

Spooner Summit

Carson River

East Fork

West Fork

Emerald Bay

Union Valley Res

Silver Creek

South Fork

Fork

American River

Silver Fork

Camp Creek

N F Consumnes R

M F Consumnes R

Pyramid Peak

Echo Summit

Freel Peak

Carson Pass

Round Top

N F Mokelumne River

Ebbetts Pass

Legend

Sierra Crest and Tahoe Rim

Direction of ice movement

Present rivers and streams

Present lakes

Glacier ice shown in light gray

0     5     10     15 miles

N

**Glacial evidence: erratic boulder, polish, striations, chatter marks**

but not always. For instance, a large glacier originating on the north slopes of Round Top Peak, in the southeastern part of our area, flowed both northwest down-canyon and northeast across the Sierra crest. The northwest lobe overflowed its canyon at a low spot and spilled into the American River drainage. A small part of this large glacier also spilled over into the Upper Truckee River basin, whose mammoth glacier, about 2000 feet thick, in turn spilled west, across Echo Summit, into the American River drainage. West of the Sierra crest large ice fields developed, burying all but the highest ridges and peaks.

When the last of the Tahoe Sierra glaciers finally retreated about 10,000 years ago, they left behind a barren land containing many rocky basins. The basins quickly filled to create today's lakes. Where the glaciers had left behind lots of sediments (ground moraines), rich forests developed. Where sediments were scarce, as in much of largely granitic Desolation Wilderness, open forests developed or the land lay bare. On these soil-free lands little has changed since the day the glaciers retreated from them. On some bare granitic slabs only ¼ inch of erosion has taken place, if that much, and the glaciers' signature, in the form of polish, striations and chatter marks, is readily discernible.

There's still a pervasive misconception that Sierra meadows are the result of glacial lakes being totally filled with incoming sediments. But in 10,000 years, lake-bed sedimentation amounts to inches, not to tens of feet. Given enough time, Sierra lakes will completely fill up with sediments, and meadows will result. But don't count on it. Odds are that long before this happens the Tahoe Sierra will once more be plunged into another glacial episode, and its glaciers will scour away the lake and meadow sediments so that in a future time the cycle can begin once again.

# Ch. 6         Botany

**Introduction** Reconnaissance satellites monitor the earth's vegetation today, and it is unfortunate they weren't around 65 million years ago, when the last of the dinosaurs became extinct. If we had a continuous video record from that time onward—in other words, for all of the Cenozoic period—what a show it would be. Back then, 65 million years ago, the earth had attained 98½% of its present age, yet in the ensuing 1½% of its aging, its surface would experience tremendous changes in landscapes, plants and animals. In the Tahoe Sierra the changes in plants were particularly dramatic.

**History of the Tahoe Sierra flora** For at least the first 15 million years of the Cenozoic period the Tahoe Sierra flora was generally tropical in nature. But with time North America drifted into higher latitudes and the flora responded by becoming subtropical. This vegetation change was brought about partly by the evolution of the existing Tahoe plants and partly by the migration of subtropical plants—from the north and northeast—into the area.

Much later, many northern species migrated into our area in response to the Sierra Nevada's volcanic upbuilding, followed by uplift beginning up to several million years ago. By 3–4 million years ago the Tahoe Sierra's crest began to form as lands east of the present crest began to sink. The area at this time had three groups of northern floral immigrants: those from polar lowlands, those from the Cascade Range and those from the Rocky Mountains.

But there were also lowland southern immigrants, which already were quite adapted to California's developing "Mediterranean" climate of hot, dry summers and cool, wet winters. In the Tahoe area the summers weren't quite as hot, but the radiation was greater—both conditions due to the higher elevation—and the summers were certainly quite dry. During this season, a plant's evapotranspiration (water loss) is high, and it needs more water.

The onset of glaciation, roughly 2 million years ago, brought even more stress to the Tahoe flora. During times of maximum glaciation, most of the area covered by this book—that is, the land above 6000 feet—lay under glacier ice. (The higher peaks and ridges, however, did protrude above the sea of ice). As with volcanic flows, glaciers swept away soils, and plants were forced downslope. In the last million years, when glaciation has been the most intense, there have been about a dozen major glacial episodes. With each one, the plants would retreat to lower elevations as the glaciers advanced, then advance toward the crest as they retreated. When the glaciers retreated, they left basins, which quickly filled to form lakes and ponds, and these provided new Tahoe-area habitats to exploit—though with each glacier readvance, the lakes and ponds were generally obliterated.

During interglacial times, such as today's, Tahoe's climate proved quite amenable to certain lower-elevation plants. Some came from the Sierra foothills, but since there was now a Sierra crest, there was a second source, the high-desert lands east of the crest. From about 6600 to 3500 years ago California's climate was a few degrees warmer than it is today, and it was probably then that some drought-resistant Great Basin plants were able to compete successfully against the resident Sierra crest plants. Similar intrusions had probably occurred during previous inter-

**Some common shrubs of the Tahoe Sierra. All have white flowers except as noted in parentheses.**
Top row, left to right: bush chinquapin (flowers inconspicuous), pinemat manzanita (pale pink), Labrador tea, bog kalmia (rose). Row 2: red mountain heather (rose), white mountain heather, creek dogwood, snow bush. Row 3: tobacco brush, mountain spiraea (rose), bitter cherry, thimbleberry. Bottom row: western serviceberry, mountain ash, red elderberry, mountain snowberry (pink).

glacial times, though with the onset of each glaciation, virtually all of the high-elevation plants would have been eradicated, the relatively few survivors eking out an existence on *nunataks*—the ridges and peaks protruding above the sea of ice. The central part of the Carson Range, lying in a significant rain shadow, was never glaciated, or if it was, it was to a very minor extent. Consequently, Great Basin plants had abundant opportunities to get established there, and today they make up a considerable percentage of that area's plant population.

The final trauma to Tahoe Sierra flora began with the Gold Rush. Particularly in the Carson Range, forests were razed to supply firewood and timber to mining settlements. Alien plants were brought in, some unintentionally and some on purpose, and their aggressive competition proved to be detrimental to some native plants. Today, ponderosa pine, and to a lesser extent its close relative the Jeffrey pine, faces a new problem—air pollution. As California's Central Valley becomes increasingly urbanized, air pollution will probably continue to increase, and the damage to these pines may eventually become quite serious, for once the trees are weakened, they are highly susceptible to death by bark-beetle infestation.

**Identifying Tahoe Sierra plants**  In the Tahoe Sierra proper, which is defined as that region mostly above 6000 feet and extending from the Carson Pass environs north to Plumas-Eureka State Park, there are about 1000 species of vascular plants. Vascular plants include trees, shrubs and herbs. Herbs include, in addition to "wildflowers" (a hard term to define) such members as grasses, sedges and rushes. However, for the aspiring botanist, and particularly for the average hiker, such herbs may be unexciting. The same applies to Tahoe's other vascular plants, the ferns, fern allies, horsetails, club mosses and quillworts.

The average hiker can't fail to notice the trees, though he or she may be more impressed with their size or shape than with what species they are. The vast majority of trees one sees in the Tahoe Sierra are conifers, and most are quite easy to identify. Since only 17 species are found along this area's trails, all are included in the next section. Nonconiferous trees, such as oaks and aspens, may be locally abundant, but certainly above 6000 feet elevation they make up a small percentage of the overall forest canopy. If you are interested in all of the area's trees but not

in the shrubs and herbs, then consider carrying Watts' 2-ounce wonder, the *Pacific Coast Tree Finder* (for this book and others, see "Recommended Reading and Source Materials," at the back of this guidebook).

*The* authoritative reference to Lake Tahoe's vascular plants is Smith's monograph and its later supplement. Unfortunately, neither is readily available to the general public, though serious botanists will want to acquire both. They list the species and their distributions, but neither has a plant key. For that you'll need Munz or Weeden. Professionals carry the fairly expensive, 4-pound Munz; most others prefer the economical, 10-ounce Weeden. Plant keys usually intimidate nonprofessionals, but Weeden's keys are as user-friendly as one could expect. Although Weeden has many more illustrations than Munz, most of the Tahoe Sierra wildflowers are not illustrated. To compensate for this, I've included over 150 species of wildflowers on 17 plates. (For scientific names, see the appendix at the back of the book.) Flowers that are found along many of this guidebook's trails are grouped together in this chapter's eight plates. Those with a more restricted, though often locally abundant, distribution are on the remaining nine plates, which are found in the hiking chapters (all plates are indexed in the "Contents"). If you are interested only in wildflowers and abhor all keys, then Niehaus and Ripper's guide is your best bet.

**The conifers: cone-bearing trees**  All of the conifers in the Tahoe Sierra have evergreen leaves, which are either needlelike or scalelike. In the key below, the conifers are listed by leaf and cone characteristics. In the descriptions that follow, the conifers in each group are listed in the order you would encounter them as you drove east up the Sierra's slopes.

1.  Pines: except for one species, pines have needles in bundles of 2-5; cones hanging (1a. 1 needle, 1b. 2 needles, 1c. 3 needles, 1d. 5 needles).
2.  True firs: needles in rows along branches; cones upright atop upper branches.
3.  False fir and hemlock: needles not in rows; cones hanging.
4.  Other conifers: leaves small, scalelike, about ⅛-¼" long.

1a.  Pine with 1 needle.
**Pinyon pine**  Needles drab, sharp-pointed, 1-1½" long. Found only along the east flank of the Carson Range, generally below its crest. Not likely to be seen.

1b. Pine with 2 needles.

**Lodgepole pine** Bark thin, scaly, sappy—don't touch it. Very common in Tahoe Sierra, especially between 6000 and 9000'.

1c. Pines with 3 needles.

**Digger pine** Needles gray-green, 7-12" long. Cones 6-10" long, on short stalks. Below 4000' (Hikes 1-7 only, especially Hike 2).

**Knobcone pine** Needles green, 3-7" long. Cones 3-6" long, stalkless. Below 4000' (Hikes 1-7 only, especially Hike 2).

**Ponderosa pine** Needles yellow-green, 5-10" long. Cones 3-5" long, with out-turned prickles. Bark yellow and platy in mature trees. Tree 150-220' tall. Common from about 1500 to 6500', occasional to 7500'.

**Jeffrey pine** Needles blue-green, 5-10" long. Cones 5-10" long, with in-turned prickles. Bark reddish brown, with butterscotch odor detected in bark furrows of mature trees. Tree 50-180' tall. Common from about 5000 to 8500'. Hybridizes with ponderosa pine, making identification difficult where the two species overlap.

**Washoe pine** Needles gray-green, 4-6" long. Cones usually less than 5" long. Hard to distinguish from its close relative, the Jeffrey pine. It occurs in significant numbers only in the Mt. Rose area (Hike 106), from about 6000 to 8500 feet.

1d. Pines with 5 needles.

**Sugar pine** Needles 3-4" long. Cones long and narrow, 10-16" long, growing at ends of long, graceful branches. Tree 150-240' tall. Common from about 3000 to 6500' west of the Sierra crest; uncommon in the Tahoe basin.

**Western white pine** Needles 2-4" long. Cones narrow, 4-8" long. Checkerboard pattern on bark of mature trees. Tree 50-150' tall. Occurs from about 6000 to 9500', but common only from 7000 to 9000'.

**Whitebark pine** Needles stiff, 1½-3" long. Cones 1½-3" long. Bark thin and scaly, like that of lodgepole pine. Tree up to 50' tall, but a prostrate shrub at highest elevations. Common from about 8500 to 10,800'.

2. True firs.

**White fir** Needles 1-2½" long, in two rows. Each needle with a half twist at base. Cones 3-5" long. Bark of mature tree grayish brown, deeply furrowed. Tree 150-230' tall. Common from about 3000 to 6500', but occasional up to 7500'.

**Red fir** Needles ¾-1½" long, stout, curving up and densely covering branches. Cones 5-8" long. Bark of mature tree reddish brown, deeply furrowed. Tree 120-200' tall. Common from about 6500 to 9000', but occasional down to 5500'.

3. False Fir and Hemlock

**Douglas-fir** Needles about 1" long, soft, and growing all around the branches. Cones 2-4" long, lightweight, with toothed bracts projecting from scales. Bark dull-brown, deeply furrowed. Tree 150-230' tall. Locally common, especially on north-facing slopes, from about 1000 to 6000'. Occasional to 6500', but rare in Tahoe basin.

**Mountain hemlock** Needles about 1" long, soft, and growing all around the branches. Cones 1-3" long, lightweight, without bracts. Bark purplish brown to reddish brown. Tree 25-100' tall. Grows in areas of deep snowpack, from about 7000 to 10,000'.

4. Other Conifers.

**Incense-cedar** Leaves yellow-green, in flat, horizontal sprays. Cones about 1" long, with only two fertile scales (two seeds each). Bark cinnamon-brown, fibrous. Tree 80-150' tall. Fairly common, it associates with white firs and ponderosa pines, growing from about 1000 to 6500', rarely higher.

**Western juniper** Leaves gray-green, clasping the branchlets. Cones, berrylike, blue-black when mature, though covered with a whitish powder. Bark cinnamon-brown, shreddy. Trunk short and broad. Locally common in dry, rocky areas, particularly in Desolation Wilderness, from about 5000 to 9500'.

**Giant sequoia** Found only in one small grove (Hike 30). When this Placer County grove was discovered, only six trees existed there, but more have been planted around them.

**Plant Distribution** Given the area covered by this guidebook, the author has divided the vegetation into four major vegetation zones. Increasing in elevation, these are: lower montane vegetation, upper montane vegetation, subalpine vegetation and alpine vegetation. (For the first three types many botanists say "forest" instead of "vegetation," but each of these zones has locally large areas of nonforest vegetation such as brush and grass.) Although many species grow in only one vegetation zone, many others grow in two zones, less in three zones, and a few in all four zones. An example from the last category is the woolly sunflower, which extends, as one variety or another, from sea level up to 12,000 feet. Obviously then, the following classification is not a perfect one.

*Lower Montane Vegetation Zone*

This zone extends from about 2000 to 6000' in elevation, broadly speaking. To the west lies the foothills vegetation zone, which barely gets a toehold in the Tahoe Sierra. The only hike described in this guidebook which passes through this lower zone is the South Yuba Trail, Hike 2.

**Wildflower Plate 1. White or pinkish white flowers of the parsley (carrot) family (photos 1-5) and the sunflower family (6-9). Note: the _scientific_ names of all the wildflowers on Plates 1-17 are listed on page 302. Flower colors are shown in parentheses.**
**1 Parish's yampah, 2 Gray's lovage, 3 Brewer's angelica, 4 cow parsnip, 5 ranger's buttons, 6 leafy thistle, 7 rosy everlasting, 8 white-flowered hawkweed, 9 hoary chaenactis.**

**Wildflower Plate 2. Whitish flowers of other plant families.**
1 Nude buckwheat, 2 western bistort, 3 alpine knotweed, 4 Nevada lewisia, 5 spreading phlox (white, pale pink or pale blue), 6 white-veined wintergreen, 7 death camas, 8 California corn lily, 9 Sierra rein orchid.

**Wildflower Plate 3. Off-yellow or partly yellow flowers.**
1 Pearly everlasting (white with yellow center), 2 yarrow (white with yellow center), 3 wandering daisy (violet with yellow center), 4 Fendler's meadow rue (yellow-green), 5 marsh marigold (white with yellow center), 6 mountain jewel flower (white-yellow to red-purple), 7 dwarf lousewort (dull yellow), 8 Leichtlin's Mariposa tulip (creamy white with yellow base), 9 Davis' knotweed (white-yellow to purple-green).

40

**Wildflower Plate 4. Yellow flowers of the sunflower family.**
1 Seep-spring arnica, 2 soft arnica, 3 arrow-leaved balsamroot, 4 Brewer's golden aster, 5 woolly sunflower, 6 nodding microseris, 7 single-stemmed senecio, 8 arrow-leaved senecio, 9 mountain mule ears.

**Wildflower Plate 5. Yellow flowers of other plant families.**
1 Sierra stonecrop, 2 golden brodiaea, 3 sticky cinquefoil, 4 sulfur flower, 5 common mullein, 6 common monkey flower, 7 Baker's violet, 8 mountain violet, 9 Sierra wallflower.

**Wildflower Plate 6. Orange, scarlet or red flowers.**
1 California fuchsia (scarlet), 2 Applegate's paintbrush (scarlet), 3 mountain pride (red), 4 alpine lily (red-orange), 5 crimson columbine (red with yellow center), 6 scarlet gilia, 7 Anderson's thistle (reddish flowers and stem), 8 pinedrops (orange-to-rust plant), 9 snow plant (red plant).

**Wildflower Plate 7. Pink, pinkish violet or rose flowers.**
1 Swamp onion, 2 Sierra onion, 3 nettle-leaved horsemint, 4 alpine shooting star, 5 Richardson's geranium, 6 baby elephant heads, 7 glaucous sidalcea, 8 pussy paws, 9 fireweed.

**Wildflower Plate 8. Blue, blue-violet, violet or purple flowers.**
1 Crest lupine (violet to blue), 2 ballhead phacelia (dull-purple to blue to brown), 3 coyote mint (violet),
4 Nuttall's larkspur (purple), 5 tall larkspur (purple), 6 monk's hood (purple), 7 velvety stickseed (blue
with white center), 8 Sierra penstemon (purple), 9 meadow penstemon (rose-purple).

45

Here, this vegetation is on dry, south-facing slopes, at elevations up to 3000 feet. But on the shady, relatively moist north-facing slopes of the South Yuba River canyon, the lower montane vegetation extends west down to 1000 feet. On the Independence Trail, Hike 1, you're traversing through a lush, verdant Douglas-fir forest.

The primary conifers of this zone are ponderosa pine and white fir, with lesser numbers of Douglas-fir, incense-cedar, sugar pine and giant sequoia, this last species growing in only the Placer County grove (Hike 30). Within this zone, as in all four zones, temperature and precipitation vary considerably. Ponderosa pine prefers the warm, dry sites, white fir and Douglas-fir prefer the cool, moist sites, and the other conifers fall in between. The occurrence of frequent fires favors ponderosa pine, black oak and their shrubby associates, such as mountain misery, deer brush and Mariposa, Indian and whiteleaf manzanitas. In any given spot in the Sierra Nevada, lightning fires tend to occur about once every 7-10 years. When fires are prevented, white fir and incense-cedar take over. This is what happened in Yosemite Valley, much to everyone's consternation, since the original, open pine-and-oak woodland provided superior views of the cliffs and waterfalls.

Near the lower end of this zone, precipitation is about 35 inches per year, with about 5% of it as snow, and the growing season is about 7 months. Near the upper end of this zone, the precipitation can double that, with about half of it as snow, and the growing season is only about 5 months. That is quite some difference. To appreciate the difference, visit Malakoff Diggins State Historic Park (Hikes 3-7), then drive up to Sierra City and explore its environs (Hikes 8-11).

### Upper Montane Vegetation Zone

At about 6000 feet the lower-montane conifers give way to their look-alikes. Ponderosa pine yields to Jeffrey pine, white fir to red fir, sugar pine to western white pine, and incense-cedar to western juniper. Shrubs do likewise, with the lower manzanitas yielding to greenleaf and pinemat manzanitas, and deer brush to tobacco brush and snow bush. Oaks are no longer trees, but rather shrubs: the bush chinquapin and the huckleberry oak. As with the previous zone, the boundary can be quite irregular. White fir may grow on sunny south-facing slopes up to 7500 feet, while red fir may grow on snowy north-facing slopes down to 5500 feet. The upper boundary too is hard to define, but it is roughly at 9000 feet.

The upper montane vegetation zone spreads across a landscape that has been severely glaciated, and this has increased the number of habitats for plants to exploit. These new habitats, listed in an order of increasing wetness, are bedrock slabs and cliffs, lateral moraines, ground moraines, meadows and lakes. Desolation Wilderness has many bedrock outcrops, and these are particularly exploited by western junipers and, to a lesser extent, by Jeffrey pines. These pines prefer instead the dry, gravelly soils of the lateral moraines, and compete for them with huckleberry oak, greenleaf manzanita, tobacco brush, snow bush, bush chinquapin and bitter cherry. The ground moraines support magnificent forests of red fir, but where the ground water is high, the lodgepole pine takes over. If the ground water is too pervasive, no tree can survive, and meadows result. Shrubs such as willows, alders and huckleberries can thrive in meadows, but typically most meadow vegetation is herbs. Here, plant diversity is at its peak, which is in stark contrast to the somber, shady red-fir forest, whose floor is largely barren. If you want to see a hundred plant species in one day, you certainly should visit at least one meadow, for it will put you well on your way toward your goal. The final new habitat, lakes, most novice botanists pass up. A number of species do grow on lake bottoms, but they are generally out of sight and reach unless you're willing to dive after them.

The upper montane vegetation zone not only spreads across severely glaciated lands, but also enters progressively drier lands the farther east one goes from the Sierra crest. In a space of about 20 miles, from the Sierra crest east to the Carson Range crest, the precipitation can be cut in half. This situation prevented the *central* Carson Range from developing glaciers. Hence, the soil there is old and relatively uniform, meadows are few and the land is lakeless except where artificially dammed by man. While the western-land shrubs and herbs can sleep through winter under a protective blanket of snow, the Carson Range plants must battle winter's icy chill head-on. With less water and more severe winters, the vegetation takes on a remarkably different character. The forest is more open, western white pines dominating over red firs. The common shrubs are gone, replaced largely by Great Basin shrubs, several species of sage-brush in particular, and also antelope bush (bitterbrush) and mountain mahogany.

Plants can also adapt to a specific kind of bedrock. In the upper montane vegetation zone there are exposures of granitic, metamorphic and volcanic bedrock, and the mule ears grow in soils derived from each. However, where volcanic soils are rich, mule ears can grow in huge colonies, forming dry meadows that are tens of acres in extent. In the Granite Chief area (Hikes 42-49), these aromatic, leafy sunflowers really put on a show.

*Subalpine Vegetation Zone*

The gradation from the upper montane vegetation zone to the subalpine vegetation zone is irregular. Red fir and Jeffrey pine of the lower zone stay mostly below 8000 feet. Not so for their associates, the lodgepole and western white pines, which can be found in abundance at 9000 feet and even reach 9500 feet. The latter is about 500 feet above the base of Tahoe's subalpine zone (though at the Sierra Buttes, to the north, this base is at about 8200 feet). Locally these pines can outnumber the subalpine zone's primary indicator, the whitebark pine. The

**Top left: cones of ponderosa pine (top), Douglas-fir (right) and sugar pine (bottom). Top right: cones of western white pine (left) and red fir (right). Bottom: white-fir branches (left) versus red-fir branches (right).**

zone's other prominent tree, the mountain hemlock, is a poor indicator, for though it can thrive at 10,000 feet, it can also thrive at 7000 feet. The problem of defining the subalpine zone isn't so much one of what trees exist, but rather of how they exist. You enter the subalpine realm where the trees no longer exist as a continuous forest, but rather in small, compact clusters.

The subalpine zone is a realm of severe environment. Almost all the precipitation is in the form of snow, and there is a lot of it, though it doesn't always stay put. Among hemlocks, which grow in snowy sites and actually help to preserve the snow by their extremely dense, shady clustering, the snow can cover the ground for 10 months of the year, In more exposed sites gusty winds can blow the snow away, leaving the ground barren and exposed to months of subfreezing temperatures. In this harsh environment the growing season is only about two months long. During that brief period, shrubs and herbs must sprout new vegetation, produce flowers and seeds, and stock up on carbohydrate reserves for the oncoming winter.

As you climb up through the subalpine realm, you'll notice that the trees decrease in stature. By 10,000 feet the whitebark pine is the only species of tree, if you can call the stunted specimens trees. They may be 20 feet high in favorable spots, but more likely they will be only a few feet high. And as you climb toward a high summit, particularly Freel Peak, Jobs Peak or Jobs Sister, the tree becomes reduced to a dense mat of knee-high vegetation.

Shrubs and herbs also decrease in stature with increasing elevation. The pine's and shrubs' adaptations are to the harsh winter climate, for keeping low allows them to stay within a blanket of protective snow. Any parts of the plants that protrude above it are pruned back by the icy, subfreezing winter winds. The herbs, on the other hand, are adapted to the summer climate, They are typically matted or prostrate, usually less than 4 inches high. By keeping low, they are protected from buffeting winds, which are rarely effective within the first few inches from the ground.

But pollination of these flowers by the wind is ineffective. The plants are too few and far between to rely on the wind for this vital process.

This is true for wildflowers *everywhere* in the Tahoe Sierra, not just above 9000 feet. However, conifers, grasses and sedges rely on wind for pollination. This mode of pollination is perhaps a clue to why the dwarfed whitebark pines grow in such dense clusters. If they were evenly spaced across the terrain, the ovules in the female cones would be far less likely to be pollinated, resulting in very few seeds. Compactness, however, assures pollination. The seeds, being heavy, are not readily distributed, but animals tend to that. The Clark nutcracker is particularly effective at this task, burying caches of seeds to last it through the year. The bird will eat most of the seeds, but some will survive to create another cluster of whitebark pines.

### Alpine Vegetation Zone

Perhaps the alpine vegetation zone does not truly exist in the Tahoe Sierra, for whitebark pines approach or reach the highest summits. In our area there are only three serious contenders for this designation: Round Top (Hike 97), Freel Peak-Jobs Sister (Hikes 102-103) and Mt. Rose (Hike 106). The author considers himself in the alpine realm when he sights the sky pilot, which he has never seen below treeline. In Yosemite, one sees this blue-flowered member of the phlox family at 12,000-13,000 feet. It does not grow north of the park.

Still, there are Tahoe shrubs and herbs that do prefer to grow on land above the trees. All of the nine wildflowers that appear on Plate 17 (Mt. Rose, Hike 106) fall into this category. Other wildflowers include silky raillardella and showy polemonium (Plate 11, Hike 16), alpine sorrel (Plate 13, Hike 71) and shaggy hawkweed (Plate 14, Hike 81). A variety of showy penstemon (Plate 15, Hike 97) also fits into this category. At high elevations this variety can form dense mats with showy clusters of brilliant blue flowers.

During glacial times, a true alpine realm existed, for Tahoe's high peaks had temperatures like those found today on the Sierra's highest peaks. The relict populations of quasialpine plants are enduring the current interglacial "heat wave," waiting for the time when they can once again expand their domain.

# Zoology

**Introduction**   We humans are unique animals. We may be the only life form in our galaxy that can comprehend nature from its least scale—the subatomic quarks and leptons—up to its grandest scale—the entire universe. We have the potential to give rise, directly or indirectly, to advanced life forms that could, theoretically, colonize our galaxy in considerably less than a million years, which is merely a tick of the universal time clock. Yet, despite our accomplishments and our potential (if we don't destroy ourselves in the near future), we are superfluous animals. But it's not only we who are superfluous; the same applies to all the vertebrates, be they fishes, amphibians, reptiles, birds or mammals. The only necessary animals are the invertebrates, those lowly animals we seldom think about unless they're pestering us, our homes or our gardens. Without pollinating insects, flowering plants would face extinction. Humans, in contrast, hold the record for causing extinctions, having eliminated innumerable plants and animals, including a former monarch of the Tahoe Sierra, the California grizzly bear.

**Invertebrates**   In a mountain meadow there can be thousands of invertebrates in every square yard. In meadow-splotched Desolation Wilderness, their numbers are in the countless billions. As in other land environments, insects make up the bulk of the species, spiders placing a poor second. California has about 30,000 species of insects and perhaps a sixth of them can be found in the Tahoe Sierra. That amounts to about five species for every species of vascular plant.

**Top: three common insects. Fir sawyer (beetle), sphinx moth at Davidson's penstemons, ceanothus sphinx moth cocoon attached to manzanita branch. Bottom: three forest arthropods. Millipede (a scavenger), tick engorged with blood, crab spider on balsamroot flower.**

Many are pollinators, including species of moths, butterflies, beetles, bees, flies and mosquitoes. Yes, mosquitoes, which, as much as we may despise them, are important pollinators. Honey bees fare poorly in the mountains, but bumblebees, which can regulate their body temperature, can thrive even in Tahoe's alpine flower gardens. Up there above 10,000 feet, they sometimes get competition from sphinx moths, which are among the Sierra's largest pollinators, being close to a hummingbird in size.

But moths lead most of their lives as larvae, which are well known for their leaf-eating habits. One equally large cousin of the sphinx moth is the ceanothus silk moth, which is found up to about 7500 feet in the Tahoe Sierra. It devours not only ceanothus leaves, but also those of other shrubs such as manzanitas and willows. Then, too, there are bark beetles, which in effect devour forests. They supposedly kill more trees than all other agents combined—fire, fungi and other insects.

Birds keep insects and other invertebrates in check, consuming impressive quantities of them, but in all liklihood insects and spiders consume even larger quantities of their brethren. For example, woodwasp larvae parasitize the larvae of bark beetles, fir sawyers and other wood borers. Crab spiders climb into flowers that match their coloration, then snatch unsuspecting creatures, such as mosquitoes, which fly too close. These spiders, in turn, are sought after by mud daubers, which are wasps. But even some wasps are subject to attack, ironically by their relatives, the ichneumonid wasps. In short, invertebrates by themselves do a commendable job of regulating their own numbers while keeping the forests and meadows healthy.

**Fish**   One kind of animal is responsible for luring thousands of visitors to the Tahoe Sierra— the trout. Originally, there were only two kinds of trout in our area, the rainbow and the cutthroat, but other species have been introduced and the rainbow has been extensively crossbred. Chapter 4 mentions these trout and their relatives, which collectively are known as salmonids, and it also indicates the lakes in which you can find them.

Some Tahoe Sierra lakes and streams also have nongame fish. In Lake Tahoe there are five species: Piute sculpin, Tahoe sucker, Tui chub, Lahontan redside and Lahontan speckled dace. The sculpin is particularly interesting. As the

female salmonid lays her eggs, sculpins may dart in and eat all the eggs they can. Most eggs, however, are successfully buried, but when the young salmonids emerge from the gravel, many are eaten by these bottom-dwelling fish. But as the surviving salmonids grow, the tables begin to turn. By the time Tahoe's lake trout reach the 5-10 inch range, about half their diet is sculpin, the other half being invertebrates. Virtually no other fish is eaten. However, when lake trout grow to the 15-20 inch range, they also consume a lot of suckers and chubs. And by the time they surpass 20 inches, their diet is 90% fish, about half of it suckers and a third of it salmonids. Cannibalism is not uncommon.

**Amphibians and reptiles**   These vertebrates, like fish, are cold-blooded, and hence do rather poorly in mountain environments. If one excludes the lower-elevation Malakoff Diggins area (Chapter 8) and looks for these animals in the rest of the Tahoe Sierra, he is likely to find only five species of amphibians and seven species of reptiles.

Two of the amphibians are salamanders. The long-toed salamander measures up to 7 inches and has a row of yellow blotches down its back. The ensatina, which is similar-sized, has some bright orange on its body and a constriction at the base of its tail. You're unlikely to see either unless you actively seek them out in ponds or under logs or leaves.

The commonest amphibian is the Pacific treefrog, whose collective, resounding choruses belie their dwarf stature. These ½-1 inch amphibians may be brown or green, but both varieties sport a black eye stripe. Larger, but less common, are the mountain yellow-legged frog, which prefers ponds, and the drab western toad, which enters water only to breed. As an adult, it prefers to forage on land, even in rocky areas.

In the Tahoe Sierra two similar lizards are quite common in dry areas: the western fence lizard and the sagebrush lizard. The adult fence lizard is about 6-9 inches long and is quite active, especially among brush and rocks. The sagebrush lizard, which is about 5 inches long, is more secretive, usually staying under or close to brush. The males of both species have blue bellies. The northern alligator lizard, which can approach one foot in total length, prefers damper habitats, such as grass.

The commonest snake is the western terrestrial garter snake, which is found in ponds as well as meadows. In water it may go after frogs

**Top: western fence lizard and western terrestrial garter snake which has just devoured a mountain yellow-legged frog. Bottom: a rubber boa, which is safely handled, and a western rattlesnake, which definitely isn't.**

or small trout, but then it may also end up a meal for a large trout. In meadows it hunts mostly treefrogs and mice. One of the many species that prey on the garter snake is the mountain king-snake, which eats—in addition to small snakes—lizards and birds. It is quite a climber. On several occasions while climbing Yosemite Valley's steep walls, the author has been upstaged by a kingsnake zipping up a vertical crack.

The blunt-tailed, smooth-skinned rubber boa is one of nature's most docile animals. Like tarantulas, which you can find down in the foothills, this snake is easily and safely handled. One reptile you won't want to handle is the western rattlesnake. While its bite usually is not fatal, don't tempt this snake, but rather give it a wide berth. It wants to avoid a confrontation as much as you do. You are most likely to see it below 6000 feet (i.e., in Chapter 8 lands). As of this writing, the author hasn't seen a single Tahoe Sierra specimen above this elevation, though they are certainly there. In the rest of the Sierra Nevada he's encountered them among bedrock, on trails, in meadows, under brush and on forest floors.

**Birds** In terms of species, birds greatly out-number all the other vertebrates. There are roughly 300 species of birds that visit or reside in our area, and that is about five times the number of their nearest rivals, the mammals. Birds are successful largely because they can fly away from bad weather. When the Tahoe Sierra becomes snowed under, birds can descend to lower elevations or fly south. Either way, they'll find food. A few, however, "dig in" and actually do quite well during the long, cold winter. The blue grouse, one of these masochists, subsists in the forest deep, eating conifer needles, staghorn lichen or some other paltry food item that most animals wouldn't consider.

The Clark nutcracker is another permanent resident. During the summer you're almost certain to meet this raucous, oversized gray jay if you are hiking through its favorite habitat, the subalpine forest. Lower down you are bound to meet its equally noisy cousin, the Steller jay.

Still, most birds make very distinct migrations. One of the commonest and most easily recognized is the dark-eyed junco, which is a small finch with a black or gray neck and head and with white outer tail feathers. Mountain chickadees, with their black cap and black eye stripe, are also very common, but they are far more often heard than seen.

Like invertebrates, birds are too plentiful for us to present a systematic description of them in a trail guide. Fortunately, excellent field guides are readily available, the guides published by Houghton Mifflin (Peterson series), Golden Press (Zim), National Geographic and the National Audubon Society. Every "birder" swears by one of these, the author preferring National Geographic's, though all are worth consideration.

**Mammals** Most of our mammalian species go unseen because they typically are nocturnal and reclusive. Grassy meadows teem with mice, voles, shrews and moles, while drier slopes attract pocket gophers, hares and rabbits. Common predatory mammals are long-tailed weasels, badgers, coyotes and red foxes.

In shady conifer forests chattering chickarees (Douglas squirrels) and their quiet cousins, the northern flying squirrels, harvest treetop crops of conifer seeds. In the lower-montane zone gray squirrels predominate. All are kept in check by martens and predatory birds.

Bear and deer are two large mammals we like to see, though on our own terms. Both can become quite tame and pesty around campgrounds; both are potentially dangerous. Campgrounds also attract other beggars, such as chipmunks and golden-mantled ground squirrels. Near treeline, these rodents are usually replaced by wilder ones—pint-sized pikas and rabbit-sized marmots.

Finally, there is one group of mammals that mountain visitors can expect to see daily—bats. In the evening you'll see them flitting among or above the trees, harvesting aerial insects. Like shrews, they can, in a few hours, voraciously consume their weight in insects, which thankfully includes a healthy dose of mosquitoes.

**Man** The most conspicuous Tahoe Sierra mammal, at least since the last retreat of glaciers, has been man. Until recent times the Maidu Indians occupied our area's western slopes, usually at the lower elevations. Here, acorns from black, golden and interior-live oaks together with sugar-pine nuts were highly prized for flour. One would imagine that the gray-squirrel population back in those days was smaller than it is today, for these animals competed with, and sometimes served as dinner for,

Top: **great blue heron, Canada geese, killdeer.** Bottom: **Steller's jay, Clark's nutcracker, mountain chickadee.**

**Top: California ground squirrel and golden-mantled ground squirrel. Bottom: gray squirrel and marmot.**

the Indians. The flour-grinding chore was relegated to the women and children, as was the procuring of ants, grasshoppers, crickets, other insects, worms, other invertebrates, and small game. Men were responsible for catching birds, trout, rabbits, deer, and—after the proper ceremony—black bears, grizzly bears (now extinct) and cougars. Coyotes, wolves, vultures, reptiles and amphibians were all avoided, for they were thought to be poisonous.

Maidu villages were located near year-round streams, and each typically had about 10 families and a total population of about 70. The total population of the Maidu people, who were divided into three dialect groups, probably never much exceeded 4000 individuals or 60 villages. Their north and south territorial boundaries were almost identical with the ones that limit the scope of this book. To the west their territory extended down to the higher foothills east of the Sacramento Valley. This valley was occupied by the Wintun, who had much in common with the Maidu, for both groups belonged to the same linguistic family, the Penutian. From the Wintun, the Maidu received beads (money), salt, Digger-pine nuts, and, in some instances, salmon. In return, they gave the Wintun bows and arrows, deer skins and sugar-pine nuts.

To the east the Maidu territory extended up to, and sometimes beyond, the Sierra crest. Their relationship with the Washoe, who belonged to the Hokan linguistic family, was a hostile one.

The Washoe lived mostly in the fault-dropped valleys east of the crest, but to them the center of their world was Lake Tahoe. They were a scarce group—perhaps 3000 individuals at most—who moved with the seasons. A family or group of families would slowly work its way up toward the Lake Tahoe high country in late spring as snow retreated and certain food came into abundance. In early June, this food was trout plus large suckers, both of which spawned in the creeks that drained into Lake Tahoe. As fish spawning declined, the Indians ascended mountain canyons in search of game, vegetable food in meadows, and trout in streams and high lakes. On these excursions, they were most likely to encounter the Maidu, who had been working east toward the crest, following in the wake of retreating snowfields.

With the approach of autumn, the Washoe returned to the Carson Valley and other east-side valleys. This season was a time of plenty, with the harvest of berries, pinyon nuts and seeds, followed by rabbit, deer and antelope hunts. Doves, quail, sage grouse and rodents were also hunted, but like the Maidu, the Washoe avoided reptiles and amphibians. Their bountiful harvest had to last until spring, when they could harvest wild lettuce, wild spinach and wild potatoes. The Washoe understood their dynamic environment and lived totally within it.

**The Maidu ground acorns in mortar holes**

The Maidu, on the other hand, modified their environment with almost annual fires, which had the distinct advantage of clearing brush that might hide a lurking enemy. (Fighting was a way of life *between* Maidu settlements as well as with the less numerous Washoe.) This practice also increased the distribution of *Ceanothus,* a genus of aromatic shrubs that sprout profusely after a fire. Since deer often browse on these plants, the size of the herd was increased.

The worlds of the Maidu and the Washoe were little changed by the coming of the Spaniards, who kept to the Coast Ranges and the Central Valley. With the discovery of gold in 1848 came lusty men who destroyed the environment to get rich quick. Maidu forests were logged for mine timbers and for boom-town shanties. Goats and cattle were turned loose in Maidu meadows that had once yielded a rich grain harvest. Professional hunters overkilled animal populations in order to supply mining settlements with food. Gravels washed by high-power monitors choked up the rivers and their fish populations. A similar fate lay in store for the Washoe when silver was discovered in the Comstock Lode in 1859. Their world in particular was severely shattered, for they lost not only their land but also their spiritual center, Lake Tahoe.

**Right: Backpacker on the Pacific Crest Trail just south of Ward Peak**

# Part Two    Ten Hiking Chapters

Cliff of quartz-rich sediments, Malakoff Diggins State Historic Park

# Ch. 8      South Yuba River and Malakoff Diggins State Historic Park

**Introduction**   "Gold!" rang out the cry in 1848, as the precious metal was discovered along the American, Feather and Trinity rivers. By 1849 the Great California Gold Rush was on, and from 1850 to 1862, during the heyday of the rush, annual production averaged 2.64 million troy ounces. (While this amount sounds phenomenal, it really amounts to only 110 tons, which would fit inside a Chevy van.) Production fell sharply in 1863, and until 1942 it usually averaged ½-1 million ounces a year. On October 8, 1942, the U.S. War Production Board issued Limitation Order L-208, closing the nation's gold mines. The order was rescinded in 1945, but the action had gravely wounded the industry, which faced postwar inflation, but still got only a fixed price for gold: $35 per ounce. Production slid from 6.2 tons in 1945 to ⅔ ton in 1968, when the government finally deregulated the price of gold. Production continued to fall, despite deregulation, bottoming out in 1971 at about 250 pounds. But then came the Arab oil embargo, double-digit inflation, and speculation in the gold market, which pushed the price per ounce over the $600 level in 1980. Prices have since subsided somewhat, but despite a still high price, California's gold production nevertheless is less than half a ton annually.

As the gold industry declined, its maze of mining trails began to disappear. Most of these often steep, utilitarian trails were abandoned or were obliterated by logging roads, reservoirs or real-estate developments. The few in active use today are sometimes guarded by gun-toting miners. Therefore, avoid active claims and instead explore the mining relicts and associated landscapes at Malakoff Diggins State Historic Park and the adjacent South Yuba Recreation Area. This chapter's first hike, the only trail outside these two areas, is nevertheless a part of mining history, for it runs along part of an old mining ditch, one that carried water to the Grass Valley mines. The second hike, along the South Yuba Trail, still gets its share of modern-day amateur miners. The remaining trails delve into the state park's nooks and crannies. Be sure to stop at the park's museum, in the partly reconstructed mining town of North Bloomfield.

This hiking area is relatively close to Nevada City, which is the author's favorite gold-mining town. Every block in this fascinating town exudes history; it is a joy to explore. Furthermore, numerous shops cater to visitors, as do community events. And finally, like the author's historic, tourist-oriented home town of Sonoma, compact Nevada City has some excellent restaurants that provide culinary delights.

# 1        Independence Trail

**Distance**   0.9 mile to Rush Creek
**Low/High Elevations**   1430'/1450'
**Classification**   Very easy
**Season**   March through November
**Map**   1

**Trailhead**   Along Highway 49, 6.3 miles west of its split from Highway 20 in Nevada City and 0.7 mile before its bridge across the South Yuba River. Parking for about one dozen cars.

**Introduction**   Becoming independent is a worthy goal for all disabled persons, such as those confined to wheelchairs. Before the 1970s, such persons were rarely, if ever, seen in campgrounds, and were never seen on mountain trails. Today, however, some of Tahoe's larger campgrounds have sites for disabled persons, and several trails in the Fallen Leaf Lake area (see Hike 56) are quite suited for them. This book's first trail, along a part of the defunct Excelsior Ditch, is the nation's first wheelchair trail to be built across rugged terrain. The meaning of its name, Independence Trail, is twofold. First, it gives those confined to wheelchairs greater independence. Second, volunteer work on the trail began in 1976, the 200th anniversary of our country's declared independ-ence. Hike 1 describes only the initial part constructed. Hopefully, the entire route of 8 miles will be completed by 1989, which is the 200th anniversary of ratification of the Constitution.

**Description**   The Excelsior Ditch, which begins about 2 miles up-river from the Highway 49 bridge, once transported water many miles to miners in Grass Valley. Today, a part of it transports hikers, both on foot and in wheelchairs, along its broad, nearly level course. The ideal time to hike this route is in the usually balmy months of April and May, when wildflowers put on a lavish display. Some of the species you'll see are illustrated in the next hike's two wildflower plates.

Live oaks, madrones, big-leaf maples, buckeyes and conifers—mainly Douglas-firs—provide shade along most of the route, so that even in midsummer, when temperatures soar well into the 90s, the hike is still tolerable. After passing a wheelchair-access viewpoint overlooking the South Yuba River canyon, then a wheelchair-access outhouse, you come to dashing Rush Creek. Small pools, suitable for bathing, are tucked between the creek's plentiful falls

**The Independence Trail is very level**

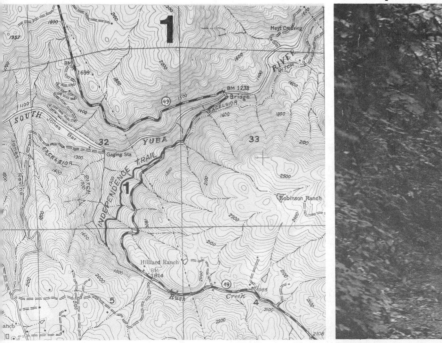

and cascades both above and below the flume crossing. Before summer, the water temperature is brisk, though refreshing. However, small aquatic worms dwell in the pools and are a minor nuisance, though not a real health problem (unlike leaches, they are easily removed from your body).

Without continued maintenance, the trail can become a bit overgrown. While this is not a problem for hikers, it can be one for those in wheelchairs, because one of the more invasive species is poison oak. Since the trail is built and maintained by volunteer labor, it could use your help.

# 2                    South Yuba Trail

**Distance**   6.1 miles, one way

**Low/High Elevations**   2140'/2560'

**Classification**   Easy to moderate

**Season**   March through November

**Map**   2

**Trailhead**   From the Highways 20/49 junction in Nevada City, drive 11¾ miles north on 49 to the paved Tyler-Foote Crossing Road, on the right. Follow it 8¼ miles northeast to North Columbia (no services), and branch right about ¼ mile past its hillside schoolhouse. Now on Grizzly Hill Road you wind 3¼ miles south to a junction ("2648" on Map 2) with the North Bloomfield-Graniteville Road. Take this road, which is a shortcut route mentioned below. You start northeast on it and quickly reach a road, on the right, that drops you momentarily to the trailhead, on the left, and the South Yuba Campground, on the right. In the past, some vehicles at the trailhead parking lot have been vandalized, so try not to leave valuables in your vehicle.

Note that the North Bloomfield-Graniteville Road takes you 2.4 miles to a junction with the Lake City Road, the route used by those going directly to Malakoff Diggins State Historic Park (Hikes 3-7).

A shortcut route to the South Yuba trailhead (and to Malakoff Diggins) is along the North Bloomfield-Graniteville Road. This leaves Highway 49 immediately west of the Tahoe National Forest headquarters, which is just west of the Highways 20/49 junction. On this steep, winding road (good brakes, no trailers or motorhomes), you go 7½ miles, negotiating hairpin turns, down to a bridge at Edwards Crossing, then climb 1.4 miles to junction "2648."

**Introduction**   While most of the Tahoe Sierra's high trails are still under spring snow, the South Yuba Trail offers day hikers and backpackers a wildflowered landscape in full bloom. During summer the afternoon temperatures are excessive, and sometimes pesky flies abound. Still, mid-July through August is the best time to sample some of the river's many swimming holes. Other summer activities include fishing, rafting and gold panning.

**Description**   The first 1.4 miles of trail, which take you to Overlook Point Picnic Site, also double as a nature trail that introduces you to the area's more prominent species. In the past the Bureau of Land Management provided a booklet that described what you saw along the nature trail's 39 posts. Since this very informative booklet probably won't be available when you hike the trail, the points it elaborates on are listed here in slightly modified form: 1, 5, Douglas-fir; 2, ponderosa pine; 3, poison oak (learn to identify and avoid this one!); 4, 27, sugar pine; 6, 22, canyon live oak; 7, California black oak; 8, California buckeye; 9, incense-cedar; 10, wood fern; 11, sword fern; 12, Kenebec Creek rock formations; 13, Pacific dogwood; 14, mock orange; 15, big-leaf maple; 16, gooseberry; 17, 34, Mariposa manzanita; 18, barberry; 19, mountain misery; 20, mistletoe on black oak; 21, mule ears; 23, mountain mahogany; 24, hollyleaf coffeeberry; 25, California laurel (bay tree); 26, 37, knobcone pine; 28, bush monkey flower; 29, toyon; 30, birds-foot fern; 31, Blue Tent and Sailor Flat hydraulic diggings southeast across the canyon; 32, buckbrush; 33, Digger pine; 35, South Yuba River canyon; 36, creeping sage; 38, deer brush; and 39, yerba santa. If you hike along this nature trail in spring, you're likely to see in flower many of the plants shown on plates 9 and 10 in this book.

During most of the summer and part of the fall, the South Yuba Trail will be dry; be sure to bring enough water. Starting from the large, day-use parking lot, our trail descends about 260 yards and joins a spur trail from the campground. Our nature trail then swings around a low, forested ridge and descends slightly to just below the base of a picturesque Kenebec Creek cascade, which flows down black slate blocks. These metamorphosed sediments underlie the entire nature trail, though in places they have

**Wildflower Plate 9. White, yellow or pale-pink foothill flowers.**
1 Trail plant (white), 2 miner's lettuce (white to pale-pink), 3 alum root (white to pink), 4 white globe lily, 5 wavy-leaved soap plant (white), 6 yellow star tulip, 7 Hartweg's iris (pale butter yellow), 8 Pacific stonecrop (yellow), 9 canyon dudleya (yellow to red).

**Wildflower Plate 10. Orange, red, violet or blue foothill flowers.**
1 California Indian pink (scarlet), 2 spotted coralroot (red and white), 3 Indian warrior (burgundy red), 4 bush monkey flower (salmon), 5 foothill penstemon (tricolor: magenta/violet/blue), 6 Kellogg's monkey flower (rose), 7 harvest brodiaea (rose to violet), 8 bleeding hearts (pink to rose), 9 purple milkweed (reddish purple flowers and stem).

61

been further metamorphosed to phyllite. We cross the creek and in 230 yards reach an old jeep road. Just 200 yards down it takes us to a junction, from which the South Yuba Trail branches left.

An interesting side trip is the 0.6-mile, moderately steep descent on the jeep road—the KENEBEC CREEK SPUR—which takes you down to the Illinois Crossing Picnic and Camping Area. This area is situated atop a level, 40-foot-high bench of gravel, cobbles and boulders which are waste products from the Malakoff Mine and other hydraulic mines (see Hike 5). Under the shade of live oaks are tables for those who like luxurious camping or picnicking. Since this bench is such an easy walk from the South Yuba Campground, you might consider carrying down a gold pan, for on BLM lands panning gold is legal. From the far end of the bench follow a narrow trail that extends almost to Kenebec Creek. Along this trail you'll spot shallow eddy pools in which you can try your luck.

From the junction with the Kenebec Creek Spur, the South Yuba Trail traverses southeast for one mile, staying high above the unseen, faintly roaring river below and arrives at a spur trail that bears south 75 yards to the Overlook Point Picnic Site. This site provides a poor view down-canyon, but it does provide tables shaded by live oaks and Douglas-firs—a welcome relief for those trudging up the South Yuba Trail on a hot summer afternoon.

Beyond this spur we traverse northward, start a descent and soon see the river below us. As we approach a head-on view of a ridge that rapidly descends to a bend in the river, we encounter our third spur trail, this one particularly worth taking. Thirteen switchback legs carry you ⅓ mile down to the mouth of North Canyon's creek, which in springtime tumbles over a sunny bedrock bench into the South Yuba. On this broad bench are open campsites, but the best attractions are the river's pools—20 feet deep in places—and the high rock ledges from which you can dive into them. In late spring and early summer the current is too fast and cold (about 50°F) to safely enjoy, but by midsummer conditions improve. Since the water barely reaches 60°F, you'll appreciate the heat of a midsummer's day, which quickly warms you after an invigorating swim.

About 100 yards past the spur, we cross North Canyon, then climb up a southwest-facing slope, start a descent, curve northward and soon drop to a junction with the Humbug Picnic Site—perched 60 feet above the river. Like the Illinois Crossing bench it is composed of gravel, cobbles and boulders wasted from the rubble created by hydraulic mining. Back in 1884, when Judge Lorenzo Sawyer issued an injunction against the dumping of mine debris into rivers, this bench *was* the South Yuba River's bottom! In the intervening time, the river has carried away most of the tailings so that it now runs clean, but a few debris segments—in the form of conglomerate-rock benches—still remain. Since this bench was built up to its present height in the late 1870s, the live oaks and ponderosa pines growing on it can be no older than that. With this in mind, you can see that at least one pine must have been growing at an average rate of about one foot per year. Before the pine can reach full maturity, however, the bench will probably be eroded away. In the meantime, we can gaze down from its edge into the cold but tempting emerald-green river pools.

Just beyond the bench and its junction with the Humbug Trail (Hike 3), our path briefly descends to a boulder crossing of milky Humbug Creek, which still suffers from mine-debris pollution. We then follow the river 0.3 mile to the South Yuba Primitive Camp. Under shady black locust trees growing on a wide, grassy bench, you'll find tables and an outhouse in this not-so-primitive setting. A nice, sandy beach—great for sunbathing when the sun's upon it—awaits those who descend the 20-foot-high bench. Both upstream and downstream from this camp you'll find deep, beautiful pools. Diving into these for trout you may see common mergansers, which are large ducks with slender, "toothed" bills that are well developed for catching their slippery prey.

Continuing onward from this camp—the last flat ground we'll see—we immediately round a bend, then climb and parallel the river 1½ miles eastward on a course that takes us past some more-remote pools. At trail's end, 30 feet above the river, we encounter a beautiful, emerald-green pool bordered by water-rounded, massive exposures of bedrock that protrude part way into the river and make ideal diving platforms. If you're bold and energetic, you might carry in a two-man raft to this trail end, inflate it, and take an exciting, 5 mile ride down the river to Illinois Bar, from which you have to hike only one mile back up to the trailhead. This alternative takes you through some pools seldom reached by other hikers.

# 3                          Humbug Trail

**Distance**   2.7 miles, one way

**Low/High Elevations**   2140'/3030'

**Classification**   Moderate

**Season**   Early April through mid-November

**Map**   2

**Trailhead**   From the Highways 20/49 junction in Nevada City, drive 11¾ miles north on 49 to the paved Tyler-Foote Crossing Road, on the right. Follow it 8¼ miles northeast to North Columbia (no services) and take the Grizzly Hill Road, which forks right about ¼ mile past the settlement's hillside schoolhouse. In another ¼ mile, before a State Forestry fire station, you take the next fork right, the Lake City Road, which winds 4 scenic miles southeast to an open-ridge junction with the North Bloomfield-Graniteville Road. You can also get to this junction by going 3¼ miles south on the Grizzly Hill Road, then driving about 2½ miles northeast on the North Bloomfield-Graniteville Road (see Hike 2's trailhead description).

From the open-ridge junction a road climbs north but you start a fairly level traverse northeast on the North Bloomfield-Graniteville Road, which then drops east into Malakoff Diggins State Historic Park. About 0.8 mile from the junction, immediately after a tight curve to the right, lies a closed road, on the left. This is the end of Hike 7. You then have a glimpse of the park's diggings before you reach the Humbug Trail, on your right, in another 0.7 mile. You'll know you missed this trailhead if you reach the conspicuous Diggins Trail, Hike 5, on your left, in 300 yards. Because parking is limited at the Humbug trailhead, you may have to park at the larger Diggins trailhead.

**Introduction**   Although this trail is occasionally steep, and in one short stretch potentially dangerous, it is nevertheless worth the effort *in spring* because of its dramatic waterfalls and diverse array of wildflowers.

**Description**   Just beyond the trailhead you'll reach a creeklet stained rusty orange by the oxidation of iron found in nearby rock deposits. Man, through hydraulic mining, has accelerated this process, and he has stained much of the state-park landscape in more ways than one. Past the creeklet you curve east and follow its waters through a lovely Douglas-fir forest in whose shade grow pink bleeding hearts, purple larkspurs, scarlet Indian pinks and white star

flowers (see plates 9 and 10 in the previous hike for the area's common wildflowers). Quickly we come to a bend and start southward down the creek from Malakoff Diggins before we encounter Humbug Creek itself.

Humbug Creek and our route now both wind southward, and we pass a rusty pool followed in a few hundred yards by an algae-choked, rusty spring. In May the dogwoods along this shady stretch of trail blossom with large, white "petals," which botanically are bracts, which surround tight clusters of small, greenish-yellow flowers. Soon we bridge a tributary creek, which has two nearby environmental campsites. The first is just above the creek, the second is below it, at the end of a 130-yard spur trail that begins just beyond the creek. There are three more environmental campsites in the park, and all are subject to reservation through the park. Not all are available for year-round use, so first check with

**Humbug Creek's upper falls**

the park by phoning (916) 265-2740. For campsite reservation, phone the park about 4-8 weeks in advance.

About ¼ mile past the spur-trail junction, we meet an old road that descends steeply to the point where our trail joins it. The road now descends 0.3 mile to its end at a seasonal creek, encountered immediately beyond a small, round pond on our left. After 50 yards we make a short, steep ascent, then roll eastward up a segment that takes us to a mossy, rocky slope with stonecrops and star flowers. The trail then rounds a ridge, bringing us back to oak- and poison-oak-lined Humbug Creek, which has some tempting pools above the brink of its upper falls. We leave the creek's side, traverse a steep, rocky slope to a small, necessary bridge, and from it obtain a spectacular view back at the cascading creek, which jumps from one churning, milky-green pothole to the next via falls ranging up to 50 feet high.

When you leave the bridge, watch your step, for there are several bad spots where the steep trail almost disappears, and at them you could take a sudden, unintentional slide down the overly steep slope; don't let the captivating scenery distract you. Into this southbound stretch of creek below us, a 7874-foot-long tunnel from Malakoff Diggins once spewed its gushing, muddy water. You'll find evidence of sediments carried down our creek when you reach a tailings bench at the junction with the South Yuba Trail, just above the river.

About ¼ mile past the upper falls' view, we pass the small, easily missed middle falls. Soon the trail curves southeast and descends almost to Humbug Creek as it passes a massive outcrop that towers above the creek's opposite bank. Here, at the brink of the creek's lower falls, are two narrow swimming pools which have been cut into a bedrock bench. On a hot midsummer day, the 2-mile hike down to these milky-green pools is more than worth the effort. In late spring and early summer, when the water flows faster, use your discretion, since a plunge over the falls could be fatal. Beyond these two oversized bathtubs, our path parallels the creek but stays well above it as it descends to meet the South Yuba Trail (see Hike 2). On it, you can hike east and enjoy the clear river's larger, colder pools.

# 4                    Missouri Bar Trail

**Distance**  1.7 miles, one way
**Low/High Elevations**  2300'/3470'
**Classification**  Moderate
**Season**  Early April through mid-November
**Map**  2
**Trailhead**  See Hike 3 for directions to Malakoff Diggins State Historic Park. Proceed east through the park to a junction immediately before the park's headquarters. Turn right, onto a road bound for Relief Hill and Washington, and drive across Humbug Creek, then past a closed road on the right before you reach another road, 0.8 mile from the headquarters' junction. Turn right and drive about 200 yards to the trailhead. Before Memorial Day, these 200 yards can be quite muddy. Parking is very limited; don't block the road.

**Introduction**  The Missouri Bar Trail, with a steady, moderate descent, takes you down to the South Yuba River in only about ½ hour. Because the trail is lightly used, you often have the trail and the river at its end all to yourself.

**Description**  The trail starts out in a mixed forest of black oak, incense-cedar, ponderosa pine and Douglas-fir. Along shadier parts of the trail, such as those typified by Douglas-fir cover, you may find large banana slugs which oh-so-slowly scavenge the moist forest floor in search of decaying organic matter—orange peels included! Our route is an obvious one which steadily descends south-southeast across metamorphic bedrock to a campsite at the confluence of Missouri Canyon creek and the South Yuba River. Down here—at Missouri Bar—the river is about 40 yards wide, and even at peak runoff it is scarcely more than knee-deep, a feature that certainly pleased old-time miners on their way between the diggings and Nevada City.

Immediately upstream from the campsite, a part of the river's flow curves clockwise back on itself, and this motion has scoured out a beautiful, deep, placid pool that remains safe—though cold—to swim in even when the river is flowing vigorously. The metamorphic bedrock near the pool is phyllite rather than slate, which is seen downstream. A trail runs east from the pool about 200 yards to another wide, knee-deep crossing that will get you to campsites above the river's opposite bank. Just up from this crossing, the river narrows somewhat and deepens to 10 feet or more, and in late summer offers additional swimming opportunities.

# 5            Diggins Trail

**Distance** Indeterminable—scramble where you wish.

**Low/High Elevations** 3000'/3080'

**Classification** Easy

**Season** Early April through mid-November

**Map** 2

**Trailhead** See Hike 3's trailhead description. There are two trails starting north from the parking area. The one above a creek's west bank goes to a nearby environmental campsite (see Hike 3's description). You want the trail above the east bank.

**Introduction** The heart of the North Bloomfield mining district is the Malakoff Diggins, which became a state historic park in 1966. The first gold to be discovered in California was found in the late 1770s in the Potholes district of Imperial County. It was, of course, James Marshall's January 1848 gold discovery at Sutter's Mill in Coloma—situated between Auburn and Placerville—that triggered the 49er gold rush to the Sierra. Most of the mining claims were established in a belt that extended from Mariposa—gateway to Yosemite—northward to the Quincy area.

In spring 1851 gold was discovered in the North Bloomfield area by an Irish prospector. He leaked his discovery to other miners in Nevada City, which was an 1849 boom town, and they secretly followed him back to his claim. When they got there, they tried their luck at mining, found nothing, and declared the project a "humbug." Because of this initial bad luck, the shanty community that grew there became known as Humbug, and the nearby creek became Humbug Creek. After several years gold was discovered, and Humbug grew to house a few hundred persons, including the inevitable saloon keepers, gamblers, "dance-hall girls" and merchants. At a mass meeting held in 1857, the populace decided Humbug was not a respectable name, and they changed it to Bloomfield. There was, however, already a California community bearing that name, so the residents changed their town's name again, to North Bloomfield.

With a change in the town name came a change in the miners' luck. At the American Hill mining district, which is about 10 miles northeast of their settlement, hydraulic mining was begun in 1852—the first in California. The following year, North Bloomfield's residents adopted this technique and by 1855 hydraulic

mining had become a major industry. In order to spray vast amounts of high-pressure water against the gold-bearing gravels of the Malakoff mine, reservoirs were constructed, but since this area, like other mining districts nearby, was rather dry, over 50 miles of canals had to be built to divert water from the Bowman Lake area down to reservoirs near the gold fields. In Nevada County as a whole, some 700 miles of canals were built for this purpose. High-pressure water eroded the gravels down into sluice boxes, in which the gold—with a density 19.3 times that of water and about 7¼ times that of its associated sediments—settled to the bottom.

A problem developed over what to do with the remaining sediments, which at the Malakoff mine amounted to a total of about 50 million tons. As profits were pouring in, sediments were pouring out—down the Yuba River. Other Sierra rivers, particularly the Feather, Bear and American, suffered similar fates. Between 1866 and 1884, the Malakoff hydraulic mine yielded about 3.5 million dollars from its 30 million cubic yards of gold-bearing gravel. The large monitors, or water nozzles, had sprayed out a hole more than 7000 feet long, 3000 feet wide and up to 600 feet deep. The gravels from this mine, and from other nearby mines, brought a great change in the lower course of the Yuba River, particularly along a 16-mile stretch from Smartville down to Marysville. The added sediments built up the river bottom, so that it easily overflowed its banks in times of high water. Not only were farmers' crops ruined by flooding, but an immense amount of fine debris was deposited on the river's adjoining plains, covering an area of 25 square miles. These deposits of fine sand and gravel rendered much farm land unfit for cultivation and caused farmers to protect adjacent land by constructing costly levees.

The farmers who were affected took their claims to court in 1884, and in a landmark case, *Woodruff vs. North Bloomfield Gravel Mining Company,* Judge Lorenzo Sawyer issued an injunction against the dumping of mine debris into the Sacramento and San Joaquin rivers and their tributaries—one of the first environmentalist victories in this country. Other injunctions soon followed, and hydraulic mining all but ended. In its heyday, North Bloomfield could boast of a population of over 1200, but by the time it was considered for incorporation in the

state historic park, its population had dwindled to nine.

Hydraulic-mining debris also changed the characteristics of rivers, thereby affecting river-barge transportation. Before the 2200 million tons of sediment choked up rivers, one could travel from Sacramento north 120 miles up the Sacramento River to Red Bluff and south 180 miles up the San Joaquin River to the Fresno area. Hydraulic-derived sediments, carried in flood waters, provided added thrust to scour away the rivers' banks, eroding good farm land in the process, but also leaving the rivers wider when the floods subsided, thereby making them shallower and less navigable.

**Description**   This trail takes you into the heart of the Malakoff Diggins. Start early if you're hiking it on a hot summer day, for there is little shade in this open pit. At the trailhead is a large sign that gives statistics of the 7874-foot-long drain tunnel engineered by Hamilton Smith, which was begun in April 1872 and completed 30 months later. At present, milky, yellow-brown water trickles from the Hiller Tunnel, which is a segment of the larger drain tunnel. During the mine's heyday, the drain tunnel transported a lot of muddy water and sediments down to Humbug Creek and along it into the South Yuba River. To finance such a tunnel plus the reservoirs and many miles of canal needed to feed them required a lot of capital. The miners who worked these diggings weren't independent souls, but rather were company pawns. Except for the first few years, when individuals flocked to the hills in search of placer gold, the extraction of this ore belonged to big business—either in the surface hudraulic mines or in the subterranean bedrock mines.

Our trail starts north across weathered Paleozoic marine sediments which long ago were metamorphosed to slate, phyllite and schist. It then tops a low saddle and presents the hiker with a sweeping panorama of the Malakoff Diggins, which are in a 600-foot-thick layer of sediments deposited from about 50 to 30 million years ago by the ancestral Yuba River. The Diggins Trail, if one can call it that, now is an abandoned east-west road along the south side of a large, shallow, muddy pond. Just 40 yards east of your junction with this road, you'll find a 30-yard-long spur trail leading north to the end of the 556-foot-long Hiller Tunnel, which provides an alternate route to the Diggins (a flashlight is recommended if you take this route). At the pond's southwest end, a footpath begins northwest and gradually curves eastward around

**Hiller Tunnel's outlet**

the iron-rich pond, dying out at its east end. From there, hike wherever you choose.

The pond is not lifeless. Cattails are invading it, and on them in spring perch male Brewer blackbirds, each singing a song that proclaims him the master of the adjacent territory he defends against landless males. Along the shore's white, quartz cobbles, the spotted sandpiper lays her eggs, which blend in perfectly with them. Invading the lower slopes above the lakeshore are alders, willows and ponderosa pines, each species dropping litter, which furthers soil development.

The Diggins resemble a miniature Bryce Canyon both in erosional patterns and in variety of colors. However, in Bryce Canyon, as in most canyons, the sediments get progressively younger toward the rim, but here, some older sediments stand above some adjacent younger ones. These older gravels were laid down by the ancestral Yuba River, which later cut down through them and then deposited the lower, younger layer of gravels in the cut. The upper layer of white gravels is called the bench gravel, since it was deposited on a wide bench cut by the ancestral river into the bedrock surface over which it flowed. That there was a wide river bench here tells us that the river had been eroding for millions of years in a low Sierra range—if the range had been higher, the river would instead have cut a gorge into the bedrock.

The Sierra was uplifted after the deposition of the bench gravel, and then the river cut a broad canyon several hundred feet deep. When the uplift ceased, the ancestral Yuba River stopped its canyon cutting and entered a second phase of depositing gravels. At Malakoff these lower gravels are divided into two colors, the upper being red and the lower pale blue. The gravels are essentially the same in composition, but the blue gravels once lay below the water-table surface, which protected them from exposure to oxygen, while the red gravels got their color from oxidation of the iron in them. It was

the blue gravels, the lowest 130 feet of sediments above the Paleozoic bedrock foundation, which contained the most gold. No wonder, then, that the first miners, who worked the uppermost sediments, declared this area "humbug."

# 6      Blair Trail

**Distance**   2.4 miles, semiloop trip
**Low/High Elevations**   3280'/3640'
**Classification**   Easy
**Season**   Early April through mid-November
**Map**   2

**Trailhead**   See Hike 3's trailhead description to the Diggins Trail (Hike 5). Continue driving east through the park to the reconstructed settlement of North Bloomfield. Your hike will descend to the Clampicnic Area, at the edge of the settlement, then will continue 0.2 mile up the road to the Blair parking lot. You can start your hike at either of these two spots, but the author has chosen to start it at the Shoot Hill Campground, whose entrance is 0.5 mile up the road. The Blair Trail starts southeast about 60 yards

before camp unit 13; the Rim Trail (Hike 7) starts west about 40 yards before it.

**Introduction**   This trail is a pleasant stroll even on hot July days, for it is short and shady, and it takes you to an old swimming hole.

**Description**   Starting in Shoot Hill Campground, we descend southeast on an old road that has been narrowed to a wide path by encroaching shrubs. Black oak, ponderosa pine, incense-cedar and Douglas-fir—typical species for this elevation and slope—provide us with a convenient canopy. Mountain misery locally appears as a sticky, calf-high ground cover, and in summer's heat it fills the air with its subtle aroma. After 300 yards our trail levels, narrows to a true trail, and curves to the gully of a

**The Hendy Giant**

trickling, seasonal creek. Ten yards before it, our trail splits. From here we'll make a loop trip, descending the steeper, creekside trail to the Clampicnic Area and returning via the shadier Blair Trail.

During spring our descent is accompanied by the refreshing song of a trickling creek, reached in a few minutes, whose banks are adorned with Indian pink, wavy-leaf soap plant, lilies and other water-loving plants. In the conifers, a woodpecker may search for bark insects while a gray squirrel may, after scrutinizing us, resume foraging for ponderosa-pine seeds and black-oak acorns.

After traversing across a drier slope covered with manzanita, we pass behind some buildings of partly reconstructed North Bloomfield, come to a bridge, cross it, and find ourselves in the Clampicnic Area, a beautiful, grassy picnic

**Incense-cedars at Clampicnic Area**

ground dominated by several immense incense-cedars. Across the road stands the silenced Hendy Giant—a 15-foot-long, nine-inch-diameter monitor, which in its day shot down many tons of gravel cliffs with its jets of high-pressure water. After a few steps up the road, we reach Cummins Hall, which serves as the park's headquarters and contains a museum that is open daily from June 1 through Labor Day. A history buff could spend many hours in it and around the settlement's buildings, reconstructing in his mind how the town might have looked and what the townfolk were like back in the 1870s.

A brief walk northeast up the town's road gets us to the parking lot for the Blair. Up a short, closed road we walk to the Blair, which is today a somewhat murky but thoroughly refreshing swimming hole. This hole was the site of early hydraulic mining; later it became a storage reservoir that provided water for one of the monitors at the Malakoff mine. In its deep, milky-green waters swim trout, other fish and kids. On less crowded days, you may find aquatic garter snakes near or in the reservoir's shallow, vegetated east end. On popular weekends you can expect all the picnic tables, under forest shade, to be occupied.

After taking a last drink from the water fountain, start northeast along the narrow earth dam that separates the Blair from the deeply cut gully down which Humbug Creek courses boisterously in the springtime. Leaving the reservoir's shore on a splendid, shady path, we follow a ditch that once fed the reservoir, and pass an iron pipe and then a wooden flume, both used to transport the canal's water across small side gullies. We near the bank of delightful Humbug Creek, then climb up an old road that first curves west up a slope before it curves north and almost dies out as it joins a road climbing northeast. We start southwest on this road, cross through a missing section of fence, and descend its westward-curving path 170 yards to a prominent, south-southwest-descending road. Don't follow it, but continue west on a trail for 120 yards to the park's main road, which you cross just 10 yards southeast of its junction with the campground's entrance road.

Found in this terrain are large but harmless alligator lizards, which slither down our path as we hike along it and parallel the entrance road above us to the creeklet down which the Clampicnic trail descends. We continue west a short way, then climb the stiff, narrow road back to our trailhead.

# 7       Rim Trail

**Distance**   3.5 miles, one way
**Low/High Elevations**   3300'/3680'
**Classification**   Easy to moderate
**Season**   Early April through mid-November
**Map**   2
**Trailhead**   See Hike 3's trailhead description for the west end of the trail, Hike 6's trailhead description for the east end—our starting point.

**Introduction**   This trail provides you with an entirely different perspective of the Malakoff Diggins than the Diggins Trail. From mid-May through mid-October, afternoon temperatures can be quite uncomfortable on this often shade-less trail, so during this season, plan to hike the trail—a good one for bird watching—early in the morning.

**Description**   The trail, starting as an old fire road, curves southwest from the campground to some open, grassy slopes, which are part of an enormous, ongoing landslide. In time, the slopes

**Author's wife standing in one of several large rifts in an active landslide**

will give way to a bowl, and the eastern part of Malakoff Diggins will lie buried under the slide's sediments. Our route soon crosses the first of many creeklets we'll see along this route, which by midsummer are all dry. Growing by most of them are water-loving big-leaf maples. On drier ground above the first creeklet grow black oaks, incense-cedars and ponderosa pines, beneath which you'll spot mountain misery, a sticky, somewhat aromatic shrub with fernlike leaves. Miwok Indians used its leaves to make a tea, which they used to treat various afflictions.

Farther along our route we encounter the first of several headward-eroding gullies, each cutting into the route. Note the recently exposed roots of plants and the steep headwall of the gully. The headwall is subject to further collapse during a heavy spring rainfall, when there may already be ground water seeping from its base. The lower sections of most of these gullies have been somewhat stabilized by the growth of shrubs, which help trap sediments. The upper, actively eroding sections, however, are usually devoid of vegetation.

Beyond a shallow gully we enter a sunny thicket of manzanita, which attracts an army of bumblebees during May when these plants are in flower. Through this thicket we descend south along our now-rocky route before coming to a level area with ponderosa pines. The rocks and boulders are derived from volcanic flows—similar to those at the Sierra crest—which were laid down about 5-10 million years ago. In this state park, these flows cap much of the older gold-bearing gravels of the ancient Yuba River. In all likelihood, less than half of this area's gold was removed by the hydraulic operations. Now the gold is protected by state park status as well as by the overlying burden of volcanic rock.

The diverse environment of brush and conifers through which we now stroll southwest provides many habitats for animals. The most conspicuous animals are birds, and here you'll see, among dozens of species, the robin, dark-eyed junco, California quail, lesser goldfinch, mourning dove, black-throated gray warbler, Steller's jay, mountain chickadee and several species of sparrows. Each species of bird has a specific dietary requirement that is at least somewhat different from that of every other species; in this way, direct head-on interspecific competition is avoided. Instead, competition is *intraspecific,* that is, among members of the same species. A principal mechanism for keeping a population in check is the establishment of territories during mating season—a practice found among other vertebrates besides birds. Only those dominant males that can establish and hold a territory will mate. Hence an overabundant surplus of young will not be produced.

Our aromatic route turns south and proceeds down a usually dry creeklet, crosses to a larger, longer-lasting one, leaves it, and then soon descends steeply back to it. We bid farewell to its cloistered grove of incense-cedar, madrone, black oak, Douglas-fir and ponderosa pine, and hike westward to an open bend, from which we get our first view of the gravel cliffs. Beyond it we wander through a 10-foot-high manzanita thicket, meet a closed road that descends southeast, and continue our brief westward, brushy traverse to a forest of ponderosa and sugar pines. Two gullies working headward into our road are passed before we encounter in a deep gully a small outcrop of cross-bedded sandstone, which is part of the gold-poor bench layer of the old gravels.

Our road traverses around the deep gully and emerges on the northwest rim above the large, shallow pond of Malakoff Diggins. Almost immediately a view opens up and we get a sweeping panorama of most of the open pit and its colorful cliffs. Old trees and shrubs grow right up to our rim's edge, indicating that the rim is retreating. Roots protruding from the tops of cliffs together with fallen trees on the slopes below confirm our suspicion. While following the Diggins Trail on the flat below us, one gets the impression that little erosion has occurred since the end of hydraulic mining. Up on the rim, however, we can see that a fair amount has occurred, and by at least three processes. First,

heavy rains can send streams of water downslope, which erode the cliffs in bits and pieces. Second, when the upper portions of the steep cliffs get wet from surface water and/or from ground water, the cliffs are likely to suffer small rockfalls. Finally, if clay is present in sufficient amounts, it can absorb enough water to weaken the cohesion of the gravels and cobbles it binds, and cause a good-sized slump. In several places our road has been eradicated by these slumps, and we can see the debris they deposited on the lower slopes 300 feet below us.

If these gravels had been 140 million years old or older, they would be much better cemented and perhaps also metamorphosed by ensuing granitic plutons. If so, the gravels would have been too solid to be mined by hydraulic methods, and their gold concentration would have been too low for any other method to have been economical. Precious and rare minerals can be found in many sites, even in soils, but unless they are sufficiently concentrated, they don't merit exploitation.

Leaving the Diggins, you commence a traverse through a fairly open field, in which you're almost certain to encounter cattle and may also see, particularly in early morning, a jackrabbit or mule deer taking off through the deer brush and past the buckeye trees. Our closed road ends at three posts along the park's main road, and you can either retrace your 3.5 miles of route or you can start down the main road. The author suggests you descend this road to a signed viewpoint, descend a closed road from it down into the Malakoff Diggins, explore them to your heart's content, and then head east from the large pond's south shore until you once again reach the main road. Hike along it into North Bloomfield, then take the shady Blair Trail back to your trailhead.

**The Sierra Buttes Fire Lookout**

# Ch. 9    Sierra City and Johnsville Gold Districts

**Introduction**    Gold was discovered at Sutter's Mill in 1848, and by 1850 frenzied miners were scouring almost every square inch of California's mountain landscape. One mountain area that proved to be quite lucrative was the upper Highway 49 region. This area extended roughly from the Sierra City environs north-northwest to Johnsville, which today is a dormant settlement within Plumas-Eureka State Park.

All the mines were located in a belt of metamorphic rocks, and while there may have been hundreds of mining claims in the 1850s, only two or three dozen eventually brought wealth to their owners. The Sierra Buttes Mine (Hike 13), which was the grandaddy that lured miners to the area, extracted about 40 tons of gold, alone accounting for about $20,000,000 of the total $50,000,000 mined in the Sierra City-Johnsville districts. The Plumas-Eureka, Jamison and Four Hills mines, all in the Hike 28 environs, accounted for about $12,000,000. The Monumental Mine, while not particularly productive, did produce, in the 1860s, two monumental nuggets—133 pounds and 158 pounds! Contrast this to milling-grade ore later on, which yielded, on the average, about ½ ounce of gold per ton of crushed rock.

Commercial mining all but died out with the start of World War 1, though the Plumas-Eureka Mine did continue intermittently until World War 2. The mining activity never returned in the postwar years, which set the stage for the creation of Plumas-Eureka State Park in 1959 and then the Lakes Basin and Sierra Buttes recreation areas.

Today, weekend miners still search for the giant nugget or the lost lode, but the area's wealth now lies in its aqueous gems—dozens of mountain lakes. Most of these are in an area bounded roughly by Highway 49 on the south, Gold Lake Road on the east, Plumas-Eureka State Park on the north and a mountain crest on the west. The bulk of this chapter's trails, Hikes 12-30, lie within this area, which is usually snow-free three or four months of the year.

The chapter's first trails, Hikes 8-11, lie in the lakeless, largely viewless canyonlands southeast of Sierra City and Highway 49. Here you'll find the gold district's southeastern-most mine, the Hilda Mine, though it is hardly the prime attraction. The prime attraction, if you can call it that, is the area's longer hiking season, generally from April through November. This extended season permits you to stretch your legs in spring and fall, when the high country is apt to be under snow.

# 8                         Haypress Creek Loop

**Distance**   2.5 miles, loop trip
**Low/High Elevations**   4390'/4840'
**Classification**   Easy
**Season**   April through November
**Map**   4

**Trailhead**   At northeast end of Sierra City, leave Highway 49, heading east on Wild Plum Road 20N13. In 1⅓ miles it forks, the left branch going to Wild Plum Forest Service Station, the right branch crossing adjacent Haypress Creek and ending in nearby Wild Plum Campground.

**Introduction**   This hike is particularly suitable from mid-April to mid-June, when the Highway 49 highlands are still largely under snow. Because it passes through a variety of habitats (mixed-conifer forest, oak woodland, shrub slope, rock outcrop, and stream bank), it offers the hiker a lavish display of vernal flowers and a large selection of song birds.

**Description**   Although you can start this loop clockwise from the Forest Service station, the preferred start is counterclockwise from the campground, for the gradient is easier and the best views then lie ahead, not behind you. From the campground's upper end, you climb moderately up a closed jeep road through a mixed-conifer forest. In ½ mile, with most of your climbing done, you reach a creek that originates on slopes above Hilda Mine. In springtime you may need a log to cross this creek. Just 50 yards beyond the creek you leave the closed road and branch left for a short climb to a minor ridge. On it you'll hear but not see Haypress Creek's low, roaring falls, which you can reach by a cautious descent from the ridge.

The well-used trail leaves the ridge for a pleasant traverse to a large bridge across Haypress Creek. Here you meet the Pacific Crest Trail, which winds ¼ mile southeast up to the jeep road on which you began your hike. Across the bridge you climb momentarily to a flat, then a bit more up to a junction.

Should you feel the need for additional exercise, you can tread northeast, climbing 600 feet in just over a mile to the Great Eastern Ravine. There you'll find a bed of light-gray, banded marble, polished by the ravine's jump-across creek. Eastward, this elective route passes through brush before penetrating a mature forest of giant conifers. About a mile past the ravine, near the east edge of Map 4, you cross a creek.

About ½ mile later, you cross three closely spaced creeks, and the trail gives way to a jeep road.

Back at the junction, you begin to climb west to an adjacent ridge, from which you can take a few steps south for a revealing view of the Haypress Creek gorge and its associated falls. Now with views of dominating Sierra Buttes, we ramble shortly over to seasonally trickling 1001 Mine creek, then in 50 yards leave the Pacific Crest Trail (Hike 11 describes the stretch of "PCT" between here and Highway 49). An array of short switchbacks now guides us down somewhat open terrain, which in summer can be quite hot. At the base of the switchbacks, near the east end of a flat, you'll hear the muted roar of some impressive cataracts, which you can see by heading a bit south from the trail. Your trail crosses the flat and ends near the Wild Plum Forest Service Station. Walk west along its road and in a couple of minutes fork left, bridging Haypress Creek and returning to Wild Plum Campground.

**Umbrella plant (Indian rhubarb) grows along Milton and Haypress creeks**

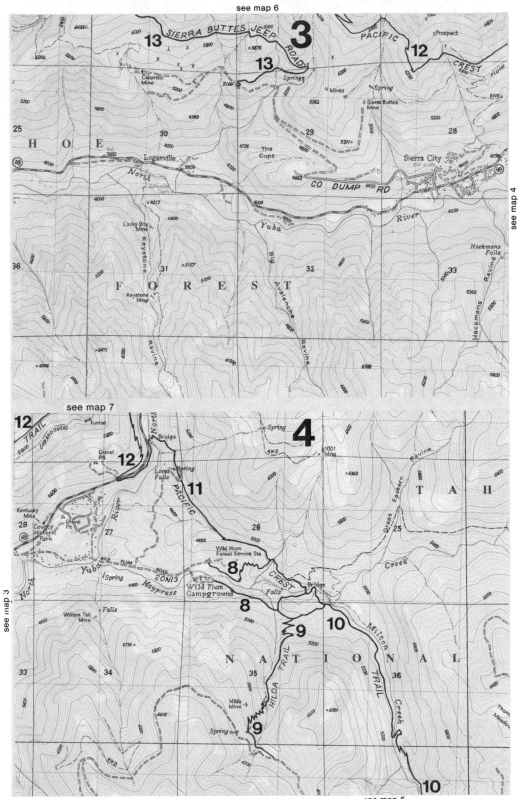

see map 7

see map 3

# 9    Hilda Mine

**Distance**   2.5 miles, one way
**Low/High Elevations**   4440'/6070'
**Classification**   Moderate
**Season**   Mid-May through early November
**Map**   4
**Trailhead**   Same as the Hike 8 trailhead.

**Introduction**   History buffs should appreciate the Hilda Mine environs, perched on public land, though they will have to expend quite a bit of energy to reach it. Fortunately, the route is shady, often cool, and blessed with spring-fed water.

**Description**   Starting from the upper end of Wild Plum Campground, the initial ½ mile follows a historic trans-Sierra route. This jeep road once went about 10 miles up Haypress Creek, via the Great Eastern Ravine (previous hike) to Church Camp, above Haypress Valley. From the camp a trail east shot through a nearby crest pass then curved north down to the south end of fault-formed Sierra Valley. We go but ½ mile up the jeep road, cross Hilda Creek—possibly a wet ford in high runoff—and then in 200 yards reach the Hilda Trail. Up it we begin, ascending steep slopes, which are made tolerable by plenty of switchbacks. After our first set of switchbacks, which approach the unseen but heard Hilda Creek, we catch a conifer-framed glimpse of Sierra Buttes as we start a ½-mile climb up the creek's canyon. The singing creek offers us a refreshing drink where we cross it, but as if its water were not good enough, someone has built a pipe spring about 100 yards up-trail from the

crossing. Beyond it we touch upon a small, usually dry gully, beside which we climb steadily upward via 12 short switchback legs.

Our trail ends at some old, dilapidated mining shacks that served as workmen's quarters for several mines that were dug in this area. The miners sought to extract gold that was trapped under the volcanic rock you see above the shacks. Beside the shacks the volcanic rock is in direct contact with the metamorphic rock on which our trail has climbed up, but small amounts of gold are found within 30-50 million-years-old sediments that are trapped between the two rock types. After lava flows buried these sediments perhaps 5-10 million years ago, the course of the ancestral North Yuba River was diverted toward the Sierra Buttes, and since that time the river has cut about 1500 feet down to where it flows today. Most of the cutting occurred within the last few million years while the northern Sierra renewed its uplift and glaciers actively scoured out the canyons.

From the mining shacks, an old jeep road replaces the trail, and up it we walk, passing an icy spring emanating from the base of a white fir located midway between the shacks and Hilda Creek. Beyond the spring we climb gently up to Hilda Creek, our last water source. Our southbound jeep road now bends eastward, paralleling a larger forest road above it and meeting that road at a HILDA TRAIL sign, which marks the end of our excursion. Here in a large clearing that is being invaded with gooseberries, we once again get a view of the towering Sierra Buttes. Hikers in late summer or early fall will find the tasty but spiny berries in season.

# 10   Pacific Crest Trail, southeast up Milton Creek

**Distance**   5.9 miles, one way
**Low/High Elevations**   4440'/6510'
**Classification**   Moderate
**Season**   June through October
**Maps**   4 and 5
**Trailhead**   Same as the Hike 8 trailhead.

**Introduction**   Although this route ends with a fine view of northern Sierra canyonlands, it is easily the long way in to that view. If you want just the view, take Hike 41, which is only 3.3

miles, one way, and has but a fraction of the elevation gain. Hike 10 is for those who enjoy hiking and aren't particularly goal-oriented. Though long, this route is mostly a gentle grade.

**Description**   As in the two previous hikes, you make a ½-mile climb moderately up a jeep road to Hilda Creek. Then, continuing up the road, you quickly meet a trail left (Hike 8), a trail right (Hike 9), and in ¼ mile another trail left (Hike 11). Ahead, your closed road goes but 40 yards east to a bend, and here it forks left, dropping to

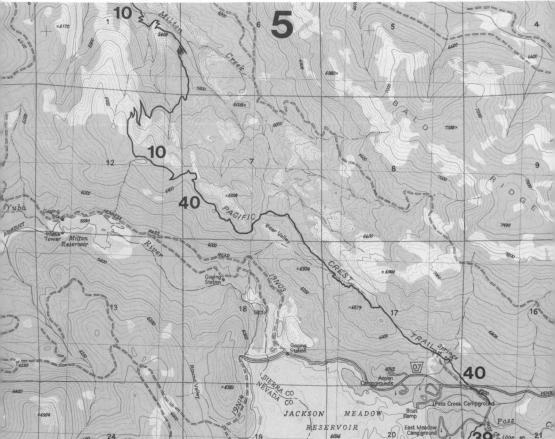

see map 17

oblivion in nearby Milton Creek. Fallen logs sprawl across the creek, providing bridges across the thrashing water.

Since the second left junction, 40 yards back, we've been on the Pacific Crest Trail, and on this tri-state route we now progress southeast up somewhat glaciated Milton Creek canyon. A thick growth of conifers usually hides the creek and muffles its song. In about a mile, after passing reclusive creekside campsites, we bridge the broad creek.

After an initial jog north, the trail parallels Milton Creek south up-canyon, recrossing the creek where it bends east. Now the climb begins in earnest, though—as you'll discover—the trail has an easy gradient, thanks to about two dozen switchbacks. If you're carrying a heavy pack, this is certainly a blessing, but for the day hiker the ascent, and certainly the return descent, can seem unnecessarily long. You negotiate more than half of the switchbacks as you leisurely knock off almost 700 feet of ascent to a saddle on a secondary ridge. You then meander west, in

and out of several gullies, before ascending longer switchbacks, largely lined with brush. Climbing higher, you have inspiring—and on hot days, perspiring—views of glaciated Milton Creek canyon, and then you contour south to a viewless saddle. A semistagnant lily-pad pond lies immediately south of it, a byproduct of a former glaciation. To dam up this body of water, a glacial moraine (and hence its glacier) had to rise 700 feet above the Middle Yuba River, hidden to the south, and into which the pond's evanescent creeklet drains.

Robbed of a crest view, you might as well continue on, heading up a shady gully to another viewless saddle, your highest point in elevation. The high point, emotionally, lies just ahead, where the trail descends out to a point. There, you have a commanding view of most of Milton Creek's canyon, and you even spy the sawtooth ridge of the Sierra Buttes, a landmark you haven't seen since you first set foot on the lower part of the Pacific Crest Trail. **Hike 40** describes the trail southeast from here.

# 11 Pacific Crest Trail,
## Highway 49 southeast to Haypress Creek

**Distance**   2.3 miles, one way
**Low/High Elevations**   4580'/4850'
**Classification**   Easy
**Season**   April through November
**Map**   4

**Trailheads**   East end: same as the Hike 8 trailhead; follow that route to the Haypress Creek bridge. West end: same as the Hike 12 trailhead.

**Introduction**   The prime attraction of this short piece of Pacific Crest Trail is Loves Falls, which is rewarding to both fishermen and sightseers alike. Few people hike southeast past it, for in summer the traverse can be hot, dry and fly-infested. However, in the first half of spring, this sunny hike may be the only one in the area that isn't snowbound.

**Description**   From the west trailhead the path parallels Highway 49 northeast, passing a usually flowing spring and an ephemeral seep before reaching the massive bridge that vaults the North Yuba River. Here the river has cut a minigorge through resistant Mesozoic-age metavolcanic rocks, and it thunders from fall to fall, collectively known as Loves Falls. (The current topo, Map 4, shows the falls *below* the bridge; earlier topos showed them above it.) A pool lies at the base of each waterfall, but most of them can be reached only by precarious scrambling. Still, fishermen insist on plying their sport in one or more of these pools, which is an exceptionally dangerous undertaking when the river runs high.

East from the bridge the trail climbs moderately to a seasonal creek, then eases off for a traverse through a live-oak woodland. This habitat has the invidious characteristic of harboring droves of obnoxious midges, which swarm about you, particularly if you're perspiring, as you're likely to on summer afternoons. However, hiking in spring or fall can be a pleasant experience, and as you advance southeast to a bedrock ridge, you're rewarded with increasingly better views over your shoulder of the Sierra Buttes. Beyond the ridge, Haypress Creek canyon captivates your attention, and soon you reach a minor ridge, down which an old trail, Hike 9, descends. Along Hike 9 (in reverse) you have at least one more fine view of the Sierra Buttes, then one of the Haypress Creek falls—if you take a few steps off-trail before you initiate a descent to the Haypress Creek bridge. The Pacific Crest Trail climbs ¼ mile southeast from the bridge, up to the Haypress Creek jeep road, while an older path, also starting from the bridge, winds southwest over to the same road. The latter route, embarking downstream, gives you an opportunity to examine the falls close-up: leave the trail as you approach a ridge, and proceed northwest.

**Fishing beneath North Yuba River's bridge**

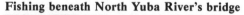

**Bridge across the North Yuba River**

# 12

# Pacific Crest Trail,
# Highway 49 west to Sierra Buttes

**Distances**  8.7 miles to lookout, 12.2 miles to
the Hike 15 trailhead above Packer Lake.

**Low/High Elevations**  4580'/8591'

**Classification**  Strenuous

**Season**  June through October

**Maps**  4, 3, and 6

**Trailheads**  Southeast end: along Highway 49,
about 1½ miles northeast of "downtown" Sierra
City and 1.0 mile northeast of a road branching
east to Wild Plum Campground. Parking limited
to several vehicles. Northwest end: same as the
Hike 15 trailhead.

**Introduction**  The longest route to the Sierra
Buttes Fire Lookout is along a northbound stretch
of the Pacific Crest Trail. Few will want to
ascend this mostly shadeless, usually dry route;
even fewer will want to retrace their steps back
down it—a lengthy 17.4 miles, round trip. If you
can arrange a shuttle, begin your hike from
Highway 49 and end it at the Hike 15 trailhead.
Sure, this direction is tougher than north to
south, but you'll end your hike with opportunities to jump into three relatively warm lakes (and
you'll certainly need a bath regardless of which
direction you hike).

**Description**  The northbound Pacific Crest
Trail (PCT) commences northeast from a closed
mining road, and it parallels Highway 49 up-
canyon. The first part of this trail section is on a
narrow, abandoned road through a forest of
black oak, ponderosa pine and incense-cedar.
Mountain misery, a low, sticky shrub, permeates
the air with a subtle fragrance as the day's
temperature rises. After the PCT bends north
onto cooler east-facing slopes, we meet Douglas-
firs and their associated vegetation. About a
mile from the start, our sporadically switchbacking trail leaves noisy Highway 49 and switchbacks relentlessly upward to a flume that today
is bone-dry. About ¼-½ mile north lie smooth,
bushy ridges, a smaller set within a larger one.
These are lateral moraines left by glaciers that
descended east from the Sierra Buttes. The
earlier glacier left the outer ridges; the later,
smaller glacier left the inner ones.

The existing permanent route 2¾ miles up to
the flume has been mostly a forested one, but we
leave all trees behind just before the switchbacking ascent tops off, in ¾ mile, on a ridge. From it
we have views both up and down the North Yuba
River canyon and views up at the east buttress of
the Sierra Buttes. Now shrubs line the trail,
mainly huckleberry oak, greenleaf manzanita,
tobacco brush and bitter cherry, but also a dab
here and there of snow bush and squaw carpet.
After weaving around several ridges and gullies
and getting saturated with views, we finally
arrive, after 3¾ miles, at a saddle and the Sierra
Buttes jeep road.

If you've stocked up on water, gear down for
the serious grind ahead. Otherwise, first continue a level ¼ mile on the PCT to a profuse
alder-lined spring, just below the trail, then return to the saddle. The road first climbs moderately to a switchback, then enters forest cover,
lending you much needed shade up the 770-foot
ascent to a near-ridge junction. You've climbed
but ¾ mile, but you'll swear it's much more.

Another ¾-mile ascent to the lookout remains,
but it is better graded and increasingly scenic.
This ascent, plus the lookout's views, are described in **Hike 16,** which is the easiest route to
the summit. After your ascent, return to the
near-ridge junction and branch right onto Sierra
Buttes Trail 12E06. This you'll descend 2¾
miles to its trailhead just above Packer Lake.

The trail begins as an abandoned jeep road,
and heads north-northeast to the ridge, while
another abandoned jeep road, misleading un-
wary hikers, strikes northwest downslope. At
the ridge, here a rim of a glacial cirque, you have
a stunning view of Young America Lake. Though
it is only ¼ mile away, it is nevertheless one of
the most inaccessible lakes in the Tahoe Sierra.

The jeep tracks quickly dwindle to a path,
and on it you briefly wind among some giant
"boulders" of pale blue-green metamorphosed,
ancient lava; then you regain the ridge. Now, in
addition to seeing Young America Lake, you see
the Sardine Lakes and their giant enclosing
moraines. Next, the trail meanders for ⅓ mile
down through a fir-and-hemlock forest where,
before August, snow patches may obscure the
trail. Then, follow blazes on the trees.

Your route meets an abandoned jeep road
and joins it for 70 yards before heading to the
adjacent ridge for a ¼-mile descent to a level
spot containing a trail junction. Had you not
taken the main jeep road up to Sierra Buttes but
rather continued north on the PCT, you would
have arrived here, after a 1.1-mile contour. The

**A virtually shadeless 3¾-mile traverse across Sierra Buttes' south slopes**

PCT continues north along the now narrow, almost level ridgecrest, heading 0.9 mile to the Hike 16 trailhead.

On the last part of your descent to the junction, you've gotten vistas of the Tamarack Lakes, which are welcome swimming holes on hot summer days. Your knee-knocking Sierra Buttes Trail heads toward them after first making a switchback down a steep slope. In ⅓ mile your fairly steep route comes to an abandoned logging road. Ahead, your descent is now a jeep road, and after ½ mile you meet a spur road over to

upper Tamarack Lake. The lower lake, being smaller and shallower, is the warmer of the two. Avoid its grassy west half and swim in its trout-inhabited east half.

Just below the lower lake, you reach a junction. Hike 14, from the Sardine Lakes area, arrives from the east, while Hike 15, ascending from the Parker Lake area, arrives from the north. You descend the latter to the ample trailhead parking lot. Packer Lake is just below you and gives you a third opportunity to take a refreshing dip.

# 13     Sierra City to Sierra Buttes

**Distance**  4.8 miles, one way

**Low/High Elevations**  5188'/8591'

**Classification**  Strenuous

**Season**  Year round; snow is an advantage for this hike.

**Maps**  3 and 6

**Trailhead**  In Sierra City turn north up County Dump Road, which in one block bends west and then climbs an easy mile up to a large flat at the edge of the dump. Turn sharply right and follow a dirt road 1.4 miles, first briefly east, then

northwest. Park at a junction, about ⅓ mile past a major gully, with the steep, narrow Sierra Buttes jeep road. Parking is limited; use nearby turnouts.

**Introduction**  With 3400 feet to climb, this route seems to be an uninviting hike. However, when the short routes to the summit, Hikes 15 and 16, are snowbound, then this route takes on a certain appeal, and it is grand on a fine winter or early spring day. Then, most of your route will be snowbound *and* you won't have to compete with off-road vehicles. Furthermore, you can make much of your descent route an exhilarating glissade.

**Description**  Winter hikers may have to start their trek from the large parking area at Sierra City's dump, 1.4 miles down the road. All others should be able to drive up to the start of the road signed STEEP and NARROW. We hike ⅔ mile eastward up this shadeless road to its tight bend west. Immediately east of this bend is a readily accessible, year-round creek, from which you should fill your water bottles. Climbing west, our steady, moderate ascent takes us past occasional incense-cedars and ponderosa pines, which provide us with convenient, shady resting spots. Along various road cuts you can't help but notice exposures of blue-green serpentine, which is the main alteration product of ultramafic rocks, such as the blue-black pyroxene you see associated with it. A once-active fault, trending northwest-southeast, approximately parallels the road we see below us. Along this fault these ultramafics, which are remnants of ancient oceanic, volcanic bedrock, were thrust upon the surrounding Paleozoic rocks. Once emplaced, these ultramafics were then invaded by superheated water under intense pressure, which forced water into their crystal structures, converting the rock to serpentine.

We think of water as being relatively harmless. We can drink it or bathe in it and it doesn't destroy us. When this same water, however, is *confined* within rocks and is subjected to temperatures that are several times greater than its boiling point, it builds up to tremendous pressures and becomes very corrosive. It then dissolves quartz, gold, silver, copper, lead, zinc and a host of other materials and carries them upward away from their plutonic, subterranean source. As it climbs farther from the pluton, its temperature—and hence its pressure—decreases, and the dissolved materials begin to precipitate out. If dissolved gold is present in the ascending fluid, it will precipitate out at the same temperature-pressure combination as the silica, which solidifies to form vein quartz. Hence miners look for quartz veins in the hope they'll find gold in them. About 30-50 million years ago, gold from quartz veins in the Sierra was eroded and transported downstream only to be redeposited where the gradient eased, the stream's velocity decreased, and the stream dropped its rich, heavy prize with other sediments. These sediments, such as those worked at the Hilda Mine (Hike 9), are the second major source of gold after veins.

The Sierra Buttes mining district is known for its large gold nuggets, and some are still occasionally found. In its heyday, this district produced at least $30 million in gold, but little has been mined since the 1930s. By far the most productive mine was the Sierra Buttes Mine—located ½ mile east of the first major bend in our road—whose gold-rich veins yielded as much as $20 million.

Our 1½-mile, sunny, westward ascent ends at a saddle atop a southwest-descending spur ridge (bottom of Map 6), which separates deeply eroded slopes to the east from barely eroded ones to the north. The jeep road up which we'll hike closely parallels this ridge. No matter what month you hike in, you'll be able to follow the road up to this saddle. Beyond the saddle, snow is likely to be encountered except from midsummer through early autumn.

After starting a walk east, we quickly encounter a road contouring north toward the Monarch Mine; then our road curves northeast and climbs ½ mile through a forest, rich in shady western white pines, to a junction with the Sierra Buttes jeep road. Winter and spring hikers will probably miss this sign, if not the entire road up to it, for both will be under fairly deep snow. The forest, however, is open enough for the snowbound hiker to pick any route he chooses. Perhaps the best route to follow under these conditions is to hike up to an obvious saddle immediately north of summit 6924, then climb northeast straight up almost to a ridge, staying near or within the forest's edge.

If you lack snow problems, then take the Sierra Buttes jeep road to a saddle crossed by the Pacific Crest Trail, both features lying immediately northeast of a low knoll, point 7179. Hike 12, which has progressed 7.2 miles along the "PCT" from Highway 49, joins our route here. With snow cover, the swath cut by the jeep trail up through the forest is not always easy to follow, not that it makes any difference. With snow, you'll probably miss the junction with Sierra Buttes Trail (Hikes 15 and 16), about ¾ mile upslope, but that too doesn't matter. You can't miss finding the fire lookout, unless you're in a whiteout, in which case you shouldn't be up here in the first place.

Hike 16 describes the summit's views plus the area's geologic history. When you're ready to descend, start down the switchbacking jeep road. If sufficient snow cover is present, you can soon leave it for a fine glissade, on boots or rear end, down toward the PCT saddle.

# 14 Sardine Lakes Moraine

**Distances** 2.5 miles to moraine crest, 3.5 miles to lower Tamarack Lake, 3.7 miles to upper Tamarack Lake.

**Low/High Elevations** 5770'/7070'

**Classification** Moderate

**Season** Late June through mid-October

**Maps** 7 and 6

**Trailhead** From Highway 49 drive 1.3 miles west up Gold Lake Road, then branch left onto Forest Route 93. In 0.3 mile this road turns right. You continue 100 yards straight ahead, on the Sardine Lakes road. Limited parking along roadside.

**Introduction** If you're staying in the Sardine Lakes area and want a trail with a lot of views, take this hike, which offers a continually changing panorama of the lakes and the Sierra Buttes. The trail provides a long way in to the Tamarack Lakes, but these are better reached by Hike 15. Therefore, most hikers will want to go only to the moraine's crest, if that.

**Description** Our shadeless route, which at first is a jeep road, climbs moderately southwest through dense manzanita up to a switchback. From this point we clearly see the sawtooth nature of the Sierra Buttes crest, and we can see that a traverse along it would be impossible without the aid of ropes and climbing equipment. Just in front of a massive wall of bedrock is deep-blue Lower Sardine Lake, which, like its twin hidden behind the wall, has been slightly raised by a low dam. In the foreground lies a favorite mid- and late-summer swimming hole, Sand Pond.

Sand Pond owes its origin to mining operations at the Young America Mine, whose large buildings once stood on a gentle slope above the lower lake's southwest shore. Higher up on our route, there will be several spots where you'll be able to take a few steps south from the trail and see the rocky, gravelly tailings left by the long-abandoned mine. The mine was a major operation as early as 1885, with a large mill in which ore blasted out of the late-Paleozoic metavolcanic bedrock was crushed to extract its gold, which, over about 50 years, amounted to $1½ million worth. The gangue, or waste material, was then flushed down via a closed conduit to the flat below Lower Sardine Lake, where it was deposited as tailings. In the early 1900s some tailings were removed and were treated by the cyanide process to recover more gold. The depression left by their removal became Sand Pond.

From the switchback, our jeep road heads north to forested slopes and a trail junction. Here we turn left onto the trail and switchback up the end of a huge lateral moraine to its long, southeast side. Because most of the moraine is clothed only in manzanita, huckleberry oak, chinquapin and snow bush, our views up the steadily climbing trail are largely continuous and unobstructed. Occasional Jeffrey pines punctuate the moraine's brushy cloak and some provide us with shady, picturesque, trailside resting spots. Looking southward across Lower Sardine Lake, we see a large lateral moraine of the same age as the one we're hiking along.

Midway along our trail's ascent we encounter a spur trail that descends steeply ¼ mile down to the rocky bench at the outlet of deep, azure-blue Upper Sardine Lake. Beyond the junction, the late-Paleozoic metavolcanic rocks making up our trail's bed gradually yield to ones of an earlier period, these rocks, like the former, coming alive with blazing colors after a rainstorm.

Soon the trail switchbacks up to the open-forested crest of the moraine, from which the buttes are still visible through firs. The 1000-foot-high moraine we've just topped shows us the *minimum* depth of the Sardine Lakes canyon glacier, which filled the canyon until about 10,000 years ago. Since this lateral moraine is composed of debris dropped by the flowing glacier, the glacier had to be higher than the moraine, perhaps by 100 feet. The glacier, whose immense thickness generated a pressure of over 35 tons per square foot, scoured out a deep basin in which lies today's Upper Sardine Lake. At its maximum thickness, then, the glacier's icy surface stood about 1200 feet above the lake basin's floor. It must have been a very dramatic, alpine sight.

Leaving the moraine's crest, the trail switchbacks steeply down to gentler slopes and becomes a closed jeep road, which undulates and winds past seasonal ponds before ending just below shallow lower Tamarack Lake. Here we encounter a second jeep road, on which vehicles are allowed, and on weekends you may see fishermen who have driven this far. This jeep road and the Tamarack lakes are described in the following route.

# 15     Packer Lake to Tamarack Lakes and Sierra Buttes

**Distances**   0.9 mile to lower Tamarack Lake, 1.1 miles to upper Tamarack Lake, 1.8 miles to Pacific Crest Trail, 3.5 miles to Sierra Buttes Fire Lookout.

**Low/High Elevations**   6260'/6760'

**Classification**   Easy (to the lakes)

**Season**   Late June through mid-October

**Map**   6

**Trailhead**   From Highway 49 drive 1.3 miles west up Gold Lake Road, then branch left onto Forest Route 93 and follow it 3.2 miles to a trailhead parking area with space for a dozen vehicles. This spot is about 250 yards past the Packer Lake Picnic Area.

**Introduction**   Like Packer Lake near the trailhead, the Tamarack Lakes provide relatively warm swimming from late July to late August. As is typical of Sierra lakes, both contain trout, and that is perhaps their greatest attraction. From the lakes you can climb to the Sierra Buttes, though such a route, while fairly popular, is 0.9 mile longer than the Hike 16 route. It also has 750 feet of additional elevation gain, some of it quite steep.

**Description**   Your route, a jeep road, starts opposite the parking area, and climbs a leisurely ¼ mile to a fork, from where a gated road swings east to Dugan Pond, which is on private land. The main road, however, continues straight ahead, in a direct fashion almost to the Tamarack Lakes. Along this moderate ascent, the road splits, only to rejoin upslope. Just below unseen lower Tamarack Lake, you reach a junc-

tion with a trail eastbound for the Sardine Lakes (Hike 14). You veer right, up the jeep road, and momentarily arrive at the northwest shore of lower Tamarack Lake. Your first view is disappointing, for the west half of the lake is largely knee-deep, little more. The east half, however, is not only swimmable but is deep enough to support a limited trout population.

A larger trout population resides in upper Tamarack Lake. Just above the lower lake, your jeep road forks, and you take the left road, which also forks, both legs reuniting by the upper lake. The Tamarack Lakes derive their name from the fringe of lodgepole pines that encircles each (as they do most Sierra lakes). Back in the 1800s, John Muir and his contemporaries called these two-needled, sappy-barked conifers *tamarack* pines.

If you're hell-bent for the Sierra Buttes, take the right road at the fork by the lower lake. The road climbs moderately, affording views across the lakes' basin, then terminates at an abandoned logging road. If you were to follow the road southeast down to its end, and then continue cross-country east-southeast up to a crest saddle, you would discover Young America Lake, which lies 300 feet below the saddle. However, almost everyone continues south from the jeep-road/logging-road junction, climbing steeply up a trail to a ridge junction with the Pacific Crest Trail. Like the jeep road below the lakes, your Sierra Buttes Trail splits and rejoins. From the ridge junction the Sierra Buttes Trail climbs southeast to the summit. This route, plus the summit views, are described in the next hike.

**Fishing at lower Tamarack Lake**

# 16     Forest Route 93 to Sierra Buttes

**Distance**   2.6 miles, one way

**Low/High Elevations**   7012'/8591'

**Classification**   Strenuous

**Season**   Mid-July through mid-October

**Map**   6

**Trailhead**   From Highway 49 drive 1.3 miles west up Gold Lake Road, then branch left onto Forest Route 93 and follow it just over 3 miles to the Packer Lake Picnic Area. Ahead, your paved route steepens as it climbs 1.6 miles to the Packer Lake Saddle, and then it heads 0.4 mile south along a ridge to a junction. Leave Route 93, which switchbacks northwest, and continue 0.2 mile south to a second saddle.

**Introduction**   After mid-July this route is virtually snow-free and therefore easy to follow. Seasoned, fanatical hikers can make the ascent in an hour's time, but most hikers will take two. This is one hike you'll want to do when visibility is great, for then you can see Lassen Peak plus most of the Tahoe Sierra. Bring lots of film, and perhaps binoculars, to capture the summit's stupendous, top-of-the-world views.

**Description**   Your route begins along the Pacific Crest Trail, which for the first half mile is not a trail at all. Rather, it is a somewhat drivable logging road that goes over to private lands being logged in the northwest part of Section 17. Just as this road starts to cut through a ridgecrest, you meet trail tread. Still on the Pacific Crest Trail, you follow the tread south, weaving along an almost level crest, which has a diverse array of wildflowers that grow on or about the phyllite outcrops. These rocks derive their sheen from an abundance of mica minerals, which are planar minerals that form crystals. The crystals became aligned more or less parallel to one another when the original volcanic rock was transformed to metamorphic rock by sustained heat and pressure.

After ⅓ mile your glistening traverse ends at a junction. From the north, **Hike 15,** originating near Packer Lake, climbs to meet us. Departing south, the Pacific Crest Trail contours 1.1 miles over to a saddle from where Hikes 12 and 13, there united, climb to the Sierra Buttes Fire Lookout. In just under a mile, we'll join that route.

Leaving the junction on the Sierra Buttes Trail, we climb moderately to steeply southeast, staying at or close to the ascending ridge. After an exhausting ¼ mile, we meet a jeep road,

steeply ascending from the west, and follow it for 70 yards to where it veers south. Here, up around 7600 feet, mountain hemlocks begin to swell in rank, creating very shady conditions that keep snow lingering through midsummer. If the trail is snowbound when you hike it, watch for blazes on the trees—though by adhering to the ascending ridge, you're bound to reach your goal.

You emerge from the forest deep for a heart-throbbing view northeast down the Sardine Lakes canyon. Young America Lake, the highest lake in view, is just ¼ mile away, yet due to the precarious nature of its surrounding canyon walls, this lake is one of the least visited in the entire Tahoe Sierra. Your views momentarily disappear as you weave among dappled, giant "boulders" of pale blue-green metamorphic rock, then you regain your views, spying the distant fire lookout that beckons you onward. Your trail reaches an old jeep road, and on it you walk a bit over to a junction with the buttes' main jeep road. Remember this stretch of route, for otherwise on your descent you may continue descending the old jeep road by mistake.

On the main jeep road, the route of Hikes 12 and 13, we now make a moderate, open, sometimes blustery ascent. Wildflower species, not seen below, begin to appear. You can't help but notice you're approaching the alpine realm. Trees, the few you see, are diminished in stature, shaven by winter's icy winds. After ½ mile of climbing, you get an awe-inspiring view of the lookout, perched atop a forbidding cliff like an eagle's aerie. Acrophobics, if they don't get weak-kneed here, certainly do when they confront the airy ladders climbing 176 steps to the lookout.

The summit area is so small that the lookout actually projects out into space, and through the iron-grating view deck you stand on, you can look straight down the 600-foot high, nearly vertical northeast escarpment. The deeply glaciated Sardine Lakes canyon to the northeast contrasts strongly with the barely eroded slopes up which the main jeep road climbs. To the south lie slopes of intermediate erosion, cut by tributaries of the North Yuba River. The views are far-ranging. On the distant northwest horizon stands snowy Lassen Peak (10,457'), the southernmost major volcano of the Cascade Range. Numerous high peaks dot the Lake Tahoe environs to the southeast. With compass in hand

**Wildflower Plate 11. Northern Sierra flowers.**
1 Nuttall's sandwort (white), 2 silky raillardella (yellow), 3 California helianthella (yellow), 4 plain-leaved fawn lily (white with yellow center), 5 northern Sierra chaenactis (cream to pink), 6 hot-rock penstemon (pale yellow with red veins), 7 California valerian (white), 8 Sierra primrose (rose with yellow center), 9 skunk-leaved (showy) polemonium (pale blue with yellow center).

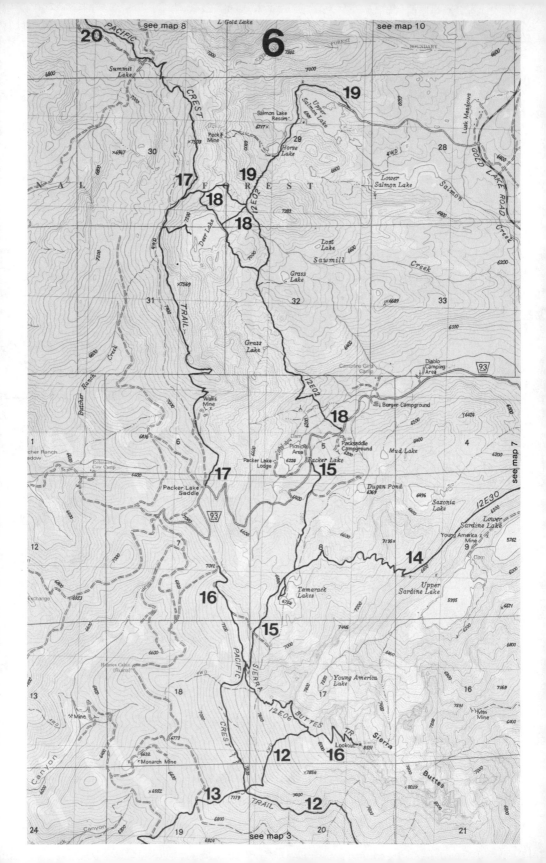

see map 8
see map 10
see map 7
see map 3

you can identify Mt. Rose (10,776'), 114°; Mt. Lola (9148'), 126°; and the light-gray Crystal Range of Desolation Wilderness (9983' maximum—Pyramid Peak), about 155°. Round Top (10,381') stands just above and left of the Crystal Range, a hefty 72½ miles from our vantage point, ranking as the southernmost peak in the Tahoe Sierra. Many lower summits and ridges, both near and far, are seen in every direction.

What immediately captivates one's attention, however, is the deep, glaciated canyon immediately northeast and ½ mile below us. It lies in stark contrast to the unglaciated, little-eroded west slope up which we hiked. That slope has changed little in the last 10 million years. Back then, the Sierra Buttes weren't a jagged crest at all, but rather a monolithic mass with minor irregularities, that was about 6 miles in diameter east-west, and about 5 miles in diameter north-south.

On the basis of the configuration of the west slope, one can determine that the original summit was located about ½ mile northeast of today's summit and stood perhaps 500 feet higher— possibly surpassing 9000 feet elevation *by today's standards*. Back then, while the southern and central Sierra was considerably lower than today, the northern Sierra was not, and the Sierra Buttes mass may have stood about 7000 feet above sea level. Today, the buttes stand about 4500 feet above the North Yuba where it flows past Sierra City. Back then, the broad mass stood 3500 feet above the ancestral North Yuba, which was as much as a mile south and a mile east of its present, southwest-curving course. The ancestral river flowed through a canyon it had cut through volcanic rocks, which was quite different from its prevolcanic predecessor. Earlier, about 30–50 million years ago, the North Yuba meandered across a low, gentle landscape, strategically depositing gold-bearing sediments after times of high runoff.

Today, Sierra City lies in a canyon deepened and steepened by the action of glacial rivers. In response to these changes, streams vigorously cut deeply into the south slope of the buttes, deeply eroding them and steepening them further. The first gold miners, who founded Sierra City in 1850, learned the dangers of over-steep slopes the hard way—a catastrophic avalanche swept down the south slope and destroyed their settlement in 1852. Not until the 1860s or later was much of the town rebuilt. Perhaps the hard life in that mining town led to the creation of the roisterous society called E. Clampus Vitus, which soon spread throughout the Mother Lode. The buttes had played a not-so-practical joke on Sierra City inhabitants, and they, in turn, formed this organization which played practical jokes upon naive newcomers. Today, the city is more of an easy-going retirement-and-vacation community rich in history, folklore and the magnificent scenery ruled over by the lordly, long-lived Sierra Buttes.

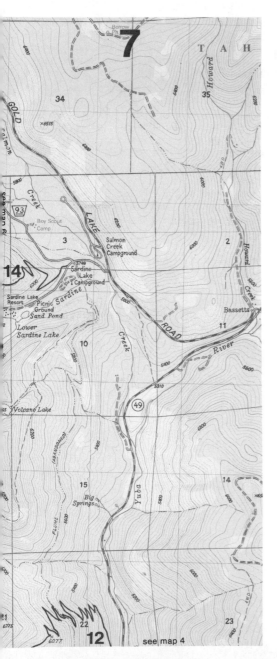

# 17 Pacific Crest Trail, from Forest Route 93 north to Summit Lake

**Distances**   2.9 miles to west shore Deer Lake, 4.5 miles to Summit Lake.

**Low/High Elevations**   7020'/7520'

**Classification**   Easy

**Season**   Mid-July through mid-October

**Map**   6

**Trailhead**   At Packer Lake Saddle—see the Hike 16 trailhead description.

**Introduction**   Of three possible routes to popular Deer Lake (Hikes 17-19), this one provides the most views. Geologically inclined hikers will find the crest views, both north and south of Deer Lake, particularly instructive.

**Description**   From the crossroads at Packer Lake Saddle, our route, the Pacific Crest Trail (PCT), climbs northeast through a red-fir/western-white-pine forest, taking us quickly to a view of Packer Lake, which lies at the base of our ridge. Soon, shady forest yields to sunny shrubland, and then we cross a jeep road bound for the Wallis Mine. The trail next curves northeast for some more views, switchbacks twice, and arrives at the edge of a clearcut. A two-minute walk north through it to a hemlock-adorned crest saddle saves you ¼ mile of walking. However, the PCT purposely deviates eastward to take you to a rocky point with truly gratifying views.

Although you've hiked but 1¼ miles so far, your climbing is essentially done. Staying near the crest of a fairly uniform ridge, you first head west, over to the top of the previously mentioned clearcut, then for ¾ mile stay at or just above its upper limit. Virgin forest returns as you round a high point on your ridge, point 7569 on the map. From its north toe you have a tree-framed view of alluring Deer Lake, then in ⅓ mile reach a jeep road that drops ⅓ mile to west-shore campsites. After the snow melts away in early or mid-July, you can expect to see 4WDs down at these sites.

An old jeep road has been paralleling our course, and in short order we twice cross it before reaching a second Deer Lake jeep road. This descends to the lake's north shore, which is also reached by the Deer Lake Trail (**Hike 18**) and the Salmon Lake Trail (**Hike 19**). The Deer Lake Trail is easily the most popular route, due to its trailhead location in the midst of "camper valley," and therefore the lake's amenities are described in that route.

Northbound, the PCT resumes its tread about 25 yards down the second Deer Lake jeep road, and weaves a course ¼ mile northeast almost to a viewpoint. At it you'll have a view of the Salmon Lakes, which you see again from just ahead on the trail. Then, just before you gain your first view of Gold Lake, you have a view south of the serrated Sierra Buttes. From the north end of those buttes, the PCT has been adhering faithfully to a crest that many would perceive as the actual Sierra Nevada crest. However, the true crest lies to the east, capped in the north by 8100+' Haskell Peak, almost due east of us, and capped many miles farther southeast along its sinuous backbone by a trio of three 9000+' summits, Mt. Lola, Basin Peak and Castle Peak. Unlike our crest, which is metamorphic, the visible Sierra crest is granitic, though its southern half is deeply mantled by volcanic flows and sediments. These volcanic deposits bury a number of faults, though because the deposits are absent in the north half, a major fault, at the east base of that massif, lies exposed to the airborne traveler. We thus have a view which covers a tremendous span of geologic history: Several hundred million years ago, this area was a sea, which was succeeded by a volcanic range. Both oceanic and volcanic rocks were then metamorphosed, in part because of the intrusion of masses of granitic rock. Much erosion took place, followed by faulting, which lifted the area, and then by renewed volcanism. Finally, glaciers repeatedly buried most of this high area, but they temporarily left it (they will return) to give us the view we see today.

Not far beyond your Gold Lake view, the PCT commences a ¾-mile descent to the Gold Lake jeep road. This viewless, partly logged stretch is unappealing, as is small, shallow Summit Lake, perched just south of a viewless crest saddle. Skip this stretch unless you plan to hike the PCT northwest along the Lakes Basin crest (Hike 20).

**A mule-deer fawn**

# 18                           Deer Lake Trail

**Distances**   1.1 miles to first Grass Lake, 1.8
miles to second Grass Lake, 2.0 miles to
Deer Lake by shortest route, 2.8 miles by
longest.

**Low/High Elevations**   6120'/7090' (by shortest route)

**Classification**   Moderate

**Season**   Early July through mid-October

**Map**   6

**Trailhead**   From Highway 49 drive 1.3 miles
west up Gold Lake Road, then branch left onto
Forest Route 93 and follow it 2¾ miles to the
trailhead, just below Packsaddle Camping Area.

**Introduction**   A short hike, this trail takes you
up to deep, sparkling Deer Lake, whose shores
see many a backpacker and fisherman. In addition, two shallow, less visited lakes are easily
reached from this trail. In a good day's walk you
can hike to four Grass Lakes in the Highway 49
region. The first two lie close to our route—the
Deer Lake Trail—another is in Lakes Basin and
the northernmost is in Plumas-Eureka State
Park.

**Description**   Leaving the trailhead, we quickly
meet and cross by various means four unequal-
sized creeks that drain Packer Lake and the
slopes north of it. Departing from the lush,
streamside vegetation, we begin to climb upward, execute two well-graded switchback legs,
and swing past a two-crest lateral moraine. Our
comfortable trail underfoot becomes rocky as
we curve over to the first Grass Lake's outlet
creek, and it remains so almost to the second
Grass Lake turnoff.

The first Grass Lake turnoff is about ¼ mile
up the trail from the outlet creek. Where you
encounter a ridge jutting 10–15 feet above the
trail's west side, you can climb up it, and from it
an easy, 100-yard, cross-country descent to the
east shore will become immediately apparent.
Of the region's four Grass Lakes, this one is the
smallest, diminished by invading grass. Two
small flats provide adequate campsites. One is
above the lake's east side, the other just southwest of its outlet creek.

From the trailside ridge, we confront a steady,
bush-lined ascent. In 0.6 mile our trail levels off
at an open-forested flat, on which you may see a
sign: GRASS LAKE ¼. If you wish to hike to the
lake, start northeast, cross a seasonal creek in 30

yards, then follow a *faint,* ducked trail that
crosses a gentle ridge and gradually descends its
north slope to the willow-lined lake, which provides warm midsummer swimming. Larger and
deeper than the first Grass Lake, this chest-
deep, grass-bottomed lake also differs in that its
water is not crystal clear. Should you decide to
camp at this sometimes hard-to-find lake, obtain
fresh water from audible Sawmill Creek, which
is 300 yards from the lake's north shore.

Only 60 yards north of the route to the
second Grass Lake, we leave the main trail as
we bear west-northwest toward a conspicuous
gully from which a seasonal creek flows. At the
gully's mouth, a rocky path, ducked and blazed,
appears and guides us ½ mile up to a moraine immediately above Deer Lake's southeast shore.
Small campsites can be found along the west,
south and northeast shores, and diving and
swimming are best from the last. If you've
brought along a fishing rod, you can try to catch
the fairly deep lake's rainbow and brook trout.

A longer route to Deer Lake, ending at the
lake's northeast shore rather than at its outlet, is
along the main trail. This climbs erratically,
crosses Sawmill Creek in just under ½ mile, then
snakes ¼ mile farther up to a saddle, where
you'll meet the Salmon Lake Trail (Hike 19).
From here you have the opportunity to strike
east, cross-country, to a rocky knoll, point 7283
on the map, which tenders a commanding panorama of basin lands from the Salmon Lakes
south to the Tamarack Lakes.

From the saddle you have a choice of two
routes to Deer Lake. The shorter is along a faint,
essentially game trail, bearing west-southwest,
which ends near the lake's northeast shore.
Cross-country hiking to this shore is easy enough
so that you need not try to follow the cryptic
trail. The longer route actually begins 15 yards
north of the saddle. It starts west up a shallow
gully, climbs and descends a slab into a larger
gully, follows it to its head, then bends southwest
across a slope to a jeep road. Upslope, this road
climbs ¼ mile to the Pacific Crest Trail (Hike
17), but you take it ¼ mile down to the lake. At
Deer Lake, ice melts rather late, entirely dis-
appearing (in average years) in time for the
Fourth of July. However, not until late July does
the lake warm enough for acceptable swimming.
The northeast shore has good basking rocks
available after an invigorating dip.

# 19                  Salmon Lake Trail

**Distance**   1.9 miles to Deer Lake (by shortest route)

**Low/High Elevations**   6510'/7140' (by shortest route)

**Classification**   Moderate

**Season**   Mid-July through mid-October

**Map**   6

**Trailhead**   From Highway 49 drive 4.0 miles northwest up Gold Lake Road, then branch left onto Salmon Lake Road. After 1.0 mile, you'll see the trailhead, on the right, about 150 yards before road's end, by Upper Salmon Lake. Ample parking here.

**Introduction**   A slightly shorter, alternative approach to popular Deer Lake, this trail provides scenic vistas across the Salmon Lakes basin.

**Description**   From the east end of the parking area, the Salmon Lake Trail begins a rocky, moderate ascent up a classic brush slope covered with huckleberry oak, western serviceberry, deer brush, snow bush, manzanita, and bitter cherry. Scattered, big-leafed mule ears—plants usually associated with volcanic soils—add their own decoration and aroma to this slope, which is the south side of a large lateral moraine. Below us, several picturesque islands, easily reached by short swims from one to another, grow more distant. Upon reaching a flat, our trail commences a moderate descent that takes us down to Salmon Lake's rocky northwest corner. As you approach outlying

buildings of Salmon Lake Resort, stay high, contouring about 50 feet above the water, and reaching a bridge over Horse Lake creek 120 yards up from the resort's main building.

Beyond the creek, our trail climbs southward, passing a small pond before arriving at shallow Horse Lake, bordered by lodgepoles, western white pines, red firs and brush. Rounding the lake's southeast shore, the trail gets swampy in places, and an abundance of corn lilies reflects this water-saturated soil condition.

A few short switchbacks carry us up to a sloping bench just south of a creeklet that descends to Horse lake, visible below us. Higher up, our steeply climbing, switchbacking trail provides us with better views of this lake plus views of Upper Salmon Lake and the massive moraine behind it. Note that the moraine isn't all that thick; rather, it covers the bedrock with just a mantle of earth and loose rock.

We soon meet the Deer Lake Trail atop a forested saddle. From here you can strike east, ¼ mile cross-country, to point 7283, for a commanding panorama of much of the terrain from the Salmon Lakes south to the Sierra Buttes. See the last paragraph of Hike 18 for two routes to nearby Deer Lake.

**Deer Lake and Sierra Buttes in June**          **Upper Salmon Lake**

# 20  Pacific Crest Trail, from Summit Lake north to Trail above Wades Lake

**Distance**  6.1 miles, one way

**Low/High Elevations**  7050'/7360'

**Classification**  Easy along the PCT; moderate along routes up to it.

**Season**  Mid-July through mid-October

**Maps**  6 and 8

**Trailhead**  None; see introduction.

**Introduction**  The most famous trail in this hiking chapter is the Pacific Crest Trail (PCT). Indeed, the trail threads a 150-mile track along the backbone of the Tahoe Sierra (plus an additional 2400 miles outside this area). Surely, this should be the trail to hike. Well, the author feels it isn't, at least not the stretch above the Lakes Basin (the Forest Service disagrees). He would have liked to see it go from lake to lake: Sardine Lakes, Tamarack Lakes, Packer Lake, Deer Lake, Summit Lake, Round Lake, Silver Lake, Mud Lake, Jamison Lake, Rock Lake and Wades Lake. What a fantastic route, one that would have few rivals in all of North America! But most of these lakes are heavily used and the entire Lakes Basin is closed to camping (except in the Lakes Basin Campground), so the trail was purposely routed high above the lakes, to discourage visitation. On this hike's 6.1-mile stretch, tempting views of the lake-studded basin have been reduced to a solitary, though impeccable, panorama from the brink of treacherous slopes above Round Lake. Obviously no hiker would try to descend to the basin from this spot.

Despite this route's limitations, you may still want to include all or part of its 6.1 miles in your hiking itinerary. You can reach or leave this stretch from: 1) the north end of Hike 17; 2) the Gold Lake jeep road; 3) Trail 12E34, climbing south from Round Lake (Hike 21); 4) Trails 12E29 and 12E30, which unite at a jeep road on a crest above the west edge of Lakes Basin (Hike 23); and 5) Trail 11E13, climbing up Little Jamison Creek (Hike 27). To avoid a shuttle, you could put together a loop route, say, by starting from the Lakes Basin Campground. First climb west to Long Lake then south past Round Lake to the Pacific Crest Trail. After 6.1 miles on it, descend Trail 11E13 north past Grass Lake to Trail 12E24. Follow that trail east past Smith Lake and down to Gray Eagle Lodge, then conclude with Trails 12E26 and 12E28 south up to your starting point.

**Description**  Small, shallow Summit Lake is immediately south of the PCT's junction with the Gold Lake jeep road (Hike 17 covers the stretch of PCT south from here). Since the lake is the only *permanent* body of water you'll encounter along your hike, you might consider camping near it, but treat its water should you drink it. Be forewarned: mosquitoes are seasonally overabundant at the lake's ample campsites.

North of the Gold Lake jeep road the PCT parallels a crest-hugging jeep road, first at a distance, then alongside it. Near the north end of the fairly level ridge, a jeep road cuts northeast across the crest and, 1⅓ miles along our hike, we have three route choices. First, we can head a few paces west to the jeep road we've been paralleling and take it ⅓ mile northwest down to Oakland Pond, which is like Summit Lake in water purity and camping potential. About 200 yards past the pond, where the road turns west, a trail climbs moderately north ⅓ mile back to the PCT. Second, one can follow the northeast-heading jeep road. The PCT route does this for a few yards before leaving it, but you can continue onward and drop to Round Lake. The road soon narrows to a trail and the route down to the lake isn't very obvious. Make sure you pass a nearby pond on its west side. Furthermore, 300 yards below the pond, be sure you curve northwest to a 5-foot-deep gap rather than descend a gully northeast toward the broad saddle above Gold Lake. This is the reverse of part of the suggested loop route. Camping is *not* allowed in Lakes Basin, so rejoin the PCT at a saddle not far east of the Four Hills Mine. The third route—the least interesting in the author's opinion—is to take the lakeless PCT.

This route leaves the northeast-bound jeep road in a few paces, then climbs almost to point 7541, switchbacking needlessly several times just south of it. From the switchbacks you get excellent views of the western Sierra, particularly of the closer terrain that includes Snake Lake, Little Deer Lake and PCT campers at Oakland Pond. North of point 7541 we have views down into well-named Lakes Basin, which has been severely glaciated. Glaciation in the entire Sierra Buttes-Lakes Basin area was quite extensive. From the Sierra Buttes, glaciers descended first northeast to the North Yuba River canyon, and then briefly down it. From the Lakes Basin and the canyons both east and west of it, glaciers extended north down to about the 4500-foot level along the western edge of fault-formed Mohawk Valley, the earlier glaciers dumping their coarse sediments into the valley's lake, which existed until about 120,000 years ago.

Steep slopes of granitelike rock prevent us from dropping into the sparkling Lakes Basin. The bedrock here, as along most of our chapter's trails, is metamorphosed volcanic rocks that were erupted west of North America about 350–450 million years ago. (They were later transported here—see the geology chapter.) At a nearby saddle, our solitary views of the Lakes Basin disappear, and we drop back into forest cover and come to a junction. Had you taken the Oakland Pond route, you'd be climbing northwest to meet the PCT here.

The PCT heads briefly west to a ridge that provides views to the south and west, then enters viewless forest for a traverse almost a mile long, Next, it curves southwest through a shady forest growing on a flat, ill-defined crest that can harbor snow patches into July. Momentarily we cross a jeep road that heads north to a ridge above the west edge of Lakes Basin. The PCT curves south to a ridge, then curves west to an excellent viewpoint above Hawley Lake. We re-enter forest again and descend ⅓ mile to a jeep-road crossing at a county-line crest saddle. A spring-fed creek lies 200 yards east along the jeep road. Those who made excursions through Lakes Basin rejoin us here. Immediately west of the saddle is a diminutive pond that nevertheless has enough staying power to hold water through most, if not all, of the summer. You could camp in this locality.

Our trail briefly parallels the road west, then swings north, taking a tortuous route that has to be hiked to be believed. Twice we almost touch the jeep road, only to veer away, but finally, after 1⅓ miles, we cross it near a high point on the Sierra crest. Leave the PCT at this intersection and take the road ¼ mile down to a junction with Trail 11E13. Follow this trail, which is described in the reverse direction in Hike 27. Alternatively, you can continue along the PCT, but such an adventure is beyond the northern limits of this book. (The entire trail is covered in a two-volume set, *The Pacific Crest Trail,* by the author and others.)

**Wades Lake, from Trail 11E13**

# 21                    Round Lake Loop

**Distance**   4.3 miles, loop trip
**Low/High Elevations**   6470'/6850'
**Classification**   Easy
**Season**   Early July through mid-October
**Map**   8
**Trailhead**   From Highway 49 drive 8 miles northwest up Gold Lake Road, then branch left at the Gold Lake Lodge spur road, which is immediately before the Plumas/Sierra county-line crest. Go 100 yards on it to a parking area for about a dozen vehicles.

**Introduction**   This relaxing trip, an easy morning hike, takes you to five lakes in the southern half of Lakes Basin. Round, Silver and Big Bear lakes are fishermen's favorites, and are also appealing to photographers and swimmers.

**Description**   Just 50 yards east of Gold Lake Lodge and only 35 yards west of the crest parking area is a closed jeep road which traverses southwest toward Round, Bear, Silver and Long lakes. We start a gentle ascent up this road, and after a few minutes' walk meet a trail that departs for Bear, Silver and Long lakes, the first

**Fishing in Round Lake**

lake reached in under ½ mile. Most hikers turn right here, since this route is the quickest way to most of the five lakes, but we'll return along it.

Over the next mile of road, our hike through a forest of white and red firs is uneventful, although we do get a glimpse of justifiably popular Big Bear Lake below. Then, our road curves left, passes two seasonal ponds, and immediately comes to a trail junction. An old trail to Gold Lake starts south up a deep gully, aborting before the crest. Walking on, we wind westward for ⅓ mile, steeply at times, up to a ridgetop.

If you want to climb to the Pacific Crest Trail (Hike 20), veer left on an old road that reaches, in about 100 yards, Trail 12E34. This ¾-mile-long connecting trail starts a steep ascent, which remains so up a ridge, passes through its low cleft, and then presents the hiker with good views of the Lakes Basin. As the ridge eases off, the trail goes through a miniature pass, swings southeast toward a gully and briefly gives one a glimpse of Gold Lake. The faint trail next turns south and climbs to a small saddle just west of a hidden, rock-rimmed pond, then soon broadens to a jeep road and reaches the crest trail.

However, the Round Lake loop, rather than forking left at the ridgetop, curves right and descends toward Round Lake, the road diminishing to a trail before it touches the south shore. Mine tailings and mechanical debris, both derived from the abandoned mine up at the ridgetop, now fill part of the deep lake's south side.

Quartz blasted from the mine's veins is recognizable among the rock fragments in the tailings, and it was in this vein quartz that miners had hoped to find gold.

A fishermen's trail skirts the lake's southeast shore, and on it we reach the jump-across outlet creek. From here an evident, rocky trail makes an open climb northwest above the lake toward the crest of a moraine. Just south of the moraine's crest—and an easy walk west from us—lies a large, triangular pond that is sometimes shaded by stately Jeffrey pines growing near it. Atop the crest, we start north and immediately see our next goal, Silver Lake, before we descend to its east shore. Fringed with western white and lodgepole pines, mountain hemlocks and red firs, this lake has considerably more appeal than Round Lake, whose shoreline tends to be more brushy. Before August, however, shade-loving mosquitoes may make you prefer Round Lake. Most of the shoreline around Silver Lake is readily accessible, if not by main trail then by fishermen's trail. Like all lakes in the Lakes Basin, Silver Lake is heavily fished. The lake's shallow, warm August water invites an enjoyable swim, but by late August the temperature begins to drop and the lake's outlet creek has already dried up. Our trail crosses this east-flowing creek, near which we have a glimpse down-basin at Cub Lake and the Bear lakes, and then it curves over to a junction just above the lake's north arm. Climbing west from here is a

**Long Lake and Mt. Elwell, viewed from a ridge above the lake's south shore**

trail that soon divides, one branch climbing to the Pacific Crest Trail, and another one rambling over to the Long Lake environs, from where another trail zigzags up to the top of Mt. Elwell (see Hikes 23 and 24).

Our sometimes vague trail rambles a bit northward, crosses a small flat, and then climbs northeast to a view of island-dotted Long Lake, which is also wide and deep. Although less than a mile long, it appears larger than it actually is, perhaps because of the stunted growth of the shoreline conifers. Leaving this ridge view, from which the east-dipping strata of Mt. Elwell are readily apparent, we descend east a few paces to a junction in a small flat that lies between two low crests. The trail going northeast takes you to Long Lake's southeast shore (next hike) before descending to Elwell Lodge and Lakes Basin Campground.

We skip southeast over a low crest, descend past a small pond on our right and approach but don't reach circular, shallow Cub Lake. Paralleling this lake's drainage eastward, our trail soon crosses above the north shore of linear, pine-rimmed Little Bear Lake. From a trailside stump about 150 yards beyond this shallow lake, a fishermen's trail departs southeast toward it, then parallels its east shore, and ends at its 10-yard-long outlet creek, which drops 4 feet into Big Bear Lake. Along this larger lake's wavy, rocky shoreline, you'll find good spots to fish, and to dive and swim from.

Back at the trailside stump, from which both Bear lakes are seen, we briefly ascend and then descend to Big Bear's north shore, and cross east over a peninsula. Momentarily paralleling this lake's north shore, we reach its northeast corner and a trail junction. Here, Hike 22, which has coincided with our route since the last trail junction, departs northeast toward Lakes Basin Campground and Elwell Lodge. We turn south, in 45 yards cross Big Bear's outlet, and then leave this extremely popular, moderately large lake behind as we start down beside its outlet creek.

At first, the outlet creek is a flowing pond, but it soon constricts before enlarging into a second pond, which is seen as the trail curves right around a ridge above it. Our trail now traverses southeast to a shallow creek in a shaded gully. After jumping across the creek, we climb east moderately and then steeply up our blazed trail, cross a boggy flat and parallel the edge of a cluster of willows as we climb northeast toward the outskirts of Gold Lake Lodge. Just before leaving the willows, we reach a steeper gradient and a trail junction. The route straight ahead climbs northeast moderately up to nearby Gold Lake. Our route veers east, climbs moderately southeast, and curves eastward back up to the closed road we first started hiking on. On it we hike 300 yards northeast to the trailhead, to the Gold Lake Lodge entrance and to the parking area.

# 22            Bear Lakes Loop

**Distance**  2.5 miles, loop trip

**Low/High Elevations**  6330'/6670'

**Classification**  Easy

**Season**  Early July through mid-October

**Map**  8

**Trailhead**  From Highway 49 drive 8 miles northwest up Gold Lake Road to its county-line crest, then 1 mile farther to the Lakes Basin Campground road. If you're driving south from Highway 89, this junction is 6¾ miles up Gold Lake Road. Drive down to the campground's hub. The Grass Lake Trail starts from the north end of the campground. Most sites, and three trailheads, are along a rutted road west, and some folks won't want to drive it. One trail starts from Elwell Lodge, whose spur road is obvious. Two trails start from road's end, about ½ mile past the campground's hub. The Long Lake Trail, with an organization campsite near its start (reservations required), traverses west, while the Bear Lake Trail climbs south. Parking for several cars.

**Introduction**  The easiest lakes loop in the Lakes Basin, this hike leads you to four lakes, including one short excursion to giant Long Lake. For those who desire a quick taste of the Lakes Basin's beauty and charm, this short hike is perfect.

**Description**  Walking west on Long Lake Trail 12E30, we immediately cross a creek, then in a few paces pass an organization campsite—flat, spacious, but mosquito-prone like the rest of Lakes Basin Campground. Climbing moderately

westward from the flat's far end, we exchange the shade of white firs and lodgepoles for fairly continuous sunlight on a more open, brushy slope. Wildflowers adorn the trail's side, and a short distance up-trail we pass a low, granitelike cliff of metarhyolite, on which rock climbers can brush up their techniques.

Just beyond the low cliff we cross a wisp of a creek, bordered here and there by western serviceberry, which is recognized in early summer by its round, fine-toothed leaves and its half-dollar-sized, five-petaled flowers. Late-summer hikers will find its white flowers replaced with purple, pulpy but edible berries. From the creek we climb to a small flat, shaded by lodgepoles, and on it meet an old trail, not well maintained, which curves southeast and then progresses eastward, crossing the Bear Lake Trail before ending at the west grounds of Elwell Lodge.

A hike equally as short as the one we've just completed takes us up almost to a ridge, and we arrive at a trail junction. Being very close to Long Lake, we continue west in its direction up a short spur trail, cresting the ridge and almost immediately dropping to a small bay on the lake's northeast shore, only ⅔ mile from our trailhead. At this bay, which is one of the huge lake's three readily accessible shores, summer visitors can rent small boats to fish from or cruise in. A use trail connects this bay with the lake's outlet, to the north.

After exploring the small bay or perhaps trying your luck at shoreline fishing, backtrack over the low ridge and cruise down to the last junction. From it the main trail climbs southwest

**Big Bear Lake**

**Cub Lake and the Lakes Basin (Sierra Nevada) crest**

and then descends a gully to a trail junction in a small flat. Hike 21, coming from the west, descends to this junction, while Hikes 23 and 24 head west up from it. You might note that although we're very close to Long Lake's south shore, which is over 100 feet below us, we can't see the lake at all. A moraine blocks our view north down it, as another moraine blocks our view southeast down toward the Bear lakes. The gully in which our trail descended to this flat separates these two linear products of glacial deposition.

The route for the next 0.8 mile coincides with that of Hike 21. Climb briefly southeast over the low, bouldery moraine, descend to Cub Lake, and pass the north shores of Little Bear and Big Bear lakes. At Big Bear's northeast corner, with barely ½ mile left to go, our trail splits from Hike 21, and we descend northward, briefly touching a meander in the lake's outlet creek. Not far beyond this meander our trail forks. The Bear *Lakes* Trail descends right to Elwell Lodge. We take the Bear *Lake* Trail, which traverses around a small ridge before descending to our trailhead. Midway along this descent, we cross the old east-west Elwell Lodge-Long Lake Trail, which we previously encountered near the start of our hike.

# 23      Long Lake Loop

**Distance**  6.7 miles, loop trip
**Low/High Elevations**  6190'/7020'
**Classification**  Moderate
**Season**  Early July through mid-October
**Map**  8
**Trailhead**  Same as the Hike 22 trailhead.

**Introduction**  All three good access points to the shores of Long Lake are encountered along this route. One need not, of course, restrict himself to these three limited shoreline segments, but rather can investigate cross-country alternatives to virtually untouched shores.

**Description**  Hike 22 describes the first mile of trail up to a junction above the south shore of Long Lake. From this junction we climb a bit southwest, then meander south over to a nearby junction above the north shore of lovely Silver Lake. This lake merits at least a brief delay, and then we scramble westward up a brushy ridge packed with pleasing panoramas that extend across virtually all of the Lakes Basin. Momentarily leaving the ridge, our trail switchbacks and then climbs back to it at a trail junction.

West, Trail 12E30 weaves and undulates a full mile over to a jeep road. This trail skirts above two nearby lakelets, the first one known as Helgramite Lake. (Nonfishermen, take note: *hellgrammites* are aquatic, predatory, toe-biting larvae of dobson flies. These larvae, up to 2 inches long, make excellent trout bait.) The trail then passes just below a third lakelet, from which rock climbers can scamper ¼ mile upslope to the base of some metarhyolite cliffs. Next the trail tops a flat ridge, and then it plunges down to a gully before climbing to a jeep road. If you were to follow its seldom used, faint stretch south, you'd reach the Pacific Crest Trail (Hike 20) in just under ½ mile. North, the more obvious stretch goes 70 yards to a trail junction. Hike 27, advancing east along the road to this junction, follows the trail about ½ mile over to a junction with our route.

Our loop route climbs northwest over to nearby Helgramite Lake. This grass-bottomed, fairly deep lakelet reflects, on tranquil days, the bold cliffs southwest of it. Attaining the high point of the climb before hurtling down toward Long Lake, one may feel compelled—particularly on a hot day—to plunge his feet into the lakelet's calm, soothing water.

Continuing onward, we quickly reach and cross the lakelet's murmuring northbound creek, and then descend its rocky gully, pausing momentarily to glance north toward domineering Mt. Elwell, which is the only *real* mountain in the Lakes Basin vicinity. The subsequently metamorphosed volcanic rocks that make up this 280-million-year-old mass appear as distinct layers—which perhaps are individual flows—all dipping, or descending, northeast. Although the rocky mass is very old, its form is not, having been largely sculptured in the last two million years.

Our somtimes steep descent northwest enters a red-fir/mountain-hemlock forest, lessens its gradient, and levels off near the crossing of a major but seasonal creek, which debouches from a striking V-shaped canyon and empties into chest-deep Mud Lake. Steering clear of the water-saturated west-shore meadow, which is being invaded and conquered by alders and willows, our trail keeps within the dry confines of red firs before curving north and climbing gently up to the base of a steeper slope, where we reach a junction. Only 25 yards beyond it, the main trail turns northwest and begins a moderate ascent. At that turn is a second junction. The trails departing east from the two junctions quickly unite into one, and on it we hike briefly up, and then descend gradually toward Long Lake. This spur trail almost reaches the shore,

and then becomes indistinct and overgrown, but a smaller path, branching left, traverses 60 yards northeast to the lake's edge. Just north of trail's end are rocks sutable for diving off or fishing from, and temptingly close lies the first of several rocky islands. Because the lake is the basin's largest, it is also the slowest to warm up, although it does get into the mid-60s by mid-August, making a swim at least to the first island feasible.

Returning to the main trail, we engage in a moderate ascent northwest up to the edge of some orange-brown metamorphic bedrock, then switchback up through a soggy, sloping meadow. Thick vegetation at times obscures the trail as it continues to switchback upslope. Eventually the trail diagonals north up to a trail junction on a small, almost level, tree-dotted bench. Hike 27, leaving a jeep road, traverses northeast along a crest to reach this bench, then commences a switchbacking route up to Mt. Elwell.

Our trail northeast is an indistinct one at first. We hike in this direction through a clump of manzanita and willows, then arrive at a gully and start northeast down it. A rocky trail descending a huge talus slope in the near distance should quickly become apparent. (Route finding is a real problem only when you are going in the opposite direction—up the gully. If you're doing this, don't yield to temptation by heading over to a conspicuous saddle and low knoll just east of the gully; the junction you are trying to reach lies on a flat about 150 yards due west of and above the saddle.)

Once on the ducked, talus-slope trail, we can concentrate our attention on the spectacular island-studded lake below us. A steady descent down the unstable talus trail takes us almost to the lake's waters, which lie just beyond a few yards of dense willows and tobacco brush. Now we climb briefly, and then traverse across a brush-covered bench to two very different, cabin-sized boulders. The first is smooth, looks granitic, and bears no resemblance to the cliffs above us or the bedrock we stand on. Where did this 100-ton boulder come from? If you've walked along the Pacific Crest Trail—a little over one mile southwest of here (Hike 20)—you'll recognize the mega-boulder as a huge chunk of Paleozoic metarhyolite, which was transported here by the Lakes Basin glacier. Glacier-transported boulders, which are usually smaller than this one, are called *erratics,* and most are easy to spot because they rest on a rock type that is quite different from their own composition.

The rough, second mega-boulder obviously broke loose from the cliffs above. It, too, is a

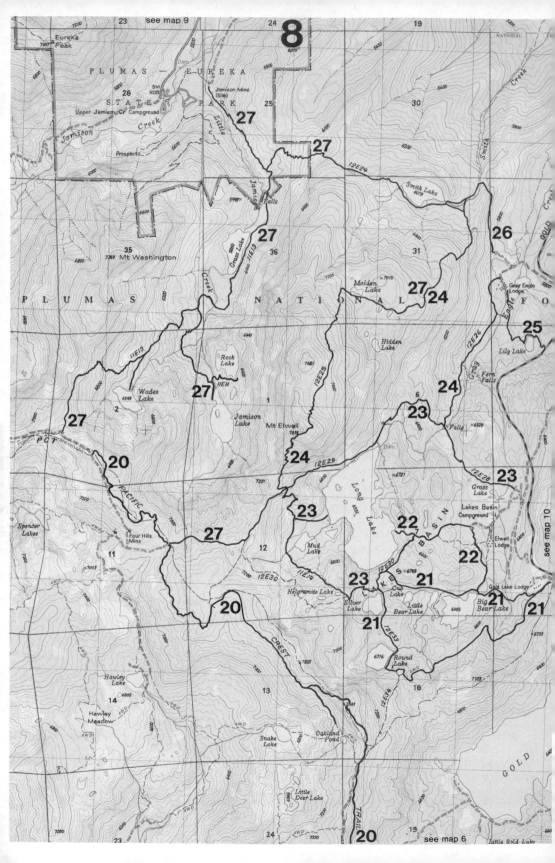

metamorphosed Paleozoic volcanic rock, but its composition is a grade of andesite or basalt. The watermelon-sized blocks within its structure bear

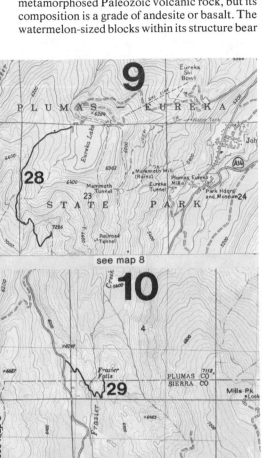

see map 8

close resemblance to the blocks in the auto-brecciated, young lava flows seen near Round Lake on Hike 92, and this large boulder probably had a similar origin.

In 120 yards, just beyond a Jeffrey pine, we come to our third and final approach to the shores of Long Lake—a short spur trail to a small check dam at the lake's north end. The shoreline vegetation is open enough for you to scramble around on bedrock to a good fishing site, a swimming area or a sunbathing slab. You may also note a faint trail, heading south from the dam, which undulates south above the lake's east shore.

Once back on the main trail, we cross some springs just after our last lake view disappears. These support an ephemeral, colorful display of wildflowers, which contrast with somber, aged junipers. These slowly growing trees send out roots that seek, and sometimes enlarge, every adjacent crack in the bedrock. Like the wildflowers, a juniper needs soil nutrients and water.

Immediately east of us we see an unmistakable "footprint" of a former glacier—a smoothed-over bedrock knoll. Closer inspection will reveal

**Long Lake**

that rocks and grit the glacier dragged along its bottom have striated the rock in the direction of glacier movement and have gouged out small, angular cavities. Seeking out all nearby cracks atop this glacier-polished knoll are the massive roots of a large Jeffrey pine.

Continuing northward, we begin a descent, immediately negotiate two switchbacks, and then descend across *joint-controlled,* shallow gullies that have been polished by glaciers. Beyond them we skirt the north edge of a grassy meadow, which cradles a small lake that diminishes greatly by Labor Day. Beyond low bedrock outcrops above the meadow's east edge, we descend northeast down a brushy slope and soon find ourselves briefly alongside a seasonal creek before we abruptly turn southeast and head for Long Lake's outlet, Gray Eagle Creek. Midway down to it, we traverse a small, spongy meadow, and by a creek near its far end we note that the trail has eroded, exposing ground water that had previously flowed through the porous soil only inches below its surface. Much of the drainage of a basin, such as Lakes Basin, is accomplished through the ground. The lakes and creeks we see are just surface exposures of ground water.

Only 25 yards before Gray Eagle Creek we come to a junction, from which a trail—poorly defined for the first few hundred yards—descends to Gray Eagle Lodge and its environs (Hike 24 comes up this route). Wide, swift Gray Eagle Creek is a dangerous ford in early season. The crossing is only 20 yards before the lively creek turns east and cascades down a rocky cliff. Be extremely careful.

Beyond the ford we have an uphill hike rich in verdant growth. Alders and dogwoods rise above thimbleberries, currants, mountain ash and willows that might hide a lurking coyote. Except in autumn, when it is blazing yellow, mountain dogbane goes unseen while ranger's buttons, corn lilies, paintbrushes and at least four species of sunflowers add their colors to the greenery. We keep our feet dry by skirting around a boggy meadow rather than slogging through it, then climb up on a ground moraine, which we'll tread upon almost every step of the way from here to trail's end.

After a climb up to a bend in the moraine, we encounter a short spur trail that descends to a shallow, reflective pond overly rich in pond lilies. Curving eastward, we now have a gently undulating path to follow, which takes us past the northern fringe of poorly defined Grass

Lake—more of a meadow in late summer. Boulder-hopping its outlet creek, we can see, 20 yards downstream, a delightful pool—molded into a swimming hole by previous owners of Lake Center Lodge. Complete with steps and a poolside grass lawn, this crystal-clear pool provides the satisfying swim needed after a long day's hike. The lodge was permanently closed by the Forest Service in autumn 1974 and later the buildings were removed.

Fifty yards beyond the creek crossing we reach the trailhead, which is located just north of campsite 7 in Lakes Basin Campground. Now we have a half-mile walk back to our original trailhead. We walk 70 yards south on the campground's road to its hub, from which the remaining route back to our vehicles is perfectly obvious.

**Girls frolicking in a pool at the Lakes Center Lodge site**

# 24        Mt. Elwell Loop, from
# Lakes Basin Campground

**Distance**   11.2 miles, round trip
**Low/High Elevations**   5790'/7750'
**Classification**   Moderate
**Season**   Mid-July through mid-October
**Map**   8
**Trailhead**   Same as the Hike 22 trailhead.

**Introduction**   Unbeatable for Lakes Basin views is a climb to Mt. Elwell's summit. This loop trip traverses lake, stream, slope and crest terrains and exposes you to all the species of trees you'll find in the basin. Rock climbers will find numerous opportunities to practice their art, particularly on the south slope of Mt. Elwell.

**Description**   The first half of Hike 23 describes our route up to a junction on a small flat on the south slope of Mt. Elwell. We go a few yards north-northwest before turning left and diagonaling west-southwest up an easy grade to the mountain's well-defined south ridge, which is usually snow-free by early July. Starting north up a trail, climbers will immediately notice that the massive metavolcanic cliffs ahead, which make up most of the south slope, offer dozens of climbing routes.

At our first switchback, red firs add a photogenic touch to our view of Long Lake, and these trees offer shade along various parts of our steep ascent. Associated with this scattered cover are the trees' usual companions, spiny-seeded chinquapin and lowly mat manzanita. About 300 feet below the top, our trail veers west far enough to present us with views of Jamison and Rock lakes. A series of short, steep zigzags now confront us, and they are being ruined by thoughtless descending hikers who are shortcutting downslope from one switchback leg to the next.

Climbers will find some easily accessible routes just below the peak's southeast summit, and not far above them the trail skirts the base of the peak's northwest summit, which has enjoyable, blocky climbing routes—some of them overhanging.

Before we know it, we're at the cleft between the two low summits, and discover aromatic tobacco brush thriving up here above the red firs we passed along the trail and the mountain hemlocks we'll soon pass.

Both of Elwell's summits are easy scrambles, although harder ways up each are very easy to find. The lower, southeast summit provides the more impressive views, for the entire, glaciated Lakes Basin, dominated by Long Lake, is spread out before you. Beyond Silver and Round lakes lies the deep canyon of unseen Gold Lake, and rising above all on the horizon are the unmistakable Sierra Buttes. The higher, northwest summit looks down on the definitely glaciated form of the Little Jamison Creek canyon, whose sides were smoothed and steepened by the ice.

From the top, the shortest way back to the trailhead is to return the way you came. Most people do. Our route, however, completes a loop trip, utilizing the less used trail from Smith Lake. Snow patches just below the summit cleft linger till September, and if you are hiking this route in July you'll have a route-finding situation waiting for you.

A brief, steep descent northeast leads us over blocks and into the outskirts of a predominantly mountain-hemlock forest—the kind of forest mosquitoes love. Red firs and western white pines soon increase their numbers along our winding, usually descending trail, and just before rounding a ridge and commencing a steeper descent, we pass through a small, sloping meadow. One-quarter mile from the ridge, we can't help but note a large, house-sized block off on our right, which certainly will appeal to climbers. It even comes with a Jeffrey pine on its summit, from which you can rappel or set up a top-rope belay. There are several scramble routes up to its summit that can be done unroped by cautious climbers, and the view from its almost-flat top is worth the brief effort. To the northeast and southeast below you lie Maiden and Hidden lakes, and between them, in the middle distance, stands Beckwourth Peak (7255'). Beyond it lies flat, fault-formed Sierra Valley and to its north rise the 8000-foot peaks of the Dixie and Diamond mountains.

Our trail now descends north, levels off and turns southeast, immediately encountering the shoreline of waist-deep, grass-lined Maiden Lake. A thoroughly integrated forest surrounds it, composed of mountain hemlock, red fir, western white pine and lodgepole pine. Beyond this small lake, an almost level, eastward-winding trail leads us past three lakelets. Between the first and second, a trail sign points the way to not-so-hidden Hidden Lake. A faint trail, blazed

**Summit view of Long Lake, Lakes Basin and the hazy Sierra Buttes**

and ducked, departs south toward it but dies out before reaching it. We'll leave this hemmed-in, green gem, which is good for swimming but not for fishing, to those who want to try a little bit of route-finding on their own.

After arcing around the north shore of the second lakelet, we climb above and away from the third, and smallest, lakelet, which dries up before summer's end. We now meander northeastward down the broad crest of a lateral moraine, shaded by an open stand of red firs, western white pines, and—amazingly—sugar pines. Foot-long cones, drooping from the ends of long branches, identify this good lumber tree. Farther down the moraine, our route becomes more brushy and open, and then we curve left, leave the crest and re-enter forest cover.

Soon we meet a short, east-curving spur trail, which ends at a viewpoint on the moraine's crest. From it we see what we just saw a few minutes earlier. Mills Peak Lookout rises above us in the southeast while flat-topped Beckwourth Peak stands in the northeast. Directly across the canyon, the large, linear, east-side lateral moraine of the Lakes Basin glaciers is readily apparent.

Back on the main trail, we descend a gully northward, and just before reaching Smith Creek come to a trail fork. The left branch, followed by those taking Hike 27, traverses over to campsites on the forested southeast side of nearby Smith Lake. Our route continues north, quickly

reaches Smith Creek, and immediately beyond it comes to a trail junction. Smith Lake's outlet is attained by following the trail that goes upstream. We hike downstream, following the creek's damp bank, whose lush vegetation provides a good home and hunting ground for orange-striped garter snakes—harmless unless you're an amphibian, a small fish or an invertebrate. One way of differentiating the aquatic Sierra garter snake from the terrestrial mountain garter snake is that, when frightened, the former tends to escape into water while the latter tends to hide on land.

Not far downstream, we come to a junction, leave the Smith Creek Trail, and immediately cross three close-spaced channels of Smith Creek before we leave the shade of red and white firs behind and top our lateral moraine's low crest. An open, steady, usually hot trail south now guides us down the moraine's brushy, bouldery slope, and we can be thankful we're not engaged in a sweaty climb up it. At first, Beckwourth and Mills peaks are visible, but both disappear before we reach trail's end at a spur-road turnaround under patriarchal Jeffrey pines.

We follow the spur road southeast, come to its union with the Gray Eagle Lodge road, and walk southwest up it to the lodge's northwesternmost cabin. From near its north side, a faint trail climbs first southwest and then south up a gully to a low saddle, from which it descends at a lesser gradient to a level area and a trail intersection. If we were to continue east, we would reach

Gray Eagle Creek in 65 yards. Its ford is always a wet one, except late in the season, and from its east bank the trail continues 95 yards southeast to the Lily Lake Trail (Hike 25).

From the intersection, we hike south-southwest on a trail from the south end of Gray Eagle Lodge, and relish its easy, almost level, up-canyon climb through a mid-Sierran forest belt of Douglas-fir, white fir, incense-cedar, sugar pine and Jeffrey pine. Midway to our reunion with Hike 23's route, we come to the Fern Falls spur trail. Certainly worth taking, this shady trail branching left arcs southeast over to nearby Gray Eagle Creek and briefly follows a chain of pools upstream to 20-foot-high Fern Falls—a cascade cutting through a narrow, fern-decked slot.

Beyond this divertissement, our main trail climbs more steeply up to a ducked ridge and crosses it, only to recross it in 200 yards. Before doing so, however, climbers will note tempting routes on the north face of Summit 6509, ¼ mile southeast. Our trail heads south, working closer toward this summit, then turns right (southwest) and climbs moderately, though briefly, across a meadowy, sometimes swampy slope. The exposed bedrock over which Gray Eagle Creek tumbles now lies ahead of us. A somewhat-ducked, hard-to-see trail up it takes us quickly to a trail junction and a reunion with Hike 23, which we follow back to the trailhead. Climbers attempting to reach the base of Summit 6509 should cross the creek before making the final bedrock climb to the junction.

# 25         Lily Lake Trail

**Distances**   0.2 mile to Lily Lake, 0.7 mile to Gray Eagle Creek

**Low/High Elevations**   5920'/5990'

**Classification**   Very easy

**Season**   Mid-June through late October

**Map**   8

**Trailhead**   At a long turnout along the Plumas County (north half) of Gold Lake Road, 1.0 mile below the Lakes Basin Campground junction and 0.6 mile above the Gray Eagle Lodge junction.

**Introduction**   This short trail is a pleasant diversion best suited for an early morning or late afternoon stroll. It also is the start of an alternative route into the Lakes Basin.

**Description**   On this short, obvious trail, you can wind down to tranquil, moraine-dammed Lily Lake in a few mintues' time. White fir, Jeffrey pine and sugar pine rim this shallow lake, which is named after the large, floating, water-lily leaves so prominent in it. Growing out of shallow water, particularly at the south end, are grasslike bulrushes.

Our trail skirts the lake's north and west shores, and then, near its southwest corner, climbs over a low ridge and in 60 yards arrives at a junction. Before the new Gold Lake Road was completed in 1973, a trail from Lakes Basin Campground descended north to here. We angle westward for a brief spurt, then, under a powerline, reach a second junction, from where a trail once climbed to Long Lake. We follow the line

north, climb over a low ridge, and end our walk at a small waterfall near the south end of Gray Eagle Lodge.

The Gray Eagle Creek Trail (Hike 24), which climbs from the lodge south up to Long Lake, can be reached by watching for a small spur-path that departs northwest about midway along our powerline traverse. This path starts in a 7-yard-wide grassy flat just before the low ridge. Look for a LILY LAKE sign that marks this junction. Cool, wide Gray Eagle Creek, which must be waded before you reach the Gray Eagle Creek Trail, turns out to be a worthwhile goal in itself.

**Yellow (Indian) pond lily**

# 26        Smith Lake Trail

**Distance**   1.0 mile to Smith Lake
**Low/High Elevations**   5820'/6090'
**Classification**   Easy
**Season**   Early July through late October
**Map**   8

**Trailhead**   From Highway 49 drive 8 miles northwest up Gold Lake Road to a crest, then 2½ miles farther to the Gray Eagle Lodge road. From Highway 89 this junction is 5 miles southwest up Gold Lake Road. Just past Gray Eagle Creek a spur road forks right from the lodge's road, and is signed for the Smith Lake and Gray Eagle Creek trails. (The latter is not described here, for it is unappealing for most people. It descends beside the usually unseen creek for about 1½ miles, crosses it, then climbs to a nearby Gold Lake Road turnout, which is 1.8 miles below the lodge-road junction.) The spur road's turnaround loop holds up to a dozen vehicles.

**Introduction**   Smith Lake is the most accessible lake in this area at which you can legally camp. (The other four lakes with legal camping are mentioned in the next hike.) However, due to Smith Lake's proximity to the trailhead, just a half-hour's hike away, you'd do better to day-hike to it, perhaps at dawn, when the trout are biting.

**Description**   From the trailhead we are confronted with a brushy, largely shadeless, 500-foot-high moraine that stands between us and Smith Lake. Fortunately, our trail doesn't tackle the moraine head-on, but rather climbs gently north along it, cresting it ½ mile later at a spot barely 200 feet above the trailhead. Now generally in forest cover, we quickly cross multi-branched Smith Creek and meet the neighboring Smith Creek Trail, which drops about 1500 feet in 2¼ miles to a loop road bound for Mohawk. On this trail we turn left, upstream, and in several minutes pass a junction with Mt. Elwell Trail 12E22, down which Hikes 24 and 27 descend. The first heads down the the route we ascended, the second heads west to Smith Lake and beyond. In several more minutes, by Smith Lake's outlet, we note a second junction with bifurcating 12E22. Along the south shore you'll find two pleasant campsites, one by the lake's outlet and another just west over a low ridge. Although Smith Lake is one of the lowest lakes in the Highway 49 area, it is not one of the warmest, for it is relatively deep and is fed by snowmelt water well into the summer. Therefore, most visitors to this lake will be fishermen in hot pursuit of trout.

# 27      Mt. Elwell Loop, from Jamison Mine

**Distances**   1.4 miles to Grass Lake, 2.1 miles to Smith Lake, 3.1 miles to Jamison and Wades lakes, 3.3 miles to Rock Lake, 15.6 miles for complete semiloop trip.
**Low/High Elevations**   5260'/7750'
**Classification**   Strenuous
**Season**   Mid-July through mid-October
**Map**   8

**Trailhead**   From Graeagle, a small Highway 89 settlement 1⅓ miles north of the Gold Lake Road junction, drive ⅓ mile north to County Road A14, heading west. Drive 4⅔ miles up it to the Jamison Mines spur road, veering left on it only ¼ mile before A14 crosses Jamison Creek. The spur road is usually locked off during the night, so park by A14 if you plan to leave after dark. Otherwise, drive 1⅓ miles up to a large trailhead parking lot among the Jamison ruins.

County Road A14 continues ¼ mile beyond Jamison Creek to a fork, located near the park's museum. For Hike 28 keep right, head through Johnsville (no services) and in almost a mile turn sharply left at a junction, from where you climb ½ mile southwest up a paved road to Eureka Ski Bowl. From the south end of the bowl's parking lot, go up a narrow dirt road, which climbs 1⅓ miles to Eureka Lake. Since this dirt road is open to motor vehicles only from Monday morning through Thursday evening, plan accordingly.

A second route to the Jamison ruins trailhead is possible. From the park's museum drive just over a mile south to Upper Jamison Creek Campground. Just after the campground's main road crosses Jamison Creek, a footpath starts north (left) from the road and takes you ⅓ mile over to the trailhead. Use this route only if you're staying at one of the campground's sites.

**Introduction**   In all of the Lakes Basin Recreation Area, there are only five lakes at which you can legally camp: Grass, Jamison, Rock, Wades and Smith. This hike includes a stop at each of them. For those who enjoy swimming, fishing, diversified landscapes, geology and flora, this hike is a must. Climbers will find the recreation area's best climbs along this backpack trip.

**Description**   Our trail begins at a large parking lot among the ruins of buildings that were the site of a bustle of activity in the late 1800s. From quartz veins in the nearby Jamison mine complex, over $1½ million worth of gold was extracted. These veins rose from a gabbro pluton that intruded the late-Paleozoic volcanic rocks of this locality.

We start up-canyon on an old mining road, which becomes a trail just past the last building. Scattered Douglas-firs and abundant manzanita and huckleberry oak at first line our trail as we parallel Little Jamison Creek, about 100 feet below. Short switchbacks soon take us away from the creek view and away from the forest's shade. Our path, over the previously mentioned gabbro pluton, has dark rocks rich in pyroxene, olivine and calcium feldspar. Before leaving this rock, we come to a junction with the Smith Lake Trail. On this trail we'll be returning.

Beyond the junction, we re-enter forest cover, receiving shade from incense-cedar, Douglas-fir, white fir, lodgepole pine and Jeffrey pine. After bending south at a gully, we climb a short distance and then are alerted to a short spur trail by a sign, JAMISON FALLS. Like ever other glaciated canyon in the Highway 49 lakes region, Little Jamison Creek canyon has its noteworthy fall—a 60-foot-high, silvery leap into freedom.

Making an easy climb up to Grass Lake, we cross a small canal—the same one we'll see along the Smith Lake Trail—which served operations down at the Jamison Mine. The campsites along the east shore near shallow Grass Lake's dam are unattractive. However, late-summer ducks, migrating south on the Pacific flyway, find this lake—and other shallow ones like it—attractive. Flowing into the south end of the lake as well as into its inlet creek are numerous creeklets. Some are lined with thimbleberry, currant and gooseberry—three shrubs producing edible berries—as well as with Bolander's yampah—a large, edible parsley that closely resembles some of its poisonous relatives. Backpackers disgruntled with the accommodations of the Grass Lake campsites set up their camps at slightly better ones on a bench above the lake's south end.

As your southbound trail heads for an obvious headwall, which supports hidden Rock Lake above it, stay alert for a sudden bend west in the trail. An older pathway continues southward before dying out. Our trail west traverses an aspen-bordered meadow, veers northwest, and for 50 yards crosses one channel after another. Look for rocks, logs or whatever to make this wet ford of not-so-little Little Jamison Creek. Early-season hikers: resign yourself to a pair of wet boots. Dry ground is welcomed as we climb west, then south up to a nearby junction. Our main trail toward Wades Lake and the Sierra crest climbs moderately southwest, but first we'll take an excursion south up to Jamison and Rock lakes.

The forested path at first climbs gently, but just beyond a collapsed log cabin it veers southwest and executes several short, steep switchbacks up brushy rock benches. Those accomplished, we soon treat ourselves to a refreshing drink from Wakes Lake's outlet creek, which crosses our path midway up this side trip to Jamison Lake. Before we reach Jamison, we have to surmount a low ridge of granitelike metarhyolite, and climbers will certainly spy short crack and face routes up it. On the west slopes above Jamison Lake, climbers will find additional appealing climbing routes, but the east slopes above Jamison, being composed of brown metabasalt or a close analog, are uninviting.

Descending the low ridge before Jamison Lake, we quickly arrive at the lake's outlet creek, frequented by water ouzels, and cross it 50 yards downstream from its broken-down dam. Just before this crossing, however, a trail splits south to the dam and the undesirable bedrock campsites not far beyond it. Of all the lakes one can camp at along this circuit, Jamison probably offers the greatest solitude, for not many hikers go cross-country to the lake's southern shore. We, like others, cross its outlet creek and follow a brief, winding trail over and across low, glaciated ridges to campsites along Rock Lake's south shore.

Aptly named Rock Lake is perhaps the most appealing lake along our circuit, and it may well be the finest of the entire Highway 49 lakes region. Photographers will certainly appreciate its beauty, and from selected rocky ledges near its southeast corner swimmers can dive into seemingly bottomless, invigorating water. Contrasting with the depth of this lake is a steep-sided rock island that rises a full 20 feet above the lake's northwest waters. Everywhere you turn, you'll find evidence of past glaciers in the

**Lodgepole pines at Rock Lake**

form of long scratches, or glacial striations, which were cut by the rock and grit that glaciers dragged along. What makes this lake so attractive is the way the glaciers sculptured its terrain, breaking off blocks of bedrock and thereby exposing dramatic bluffs. You'll certainly be tempted to linger awhile in this rockbound paradise.

Returning to the main trail, we begin a steep ascent that leads us up past an outcrop of white, vertically foliated metarhyolite before reaching the signed Wades Lake spur trail.

Our hike up the Wades Lake spur trail is an easy ¼-mile stroll. Just before reaching the lake's outlet, we pass a very good campsite—beneath red fir, lodgepole pine and western white pine—located on our left. Like Jamison, Wades has had its dam mostly removed, and the lake has returned to its natural level. Our lake, resting in a bowl of greenish-tinted, light-gray metarhyolite, has a shallow north end which slowly gets deeper, allowing the reluctant swimmer to gradually get used to this fairly deep lake's usually chilly water.

Back again on the main trail, we start southwest, immediately pass a flat meadow on our right, and engage in a steep ascent up the crest of a lateral moraine, occasionally scented with tobacco brush, before traversing across slopes up to a saddle. A grove of red firs, ascending east to this saddle, obstructs our view west down into glaciated Florentine Canyon, but our sweeping view east toward Mt. Elwell reveals the 4 miles of crest we'll have to circle to reach the peak's two summits. The saddle also marks the boundary between the metamorphic rocks we've just climbed and volcanic ones to be ascended. These rocks—the only geologically young

volcanics we'll walk upon in the Plumas-Eureka/Lakes Basin landscape—are auto-brecciated andesitic mud flows about 5-10 million years old, and are similar in origin to the flows that are very common south of Highway 50's Echo Summit (see the geology chapter's "Tahoe Sierra volcanism"). We struggle south steeply up a ridgecrest made of this loose material before attaining the Sierra crest.

On the crest we turn left and climb—steeply at first—up a dusty jeep road, which parallels the mighty Pacific Crest Trail, below on our right. Our climb southeast through a field of mule ears and volcanic rocks quickly levels off, and ¼ mile from our trail junction our jeep road intersects the Pacific Crest Trail (Hike 20, north end). If you haven't had serious snow problems so far, turn left onto it for a very meandering, forested, 1.3-mile traverse back to the jeep road. If you've had snow problems, keep to the jeep road, since it is easier to follow. It soon starts to descend, then in ½ mile passes the Four Hills Mine. Now abandoned, this mine in its day produced $2 million in gold from its quartz veins. A ¼-mile descent south gets us to a junction with the Spencer Lakes jeep road. Down this road, about ½ mile west of us, lie pockets of magnetite, which is a magnetic, iron-rich ore. The composition of iron in these pockets is pretty high, about 40%, but the quantity, under 5000 tons, is unprofitable to extract.

If you've taken the jeep road, you climb ⅓ mile east from the junction to arrive at a second intersection of the Pacific Crest Trail. Here, on a broad crest saddle, marked by a small, circular, semistagnant pond, we enter the Lakes Basin Recreation Area, and after a few minutes' walk on our road we cross a spring-fed creek, which provides the only pure, year-round water we'll find between Wades and Smith lakes (Maiden and Hidden lakes are usually tolerable). Beyond it, we hike a steady ⅓-mile ascent east to a sharp bend where the road turns south. Near it are two trail junctions only 70 yards apart. From the southern one Trail 12E30 rollercoasters wildly east over to Helgramite Lake.

Our route starts from the northern (first) junction, traverses north along a knife-edge crest when it is not immediately below it, and then briefly contours over to a junction on a tree-shaded bench ½ mile south of the top of Mt. Elwell. Our traverse across this ridgecrest, which exhibits nearly vertical foliation like that of the Wades Lake area, exposes us to our first good views of the Lakes Basin topography. From the junction we now follow the trail description in Hike 24 up to the two summits, over to Maiden Lake and finally down to a trail junction immediately before reaching Smith Creek.

Hike 24 crosses Smith Creek, but our route veers northwest and quickly arrives at a good, large, pine-shaded campsite near Smith Lake's outlet. Beyond it over a low ridge lies a second good campsite, which is nestled beside a lively creek lined with alder and dogwood. Our roller-coaster trail west climbs another low ridge, this time over blue-green-gray metavolcanic bedrock, then descends close to the lake's shallow south arm, which is being choked with grasses and rushes. A third and final ridge climb leads us over to the cascading creek that empties into this clear, green lake. Seeking the creek's life-giving water are alder, dogwood, mountain ash, vine maple, thimbleberry and many wildflowers.

West of Smith Lake our trail snakes ¼ mile up to a small notch on a broad, ill-defined saddle, then makes a gradual descent through a forest of red fir and western white pine that also contains sugar pine—an unusual bedfellow for them. Beyond a shallow pond, our trail west drops more steeply and crosses the north-heading, bouldery crest of a lateral moraine midway down to an old mining canal that originates at Grass Lake. A brief descent southwest now takes us to the end of our loop, and on the main trail we descend Little Jamison Creek's canyon trail back to our trailhead.

# 28       Eureka Peak Trail

**Distance**   1.5 miles, one way
**Low/High Elevations**   6170'/7286'
**Classification**   Moderate
**Season**   Early July through mid-October
**Map**   9
**Trailhead**   See the Hike 27 trailhead.

**Introduction**   This summit climb is the shortest one in the Highway 49 region, and it provides views that are more than worth the effort. Peak 7286's north slopes contain steep, solid rock, which should attract any nearby rock climbers.

**Description**   First we cross over Eureka Lake's earth-fill dam to the start of an old, overgrown road. Snags within the lake's shallow water indicate the position of its shoreline before the dam was built. Leaving this popular fishing lake, we immediately pass the branching west-shore road as we climb to a forested slope of a lateral moraine and pass a snow-survey shelter. Along our moderately climbing road, we find rocks of almost every color: from blue, green and gray to red, brown and white. The reason for this diversity in color is, simply enough, the diversity in rock types: various metasediments, metavol-

canics and mafic intrusives (igneous rocks rich in magnesium and iron).

Beyond a steep, open ascent past a red-brown cliff, our road reaches, and dies out upon, a forested, gentle slope. Replacing it is a trail, heading south, which stays close to the dropping edge of the main canyon. In this forest of red fir and western white pine you may encounter two furry predators, the long-tailed weasel and the pine marten. Both feed mainly on rodents, but the weasel also attacks small birds. Look for them in tree cavities or ground burrows among rocks or logs or under tree roots—particularly those of red fir.

Our trail up-canyon gives us glimpses of Eureka Lake just after we cross a small, splashing creek and start to parallel its east bank. As we approach a cluster of the creek's willows, we leave the creek, cross an often dry gully, and climb steeply to a minor ridge, on which, by taking a few steps northeast, we get a good view of the lake and the countryside beyond. Two distinct rock types now confront us as we climb southeast up the trail: granitelike metarhyolite on our left and nearly vertical beds of metasediments on our right.

Stimulating our olfactory nerves are tantalizing aromas of a few plants of tobacco brush, which are encountered as we enter a classic forest assemblage of magnificent red fir, delicate mountain hemlock, checker-barked western white pine and lowly mat manzanita. Our southward, shady trail up the southwest slope of Peak 7286 soon turns northeast and climbs to a saddle south of the peak's rocky summit. Standing between us and the summit is a rocky crest, which drops off to a low saddle immediately below the summit. The safest, easiest way to this second saddle is to round the crest on its east side. First descend briefly, then parallel the base of the crest over to a gully, which you ascend to the saddle. The short, easy scramble to the top is evident and not exposed.

The summit is cleaved in half, and through the cleft we get a framed view of Eureka Lake. Standing on either half of the summit, we get a more complete view, which includes not only Eureka Lake and its distinctive moraines, but also the huge lateral moraines of Jamison Creek canyon, whose floor lies almost ½ mile below our summit. The 500-foot-high moraines extend up to 2 miles beyond the old mining town of Johnsville. Placer gold was first discovered near this site in the first days of the 1849 gold rush, and gold in vein quartz was discovered two years later. The placer gold never amounted to much, but the bedrock gold, mostly mined from 1872 to 1890, brought in about $8 million to the Sierra Buttes Mining Company. Beneath our feet, into the bowels of Eureka Peak, were sunk 70 mine shafts, all now closed.

If you want to climb to the top of Eureka Peak, you can reach it by hiking ½ mile up the crest that curves southwest up from Peak 7286's first saddle. Eureka's summit, however, is less defined and doesn't offer as good views as those from Peak 7286. Beyond the nearby landscape, we see flat-topped Beckwourth Peak (7255') in the east, the pointed Sierra Buttes (8591') in the distant south-southeast, and closer Mt. Elwell (7818') just left of the buttes. Dominating the northwest horizon is snowy, royal Lassen Peak (10,457'), the southernmost active volcano of the Cascade Range.

Botanists will be pleased to find that plants grow on this rocky, inhospitable-seeming summit. Phlox, buckwheat, cream bush, and—surprisingly—rabbit brush manage to survive. Rabbit brush is usually associated with a closely related high-desert sunflower, sagebrush.

**A summit view of Eureka Lake**

Descending to the saddle above the gully, you'll see just west of it—if you haven't already noticed—a small, natural window, which was formed when a block of bedrock lodged between the summit's slope and a resistant pinnacle. Climbers will find many opportunities to either boulder or rope-climb near the summit or its dramatic north escarpment. The metarhyolite rock, superficially resembling granite in color and texture, also has similar rock-climbing characteristics.

# 29                              Frazier Falls

**Distance**   0.6 mile, one way
**Low/High Elevations**   6160'/6210'
**Classification**   Very easy
**Season**   Late June through late October
**Map**   10

**Trailhead**   From Highway 49 drive 7 miles northwest up Gold Lake Road, then branch right onto the *old* Gold Lake Road for a 2-mile drive north to the trailhead. From Highway 89, drive 2½ miles southwest up Gold Lake Road, then at a prominent moraine crest branch left onto the old road for a 4-mile drive up to the trailhead.

**Introduction**   Easily the highest falls in the Highway 49 region, this sheet of water continues to impress visitors late into summer. Standing at the viewpoint opposite the perennial falls, you can study the canyon that drops before you and imagine what it must have looked like when an enormous glacier filled it.

**Description**   From the roadside picnic area—complete with tables and toilets—we start to walk southeast, shaded by firs and pines. Brush becomes more prominent as we wind around and over low, glacier-polished ridges before coming to Frazier Creek, which is lined with aspen, dogwood and willow. The dark, blue-gray bedrocks over which we walk are lava flows that were derived from distant, oceanic sources back in the late Paleozoic era, about 280 million years ago. In the process of transport they were severely tilted so that now, rather than being almost horizontal, they dip almost vertically down. The texture of these flows, which are approximately basaltic in composition, has been altered by heat and pressure generated by the earth's shifting crust. Initially richer in dark minerals, these metabasalts differ in color and texture from the granitelike metarhyolites seen on Mt. Elwell and on the crest above Lakes Basin.

After crossing the bridge over Frazier Creek, we wind among some more low ridges, whose bedrock has been split and intruded with white

vein quartz, then turn north and descend to a fenced-off viewpoint directly opposite 248-foot-high Frazier Falls. Located 1.9 miles downstream from Gold Lake's outlet, this cascade marks the resistant midpoint in a canyon that once contained a 7-mile-long, 800-foot-thick glacier. Originating at the crest above Gold Lake's southwest shore, the glacier had a tortuous path to follow. Gold Lake, of course, didn't exist back then, but ½ mile beyond the site of its outlet the glacier was forced to bend northward, and the bend undoubtedly caused crevasses, or deep cracks, to form at this stress point. Then, straightening its course, the icy mass traveled less than a mile before it tumbled—in very slow, frozen motion—down the bedrock that Frazier Falls cascades over today.

Just how fast did the glacier cascade over this brink? On the basis of large, present-day glaciers existing in more northern latitudes, we can estimate that the glacier ice might have "fallen" at the rate of about 30 feet per day, or about ¼ inch per minute. This rate of motion would have been barely noticeable if it were constant. It wasn't. If we had been present, we would have heard the glacier groan as crevasses slowly opened and closed, and ice broke off, fell and was buried under the slow onslaught of ice behind it. The rate of ice movement at less steep locations, such as the area where Gold Lake is today, was much less, probably being on the order of 1-3 feet per day.

Standing at the viewpoint, you can look down-canyon and see the high lateral moraine that makes up the canyon's west wall. About 20,000 years ago, a glacier filled this canyon to the moraine's height, if not higher. Try to imagine what a different landscape this area must have been back then! On your way back, note how glacial action, exerting a pressure of 20 tons per square foot, has abraded and smoothed the low ridges you wind along. Remember also that all the soil and vegetation you see before you have appeared in the last 10,000 years, that is, since the mammoth glacier finally retreated back up Frazier Creek canyon.

Devils Oven Lake and Paradise Lake, from just off the Warren Lake Trail

# Ch. 10   Interstate 80's Recreation Lands

**Introduction**   This chapter's first route, Hike 30, is a pleasant stroll along the wooded trails of isolated Placer County Big Tree Grove. Today, this is the northernmost of a scattering of western Sierra giant-sequoia groves. In the geologic past these trees ranged over a far greater area. A similar story can be told of the Tahoe Sierra trails, which in the historic past were far more extensive.

Take, for example, the trails about Green Valley, which is 2 miles southeast of Interstate 80's settlement of Alta. The valley lies in the bottom of a deep, spectacular canyon cut by the North Fork American River. The *Colfax* 15-minute topographic map (1950) shows Green Valley and its immediate environs ramified with trails. What really exists: The trail from near Interstate 80 to Green Valley does exist, but like virtually all of the old, utilitarian trails that are so typical of the western Sierra canyon country, it is uncomfortably steep. Furthermore, this trail, like so many others, is unmaintained, and it dies out before reaching the river. If you did plow down to the river through the brush— thereby running the risk of encountering rattlesnakes, ticks or perhaps poison oak—you would be disappointed with the debris earlier travelers have left behind. Two trails that once traversed east across Green Valley to other trails no longer exist. Another mapped trail, heading down-river from Green Valley, quickly reaches private property.

Trespassing at lower elevations is definitely *not* recommended. As one sign points out, "Survivors will be prosecuted," and the gun-toting owners mean it. Hundreds of small mining claims dot the lower Tahoe Sierra, and the prospectors that work them are often trigger-happy. As one old prospector told the author, he would kill anyone he *thought* might want to steal his gold (he had less than an ounce worth). Armed natives, then, are the greatest danger to hikers who want to explore anywhere in the lower Tahoe Sierra. If you still decide to explore these elevations, then be prepared to find only a small fraction of their trails in existence. New roads plus logging operations have taken their toll of trails.

For the hiker in search of lakes, there are basically two I-80 recreation areas available: largely metamorphic-rock Grouse Ridge and largely volcanic-rock Castle Peak. Hikes 31–33, which are partly along old jeep roads, explore the former, while Hikes 35–38 explore the latter. Hike 34, to the lone, clustered Loch Leven Lakes, visits a granitic-rock terrain.

Hikes 35 and 38-41 describe the Pacific Crest Trail, which was built through this area mostly from 1978 to 1982. This trail, which accounts for about half of the chapter's 70-odd miles of described trail, offers views but no lakes, except via side trips. True to its name, the trail generally stays at or close to the crest, which in the I-80 region is mostly volcanic. These rocks in large part explain the lack of trailside lakes, for in the Tahoe Sierra, the lake basins have been cut by glaciers in granitic and metamorphic bedrock, not in the relatively soft volcanic bedrock.

One route deserves special attention: Hike 36 to Warren and Devils Oven lakes. It is one of the most spectacular routes in all of the Tahoe Sierra. However, due to the difficult terrain, this hike lies solely in the domain of the rugged backpacker or mountaineer.

# 30     Placer County Big Trees Grove

**Distance**   1.8 miles of trail in the grove
**Low/High Elevations**   5190'/5310'
**Classification**   Very easy
**Season**   May through October
**Map**   11

**Trailhead**   Leave Interstate 80 just 2 miles northeast of its Highway 49 intersection, as you branch east on the Auburn Ravine Road off-ramp. Here you'll find a plethora of gas stations and fast-food establishments. Take the Auburn-Foresthill Road 15½ miles northeast to the Foresthill Ranger Station. In Foresthill, 1.2 miles later, fork right on Mosquito Ridge Road 96 and follow it 24 miles to the Placer County Big Tree Grove spur road.

**Introduction**   Located about 41 miles from I-80, this grove of giant sequoias is certainly remote for most visitors. However, if you are bound for French Meadows or Hell Hole recreation area, or for Granite Chief Wilderness (Hike 42), then this grove will be right along your route. This is the northernmost and most isolated grove, lying a distant 55 air miles north of the next grove, in Highway 4's Calaveras Big Trees State Park.

Naturalists originally thought that these sequoia groves, roughly 75 of them, were remnants of a once-continuous sequoia forest. During the Ice Age, it was thought, major glaciers descended through major canyons, supposedly breaking the forest into several large groves, and these then dwindled to today's current groves. However, such a scenario runs contrary to well-established geologic evidence. In all probability, this Placer County grove is the end product of a sequoia migration that may have begun 10-15 million years ago. Starting near the Nevada border, some trees migrated southwest in response to the volcanic upbuilding and subsequent rising of the Sierra Nevada. These changes put the former groves at higher, less desirable elevations, ones with cooler temperatures. Consequently, it was to the trees' advantage to seek out their favored environment, which now lay farther west. Seedlings at the west edge of a sequoia forest would have a better survival rate than those at the east edge, and over time the population would shift westward.

Today's Tahoe Sierra crest began to form about 3–4 million years ago, and at least some sequoias must have migrated west at least this far. Those that hadn't were trapped on subsiding eastern lands that were becoming increasingly arid. There, sequoia seedlings eventually could not get established, and the sequoia forest, with its associated plants and animals, disappeared.

The author has determined that the part of the Sierra Nevada covered in this chapter began to rise in earnest about 2 million years ago. Significant, but not major, glaciation may have begun by then, though glaciers didn't necessarily eradicate migrating groves. More likely, the lower temperatures of the glacial times spurred the westward migration toward the Placer County site. The author has calculated that this site in the future will ultimately rise about 3700 feet, and to maintain its current environmental conditions the grove will have to migrate about 14 miles southwest to what is today the town of Foresthill. But given the small size of today's grove, all the trees are likely to die out in the relatively near future unless man intervenes on their behalf and increases their distribution.

**Description**   At the trailhead beside the parking lot is a map of this grove's Forest View Trail and Big Trees Trail. The Forest View Trail, starting near the drinking fountain, is exactly what it claims to be: a view of trees and the interesting plant life beneath them, not a view of scenic panoramas. The Big Trees Trail, starting at the map, has signs that identify trees, shrubs and features, and give the dimensions of the larger sequoias. Since both trails are so obvious, no trail description is necessary. Take the Big Trees Trail first, so that you will recognize some of the species you'll see along the Forest View Trail.

Two trail signs deserve elaboration. The first one is the FALLEN TREE sign, which states that this sequoia trunk, 154 feet long by 10 feet in diameter, fell in 1861. Had the trunk belonged to any other species of tree that grows in this grove, it would have long since decayed into oblivion. The bark and wood of the sequoia, however, are very resistant to insect infestation and fungal attack. That this trunk—and the larger Roosevelt Tree trunk near it—has survived over a century is amazing when you consider that chemical and biochemical processes in this area are quite strong.

Only one other tree, the bristlecone pine, can withstand decay better. Preferring timberline slopes in drier ranges east of the Sierra, this pine has an extremely short growing season—a month or so—and consequently it grows very

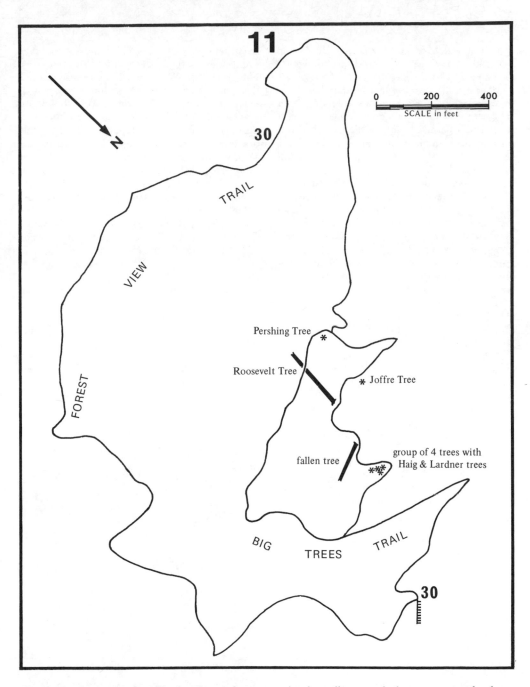

SCALE in feet
0   200   400

30

TRAIL

VIEW

FOREST

Pershing Tree ✳

Roosevelt Tree

✳ Joffre Tree

fallen tree

group of 4 trees with
Haig & Lardner trees
✳✳✳

BIG   TREES   TRAIL

30

slowly, producing extremely close-spaced annual rings that are very resistant to all kinds of
attack. Until the 1950s it had been thought that
the sequoia was the world's longest-living tree,
but not now. The bristlecone pine not only lives
longer—5000 years versus 3000 years—but its
dead trunks also survive longer. By counting and
matching tree rings in both living and dead pines,
scientists discovered that some trunks have
survived thousands of years; a few pines whose
seeds germinated 9000 years ago have their
dead trunks lying around today. Since this tree's
annual rings reflect precipitation—rings spaced
farther apart when there is more of it—scientists
have been able to piece together a 9000-year-
long climatic history for the Basin and Range

province, which includes most of Nevada and adjacent parts of neighboring states.

The second trail sign worth noting is STREAMS UNDERGROUND, next to which we can look down into some small holes, one or two feet deep, and see water flowing in an underground channel. It is channels like these from which the shallow, far-ranging sequoia roots get the water they need. If you hike both trails in this grove, you'll notice that the sequoias are found only on the lower slopes, which are laced with ephemeral creeklets—sure signs of abundant groundwater below. Note that the vegetation in the sequoia grove is composed of water-loving species such as dogwood, alder and azalea, while the slopes above have manzanita. Throughout this small grove you'll see trees found in virtually every one of California's sequoia groves: sugar pine, ponderosa pine and white fir. Also seen in this locality are scrub tanbark oak, black oak and Douglas-fir.

The present boundaries of California's sequoia groves appear to be quite stable; they are neither expanding nor contracting. Because few seeds are sprouting, however, most of these groves are undergoing a gradual decrease in numbers of sequoias. This gradual decrease in numbers has been going on for at least 500 years, so Western man isn't really at fault—although early entrepreneurs tried to lumber the groves. The sheer bulk of these giants caused them to shatter into useless splinters when they hit the ground, so most of the sequoia trees—unlike their close cousin, the coast redwood—were spared from the ax. This Placer County grove was discovered in 1855 by miners who were searching for gold among the quartz veins which infuse the Paleozoic marine sediments that underlie its fairly deep mineral soil.

It is this moist mineral soil that the sequoia seedling needs to survive, not the mat of drier litter atop it. A survey of three controlled burns in Kings Canyon National Park showed that a year after the fires burned off the litter, there were about 1500 sequoia seedlings sprouting in the mineral soil for every mature sequoia in the burns. In an adjacent, unburned grove, no seedlings sprouted. Burned sequoia litter holds up to three times more water than does unburned litter. Fires also aid seedlings by killing fungi, eliminating some plant competition and driving off small rodents that feed on the seedlings. Still, mortality is high: only about 30 seedlings per parent survive by the end of the third year.

Once the sequoia grows large enough to develop a good, protective bark, which will eventually get to be over a foot thick, it becomes immune to virtually everything, fire and lightning included. What, then, kills these giants? The author concludes, after having visited at least half a dozen sequoia groves, that these giants die due to loosening of their roots by erosion of the soil that supports them. The soils are typically about 3-5 feet deep, and in this shallow layer the roots radiate out 100 feet or more from the trunk. Over a 2000-year period, easily half of this soil can be eroded away, exposing many roots and leaving the tree defenseless against a large windstorm, such as the one in 1861 that toppled two giants in this Placer County grove. Unlike short-lived giants such as sugar and ponderosa pines, sequoias do not reach old age and die to leave a snag that eventually falls over. Rather, these giants are *undercut* while in their prime—they don't reach old age. Overuse by people can accelerate erosion, although they probably were not a factor in the felling of Yosemite's popular Tunnel Tree. Bristlecone pines, such as those in California's White Mountains, grow on slower-eroding slopes, and this may increase their longevity. Nevertheless, they too, because of their long lives, are faced with the same problem.

## The 225-foot-high Pershing Tree

# 31       Round Lake Trail to Milk Lake

**Distances**   1.2 miles to Island Lake, 1.7 miles to Round Lake; 1.8 miles to Long Lake, 2.1 miles to Milk Lake.

**Low/High Elevations**   6670'/7010'

**Classification**   Easy

**Season**   Late June through late October

**Map**   12

**Trailhead**   Leave Interstate 80 about 45 miles northeast of Auburn (16 miles west of Donner Pass), and head west on Highway 20. In 3.9 miles you come to Forest Route 18 (Bowman Road), turn right onto it, and after 3.6 winding miles reach Fuller Lake. Over the next 2.7 miles, you climb to the Fuller Lake Campground entrance, pass a road to Rucker and Blue lakes, then arrive at Forest Route 14 (Grouse Ridge Road). Hike 33 begins near the end of this rough road. Still on F.R. 18, you go a full 2 miles before branching right onto F.R. 17. Drive 2.1 miles up this good-to-fair road to a junction with a logging road branching left. Keep right here, and again 0.4 mile farther, where a dead-end road branches left. In 0.3 mile you'll reach Carr Lake Campground, and just beyond it will park at the Carr Lake Trailhead Parking Area, which is 3.0 miles from the start of F.R. 17. Don't park in the cramped space just beneath the Feeley Lake dam, about 160 yards farther. Leave this for fishermen who have to carry their small boats up to the lake.

**Introduction**   One lake right after another greets the hiker along this short, varicolored, enjoyable route. Because Hike 31 is so short, you'll probably want to do it as a day hike, even though campsites are at every lake. No lake is farther than an hour's walk from the trailhead. From Island Lake you can head north and visit another group of lakes, which are described in the next hike. The Round Lake Trail also provides an alternate way in to Glacier Lake, the Five Lakes Basin and Beyers Lakes. This route is well suited for hikes in early summer and again in October, when the road up to the Grouse Ridge trailhead may have snow patches or may be quite muddy.

**Description**   From the trailhead parking area, walk 160 yards east along the last bit of Forest Route 17—a rough road for cars—to Feeley Lake's outlet creek. Keeping your feet dry can sometimes be a problem; the route could use a footbridge across the spillway at the north end of Feeley Lake's dam. At the dam's south end you'll find the official start of Round Lake Trail 12E26, which originally was a jeep road, though the tread has narrowed with time and parts of it have been replaced with short segments of trail to yield a better route.

We start east beside Feeley Lake, which is a fairly large, moderately deep, clear lake that in the still of the morning vibrantly reflects the red-brown colors of dominating Fall Creek Mountain. However, by late summer or early fall, the lake drops 5 or so feet, close to its natural, pre-dam level, and then the shoreline becomes a "bathtub ring." Regardless of which month you visit the lake, you're likely to see fishermen in their small boats hoping to catch a good trout breakfast.

After about ⅓ mile we leave the shoreline and make a short, moderate climb through a red fir/western white pine forest, top a minor ridge, and quickly arrive at a tranquil, acre-size, lily-pad lakelet. We jump its outlet creek and parallel first the lakelet's shore and then a wet meadow's edge, our views north being obstructed by a low bedrock ridge. At the meadow's end we cross a small gap and are greeted by a pleasant, small lake with a photogenic, lodgepole-covered island. Being mostly waist-to-chest deep, it is a warm lake suited for swimming, but is too shallow to maintain fish. From just above its southeast corner Crooked Lakes Trail 12E11—Hike 32—branches north.

Keeping to the Round Lake Trail, we quickly encounter a view of the nearby southwest tip of Island Lake. Along its south shore you can find some fair campsites. From granitic benches of varying height that border the southeast edge of the lake, one can dive into the cool, deep, refreshing water. Also from these benches one can gaze down toward the lake's bottom, which is 15 feet or more beneath the surface, and see trout swimming lazily. Farther from the shoreline, the lake attains a depth of 80 feet, which easily makes it the deepest lake in this recreation area.

Island Lake floods most of a narrow, north-south mass of 250–300 million-year-old volcanic rock, which was intruded and metamorphosed in part by the somewhat younger granitic rock that makes up the lake's east shore. In contact with the metamorphosed rock along the lake's west shore are 400–500 million-year-old marine metasediments and metavolcanics, whose iron-rich content accounts for the red-brown color of Fall Creek Mountain and the adjoining landscape.

From the trail view of Island Lake's southwest corner, we climb east to a north-trending, open bedrock ridge, from which we can see the island-speckled lake below us, and can also see, on the north horizon, the unmistakable sawtooth crest of towering Sierra Buttes, about 13½ miles distant. Leaving the ridge, we descend shortly northeast to a creeklet that drains from Round Lake to Long Lake. If you were to follow the creeklet north, you'd reach the south tip of Long Lake in about 130 yards. Just a few steps beyond the creeklet on the Round Lake Trail you'll spy a footpath. This parallels the creeklet upstream to nearby Round Lake, along whose northwest shore you may find three campsites that are really too close to the lake for environmentally sound camping.

If you're on horseback or want to continue onward, stay on the Round Lake Trail (which doesn't visit Round Lake), and make a brief climb to a small gap before making an even briefer descent to the head of a gully. From here, where the trail turns from northeast to southeast, you can head 100 yards down the gully to Long Lake. This scenic lake appears to be purposely designed for the best visual effect, for it has a pleasing balance between conifers and granitic benches. The lake's rocky shore, however, precludes spacious camping.

About 70 yards southeast from the Long Lake cutoff, the Round Lake Trail spawns a trail that heads 50 yards south, up a creeklet, to the north corner of *noncircular* Round Lake. Note that this lake has two outlets, one at the north shore and one at the west, and a shoreline trail

runs between the two. During midsummer, Round Lake is warm enough for some enjoyable swimming.

From the Round Lake spur junction, we go down the north-outlet creeklet a few yards, cross it, and climb rather steeply to an easily missed junction just below a ridgecrest. Here, a faint footpath start south, traversing 160 yards over to the northwest corner of shallow, greenish Milk Lake. In this vicinity you'll find a fair campsite under forest cover. From it a narrow footpath heads east across slopes densely vegetated with bracken ferns, wildflowers and shrubs. The trail is barely above the lake's waterline in places, and the thick vegetation at times almost forces you into the lake. By the lake's northeast corner you'll find another fair campsite, the one often used by those who descend from Grouse Ridge Campground.

Hike 31 ends at Milk Lake, but from this lake's spur-trail junction, the Round Lake Trail continues east. After a relatively easy ¼-mile climb, it almost tops a shallow saddle at the east end of the previously mentioned ridgecrest. From this locale, a spur trail strikes southwest, vaults the saddle in 45 yards, and then makes a short, steep descent to the northeast corner of Milk Lake. Beyond the spur trail, the Round Lake Trail climbs 120 yards east to its end at a junction, 2.3 miles from your trailhead parking area. Here, on a descending, forested ridge, you meet Grouse Ridge Trail 13E28, which gains 400 feet in elevation in a rather steep, southward climb of ⅔ mile to its trailhead near Grouse Ridge Campground. Northeast, this trail descends ⅔ mile to a junction with Glacier Lake Trail 13E13. The lake, at trail's end, lies about 2.5 miles farther, and the route to it is described in Hike 33.

**Feeley Lake (left), Island Lake (center) and Fall Creek Mountain**

# 32   Crooked Lakes Trail to Penner Lake and beyond

**Distances**   1.2 miles to Island Lake, 1.5 miles to Hidden Lake, 2.4 miles to Crooked Lakes spur trail, 3.4 miles to Penner Lake's outlet, 4.5 miles to junction near Rock Lake.

**Low/High Elevations**   6670'/6920' to Penner Lake; 7060' to Rock Lake.

**Classification**   Easy

**Season**   Late June through late October

**Map**   12

**Trailhead**   Same as the Hike 31 trailhead.

**Introduction**   Penner Lake is a fine goal for the novice backpacker, for it is reached with relatively little effort, yet its setting is more akin to that found in more-remote parts of the Sierra. And those who like off-trail exploration can check out about a dozen lakelets that lie just off the Crooked Lakes Trail. Granted, most are not too appealing, but still a few are quite rewarding.

**Description**   Follow Hike 31's description 1.1 miles east to your first junction, which is with northbound Crooked Lakes Trail 12E11. You descend a few yards to the southeast corner of a lake that would do well to be named "Little Island Lake." The lake and its island are both little. Because it is quite shallow, it provides relatively warm swimming over most of the summer. Your trail follows the shoreline over to the lake's east corner, from which you have barely a hop, skip and jump east to the west shore of Island Lake. Having an area of 35 acres and a depth of 80 feet, it is the largest, deepest lake you can hike to in the Grouse Ridge Recreation Area (you can of course drive to larger, deeper reservoirs, such as Faucherie Lake). Given its size, Island Lake can hold quite a lot of trout. However, given its proximity to the trailhead, the lake sees a lot of fishermen. The lake is also a great one for swimming, though mainly from late July through mid-August, when its temperature is at a maximum.

The trail leaves "Little Island Lake" at its northeast corner, and after you go 150 yards north, you reach a one-tent campsite that is nestled among lodgepole pines just left of the trail. Within a minute beyond it, we almost touch a corner of Island Lake, and if you want to check out tree-ringed Hidden Lake, leave the trail here and climb 0.1 mile northwest.

Those keeping to the Crooked Lakes Trail now follow it northeast, and momentarily top a low ridge that juts halfway across Island Lake. Swimmers in particular, take note: you can swim to three islands, or to the east shore, on which you can find "diving platforms" of varying heights. Hiking onward, you may spy a tiny campsite near the lake's northeast tip, and a slightly larger one—on sloping ground—at the tip. From that tip you can usually jump across the lake's outlet creek and then meander over to open benches above the lake's east shore in search of isolated campsites.

Immediately north of Island Lake we drop to a small lake and walk along its uninviting, lodgepole-and-willow-lined west shore. However, the east shore is quite inviting, at least to swimmers, since it has some good diving *and* sunbathing potential. To reach the east-shore cliffs and slabs, cross the dam at the lake's north end. Also note that a lakelet lies about 200 yards east of the cliffs, just over a minor ridge.

Only 120 yards beyond the small lake, where the Crooked Lakes Trail jogs east a few yards, you'll find a good campsite, whose only liability is that it is too close to the trail for privacy. Ahead, we ramble for ¼ mile, basically northward, through a shady red-fir forest to the first of many Crooked Lakes, this one small, grassy and unappealing. Three more of similar quality lie out of sight just southeast of the lake.

We continue briefly northward, round a seasonal pond, and then make a short descent northeast. You'll be heading toward a fairly shallow lakelet, but the best of the Crooked Lakes lies out of sight. Immediately before reaching the lakelet, near the bottom of your descent, you should spot a use trail that weaves eastward for 150 yards over to a fine campsite above the west end of one of the larger Crooked Lakes. From the campsite you have a fine view east-southeast toward the Black Buttes, the scenery marred somewhat by the lake's stained, higher shoreline, which marks the lake's former level when it had a dam. By continuing cross-country southeast downstream from the dam, you'll encounter three small, shallow lakelets, then briefly east of the last will reach a larger, more inviting one. From its outlet one can head 0.2 mile east and find Grouse Ridge Trail 13E28 along the base of a small hill.

If you choose not to visit any of these Crooked Lakes, you'll continue past the fairly shallow lakelet and quickly begin a climb to Penner Lake. Along this 260-foot elevation gain, you're bound to see an attractive, northern member of the Crooked Lakes, which too is a worthy goal. Your climb eases as you curve

north and leave views of this lake-blessed area behind. You make a short traverse across a bench to a dumbbell-shaped pond, then conclude your climb with an equally short stretch up to a ridge. Penner Lake spreads out below you.

The stretch of trail down to the lake and past its east shore is generally faint, so make mental notes of the route for your return trip. You first start north down the ridge, quickly enter a shallow gully and follow it 120 yards northeast down to its base, then curve left over to Penner Lake's southeast shore. Here you can fish or swim, but you won't find a suitable campsite. The trail wanders northward across barren, metamorphic bedrock and passes a small, shady campsite that is just above a shallow bay.

Here you'll see a metamorphic-rock ridge jutting out into the lake, almost cutting it in two. Were the bay deeper, the ridge would be a good one for high-diving, but such water sport is best at the lake's south end. You'll note that atop the ridge is a monstrous granitic boulder, about 100 tons in weight. This was transported here by a westward-moving glacier.

From the shallow bay the trail briefly winds along a low ridge, then descends to a moderate-sized campsite by the lake's outlet creek. Just across and down the creek lies a smaller campsite. Here, at the lake's northeast corner, a shoreline trail starts west, while the Crooked Lakes Trail makes an unnecessary climb and descent north to Rock Lake. The former is more interesting, for it gives you fishing and swimming access plus some nice views from a gap above the lake's west shore, including a view east-southeast of the rugged Black Buttes.

If you take the latter, you'll be mostly following an old road, which first climbs 160 feet in elevation up a brushy slope to a gentle ridge with an open red-fir forest. If you're willing to climb an extra 200 feet, continue northwest up to nearby peak 7254 for a commanding view of much of the Grouse Ridge Recreation Area. Otherwise, follow the winding road down to Rock Lake, the tread diminishing to a faint trail where it levels off just before the lake. You may spot a use trail that curves westward over to a good campsite. About 140 yards past this indistinct trail you'll come to an official one, which begins just southeast of a nearby pond. This trail descends moderately, indistinct in places, 0.6 mile southeast to Grouse Ridge Trail 13E28. South, that trail makes an uninteresting ascent past Shotgun Lake, which is more meadow than lake, then past the site of former Middle Lake, which now is a meadow with a lot of tree stumps. After 2.3 miles it reaches a junction with Glacier Lake Trail 13E13. North, it goes down-canyon 0.5 mile to a junction with an east-descending 0.5-mile-long trail from Rock Lake, then descends an additional 1.3 miles to the west end of a dam across Sawmill Lake.

Finally, after the last 60 yards along Crooked Lakes Trail 12E11, you end at a trail junction that is just northeast of the nearby pond. The previously mentioned trail that leads east from here descends rather steeply 0.5 mile to the Grouse Ridge Trail. West, it contours over to and then along Rock Lake's north shore. Beyond the lake, it widens to a jeep road. Near the lake's east end are at least two adequate campsites. The lake is a good one for both fishing and swimming, though after mid-August the lake's level begins to drop quite a bit, and it becomes quite unsightly by mid-September, as do many other dammed lakes.

# 33    Grouse Ridge, Glacier Lake and Sand Ridge Trails

**Distances**   0.7 mile to Sanford Lake, 0.8 mile to Milk Lake, 1.2 miles to Downey Lake, 3.3 miles to westernmost lake in Five Lakes Basin, 3.5 miles to Glacier Lake, 3.9 miles to center of Five Lakes Basin.

**Low/High Elevations**   6940'/7570' to Glacier Lake; 7428' to Five Lakes Basin.

**Classification**   Moderate

**Season**   Mid-July through early October

**Map**   12

**Trailhead**   See Hike 31's trailhead directions to Forest Route 14 (Grouse Ridge Road). Drive up this road, which deteriorates to a sorry state by the time you reach a high ridge, 5¼ miles up from F.R. 18. Immediately beyond the ridge the road forks, the right branch descending slightly to nearby, primitive Grouse Ridge Campground, the left branch traversing ¼ mile to a descending ridge. On it, just below the road, is a rocky parking area, with room for a few vehicles. The Forest Service requests that you park here, not at the nearby campground, which can fill to capacity on summer weekends.

**Introduction** Sanford, Milk and Downey lakes are easily less than an hour's hike away, and each is a suitable goal for day hikers. Indeed, you can visit all three and return to your trailhead in under 4 miles—not a bad day hike. While Glacier Lake and the Five Lakes Basin can both be reached in about 2 hours' time, each goal is more suited to an overnight hike. With Glacier Lake as a base camp, you can climb the Black Buttes and even drop to the Beyers Lakes. With the westernmost of the Five Lakes as a base camp, you can explore Five Lakes Basin.

**Description** The Grouse Ridge Recreation Area has such an abundance of lakes within its complex, though not difficult, topography that you may first want to make an easy hike ⅓ mile up from the trailhead to road's end at the Grouse Ridge fire lookout and study the terrain. From it you'll see a much larger landscape, one that extends from Lassen Peak (10,457'), in the north, to the Crystal Range (almost 10,000') of Desolation Wilderness, in the south.

Our route, which was once a jeep road like most of the trails in this area, starts down a bedrock ridge, and is quickly joined by a trail from nearby Grouse Ridge Campground. Then, in several minutes, we reach a second junction, from where a trail descends southeast to a ridge above Sanford Lake's north shore. A use trail continues down to a campsite on that shore, then winds around the lake's north arm to a crossing of the outlet creek. It then quickly terminates at the east arm which, surprisingly, also has an outlet.

Of interest to climbers is the 500-foot-high, low-angle cliff immediately south of Sanford Lake. Almost countless climbing routes exist up it, for hundreds of shallow, steep cracks striate this wall of fine-grained granitic rock. Because the cracks are shallow, however, protection along many routes is quite difficult with climbing nuts.

From the Sanford Lake trail junction, our ridge route swings north and descends to a junction with Round Lake Trail 12E26. If you head 120 yards west down this trail, you'll reach a junction with another trail, which crosses a nearby saddle and makes a brief descent to the northeast corner of Milk Lake. For lakes west of

Milk Lake, you'll expend less energy if you start east from the Carr Lake trailhead (Hike 31).

Keeping to Grouse Ridge Trail 13E28, you cross from west of the ridgecrest to just east of it in 0.2 mile. If you want to visit one of the area's best swimming lakes, leave the forested ridge in this vicinity and head straight downslope (southeast). You'll soon see Downey Lake. From rock benches above its north shore, you can high dive into refreshing, deep water. Because the lake lies in fairly open, relatively flat terrain and not in a shadowy cirque, it offers a relatively long, warm swimming season, from about the July 4th to Labor Day. In contrast, Milk Lake, which is ½ mile west, is often fed by shoreline snowfields well into July.

If you don't visit Downey Lake, you'll reach a trail junction, on a broad, level, viewless saddle, about ⅔ mile beyond the Round Lake Trail junction. From the saddle, the Grouse Ridge Trail continues northward. On this lightly used, unappealing route, you'll reach a junction in ½ mile, turn left, and descend to the east edge of the Crooked Lakes basin. You can do some interesting lake hunting if you leave the trail here and head due west. On the trail, you'll quickly pass through a small meadow, then make a gentle descent along a creek to the easily missed site of Middle Lake, which has been a stump-filled, grassy meadow since the shallow lake's dam was destroyed. About ¾ mile beyond this meadow, you'll pass through another meadow, this one holding grassy Shotgun Lake, which is more meadow than lake. Then, in about 270 yards, you'll meet a primitive trail that climbs, indistinctly in several spots, 0.6 mile northwest to the north end of Crooked Lakes Trail 12E11, near Rock Lake (see end of Hike 32).

Few people will take the above route. Rather, most will choose either Glacier Lake and environs or the Five Lakes Basin. The latter can accommodate more people. From the broad, viewless saddle, you arc east, spying to your right one of many shallow lakelets in the Downey Lake environs (the lake is ⅓ mile south of the saddle). After only 110 yards, you arrive at another junction, this one in a small meadow. From here, the older Sand Ridge Trail (formerly Trail 13E13) climbs northeast while the newer Glacier Lake Trail (the current Trail 13E13) traverses east. The older route will be described first.

The Sand Ridge Trail quickly starts a moderate-to-steep ascent, the gradient holding all the way to a high point, 7372, at the west end of Sand Ridge. With the 430-foot elevation gain behind you, the rest of the hike is a breeze, sometimes literally, for your ridgecrest route is mostly open. Sand Ridge, which is all that remains of some lava flows, is clothed with mule ears—a sunflower that is almost inevitably associated with all of the Tahoe Sierra's volcanic soils. Our pleasant ridgecrest stroll does include some open clusters of red fir, mountain hemlock, lodgepole pine and western white pine, and between the conifers grow aromatic plants other than mule ears: coyote mint, tobacco brush and wild parsley.

The largely open vegetation allows us to constantly watch the changing perspectives around us. The serrated Sierra Buttes (8591'), north of us, contrast with more subdued, closer English Mountain (8373'), in the northeast. The former is constructed of older rocks than the latter—Paleozoic metavolcanic rocks versus late Paleozoic ones. To the southeast rise the rugged Black Buttes, composed of *mafic* intrusive rocks, which are similar to granite in origin and texture, but are rich in dark minerals, such as pyroxene and olivine. In addition to these summits, we can see Sanford and Downey lakes plus Interstate 80, and we can trace most of our route from Grouse Ridge.

From the east end of Sand Ridge we make a short descent to a granitic saddle, from which experienced hikers will have little trouble hiking cross-country ¾ mile southeast up to Glacier Lake, which lies just below a conspicuous saddle in the Black Buttes' crest. You may see vestiges of an old jeep road as you climb to the lake, but virtually any cross-country route you choose is about as easy as trying to follow the road.

Those keeping to the trail from the saddle have a short descent northeast to the western-most lake in the Five Lakes Basin. This shallow, trout-stocked lake sits west of and about 200–250 feet above the five lakes proper. From a point on low, granitic ridges just east of your lake, you can easily view the three central, most inviting lakes. You'll also see that the open-slab descent east to them is quite easy. You may want to spend a few days exploring around and relaxing at the other lakes and lakelets in this glacier-scoured, largely treeless basin.

Those taking the newer Glacier Lake Trail face an often boggy, mosquito-ridden, viewless route that requires only a bit less energy than did the Sand Ridge Trail when it branched up to Glacier Lake. One wonders whether the new route was really worth building. The first half mile is quite flat, then you climb for several minutes almost to the edge of a fairly large, willowy meadow. Immediately right of the trail is a low ridge, clothed with pinemat manzanita, from which you have an inspiring view of the looming Black Buttes. With this view and a general lack of mosquitoes, this low ridge makes a nice lunch stop.

Just beyond the willowy meadow you skirt a seasonal lakelet, and have a few minutes of contouring before you begin your climb of 500+ feet to Glacier Lake. You end your eastward traverse in ¼ mile, where you cross a creek that originates at the base of the Black Buttes. Now you climb southeast and in just over ¼ mile recross the creek. After an initial start upstream, you switchback, then resume your southeast course for 0.2 mile to the base of point 7547. The trail now can be vague as it snakes briefly

**A Black Buttes' view down into the Beyers Lakes basin**

eastward up talus, then angles northeast across a bedrock ridge and drops to the south shore of a seasonal pond that lies immediately east of point 7547. The final ½ mile of trail is more obvious. It climbs, generally east-southeast, into a red-fir/western-white-pine forest and terminates by campsites on a bluff that stands above the west shore of Glacier Lake.

While *all* the natural lakes in the Grouse Ridge Recreation Area owe their existence to glacial processes, Glacier Lake is the only one that retains an icy chill about it. Being the highest and chilliest lake in the area, it's perhaps the only lake you won't want to swim in. And, although it's been planted with trout, the lake, with its cold, pure water, is an unsuitable habitat for a thriving population (in other words, don't count on a trout dinner).

Still, the lake is a scenic site for a base camp. From it you can make a day hike down to the previously mentioned Five Lakes Basin, or you can climb the buttes or explore the Beyers Lakes

vicinity. The highest of these dark buttes, which are composed of gabbro and diorite, is reached from the lake by hiking southeast up the steep, matted slope to a conspicuous saddle. From it, a short climb west, which is no more than a scramble, gets you atop summit 8028, and this provides you with a commanding panoramic sweep across miles of glaciated lands.

The shallow, warm Beyers Lakes, which are immediately apparent from the saddle, can be reached by a fairly easy cross-country route. Rather than descend steep slopes directly to them, first diagonal east about ½ mile down to a rocky bench and then parallel a usually dry creek south another ½ mile down to the eastern-most lake. Our approach to these lakes via the Glacier Lake Trail is about 2½ miles shorter than a route that is partly along the Beyers Lakes Trail. This route begins at the Indian Springs Off-Highway Vehicle Trailhead, which is ¼ mile northwest of the entrance to Indian Springs Campground.

# 34    Loch Leven Lakes Trail

**Distances**   2.0 miles to Upper Loch Leven Lake, 2.4 miles to Lower Loch Leven Lake, 3.1 miles to Salmon Lake, 3.5 miles to High Loch Leven Lake.
**Low/High Elevations**   5720′/6870′
**Classification**   Moderate
**Season**   Late June through late October
**Map**   13

**Trailhead**   Leave Interstate 80 at the Big Bend exit which, for eastbound travelers, is 1½ miles east of the more popular Cisco Grove exit. Westbound travelers: this exit is 6 miles west of the more popular Soda Springs exit. On Hampshire Rocks Road (a part of old Highway 40), drive to the Big Bend Visitor Information Center, which has the Big Bend Campground on its premises. Your trailhead begins 140 yards southwest of the visitor center, at the start of a private road that is also used as a public trail. Park near this road.

**Introduction**   The popular Loch Leven Lakes Trail is probably the best constructed trail in the Tahoe Sierra. Granitic rocks line and buttress the trail all the way from the railroad tracks to the Loch Leven Lakes basin. The ascending

route up to the lakes is never more than moderately steep.

**Description**   From the sign along old Highway 40, hike south 0.2 mile on the private road, to where it bends west. Here at this bend, the signed Loch Leven Lakes Trail takes off through a forest of lodgepole and Jeffrey pines, then climbs more-open granitic slabs adorned with snow bush, huckleberry oak, bitter cherry and scattered conifers. Looking west from a ridge we can see a change in the color of the bedrock, for the granitic rock beneath us gives way to an older assemblage of rocks that are mostly metamorphic in character. Solitary granitic boulders near us bear witness to the past presence of glaciers.

Beyond these boulders, we drop slightly to an alder-lined creeklet that has scattered junipers and incense-cedars growing on slopes above it. An easy climb from the creek takes us past bracken ferns, sagebrush and lodgepoles to the Southern Pacific railroad tracks. On these we walk 50 yards east, almost to the large overhead lights, near which we discover the continuation of our trial, curving west. Well-graded switchbacks take us up through a forest of incense-cedar, white fir, lodgepole pine, Jeffrey pine and western white pine. Interspersed beneath the

shady conifers—particularly near seasonal creeklets—are tall vine maples and creeping thimbleberries.

Above a small hill in the north, we can see through the opening forest a metamorphic landscape in which desolate Red Mountain looms above scrubby, reddish-brown Rattlesnake Mountain, which itself rises above Interstate 80. About 50 yards beyond this view is a spring that provides water for late-season hikers. We leave the forest's pleasant, peaceful cover and soon

reach Loch Leven Summit, a ridge point above Upper Loch Leven Lake. Down a shrubby slope we descend a short, steep trail segment to this shallow lake's shore, along which we can find small, fair campsites. North-south striations on its shoreline bedrock indicate the direction of movement of a past glacier. Late in the season, this trout-stocked lake becomes somewhat cloudy.

Near the pond lilies at the lake's south end, we encounter a junction with the Salmon Lake

High Loch Leven Lake

Trail. This faint trail—a good side trip—starts west-southwest, but quickly veers northwest up a low ridge, crosses it and descends slightly to an open swale before winding south-southwest down to the base of a low, rocky notch. After crossing this notch the trail continues briefly south down a gully that disgorges on the fairly flat east bench of Salmon Lake. Climbers will find short cliffs northwest of the lake, which require a half-length rope (75 feet) for safety. Fishermen can compete with the belted kingfishers that dart across the lake in search of its small trout.

From the junction with the Salmon Lake Trail, our Loch Leven Lakes Trail quickly crosses the upper lake's ephemeral outlet creek and climbs through a small notch to island-dotted Lower Loch Leven Lake. Immediately north of where our trail meets this lake, there is a fair-to-good campsite, and from it our trail traverses south, passing a large campsite. As you head along the shallow lake's rocky shore, you'll note some tempting slabs, which are great for sunbathing after a dip in this relatively warm lake.

At the lake's southwest corner is an easily missed junction. From it, the old Cherry Point Trail descends—steeply at times—2¼ miles to a grassy meadow along a seasonal tributary of Little Granite Creek. Because the total drop to it is substantial, about 800 feet, it is not worth your effort except perhaps in mid-October, when the abundant aspens just north of it turn the canyon gold with color.

After rounding Lower Loch Leven Lake's southern tip, our trail curves northeast, traverses through a narrow, shady gully, crosses its creek, and climbs moderately up to trail's end at High Loch Leven Lake. This lake, purest of all the Loch Leven lakes, is also good for swimming, and it has a beautiful little island which one can sunbathe on or dive from. The combination of cliffs and conifers that border this heather-lined lake makes it perhaps the most scenic, and its southeast shore has sites that can hold dozens of campers.

Hikers expert with map and compass can continue one mile farther, going east cross-country to seldom visited Fisher Lake, which is nestled on a viewful granitic bench. Unlike most of the lakes between the Loch Leven Lakes and Donner Pass, isolated Fisher Lake is on public land.

# 35   Pacific Crest Trail, north to Paradise Lake

**Distances**   2.8 miles to Castle Pass, 3.7 miles to Peter Grubb Hut, 5.5 miles to Sand Ridge Lake, 8.9 miles to Paradise Lake, 9.5 miles to Paradise Lake saddle, 9.9 miles to Devils Oven Lake.

**Low/High Elevations**   7230'/8350'
**Classification**   Moderate
**Season**   Mid-July through mid-October
**Map**   14

**Trailhead** Take Interstate 80's Castle Peak/ Boreal Ridge exit, which is immediately west of the highway's Donner Summit Safety Roadside Rest Area. From the north side of the highway, drive 0.2 mile northeast up a paved road and park at its end. On popular weekends, you'll find cars parked along this entire length of road. This trailhead may be closed after a new one, on the other side of I-80, is completed in summer 1987. See the Hike 41 trailhead (page 136).

From pavement's end, some folks drive up a severely rutted jeep road to an upper parking area, which is only 250 yards below Castle Pass. The Forest Service may close this road, which crosses private land, but until they do, motorists who make it to the upper parking area can subtract 2.7 miles from all of the above distances.

**Introduction** In the past, Paradise Lake was too accessible to motorcycles and other ORVs, which took an old jeep road that more or less parallels your route to this lake. Although ORVs have been banned along this route since 1977, the author, re-hiking this area in 1983, found fresh cycle tracks along the last mile to the lake. Nevertheless, you're unlikely to find vehicles at this island-blessed lake. To *guarantee* tranquility, you can take the difficult cross-country routes to Warren and Devils Oven lakes.

**Description** From where the paved road ends, a jeep road continues ahead and an abandoned road forks right. The old route to Castle Pass is up the jeep road, and it is considerably shorter than the new route. If you take it, you can shave 1.2 miles off all of the above distances. After 0.6 mile up this road, another road branches right, crosses Upper Castle Creek, and winds up to the new route, the Pacific Crest Trail (PCT). This intermediate route, across the creek, shaves 0.4 mile off all of the above distances. Its advantage is that you hike along the scenic, well-graded, upper half of the Castle Valley PCT segment, avoiding the steep upper part of the lackluster jeep road. Its disadvantage is that the creek crossing is usually a wet one unless you're a world-class long jumper.

The new route, the PCT, in 1983 was within shouting distance of the main trailhead, yet somewhat inaccessible. The Forest Service plans to build a fairly large trailhead parking area just west of the *eastbound* I-80 rest area, to be completed in 1985 or '86, and this will tie in to the PCT. All of the above mileages will then be about a mile longer. Until they build it, take the following temporary route. From pavement's end, head east down a short, abandoned road, peeling right onto a *de facto* trail just before the road ends. This poorly defined trail basically heads downstream, and you'll probably have to cross Upper Castle Creek via the I-80 shoulder. Once across, head back upstream about 50 yards, turn right, then more or less parallel I-80 to the west end of a linear lake. A trail from the I-80 rest stop circles the lake, and on it you walk clockwise but 80 yards north, to where you find the PCT striking west-southwest—your route. If you stay on the lake trail, you'll meet, in about 150 yards, the "southbound" PCT, which makes a climb northeast over a granitic ridge before dropping east to close-by Summit Lake Trail. For those on Hikes 36 and 37, this is the hard way to Warren and Summit lakes. Rather, continue around the lake to the Summit Lake trailhead, which is immediately east of the lake, near the rest area's building. This trail crosses the granitic ridge at a lower spot, then momentarily intersects the PCT.

Hike 35, along the "northbound" PCT, strikes west-southwest across glaciated granitic slabs, then turns northwest and parallels a major fracture in the bedrock. Beyond it the trail veers west toward Castle Valley and, staying within tree cover, follows the valley's meadow northwest to a road. If you've taken the Upper Castle Creek ford route, you join us here. Over the next well-graded 1.4 miles to Castle Pass, the early-season hiker crosses at least a dozen streams, some of them quite impressive. Before mid-July you just might get wet feet—and find much of the trail under snow.

At Castle Pass we join the much shorter old route, a jeep road. From this point onward the jeep road is abandoned, though it is certainly followable all the way to the Paradise Valley environs. For a nonpareil view of this part of the Sierra Nevada, start north along the ridge from Castle Pass. After about a mile and an 1100' elevation gain, you'll reach the base of the three Castle Peak summits. Up there, with wind-swept alpine wildflowers and soaring golden eagles, you can examine the countryside from the Sierra Buttes to Lake Tahoe's rim peaks.

From Castle Pass the PCT stays just above the old jeep road for ¼ mile, coincides with it for 100 yards, then stays just below it. Soon both drop into Round Valley, the PCT switchbacking down to Peter Grubb Hut, which is one of several Sierra Club cabins in the Sierra Nevada. It is open for public use, but please treat it properly. (Reservations should first be made at the Clair Tappan Lodge.) Just southwest of the hut grow some fine specimens of western white pine. When mature, these trees have a conspicuous checkerboard pattern on their trunks, which makes them readily distinguishable. The hut, the pines and the floor of Round Valley all rest on a granitic bench. Note, across the valley, where the granite gives way to horizontal volcanic flows. Roughly the upper 700 feet of Basin Peak is composed of flows, the upper ones basaltic and the lower ones andesitic. These flows were laid down across a rolling granitic landscape from roughly 10 to 5 million years ago. Surveying these flows, late-season hikers have a bonus, for then Basin Peak's slopes turn rusty red as several million lowly Davis' knotweeds don their fall colors.

Just past the hut we jump across Lower Castle Creek and come to the primitive Sand Ridge Lake Trail 14E11. The lake and its environs, neither one very attractive, lie at the end of this 1.7-mile trail.

North from the junction the PCT climbs shortly to the back side of a glacier-smoothed-and-striated granitic outcrop which, on the map, is elevation "7920." From it you have westward views of the Sand Ridge environs. Your climb continues, first up along a persisting creeklet, and then you cross and recross the old jeep road. If you want a shortcut route to Warren Lake, take the road, which steeply gains 300 feet in elevation before initiating an undulating course north. After ½ mile the road starts to plunge northwest, and here you leave it, traversing cross-country one mile east, more or less on the 8500' contour, to the Warren Lake Trail.

The PCT also takes an undulating course north, and in 1¼ miles it intersects the plunging jeep road. Apply the repellent, folks, for you're about to enter prime mosquito land. You switchback down through a forest dominated by mountain hemlocks, leap across North Creek, then pass mosquito ponds along a short traverse to the Magonigal Camp jeep road. Note this junction, which is immediately west of a large, boggy meadow. Pursued by mosquitoes on your return trip, you could easily speed past this junction.

Hike 38, which has come 7⅔ miles east along the PCT from the Meadow Lake Road, joins our route here for the last mile to Paradise Lake. Your road, which is often muddy before September, first circles the boggy meadow, then contorts among trees, mudholes and boulders before vanishing just before the lake. Since the lake spans a broad bench above Paradise Valley, you need not fret over finding it; it's impossible to miss.

While Paradise Valley is paradise for mosquitoes, Paradise Lake, or at least its east shore, can be paradise for backpackers (its west shore is mosquito-prone and on weekends may have ORVs). To reach that shore, round the lake at its south tip, not along the brushy north shore. Just before the south tip you'll hit some bedrock cliffs, but these are quite safely negotiated with a bit of prudent route finding. Look for small campsites along the low, broad saddle above the lake. On it you have a superlative view of Warren Lake, to the east well below you, and you have plenty of slabs for sunbathing after a quick dip in refreshing Paradise Lake.

Experienced mountaineers can descend to Warren Lake along a ducked, vigorous—and potentially dangerous—cross-country route. From the low point of the saddle, this route quickly drops to the north end of a granitic bench the size of a football field. The crux is the first 100 yards down from its south end; it's rather steep. Alternatively, experienced mountaineers can head south from the saddle, hopscotching from bench to bench over to tightly confined Devils Oven Lake. However, this stark, rarely visited lake is best approached from the Warren Lake Trail, for the cross-country route from that trail down to the lake is much more obvious.

# 36    Warren Lake and Devils Oven Lake

**Distances**  2.0 miles to Summit Lake, 3.6 miles to Frog Lake point, 7.2 miles to Devils Oven Lake, 7.7 miles to Warren Lake, 8.5 miles to Paradise Lake saddle.
**Low/High Elevations**  7210'/8555'
**Classification**  Strenuous
**Season**  Late July through early October

**Map**  14
**Trailhead**  Same as the Hike 36 trailhead.

**Introduction**  This hike's major goal, Warren Lake, is at almost the same elevation as the trailhead. Only a mountain of climbing—over 2000 feet in either direction—stands in the way. The hike, then, is not for the weak-hearted.

Since most of the Tahoe Sierra's lakes are considerably easier to reach, why visit Warren Lake? The lake, while interesting, is not particularly outstanding. However, the route to it is. The trail contains a 3-mile rambling traverse of a multifaceted, glaciated basin that is reminiscent of Washington's North Cascades, conveying a sense of unbridled wilderness not found in most of the Tahoe Sierra.

**Description**   For the first ¾ mile of route, see the second paragraph of the Hike 35 description. From where the Summit Lake Trail intersects the Pacific Crest Trail, you climb northeast, quickly crossing two creeklets before paralleling the vertical east side of a minor granitic ridge. With a short rope, rock climbers can practice some difficult routes up it. Nonclimbers cross two more creeklets, arc through a crescentic meadow, and quickly arrive at a junction. Here the Summit Lake Trail veers right, finding its namesake in under ½ mile.

Now on the Warren Lake Trail, you begin to climb in earnest. A largely brushy, moderate climb ends as you crest a minor ridge just west of point 7888, a low granitic knoll. Take a breather, walk over to it, and enjoy the scenery. You then

traverse around a wet meadow just north of the knoll, eyeing the lofty Frog Lake point, 800 feet above you, to which you'll climb. Spurred on, you expend energy exponentially as the trail grades from level to steep. Fortunately, the steep grade persists but ¼ mile, and then on a moderate grade you exchange forest shade for an open field of mule ears, lupines, knotweeds, sidalceas and other wildflowers.

The trail peaks out on an often windblown saddle, which lies just west of Frog Lake point. Take the 120-yard *de facto* trail up to its summit, even though it will add a bit to your overall mileage. The panoramic views from it more than compensate for the minor effort. From the point note the irregular contact between the dark, layered volcanic rocks of Castle and Basin peaks and the underlying granitic rocks. When the volcanic rocks were laid down, perhaps 5-10 million years ago, they buried many a granitic valley. Also note the next 3-mile stretch of route across basin slopes. This rambling traverse ends by a far saddle to the northwest of your viewpoint.

With that saddle as a next goal, you switchback down to a ridge junction with an unmaintained trail from the Frog Lake environs. A brief

**Paradise Lake, from bedrock cliffs by its south tip**

**Warren Lake, from a broad saddle just east of Paradise Lake**

traverse southwest takes you to a second ridge, from where the route ahead is amply spread before you. Before mid-July the route ahead can be smothered in snow, and has over two dozen creeklets to cross. By mid-August, some of the creeklets dry up, and the subalpine wildflowers locally dazzle the eye.

Near the end of your traverse, you cross two low granitic ridges, enter a shallow gully, and curve east. If you're bound for Devils Oven Lake, leave the trail here and walk north up to an adjacent ridge. From it you can identify a curving, descending route along a ridge down to this remote, cliffbound lake. You can also delineate a highly feasible traverse from this lake over to Paradise Lake. Also, if you plan to climb from Warren Lake up to Paradise Lake, take a look at what's in store.

Trailbound travelers head east briefly, reach a crest, then quickly leave it before reaching a saddle. Ahead, you'll drop over 1000 feet down

one of the steepest knee-jarring trails imaginable. Constrained by encroaching bedrock, the trail tries vainly to ease the grade with dozens of miniscule switchbacks. By the time you reach several campsites at trail's end, you'll need a well-earned layover day at Warren Lake. Less used campsites lie about the lake, particularly along its western half (thickets impede a traverse around the eastern half).

The cross-country climb up to Paradise Lake involves only half as much elevation gain as the trail's steep return route. Consequently, hikers reluctant to retrace their steps up it may be sorely tempted to opt for the cross-country route, which starts at the end of a *de facto* trail near Warren Lake's southwest corner. Be forewarned: the ducked route can be hard to follow, and in several places you'll have to use your hands as well as feet. This is no route for novices or for hikers with heavy frame packs. If you reach a large bench the size of a football field, you've got the rest of the route made.

# 37 Summit Lake, from I-80 Rest Stop

**Distance**   1.5 miles, one way
**Low/High Elevations**   7240'/7440'
**Classification**   Easy
**Season**   Early July through mid-October
**Map**   14

**Trailhead**   At *westbound* Interstate 80's Donner Summit Safety Roadside Rest Area.

**Introduction**   Less than ½ mile away from I-80, naive campers at Summit Lake are serenaded with the incessant drone of large trucks lumbering up the Donner grade. However, as a day-hiking goal, this fairly shallow lake is more enticing, for splashing about in its relatively warm water masks the highway's noise.

**Description**   Paradoxically, the trailhead sign is located near another sign, one that says you can't use the parking lot for trailhead parking. You can park for 4 hours, using the rest area's toilets, its phones or its picnic tables, but you can't hike! But who's checking?

From the east side of the rest area's building, the Summit Lake Trail makes a brief climb northeast over a low, brushy ridge, then drops for a few heartbeats to an intersection with the Pacific Crest Trail. You continue ahead, crossing two sets of creeklets that are separated by a low, glaciated, granitic ridge. Along its east side, rock climbers can find various routes, up to about 25 feet high, to challenge them.

Beyond the sets of creeks, you soon emerge from brush, arc through a crescentic meadow, and quickly reach a junction, at which you veer right. Your trail leads out to the nose of a bald, descending ridge, proffering a view of I-80 traffic, then retreats to forest cover. In a couple of minutes you cross the sometimes flowing outlet of Summit Lake, then in an equal time arrive at the lake's south corner. Midway between this corner and the outlet, you'll find a shoreline rock which permits you to shallow-dive into the lake's warmer-than-average water. This splashing entry beats wading out to deep water, for the muddy wade is not particularly pleasant. Don't expect noteworthy fishing at this shallow, popular lake.

# 38 Pacific Crest Trail, east to Paradise Lake

**Distance**   8.7 miles, one way (5.6 miles, one way, from second trailhead).
**Low/High Elevations**   7530'/8110'
**Classification**   Moderate
**Season**   Mid-July through mid-October
**Maps**   15 and 14

**Trailhead**   Leave Interstate 80 near the east end of Truckee and drive 14½ miles north on Highway 89 to Forest Route 07 (this junction is 9 miles southeast of Sierraville). Take this paved, heavily used logging road 9½ miles west, branch left onto Road 19N11, and on it drive 5½ miles up, down and across slopes before you parallel a stream, which is cutting along a fault, as you make a one-mile climb south. This climb ends at the north edge of a nearly level meadow, and you backtrack about 60 yards to find the Pacific Crest Trail (PCT). Park along the road.

A second trailhead, closer to Paradise Lake, reduces your hiking distance by a third. From the north end of the meadow, drive 0.2 mile to a road junction near its south end. Veer left and take a good road over to Bear Valley, passing two road junctions near the valley's lower end. Drive northeast to the head of the valley, almost touching the PCT, curve south above the valley's east side, and then turn east into another valley. In 0.4 mile you'll reach a minor road, which climbs ⅓ mile up to a saddle and the PCT. Parking limited.

**Introduction**   Unless you've got an ORV, the shortest way in to Paradise Lake is along this route, starting from its second trailhead. From the first trailhead, you do add a considerable 3.1 miles each way, but this stretch of trail is easy walking and is quite scenic. As on Hike 35, be prepared for lots of mosquitoes in the area's wet lowlands.

**Description**   The eastbound PCT begins a few paces down Road 19N11 from the westbound PCT (Hike 39). You immediately cross a usually flowing creek, which drains the adjacent meadow, then pass a small outcrop of metamorphic rock. This rock gives way to granitic rock, but you won't see the contact between the two, since a much younger layer of volcanic rocks, roughly

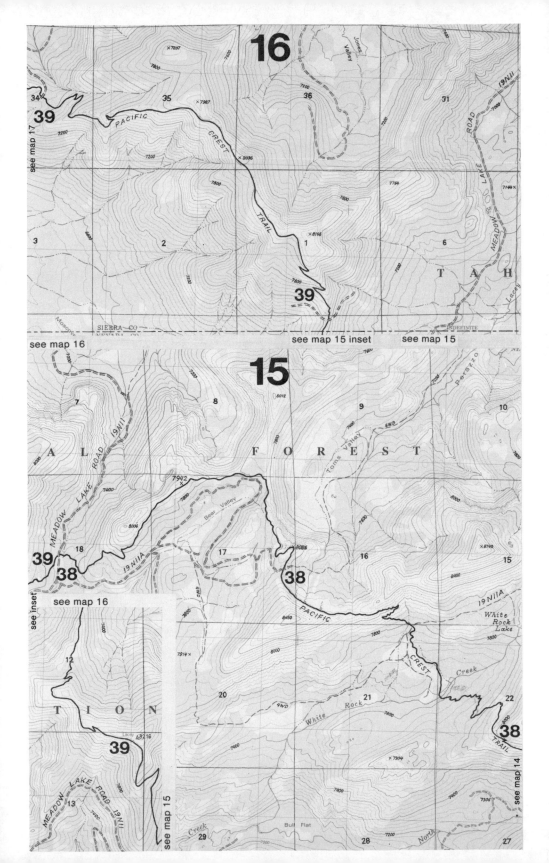

see map 16 see map 15 inset see map 15

see map 17

see map 16

see inset

see map 15

see map 14

10 million years old, covers most of the terrain. You climb through a selectively logged forest of red firs and western white pines, then traverse across open volcanic slopes. Because volcanic rocks decompose to clay soils, this traverse (and most of the route) can be quite muddy when the ground is wet. Note some light-gray granitic boulders, which are certainly out of place here. These were left by a giant glacier which, combined with others, covered nearly all the lands you see. Near the end of your traverse, leave the trail for a brief climb to point 7942 for fine views. To the northwest you see a tree-lined lakelet, below you, and the distant Sierra Buttes, on the horizon.

Your trail now traverses east along a volcanic ridge, almost touching the Bear Valley loop road before turning south to climb up a similar ridge. The climb ends at precarious point 8086, which has superb views to the north and northwest—the best such views on the hike. Your viewpoint stands at the head of a glaciated valley. From here, glaciers repeatedly flowed 4 miles north-northwest down Perazzo Canyon to a main canyon, through which an 800-foot-thick glacier flowed east along Forest Route 07 almost to Highway 89. Leaving the knobby viewpoint, which is composed of autobrecciated lava, we descend into a forest and in a couple of minutes reach a viewless saddle—the second trailhead. If you're starting your hike here, take a few minutes to climb up to point 8086 and admire the views.

From the trans-crest road at the saddle, we meet our first sizable population of mountain hemlocks, which shelter snow, in some years, until September. The tread can be vague, but the trail essentially climbs south for 0.1 mile before contouring southeast. You soon emerge from the dense forest and contour across the head of a boggy, sloping meadow. The contour continues around a low crest point, then you meet a crest saddle, which has your first good views south. On the southeast skyline stands rounded Basin Peak, with three-turreted Castle Peak just to the right behind it. Beneath both lies straight, deep, granite-walled Paradise Lake canyon. A more important objective lies much closer: a large meadow. The PCT stays within tree cover along its left edge, but if you can't follow the trail, then walk through this meadow to its end.

To reach the meadow, your trail first switchbacks down profusely gullied slopes to a bend in the White Rock Lake jeep road (19N11A). The trail then winds southward down a bit, almost touching a road junction at the north tip of the

meadow. Here, you can hop onto the road and proceed southeast through the meadow to White Rock Creek. In 1983 the newly constructed, unmarked PCT segment paralleled the meadow's edge southeast, slogged through a boggy stretch near the lower end, invisibly headed south about 100 yards, then reappeared immediately before White Rock Creek. Jeep tracks and cow tracks added to the confusion. Hopefully, by the time you hike through, the Forest Service will have made the route more visible and will have built a bridge across the creek. Until a bridge is built, the creek crossing will probably be a wet one for all but late-season hikers. If you've driven in on jeep roads to campsites in this locality, you have only 3½ miles to hike to Paradise Lake.

From White Rock Creek the PCT traverses initially east, then switchbacks up increasingly steep slopes, these largely cloaked in a dense, snow-harboring forest. Probably through lack of funds (hopefully not through lack of insight), the Forest Service has routed the PCT very close to an old trail, and both peak out beside a granitic knoll. Had the author routed the trail, he'd have sent it south from the creek for a 150-foot climb to a broad saddle, then would have contoured it 2 miles east to Paradise Lake. Instead, the actual trail climbs over 400 feet to the knoll, drops over 400 feet to Paradise Valley, then climbs almost 200 feet to the lake.

Oh well, at least the knoll provides you with a fine lunch stop—one with an excellent view of Paradise Lake canyon. Does this canyon look a little different from most High Sierra canyons? It's lacking one important feature, a headwall. What you see here is only part of a canyon, for the upper part has vanished. How so? Perhaps 10 million years ago and possibly earlier, a river or large stream flowed west down this canyon, and it continued to do so until at least 4 million years ago. But around then or possibly a bit later, the lands to the east began to sink downward, along faults, a process that may have taken 1 or 2 million years. New creeks developed on the east side of the newly formed crest, and these flowed east into fault-formed basins. The upper part of Paradise Lake canyon had faulted down and was largely eroded away. In the last 2 million years glaciers have waxed and waned in our landscape, and we can be thankful for them. Locally, they gouged basins in granitic bedrock to give us Paradise, Warren and Devils Oven lakes.

With these goals in mind, we speed down the PCT, quickly enter forest, and finally pass a

The "headless," glaciated Paradise Lake canyon

stagnant pond just before reaching the Magonigal Camp jeep road. The pond heralds your entrance to mosquitoland. Apply repellent. For the rest of the route to Paradise Lake, turn to the last two paragraphs of **Hike 35** for a description. Note your junction with the jeep road, for until it is better signed, you could easily miss it on your return trip.

# 39 Pacific Crest Trail, Meadow Lake Road northeast to Jackson Meadow Reservoir

**Distances**   1.5 miles to peak 8216 from south trailhead, 9.7 miles to same from north trailhead, 11.2 miles total, one way.

**Low/High Elevations**   7540' (s. trhd.), 6200' (n. trhd.)/8216'

**Classification**   Easy (from s. trhd.), moderate (from n. trhd.)

**Season**   July through October

**Maps**   15-17, 5

**Trailheads**   South: same as the Hike 38 trailhead. North: same as the Hike 40 trailhead.

**Introduction**   For an excellent view of the Sierra-crest lands between Highway 49 and Interstate 80, take this hike to peak 8216. Since the south trailhead is higher and much closer to this peak than is the north trailhead, it is the logical starting point.

**Description**   From Meadow Lake Road 19N11 our trail, the Pacific Crest Trail (PCT), heads southwest over to a small meadow, then switchbacks not too far beyond it. We now climb north, and views soon appear, growing better as we climb through a thinning forest. We switchback over to an adjacent ridge and climb north up it. Where the PCT leaves the ridge for an open traverse west, you leave the trail for a three-minute climb to peak 8216.

From the summit you have a 360° panorama of a landscape that in former times was almost entirely hidden beneath glacial ice; only the highest peaks and ridges protruded above it. You'll see, to the north-northeast, shallow, spreading Webber Lake, which lies at the lower end of a glaciated canyon. Above its left shore is a forested gap, through which you see part of giant, flat-floored Sierra Valley. This *graben,* or fault-formed valley, has been receiving sediments for several million years, the sediments being thousands of feet thick in some places. The valley's flatness is due to the fact that in former times it held a shallow lake (see the geology chapter's "Glaciation").

Looking 5 miles due east, you'll note 9148′ Mt. Lola. It is the highest peak between Tahoe's Mt. Rose and the Cascades' Lassen Peak, and is the remnant of an old volcano. Gently rounded Basin Peak stands in the southeast, joined by triple-turreted Castle Peak, the latter also the ruins of an old volcano. A few miles south of your summit, atop a flat, granitic bench, lie a slew of glacial lakes and ponds. Just right and below them lies man-made Fordyce Lake and, but 2 miles southwest from us, Meadow Lake. Dozens of lakes lie among lands to the west, but most are hidden from view. Our last major landmark, to the northwest, is the serrated 8591′ Sierra Buttes. On very clear days you should be able to discern 10,457′ Lassen Peak, just right of the buttes.

Leaving the summit, most folks will want to retrace their steps back to the south trailhead. However, if some kind soul has dropped you off at that trailhead and is waiting for you down by Jackson Meadow Reservoir, then you'll have an enjoyable, mostly downhill route to that goal.

You begin by traversing a viewful ¾ mile west on the PCT, then round a ridge and descend briefly northeast through a shady forest. If you're going to find snow along your route, it will be here. The descent quickly abates, and you walk north along a ridge, crossing a logging road at its north end. Ahead, your only real climb begins— about 450′ worth—which in about a mile takes you to a crest immediately west of peak 8166. A short jaunt up to it tenders views similar to those from peak 8216.

Now the route is essentially downhill all the way to Jackson Meadow Reservoir. Views along our descending volcanic crest are plentiful and interesting, though not on a par with those from peak 8166 or 8216. After a descent west past knobs of autobrecciated (broken-up) lava, the PCT heads north, descending 0.2 mile almost to a creek that flows through most of the summer. We switchback almost to it a second time, then descend to a major road that crosses a minor saddle. You could get water from the seasonal creek by walking about ¼ mile north down the road.

Westward, we climb just a bit before skirting past autobrecciated lava buttes on peak 7348. As our descending route curves north down a ridge, we enter an area of selective logging, cross a good road, and in ⅓ mile recross it. Now hiking on slopes of metamorphic rocks, we leave the ridge, parallel the west edge of an old road for 0.4 mile, then drop ever closer to the northeast shore of spreading Jackson Meadow Reservoir. Nearing the lake, the PCT almost touches a south-climbing road, and if you plan to visit East Meadow Campground, head 0.1 mile down the road to the paved campground road. The PCT curves northeast away from the campground,

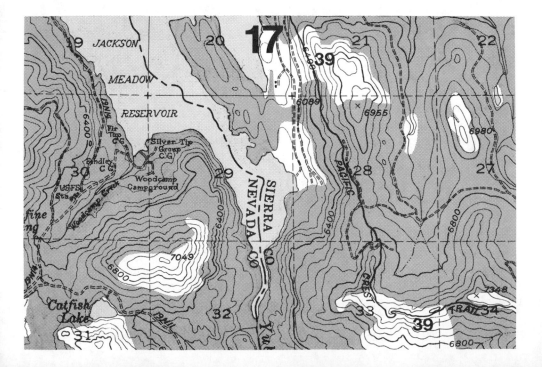

**Heading northwest toward Jackson Meadow Reservoir and the Sierra Buttes**

then quickly reaches its paved road only a few yards west of a junction with southeast-heading Pass Creek Loop Road. This junction is the hike's north trailhead. East Meadow Camp-ground lies ⅓ mile west along the paved road, and it is perched just above the welcome, fairly warm waters of Jackson Meadow Reservoir, a boaters' mecca.

# 40   Pacific Crest Trail, northwest from Jackson Meadow Reservoir

**Distance**   3.3 miles to viewpoint
**Low/High Elevations**   6190'/6450'
**Classification**   Easy
**Season**   Late June through October
**Map**   5

**Trailhead**   Leave Interstate 80 near the east end of Truckee and drive 14½ miles north on Highway 89 to Forest Route 07 (this junction is 9 miles southeast of Sierraville). Take this paved road 9½ miles west to a junction with Road 19N11 (Hikes 38 and 39 start 6½ miles up it). Continue about 5¾ miles west on 07 to a junction with a paved road, on your left, which curves over to Jackson Meadow Reservoir's East Meadow Campground. Your trail begins about a minute's walk east on F.R. 07 from the junction. If you don't want to park along this busy logging road, then park along the campground road. Your route, the Pacific Crest Trail, parallels this road, as you'll discover if you walk but a few yards northeast from the road. Hike 39's north trailhead lies 0.4 mile along this road, only 40 feet west of where Pass Creek Loop Road splits left.

**Introduction**   If you're vacationing in the popular, boater-oriented Jackson Meadow Recreation Area, you might enjoy this pleasant, easy diversion.

**Description**   Once you've located where the Pacific Crest Trail (PCT) crosses Forest Route 07, you start an easy climb northwest. Early-season hikers pass more than a half dozen trickling springs, but near summer's end many may be dry. The springs more or less mark the contact between volcanic soils and hidden, metamorphic bedrock. The forest, of white firs and Jeffrey pines, shows signs of former logging as we approach a minor saddle. Descending from it, we see the Sierra Buttes, framed by a linear minicanyon, through which we descend. This steep-walled canyon is in itself worth investigating.

A series of short, descending switchbacks take us out of the minicanyon, and then we cross its usually dry creek. Water here may flow underground, for rocks on the southwest wall appear to be marble (the stuff caves are formed from). The rocks on the opposite side appear to be metavolcanic.

Next, we contour across slopes above miniature Bear Valley. Today, Cow Valley would be a more appropriate name. Beyond a ridge west and above Bear Valley, we traverse northwest, have backward views of Jackson Meadow Reservoir, then cut through a minor gap and make a winding, gentle climb to a shallow crest saddle. Just north of it we reach our viewpoint: the Sierra Buttes rise in majesty above deep, mildly glaciated Milton Creek canyon. Ahead is the upper end of Hike 10, which ends with a ⅔-mile meander along a viewless crest to our viewpoint.

# 41 Pacific Crest Trail, I-80 southeast to Hwy. 40

**Distances** From eastbound I-80 rest area: 3.4 miles; from westbound I-80 rest area: 3.7 miles; from USFS proposed I-80 trailhead: about 3.7 miles.

**Low/High Elevations** 7020'/7270'

**Classification** Easy

**Season** Mid-July through mid-October

**Maps** 14 and 18

**Trailheads** North: Currently along the Sierra crest at Interstate 80's Donner Summit Safety Roadside Rest Areas (one for each direction). The parking limit at each rest area is 4 hours, which is too restrictive for some hikers. Consequently, the Forest Service is building a fairly large trailhead parking area just west of the *eastbound* I-80 rest area (you'll take the Boreal Ridge exit). This parking area, plus a connecting trail east to the Pacific Crest Trail (PCT), is due to be completed in summer 1987.

South: If you plan to be on the trail for more than 4 hours, then start from this trailhead, which is along old Highway 40 at the true Donner Pass, opposite a junction with a paved, south-heading road. Eastbound drivers reach this spot by taking the Soda Springs exit from I-80; westbound drivers reach it by climbing west from Donner Lake up the old Highway 40 grade. No parking area exists, so park nearby, along the roadside.

**Introduction** This 1982 route is most likely to appeal to rock climbers, since it provides easy access to some challenging cliffs that lie close to the south trailhead. From mid-July through early August, wildflowers are at their peak, which should attract the botanically inclined, though since the terrain is exclusively granitic, the diversity of plant species is quite limited. Finally, this hike may appeal to day hikers looking for an easy stroll or for a picnic with a Donner Lake view.

**Description** The route description begins at the eastbound I-80 rest area, since it is closest to the proposed USFS trailhead, which will lie between this rest area and the Boreal Ridge Hotel. (However, rock climbers will want to start from the old Highway 80 trailhead, since most of the cliffs lie near it.) Just west of the rest area's building, the Glacier Meadow Loop Trail starts south to make a 0.6-mile counterclockwise loop, which ends near the east side of the building. If time is of the essence, start at the trail's end, the east side, since you'll reach the PCT faster. In about 250 yards you'll come to a junction just above a shallow, murky lakelet. Leave the nature trail and head 200 yards east to a junction with the PCT.

If you've started from the westbound I-80 rest stop, you'll end up here. From the east side of that rest stop's building, you take the Summit Lake Trail 400 yards northeast up over a low ridge to an intersection with the PCT. Turn right, climb over a lower ridge and head downstream to nearby I-80. A horse tunnel has been constructed under both the westbound and eastbound lanes—a decided plus for equestrians.

**Donner Lake and old Highway 40**

However, the stream's culverts under the lanes are sorely inadequate in times of high runoff; consequently the stream overflows through the horse tunnels. Under these circumstances, hikers may opt for a dash across I-80. From the south tunnel the PCT skirts the west edge of a wet, willowy meadow and in ¼ mile reaches the previously mentioned junction.

You leave the meadow and curve up a forested swale, passing a small pond just before emerging from forest cover. You immediately approach a shallow gap, on your right, but then switchback down away from it. Ideally, the PCT should have crested the gap, then followed an old path past attractive Azalea and Flora lakes to unattractive Lake Angela. However, these lakes, all on private land, flow into creeks that provide domestic water for homes in this area, and horse traffic along the PCT might have quickly contaminated the lakes, perhaps with hard-to-eradicate *Giardia lamblia* microorganisms. Therefore, the Forest Service correctly located the PCT below and east of these lakes.

The PCT route heads east along the base of a large granitic knoll, then turns south, heading past its large cliff. Climbing routes up it are definitely inferior to those up the Highway 40 cliffs. You now make a switchbacking descent south, leaving behind most of the I-80 traffic noise. You bottom out near the brush-lined Flora Lake outlet creek, then traverse a few minutes southeast to a stale pond. Two sets of converging powerlines lie past it, then you switchback up to a second pond, having a view or two of I-80 country along the way. In a few minutes you reach a shallow saddle just northwest of point 7389, which is the top of Grouse Slabs—popular among climbers. From that summit you have the best view of the Donner Pass-Donner Lake landscape.

**Two climbers on School Rock**

You next engage a multitude of short, gentle switchbacks, descending near a cliff that offers more climbing opportunities. You then cross a flat-floored bowl and arrive at one of the Donner area's most popular climbing spots. On any sunny summer weekend, you're likely to see roped climbers practicing their sport. Past the climbing rocks, you conclude on a stretch blasted out of bedrock, the trail contouring just above old Highway 40. While not too intimidating to the hiker, one overhanging wall above the trail would certainly make the author nervous if he were on horseback.

A Jeffrey pine—one of many giant conifers in Five Lakes Creek canyon

# Ch. 11    Granite Chief Wilderness

**Introduction**    The idea of a Granite Chief Wilderness developed in the 1930s, but a half-century would pass until, in 1984, the high lands south of Interstate 80 and west of Lake Tahoe's northwest shore finally became official wilderness. The reason for such a protracted "birth" lay in the pattern of public and private ownership of the proposed wilderness. If you were to look at a 1960s or '70s map of Tahoe National Forest, you'd see that much of it was quite discontinuous. Over much of its domain a checkerboard pattern existed, every other township section (each roughly one mile square) being in private hands. Most of this private land belonged to logging-oriented Southern Pacific Land Company, which today is California's largest private landowner. Owing a total area about the size of Los Angeles County or the San Francisco Bay Area, it indeed had a sizable holding, in fact, about 40% more area than the combined total of Lassen, Yosemite, Sequoia and Kings Canyon national parks.

The checkerboard pattern in the national forests was inherited from a 19th century U.S. government policy. To induce the construction of major railroad lines, the government back then donated large tracts of land to railroads along their rights of way, albeit in a checkerboard pattern. Can you imagine what Yosemite National Park would be like if every second square mile lay in private hands? An administrator's nightmare. As you might conclude, such a land pattern benefits neither Southern Pacific Land Company nor Tahoe National Forest. Consequently, since the 1930s they have gradually traded more and more sections of land. For the Forest Service, this led to the eventual consolidation of the necessary land to create Granite Chief Wilderness. Ongoing trading east of here should lead, in a few years, to the creation of a Mt. Rose Wilderness in the northern Carson Range (Chapter 16).

The acquisition of private land might have occurred much more rapidly if the Granite Chief terrain had lived up to its name by being largely granitic, as is most of Desolation Wilderness. Instead, it is largely volcanic, and where granitic and metamorphic rocks are exposed, they are often veneered with volcanic soil. And it is this volcanic soil which is largely responsible for the area's magnificent forests. It is difficult for a lumber company to give up such prime real estate. Hence, a section is likely to be logged before it is exchanged for a section of National Forest Land. This may seem unfair, but living in wood-framed houses, the great majority of us can't complain.

One disadvantage of a volcanic terrain is that it develops lakes only reluctantly. Of the few that do exist in the wilderness, almost all are on granitic or metamorphic benches. For lakes, you'll have to go to Desolation Wilderness. Hiking in Granite Chief Wilderness is largely of two kinds: along open, volcanic ridgecrests and through forested canyon lands. Obviously, the first kind is more scenic, and this chapter offers two exceptionally fine routes: Hike 43, from Donner Pass south to Tinker Knob, and Hike 50, from Barker Pass north to Twin Peaks and the Five Lakes basin. Hike 51 offers a longer route to Twin Peaks, while Hike 46 offers a shorter route to the very popular Five Lakes basin. The remaining trails are largely devoid of views, lakes and, fortunately, campers.

# 42       Picayune Valley Trail

**Distances**   4.7 miles to north edge of Picayune Valley, 7.2 miles to junction with Trail 15E08 to Whiskey Creek Camp.

**Trailhead**   First, follow Hike 30's trailhead directions to Placer County Big Trees Grove's spur road. Staying on the main road, Mosquito Ridge Road 96, you drive about 10¾ miles to the far (south) end of French Meadows Reservoir's dam. Still on Road 96, you turn left and pass several recreational facilities before bridging Middle Fork American River, almost 5 miles from the dam. In one mile you pass Ahart Campground, and then in 2 miles reach a junction with a road that climbs tortuously 5.7 miles northwest to a junction with the Soda Springs Road. Starting just off Interstate 80 at Soda Springs, this road appears on the Tahoe National Forest map to be a short way in to French Meadows Reservoir. It isn't. The 19-mile drive along this road to the previously mentioned junction is a grueling, hour-long ordeal. Don't be misled.

Onward, you go 1.4 miles to a junction with Road 15E10, on the right, which is 5.4 miles from the bridge across Middle Fork American River. Ahead, the main road looks like an alluring route out to Soda Springs, but it becomes a jeep road in 1.5 miles and an abandoned road near Forest Hill Divide.

On Road 15E10 you go almost ½ mile to Talbot Campground, which is small and primitive, but nevertheless has some charm. Immediately beyond, a bridge crosses the main branch of Talbot Creek, but the road is initially rough, and some folks may want to park at the campground. You go ⅓ mile past the creek to a fork left and in 120 yards reach the "trailhead"—boulders across your road.

**Introduction**   The Picayune Valley Trail is the most popular of three west side trails leading into Granite Chief Wilderness. (The two others are the Western States/Tevis Cup Trail, mentioned in Hike 45, and the Grayhorse Valley Shanks Cove Trail 15E11, mentioned in Hike 49.) Certainly it isn't the shortest trail into the heart of the wilderness, but if you're camping in the French Meadows area, it is the most convenient. Overall, the climb up the Middle Fork American River canyon to Picayune Valley is an easy one, and most people won't want to continue farther, for the climb out of the deep, steep-walled canyon is strenuous. Along the canyon's route and up at Picayune Valley you

can find some fair-to-good isolated campsites. Strong, adventurous hikers can visit the Mildred Lakes or climb Mount Mildred, these goals requiring a great deal of effort for modest rewards—the wilderness has better lakes and higher summits.

**Description**   From the boulders blocking the road, we head east along a former road and after 0.6 mile we angle right, away from an older road that continues ahead. In about 320 yards our road ends at the real start of the Picayune Valley Trail, and on it we go an equal distance to the east edge of Section 1, where we leave private land and enter Granite Chief Wilderness. Now we make a short, moderate climb past white firs, incense-cedars, ponderosa pines and Jeffrey pines to a notch that separates a low knoll from the canyon's north slopes. A minor descent southeast from the notch takes us down to the start of a gently undulating eastward ascent that parallels the unseen Middle Fork American River for about one mile. By walking south 100–200 yards along the forest's open floor, you can reach this lightly visited section of river and find a place to establish a good campsite for yourself.

Just after we begin our second, relatively short, moderate ascent, we pass our first usually flowing tributary, then in 0.4 mile cross the Middle Fork, which here makes a short fall into a churning, refreshing pool that supplies us with what may be the best trailside water.

Our trail now veers southeast and climbs up to a second low notch, from which we can look north and see a skyline cliff of light-gray granitic rock, this cliff being a spur ridge that was severely abraded by glaciers. To the southwest, dark-gray metamorphic cliffs rise above the canyon's floor. Our trail toward Picayune Valley now stays close to the contact between these two very different rock types. From the notch we make a rolling traverse and quickly reach a small, pleasant campsite, which lies among lodgepole pines and white firs between the trail and some nearby small pools on Picayune Valley creek. Our southbound adventure now enters its first field of mule ears, then proceeds through several flowery, wet meadows, which are separated by stands of aspen, cottonwood, alder and willow.

The sometimes boggy trail tread gives way to a rocky tread as we start our third short, moderate ascent. Near the top, we approach some waterworn bedrock, and here it's worth your effort—at least before August—to walk a few yards west to a view of the creek's 60-foot-high waterfall. Standing here at a rocky brink just before the north end of Picayune Valley, we can gaze northward down-canyon and identify three major rock types.

The multihued rocks of the canyon's west slopes originally were sediments, most of which were deposited as volcanic sand and silt in an ocean basin about 180–200 million years ago. Later, these sediments were compacted through deep burial and folding into metasediments. Then magma, which is molten material that solidifies to form granitic rocks, worked upward through the earth's crust between 100 and 140 million years ago and intruded these meta-sediments, altering them even further. Some of the magma worked its way to the earth's surface, and erupted over eons to construct a volcanic mountain range like today's Cascade Range. Over tens of millions of years, that range was eroded away, together with much of the meta-sediments, so that today granitic rocks, chiefly granodiorite, make up most of the steep, brushy east slopes of the canyon. Atop the granitic band rest dark-brown deposits of andesite lava that likely formed 5–10 million years ago.

If you want a breathless experience, you can make a very steep climb from Picayune Valley to the Mildred Lakes. From the rocky brink with down-canyon views, you quickly enter the valley as you curve around a low knoll and meet a small creekside camp where you enter a stand of aspens. Then in ¼ mile you enter a meadow of lupines, sidalceas and mule ears, from which you'll see a shallow side canyon at a 260° bearing. Climb up slopes just south of it. The first 200 feet or so of elevation gain is through dense huckleberry-oak brush, which will stop all but the most determined hikers. Above, the going, though steep, is basically without obstacles. Of the three Mildred Lakes, two are

**Middle Mildred Lake**

waist-deep ponds, the middle lake being the only one large enough to warrant the title of lake. At about 7950 feet elevation below a snow-harboring slope, the lake can have shoreline snowbanks into July, and by early August will warm up to the mid-60s. This is adequate, but not ideal, for swimming, though after the strenuous climb, you'll probably want to jump in. Fishing may be good, since few people fish the lake, but there are no guarantees. Poor, cramped campsites are another negative factor. Still, should you want to visit the lake, but are not up to bushwhacking and overly steep slopes, you can take a longer way to the lake. From the end of Picayune Valley, follow the main, wildflower-banked stream west up toward a conspicuous saddle, Heaven's Gate, and about ¼ mile before it diagonal north up variable slopes to the bench holding the lakes. Most folks will be content to avoid the lakes and enjoy Picayune Valley or continue on the trail toward Whiskey Creek Camp or Five Lakes Creek.

Our trail once climbed up an extremely steep volcanic slope above Picayune Valley's south end, but now it switchbacks up to a saddle just north of an impressive band of deeply grooved andesite cliffs of autobrecciated lava flows. Climbers will find an abundance of handholds up the two dozen or so deep grooves of these nearly vertical, 200-foot-high cliffs, which require expansion bolts to protect the leader.

Leaving the saddle, we follow an ascending crest route that takes us past much lower volcanic cliffs, which for the climber are alone worth the relatively long hike up to them. Non-climbers will appreciate the interesting composition of these stark landforms as well as the ridgecrest views obtained. On the horizon in the south-southeast, the high peaks of the granitic Crystal Range poke up above the notch that marks the head of Big Powderhorn canyon.

Our crest route levels off, we enter a red-fir forest, and then we make a short descent to a trail junction amid a tremendous field of mule ears that covers the slopes. No single plant in the Granite Chief area so dominates its volcanic slopes as does this aromatic, large-leaved sunflower. Hike 42 ends at this junction, but you, of course, can continue northeast toward Whiskey Creek Camp or southwest toward Shanks Cove, both directions of this trail being covered in Hike 49. If you're heading southwest, you'll want to descend cross-country straight down to the trail from where our trail crosses the crest at the saddle, thereby saving a mile of needless ascending and descending.

# 43  Pacific Crest Trail, south to Tinker Knob

**Distances**  2.3 miles to Mt. Judah, 2.5 miles to Mt. Lincoln, 6.2 miles to Anderson Peak, 7.2 miles to Tinker Knob.

**Low/High Elevations**  7060'/8949'

**Classification**  Moderate

**Season**  Mid-July through mid-October

**Maps**  18 and 20

**Trailhead**  Eastbound drivers take Interstate 80's Soda Springs exit and drive about 4 miles east on old Highway 40 to Donner Pass. From the west shore of Donner Lake westbound drivers climb a similar distance to the pass. From the pass drive south 0.2 mile on a paved road to where it bends west. Here, a pole-line road starts east, reaching in 40 yards a private road, which forks right. Park in this vicinity, which is limited to several cars at most, or along the nearby paved road.

**Introduction**  In the entire Tahoe Sierra, perhaps no other stretch of Pacific Crest Trail provides better views than does this hike. Once this route climbs to the crest, it stays at or very near it for over 5 miles, and since the terrain is largely unforested, your views are a cornucopia of optic delight. The hike is the epitome of what the Pacific Crest Trail should be, thanks to Mother Nature and to a minimal infringement of private property. The only drawback is lack of realistic campsites: along the crest, level land and flowing water are virtually nonexistent. Therefore, you'll want to day-hike this route. If you prefer backpacking, take the next route.

**Description**  Our route, the Pacific Crest Trail (PCT), begins at the junction of the pole-line road and the private road. If you are hiking before mid-July in a typical year, the first ¼ mile may be entirely snowbound. If you have snow problems on this initial stretch, then you can expect more along the east slopes of Mt. Lincoln and in a wooded area north of Anderson Peak.

Almost immediately, you enter a 50-yard-long swath of lush vegetation, with wildflowers at their prime in mid-August. Tallest, though not showiest, of these is alpine knotweed, a head-high, scarce relative of lowly Davis' knotweed, which pervades the volcanic terrain we'll soon see.

First we climb a granitic headwall via short switchbacks, and soon have westward views of Lake Mary and northward views of Lake Angela. The latter lies at the headwaters of the South Yuba River. View-rich huckleberry-oak scrub on granitic terrain yields to nearly viewless red-fir forest on volcanic terrain before we cross a private road, which is about 1 mile from the trailhead. The forest, where open, provides seasonally lavish displays of wildflowers, sometimes accompanied by a trickling creeklet or a seeping spring, and in these spots we have a glimpse of the local scenery.

When you reach a crest saddle, about 1¾ miles from the trailhead, you can strike northeast cross-country up a ridge to 8243' Mt. Judah. From there, scanning the landscape from northwest to northeast, you see shallow, spreading Lake Van Norden, dark, volcanic Boreal Ridge burying granitic rocks, rugged 9103' Castle Peak in the distance above it and, of course, giant Donner Lake. Note the relatively flat lands west from Donner Pass, which are drained by the South Yuba River. At one time this river extended for miles east of today's pass. But that was before 4 million years ago, when the crest began to form as eastern lands started downfaulting.

From the saddle the PCT climbs south briefly up the crest before leaving it for a traverse across Mt. Lincoln's gullied east slopes. To climb this 8383' peak, which is the remnants of an old volcano, continue cross-country up the steepening crest, soon reaching a road from Sugar Bowl Ski Area which takes you to the nearby summit. Although you're only a mile from Mt. Judah, your views are very different. Your best views are to the south and west, a landscape unseen from Mt. Judah. You can look straight down the North Fork American River, which has cut a mammoth canyon. In its deepest section, Royal Gorge, the river lies over 4000 feet below its north rim, Snow Mountain. Obviously, the river has been cutting through this metamorphic terrain a long, long time.

Beyond Mt. Lincoln's gullied slopes you enter Section 33, which is largely private land. We switchback down to a crest saddle, then have a long, though easy, near-crest ascent to point 8043, just within Section 34. From it we descend just a mite then switchback almost to the top of Section 3's point 8210. At the first switchback is a volcanic pinnacle, whose short, 40-foot-high, east-side route tempts rock climbers. Other sides are higher. Bring rope and expansion bolts.

From near the top of point 8210 you have a splendid view of hulking Anderson Peak, our

**18**

View southeast toward Anderson Peak

next major goal. This is composed of dipping lava flows, which are about all that is left of a former volcano. In front and just left of the peak is somewhat forested point 8374. Part of the vent of the volcano lies immediately east of this point, and the vent marks the location of the volcano's center. This volcano may have been active when or just before the Sierra crest began to form.

We traverse past point 8374, climb up Anderson Peak's forested north slopes, and then contour around its west and south slopes. Where the trail makes a short jog, you can leave it and climb breathlessly about 10 minutes to the nearby summit. This is for peak baggers only, since its views are very similar to those along the trail.

Dwarfish, drought-tolerant subalpine wildflowers now line our crest route southeast toward Tinker Knob, which was once part of the throat of an old volcano. Just before the knob the trail veers east, and from this point you climb south

cross-country, carefully up to the highly fractured summit, which you'll reach in 5-10 minutes. Inspecting the terrain seen from today's summit, you view a volcanic landscape that has undergone severe erosion, in large part due to glaciers, which have exposed the underlying granitic and metamorphic bedrock. Among the more prominent landmarks is 10,776' Mt. Rose, which stands high above Lake Tahoe's north shore. To the south rises aptly named Granite Chief, devoid of volcanic rock. It is one part of the old granitic-and-metamorphic landscape that escaped burial by successive waves of volcanic flows that flooded the north Tahoe landscape in the last 33 million years. You'll see, in the distant south, the snowy, granitic Crystal Range, which forms the backbone of Desolation Wilderness. In the west lies a deep gash in the landscape, Royal Gorge. Compare this canyon to the shallow South Yuba River canyon, hardly detectable in the west-northwest.

# 44     Squaw Valley to Tinker Knob

**Distances**   3.8 miles to Pacific Crest Trail, 8.0 miles to summit of Tinker Knob.
**Low/High Elevations**   6240'/8949'
**Classification**   Strenuous
**Season**   Mid-July through mid-October
**Maps**   21 and 20

**Trailhead**   From Interstate 80's Highway 89 exit in western Truckee, drive about 8½ miles south up 89 to the Squaw Valley junction. If you're coming from Lake Tahoe, this junction is

just over 5 miles down 89 from the Tahoe City Y. Drive 2.2 miles up Squaw Valley Road to a fire station, on your right, which is immediately before the ostentatious Olympic Village Inn. No trailhead parking area is set aside, so check at the fire station for the best place to park.

**Introduction**   The best route to Tinker Knob is along the previous hike. However, the Squaw Valley route to Tinker Knob offers relatively secluded camping along the upper reaches of the North Fork American River canyon. Rock climbers may want to go only 2½ miles up the trail, to an assortment of moderate-to-difficult climbs up small, granitic cliffs.

**Description** From the east (right) side of the Squaw Valley Fire Station, our Granite Chief Trail 15E23 (old 15E08) starts a climb up-canyon. You're likely to see old, abandoned segments of Trail 15E08 plus a couple of feeder trails from the Squaw Valley environs. After a few minutes you come beside a chorusing creek, lined with aspens and cottonwoods, and you parallel it about 90 yards to a junction. Upstream, a trail continues toward one of Squaw Valley's many chair lifts.

We turn right, climb away from the creek, and with elevation cross a seasonal creeklet before reaching the edge of an opening that is carpeted with leafy, aromatic mule ears. Here, about a mile from your trailhead, a conspicuous trail comes in on the right. Be sure on your descent to bear left at this junction. From the opening we recross the seasonal creeklet and start a climb up sloping, granitic benches. Below these benches the midsummer hiker will have seen quite a diverse display of wildflowers, thanks in part to a wealth of minerals supplied by volcanic soils derived from volcanic rocks above. On the sloping benches, however, a former glacier removed all the soil, and very little new soil has formed in the ensuing 10,000 years.

From the benches you have views of the burgeoning Squaw Valley ski complex, and more views of it lie ahead. As long as you're looking in that direction, note the trail's route. On your descent you can easily lose the trail across this barren bedrock. With elevation, Lake Tahoe comes into view, and then we curve into a side canyon with a refreshing creek. Better views appear as we climb southwest up to a set of major, sloping benches with cliffs up to 50 feet high. Rock climbers: climbing here is fair to good.

Beyond the last, polished, striated bench, we turn our backs on materialistic Squaw Valley, cross and recross a persistent creeklet, note an abandoned, former trail segment, and enter a forested, hanging side canyon. From it a former trail segment once climbed up to a crest saddle at the canyon's end and then descended briefly to nearby Mountain Meadow Lake. However, that lake and its surroundings are on private land, which also doubles as a University of California Ecological Study Area. Consequently, the trail was rerouted so now it curves west and then switchbacks up to a junction with the Pacific Crest Trail, immediately east of a north-sloping ridgecrest.

Here we turn north, then cross the crest at a nearby saddle, and soon our high route opens up and offers us views south toward Granite Chief, southwest toward Needle and Lyon peaks, northwest down the North Fork American River canyon, and north across the canyon toward our goal, Tinker Knob. The views actually improve as we get lower, and then we leave the crest and switchback down to a junction with Painted Rock Trail 15E06, reached 1.5 miles after the previous junction. This old route, climbing 3¾ miles up from the old Soda Springs, was described in the original edition of *The Tahoe Sierra*. However, by 1983 the roads to the trailhead had become so plastered with NO TRESPASSING signs that the author felt compelled to strike this public trail from the book.

On the PCT we descend to the nearby headwaters of the North Fork American River, then climb around and over granitic outcrops, reaching a bowl with water and a campsite in ⅔ mile. About ⅓ mile past this bowl, the trail enters a larger one, with more-spacious camping on a waterless flat below the trail. Beyond the bowl you contour past two usually flowing springs and then, in ¼ mile, switchback for a sustained 0.6-mile climb to Tinker Knob saddle. Sharp-crested ridge 8761, just south of us, divides the impressive panorama we have to the south and east. Descending north is the abandoned Cold Stream Trail 15E05, largely on private land and closed to the public. It used to be the shortest route up to Tinker Knob.

With that goal in mind, head ⅓ mile northwest on the PCT to where it starts to drop along the Sierra crest. Leave the trail and climb south carefully up to the highly fractured summit of Tinker Knob. The summit's main views are described in the last paragraph of Hike 43.

**Tinker Knob, from the Pacific Crest Trail**

# 45 Squaw Valley to Granite Chief, Little Needle Lake and Whiskey Creek Camp

**Distances** 5.2 miles to Granite Chief ridge, 5.6 miles to Granite Chief's summit, 7.3 miles to Little Needle Lake, 9.2 miles to Whiskey Creek Camp.

**Low/High Elevations** 6240'/8550' at ridge

**Classification** Moderate

**Season** Late July through early October

**Maps** 21, 20, 19 and 23.

**Trailhead** Same as the Hike 44 trailhead.

**Introduction** This rugged, varied hike visits the highest lands of the Granite Chief Wilderness. Its last goal, Whiskey Creek Camp, can certainly be reached more easily, and those in a hurry should instead take Hike 46 to it. The adventuresome can leave Hike 45's main route and make visits to Granite Chief, Needle and Lyon peaks, and Needle and Little Needle lakes—all lying in the cool, subalpine realm. Note that you can *greatly* reduce the amount of initial climbing by taking Squaw Valley's aerial tramway and then hiking about a mile up to the Watson Monument at Emigrant Pass. Doing so cuts your distance by about 4 miles and the amount of climbing to Granite Chief ridge by about 75%.

**Description** The first 3.8 miles of Granite Chief Trail 15E23 up to a near-saddle junction with the Pacific Crest Trail are described in detail in Hike 44. From the junction we head south, initially up a broad, gentle ridgecrest, then along its eastern slopes. At first we traverse beneath granitic cliffs that are laced with veins. Just beyond them we get views of Squaw Valley and Lake Tahoe, which continue as we climb through a forest that is increasingly rich in mountain hemlock. Along this usually ascending traverse, one sees plenty of short cracks on the cliffs, which would tempt the rock climber were they closer to the trailhead. We cross a small flat, covered with grus (granitic "gravel"), just before we descend momentarily to the eastern edge of a fragile, subalpine meadow, which harbors the headwaters of Squaw Creek. Rising above it is the northeast face of Granite Chief. We cross the creek, briefly skirt the meadow's edge, and then climb on short, steep switchbacks toward a ski-lift tower on the east ridge of Granite Chief. The Pacific Crest Trail reaches the windswept Sierra crest immediately east of the tower, and if you've successfully carried a backpack up to here, you can cele-

brate, for now almost every step of the way to Whiskey Creek Camp is downhill.

Only a few paces down, and just before the Granite Chief Wilderness boundary, you'll meet two trails. Left, a trail arcs southwest, climbing moderately in just over ⅓ mile to the Watson Monument at Emigrant Pass. If you've taken the aerial tramway, you'll follow a road one mile to the pass, then take this trail to reach the summit of Granite Chief. To the right of our Pacific Crest Trail, a steep, primitive trail climbs a similar distance to the summit. Being the highest point (barely) for miles around, Granite Chief offers worthy views. To the southeast is relatively close-by, flat-topped Squaw Peak, standing high above Whiskey Creek. Farther away and right of the peak are the Twin Peaks, and right of them are the distant, often snowy peaks of Desolation Wilderness. To the left of Squaw Peak is much of the Squaw Valley Ski Area plus Lake Tahoe. Tinker Knob is a prominent point on the northern skyline, while Needle Peak, under a mile west of us, is a closer point that is bound to tempt peak baggers.

Should you be so tempted, descend west to a nearby saddle, then traverse the south slopes of a crest summit to a second saddle, this one above Needle Lake. It would be hard to find a colder lake in the entire Tahoe Sierra, for this lake can be mostly or partly snowbound well into August, when virtually every other lake has warmed to the 60s or low 70s. From the saddle, you're confronted with a headwall, and can go around either side. With a lot of exertion, but not much exposure, you'll reach the base of Needle Peak. If you're looking for the easiest route up it, head for its west side and cautiously scramble up it. Should you try the steep east side, use extreme caution and/or a rope. Views are similar to those from Granite Chief, except that Lake Tahoe is largely obscured.

Back on the Pacific Crest Trail near Granite Chief's east ridge, we reach, after about a minute's descent, a snowmelt creeklet, and then in a similar distance intersect the Western States Trail. East, it goes 0.2 mile to the Sierra-crest saddle, where it meets the previously mentioned trail to Emigrant Pass. West, it fluctuates wildly for 1⅓ miles over to a junction with the Tevis Cup Trail. This stretch, constructed by horsemen in the 1980s, was apparently built without any forethought, since the steep ups and downs are random and have nothing to do with topography or obstacles.

Onward, we have an open, switchbacking descent to the miniscule headwaters of Middle Fork American River. You'll find a well-used campsite just above its south bank, and a few yards past it is a junction with part of the old Tevis Cup Trail, which climbs rather steeply 0.6 mile east to Emigrant Pass.

From the junction our trail winds through forest down to a saddle that separates the American River and Whiskey Creek drainages. Here the Tevis Cup Trail resumes. Just 100 yards northwest down this trail, by the edge of a meadow, one sees a faint, unmarked trail climbing west-southwest upslope. This trail becomes more prominent higher up, and after ⅔ mile crosses the north outlet of Little Needle Lake (there is also a west outlet). The trail fades away about 140 yards southwest past the outlet, at a small campsite above the lake's northwest shore. If you continue cross-country southwest, you'll find a second campsite near the west outlet.

The Tevis Cup Trail continues beyond the Little Needle Lake spur trail, crossing the American River in about 0.7 mile, then climbs, in 0.6 mile, all too steeply to a junction with the previously mentioned Western States Trail. United as one, the trails in 0.8 mile first traverse springy slopes, then drop to a spur ridge—the top of the wilderness' most prominent granitic cliff. Serious climbers can camp among red firs atop the ridge, getting water from the last spring they passed. But climbers aren't the trail's main users. Each year, a grueling footrace is run along

this course, starting in Squaw Valley and ending 100 miles west. And, since 1955, equestrian groups have annually made a similar trek, some starting as far east as Carson City and ending in Sacramento. West from the granitic ridge, the trail fluctuates madly to avoid dense alder thickets, and along this stretch one can do some exceptionally fine botanizing. The author mapped the trail all the way to a primitive road, as shown on Maps 19 and 20, but since the user enters private property from the east edge of Section 29, he doesn't encourage the trail's use.

From the American River/Whiskey Creek divide the Pacific Crest Trail heads south over to a nearby flowery—though often boggy—meadow, then switchbacks down forested slopes to the headwaters of Whiskey Creek. Soon views open up as we descend into one of the Sierra's largest fields of mule ears. On the floor of a hanging valley we approach Whiskey Creek and some small campsites that are hidden under the dense cover of trees beside it. We parallel the usually unseen creek east to where the valley floor drops off sharply; then views soon reappear, down-canyon toward the obvious, closely spaced summits of Twin Peaks.

After a 0.6-mile traverse across mostly scrubby slopes, we come to a shaded junction with a trail that switchbacks and winds ½ mile down to Whiskey Creek Camp, situated above the west bank of the creek. This very spacious camp, with a bunkhouse, a storage shed and a roofed stove, is a favorite among equestrians. Backpackers objecting to the pervasive aroma of horse manure can erect tents on level ground just north or west of the camp.

**Little Needle Peak above Little Needle Lake**

# 46 Five Lakes Trail to Five Lakes Basin and Whiskey Creek Camp

**Distances**  2.1 miles to largest lake, 4.1 miles to camp.

**Low/High Elevations**  6560'/7600'

**Classification**  Moderate

**Season**  Early July through mid-October

**Maps**  21, 20 and 23.

**Trailhead**  From Interstate 80's Highway 89 exit in western Truckee, drive about 10 miles south up 89 to the Alpine Meadows Ski Area

junction. If you're coming from Lake Tahoe, this junction is just under 4 miles down 89 from the Tahoe City **Y.** Drive 2.1 miles up Alpine Meadows Road to the Five Lakes Trail, on the right, which is opposite a junction with the upper end of Deer Park Drive.

**Introduction**  Ascending this wide, well-graded, popular trail, you can reach the Five Lakes basin in only an hour's time, leaving many hours to fish, swim, explore or relax around these

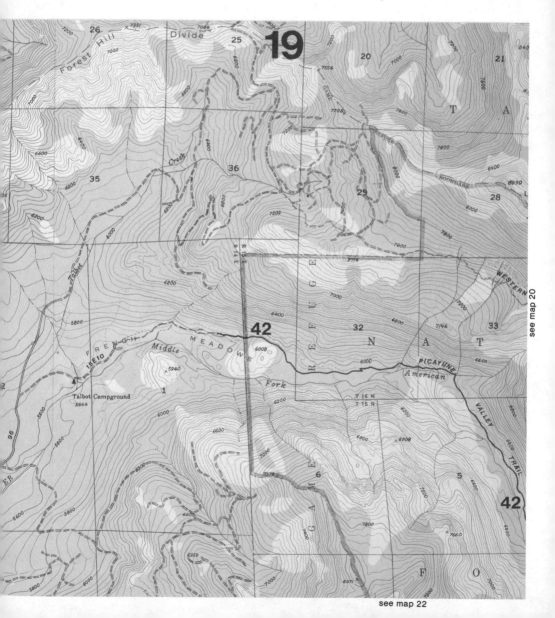

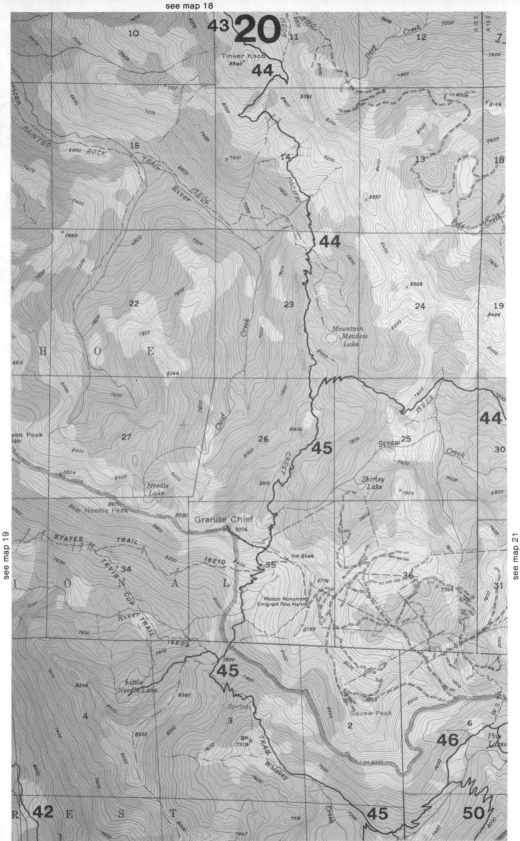

see map 18

**43** **20**

**44**

**44**

**44**

**45**

**44**

**45**

**45**

**46**

**50**

**42**

see map 19

see map 21

see map 23

10 11 12 7

Tinker Knob

15 14 13 18

22 23 24 19

Mountain
Meadow
Lake

27 26 45 Squaw 25 30

Needle
Lake

Granite Chief Shirley
Lake

Needle Peak

STATES TRAIL

34 35 36 31

16E10

River TRAIL

Watson Monument
Emigrant Pass Marker

Little
Needle Lake

Spring

4 3 2 6

Squaw Peak

Five
Lakes

BM

E S T 45

PACIFIC

CREST

TRAIL

Whiskey

**Squaw Peak and the westernmost of the Five Lakes**

lakes. Whiskey Creek Camp, a favorite among equestrians, is an easy 2-mile descent farther.

**Description** We start west along volcanic talus, derived from the andesite cliffs above us, and hike past dense stands of huckleberry oak beneath a scattered cover of Jeffrey pines and white firs. Rounding a broad ridge, we can look south toward the upper canyon, whose slopes support the hardly visible ski lifts of forested Alpine Meadows—quite a contrast to the many highly visible lifts in open Squaw Valley, north of us.

Our dusty Trail 16E13 becomes a gravelly one as volcanic rocks give way to granitic ones, some of them stained reddish by iron oxide in the rock. A few switchbacks through dense brush transport us higher up the slope, and then we arc southwest to a switchback on a weathered granitic ridge. From it we can look east, back the way we came, and see the clear contact between the medium-gray young volcanic rocks and the lighter, much older granitic bedrock west of them.

After passing stunted Jeffrey pines and some western white pines that struggle in the shallow soils of this dry granitic ridge, we climb moderately northwest. The grade then eases, and we arc west across brushy slopes, then southwest past red firs and lodgepole pines up to the east boundary of Granite Chief Wilderness. Our path quickly levels off, and from where it

curves from southwest to west, a faint spur trail descends to the northernmost of the Five Lakes—a shallow, grassy body of water dotted with granitic boulders.

After a few minutes' walk beyond this spur, we come to a second one, descending to the Five Lakes proper. We take this trail, which in 2 minutes bifurcates just above the basin's largest, westernmost lake. A short trail west heads along north-shore campsites, a longer trail south heads along east-shore sites. This trail, in turn, gives rise to another spur trail, which traverses east to a second lake, which at high water is actually a lobe of the westernmost lake. Draining into the north and southeast corners of this "lobe" are creeklets from two of the basin's other lakes, which can be reached by heading up the creeklets. Within this glaciated granodiorite basin, plenty of campsites can be found around the warm, shallow lakes. Late-season hikers will find the best drinking water along Five Lakes Creek, which emanates near campsites above the north end of the westernmost lake.

Although campsites abound in the Five Lakes basin, this area receives too much use, at least on summer weekends, for a wilderness camping experience. To get away from the crowd, head over to the Whiskey Creek Camp environs. On the main trail we start west and in a minute reach a junction with the W S (Western States) Trail. This little-used trail climbs north to a nearby crest, then descends into Squaw Valley, ending at an old road. The unmaintained trail is abundantly signed NO TRESPASSING, VIOLATORS WILL BE PROSECUTED. SQUAW VALLEY SKI CORP., and this must scare off many would-be hikers. Actually, the trail's right of way was established long before the anti-environment, pro-megabucks corporation was born. Still, no one would want to take this trail, which presents a sore sight to the eyes. The Forest Service hopes to relocate the trail to avoid the Squaw Valley complex, and if this does happen, then hikers will have a good loop route: Hike 45 to Whiskey Creek Camp, 2 miles east to the W S Trail, then down that route to a trailhead near the original one.

Moving on, we soon cross a lively creek, which is fed by snowfields on the east slopes of volcanic Squaw Peak. Next, we traverse southwest, then descend south, reaching a junction with the Pacific Crest Trail (PCT) 2.6 miles from our trailhead. Hike 50 branches left here, for a climb south to Twin Peaks. On the PCT we head down-canyon across generally open, picturesque slopes, which offer both dry-land and wet-land floral displays. As we're about to curve west through a forest, we come to a junction. Here an old trail starts south, winding 220 yards down to a fork, the left, rocky branch reaching brush-lined Five Lakes Creek in 25 yards. Hike 48, from Diamond Crossing, descends this route. The old trail's right branch once traversed west to Whiskey Creek Camp, but was abandoned in 1983.

On the PCT we make a forested 250-yard traverse west to another junction, branch left, and snake 0.4 mile down Whiskey Creek Trail 16E06 to Whiskey Creek. The camp, with bunkhouse, storage shed and a roofed stove, lies on a spacious flat above the creek's west bank. Horse manure can be a problem for hikers with sensitive noses, but they can head west or north 100-200 yards and establish a more sanitary camp. You'll find a junction in the west part of Whiskey Creek Camp. Hike 48, from Diamond Crossing, climbs north to this junction, while Hike 49 climbs west from it.

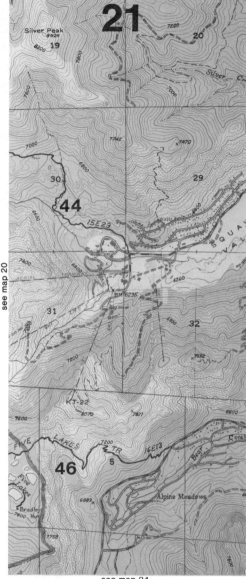

see map 24

# 47    Powderhorn Trail to Diamond Crossing

**Distances**   4.0 miles to Diamond Crossing, 7.4 miles to Steamboat Canyon creek.

**Low/High Elevations**   6030'/7820'

**Classification**   Moderate

**Season**   Mid-July through early October

**Maps**   26, 23 and 21

**Trailhead**   Leave Highway 89 opposite Kaspian Beach, at a junction with Road 15N03. This junction is 4.3 miles south of the Tahoe City **Y**, and only 0.4 mile north of overhanging roadside Eagle Rock, which in turn is about 4 miles north of the town of Tahoma. Drive 2.3

miles west on Road 15N03 (Forest Route 3), branch right across Blackwood Creek and climb 4.8 miles to the Sierra crest. Descend 0.5 mile along it to the Barker Pass environs, where the Pacific Crest Trail crosses your road. Hike 51 climbs west from here, Hike 75 descends south. Traverse 1.3 miles west to a major logging road (Road 32), descending to Barker Creek, then past this road a final 0.3 mile to the Powderhorn trailhead, with roadside parking for a few cars.

**Introduction** This somewhat popular trail down to Diamond Crossing takes you to some good creek campsites—ideal spots for just relaxing. From Diamond Crossing a route west heads into a more isolated part of the Tahoe Sierra, in which the inquisitive backpacker or equestrian can do some exploring on his own.

**Description** By a gully carved from loose volcanic rocks, our Powderhorn Trail 15E15 switchbacks up a mule-ears slope to a broad saddle clothed in red fir. You'll note some selective logging nearby, and the red fir is the tree the loggers were after. In addition to the fir, we see western white pine and mountain hemlock as our trail descends west, its tread snowbound into early August in some years. Steep switchbacks take us quickly down to the headwaters of Powderhorn Creek, and here, at the bottom of loose, volcanic boulders and sediments of its sometimes dry channel, one will always find water flowing through this porous rock. We cross to the creek's west bank, which we'll parallel—though at a distance—all the way down to a flat meadow just south of Diamond Crossing.

Our gradient is now mostly a moderate one as our trail leads us north down through more open areas that are abundant in lupine, mule ears, coyote mint and, soon, sagebrush. In one of these clearings we pass a huge trailside boulder on our right that broke loose from the slopes above us. This boulder is a characteristic part of an autobrecciated lava flow (see the geology chapter's "Tahoe Sierra volcanism"), for it is composed of a wide assortment of smaller, angular boulders that range up to 2 feet in diameter. Some flows also contain nonvolcanic rocks, because surface rocks get intermixed with them later on if they travel as mudflows down-canyon. Notice how the texture of this huge boulder differs from the smaller boulders that were derived from massive lava flows composing the cliffs way above us.

After crossing several ephemeral creeklets and touching the lower edge of the talus slope derived from the cliffs, our trail enters a moderately dense forest. After descending gentle slopes, we enter a level meadow, which is rich in grass in early season, in corn lilies and yampah in late season. We start west through it, then turn north, and leave the meadow and an adjacent campsite for an immediate boulderhop of Powderhorn Creek. Early-season hikers may find the creek 10 yards wide and more than a boulderhop. About 280 yards beyond the creek, we reach the outskirts of open, sloping Diamond Crossing. Hike 48 continues the route description north from here.

You can find campsites in the vicinity of Diamond Crossing, but more lie to the west. To explore the Granite Chief hinterlands, start from a junction within the crossing and head west down a trail which is joined by a faint shortcut trail after about 250 yards. We continue westward and soon pass cottonwoods, lodgepoles, alders, Jeffrey pines and white firs that line boulder-bottomed Five Lakes Creek, which can be a 20-yard-wide, very wet ford in early season. On the creek's west bank you'll discover a good campsite, but more-secluded ones that are just as good or better can be found by spending a few minutes looking upstream or downstream. Most backpackers will be content to stay at the campsites they find around here, but you can continue down-canyon. In that direction the trail makes an initial ascent southwest, undulates through a sometimes shady forest as it passes four low knolls on the left, and then makes a moderate descent to Little Buckskin Creek. We no sooner climb out of its shallow gully than we find ourselves making a brief descent to Buckskin Creek. Just 30 yards beyond it we reach a fair campsite on a small flat, then in 60 yards reach a junction from which two unmaintained trails head off to oblivion.

**A boulder of autobrecciated lava**

# 48    Diamond Crossing to Whiskey Creek Camp

**Distances**  5.0 miles by west-side route, 5.6 miles by east-side route, 18.5 miles for complete semiloop trip from Powderhorn trailhead.

**Low/High Elevations**  6050'/7190'

**Classification**  Moderate

**Season**  Mid-July through early October

**Maps**  23 and 20

**Trailhead**  None; see introduction.

**Introduction**  This hike, north up Five Lakes Creek to Whiskey Creek Camp, takes off from Hike 47's Diamond Crossing. From that hike's trailhead, the camp lies a distant 9.0 miles away via the west-side route. Like Hike 45, this route is certainly a long route to the camp. Most travelers will reach it via Hike 46. If you come in by either long route, you can make a looping excursion along Five Lakes Creek, descending either bank, then ascending the other. Of greatest interest to the author along this 5.1-mile loop trip was the giant size of many of the trailside trees and wildflowers. The area seems conducive to maximum growth.

**Description**  Hike 47 describes the route to Diamond Crossing, which is a large, usually dry meadow with a trail junction. From it Hike 47 heads down the meadow, west to Five Lakes Creek and beyond. We climb gently northeast through the meadow, which is bordered by some tall Jeffrey pines, and in 150 yards of shady walking reach a junction with Bear Pen Trail 16E26. If you were to follow this moderately climbing trail 2.7 miles east, you'd reach the Bear Pen, which is a small, meadowy cove at the upper end of a boxed-in canyon. Vegetation up there is like that along the start of Powderhorn Trail's descent—rich in hemlock. Up there, by the meadow's north edge, you would find a campsite just east of trickling, alder-lined Bear Pen Creek.

On the Five Lakes Creek trail we go another 150 yards to cross that creek immediately east of a miniature gorge. Soon we enter a meadowy stretch, which can be quite boggy in early season. However, by late August the soil is reasonably dry and the wildflowers have achieved their maximum height. Here the tall larkspur lives up to its name, growing 7 feet tall, and the arrowhead senecio, which usually tops out at 3-4 feet, reaches 5-6 feet.

Just beyond the seasonally wet area we pass some mammoth Jeffrey pines, which stand out among the smaller, far-more-common red firs.

Note the chartreuse-colored staghorn lichens growing profusely on these firs (and note that they grow very poorly on the pines, which are largely devoid of them). The lichens grow down to within a few feet of the ground, this lower limit more or less marking the depth of the average winter snowpack.

We next cross Grouse Canyon's sizable creek, doing so within sight and sound of Five Lakes Creek. In ¼ mile we jump across a spring-fed creek, then in ½ mile come to a junction. The 5.1-mile Five Lakes Creek loop to Whiskey Creek Camp and back starts here, by the south end of a sloping meadow. The shortest route is up the creek's west bank, so we branch left and descend 400 yards to the bouldery creek. If you want secluded campsites on fairly level terrain, look around in this vicinity.

From the creek, which is an often-wet ford in early season, we walk 170 yards west to a junction. Hike 49, a loop trail from Whiskey Creek Camp to Shanks Cove and back, joins us here for its remaining 2.0-mile climb. In 0.6 mile this climbing route of ours forks. If you're not satisfied with the route so far, you can keep right, descend northeast to the nearby creek, then climb northeast to just 15 yards north of the Big Spring meadow, where you'll meet the east-side route. Keeping left, our generally shady route is uneventful. The trail climbs gently at first, then moderately up the crest of a lateral moraine, which it briefly leaves to weave over to a small meadow by the union of Whiskey and Five Lakes creeks. The trail wanders back to the moraine's crest, now rather amorphous, and climbs ¼ mile to its northern end, which you top immediately south of spreading Whiskey Creek Camp. From a trail junction by the west end of the camp, you head west or north for secluded sites. Equestrians generally camp at the east end, by the camp's three structures.

Our loop route heads east from these, immediately crossing Whiskey Creek, then meandering almost ½ mile up to the Pacific Crest Trail (this ascent is the reverse of the conclusions of Hikes 45 and 46). On the famous Pacific Crest Trail we go but 250 yards east to a junction, branch right and wind 220 yards down to a trail fork. Five Lake Creek's east-side trail climbs to here, then, in the past, it headed directly over to Whiskey Creek Camp. We ignore this abandoned route, and descend 25 yards to the brush-lined creek.

The route south is not unlike our route north, except that it is unmaintained (though still easily followed). We descend moderately past white firs and Jeffrey pines, occasionally having glimpses of Five Lakes Creek, which is mostly hidden by alders, aspens, cottonwoods and lodgepoles, the first three adding a golden color to the hike in September. After 1¼ miles we come to a junction with a diagonaling trail—a route to the west-side trail. In 15 yards our east-side trail enters the Big Spring meadow. Look for the spring, just below the trail, by the meadow's south end.

Leaving the meadow, fringed with Jeffrey pines and sagebrush, we resume our descent, reaching another meadow in ½ mile. This one, with a seasonal creeklet along its north and south borders, signals the end of our loop, for we recognize a familiar junction a few yards into tree cover. Now we retrace our steps 2.7 miles south to Diamond Crossing, then 4.0 miles from it back up to the trailhead.

# 49  Whiskey Creek Camp-Shanks Cove Loop

**Distances**  1.5 miles to Picayune Valley Trail junction, 8.3 miles for complete loop.

**Low/High Elevations**  6350'/8180'

**Classification**  Strenuous

**Season**  Mid-July through early October

**Maps**  23 and 22

**Trailhead**  None. Start from Whiskey Creek Camp, which is the end point of Hikes 45, 46 and 48.

**Introduction**  If you've got an extra day at Whiskey Creek Camp and are up to an energetic hike, take this loop. It circles in a counter-clockwise direction, challenging you with the difficult stretches of trail first, while you are still fresh. However, this section up to crest views is also the most rewarding. Cross-country aficionados can extend the route, making a top-of-the-world excursion over to the remote Mildred Lakes.

**Description**  This route begins and ends at a trail junction in the western part of Whiskey Creek Camp. A level traverse west leads us past a large, obvious campsite before we hit a small, steep slope. Short switchbacks take us to a gentler slope above, colored and scented by mule ears. Beyond it, our trail climbs steeply once again, entering a forest of red firs and western white pines. Midway up our haul to a ridge, we encounter an alder-lined trickling creeklet, which gives us an excuse to rest. Since this is the last dependable water before an iso-lated campsite, almost 4 miles farther, you might fill up.

Once on the fairly open ridge, we have another excuse to pause, for we can admire a panorama that extends from Granite Chief, north of us, southward along the ridgecrest ande-site flows that cap Squaw, Ward and Twin peaks. A low ridgecrest notch to the south is the saddle over which the Powderhorn Trail climbs. Looking through the Five Lakes basin notch, we can see the distant, broad, saddle-shaped sum-mit of Mt. Rose (10,776'), third highest of the Tahoe Basin peaks.

We climb up the ridge briefly, then make a descending, westward traverse through one of the Sierra's largest fields of mule ears (a larger one is crossed in Hike 46). This 40+ acre spread of large-leaved sunflowers saturates our visual and olfactory senses. Characteristic of, but not limited to, slopes of volcanic soils, mule ears tend to grow in almost pure stands, leading one to suspect that their aromatic leaves produce substances that reach the topsoil and prevent the germination or growth of competing wildflowers. This phenomenon has been observed in other plants—particularly in aromatic ones—and it is interesting to note that where there are plants associated with mule ears, they are usually sage-brush, coyote mint or some other aromatic species.

After rounding a forested slope, we traverse through a second large field of mule ears and come to a junction, near a shallow gully, with a trail that makes a short ascent before descending along the ridgecrest and down into Picayune Valley (see Hike 42). Beyond the junction, we descend through a red-fir forest to an open, sometimes wet cove below an impressive array of deep, vertical grooves that striate a huge cliff of volcanic deposits above us. Were this deeply grooved rock more solid and closer to the trailhead, it would attract rock climbers. Leav-ing the cove, we follow our blazed path past red firs, then scramble up as it climbs steeply toward a ridge. The firs on this shaded ascent allow snow patches to remain as long as late July. Because the trail is composed of volcanic

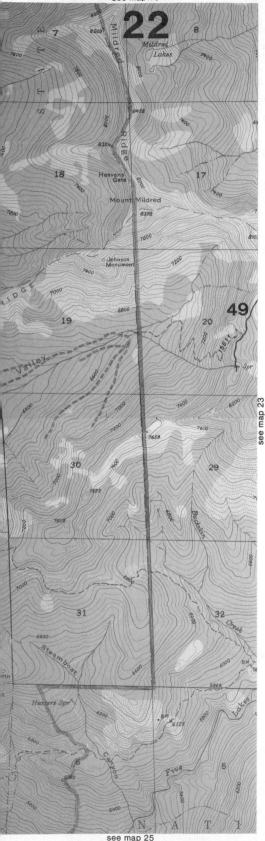

rubble, it can be slippery, so watch your footing up to the ridge and beyond.

Struggling up the ridge of blocky volcanic rock, we pass some grotesque formations before the trail eases its ascent and reaches an east-west saddle from which we can gaze down through Picayune Valley. Bordered by brown metamorphic rocks on its west slope and light-gray granitic rocks on its east slope, this valley sits deep beneath the dark-gray andesite flows that cap the two ridges above its slopes (see Hike 42 for a geologic interpretation). From this viewpoint we climb southwest through a forest of hemlock and pine to a long north-south saddle. From it we can see—due west of us—Johnson Monument, which is a large, isolated, severely overhanging volcanic block atop a narrow pedestal. In the northeast, Mt. Rose again projects its broad summit above the Five Lakes basin gap.

To reach Johnson Monument, Mt. Mildred or the Mildred Lakes, cross-country explorers should leave the trail at the north end of the long saddle, head northwest across flat-topped summit 8109, then descend, steeply at first, to a saddle separating Picayune Valley, to the north, from Grayhorse Valley, to the southwest. If you're curious as to how tall the Johnson Monument actually is, then contour almost a mile across brushy, rubbly slopes and see for yourself (the author judged it at about 100 feet). Your saddle offers a view southwest down heavily logged Grayhorse Valley, a hanging valley that obscures a view of Hell Hole Reservoir, about 1800 feet below it. To get a glimpse of that reservoir, you'll have to climb to the summit of Mt. Mildred.

Only peak baggers can justify this 650-foot climb. Others climb just a bit, then leave the crest for a traverse northwest to the base of steep slopes beneath Heavens Gate, which is the saddle immediately north of Mt. Mildred. A scramble up to the saddle will earn you a view of French Meadows Reservoir. By keeping just below the base of steep slopes, you can reach Mildred Lakes in about a ¾-mile traverse north. The middle lake is deep enough for a brisk swim, while the north and south lakes are mere ponds. Camping space is very limited, but the isolation of these lakes does offer you a true wilderness feeling.

Most of this hike's travelers won't take the side trip just described. They continue south on the long saddle with a view of the Johnson Monument and reach a trail fork. To the right a trail descends ⅓ mile southwest to a junction, from which our Grayhorse Valley-Shanks Cove

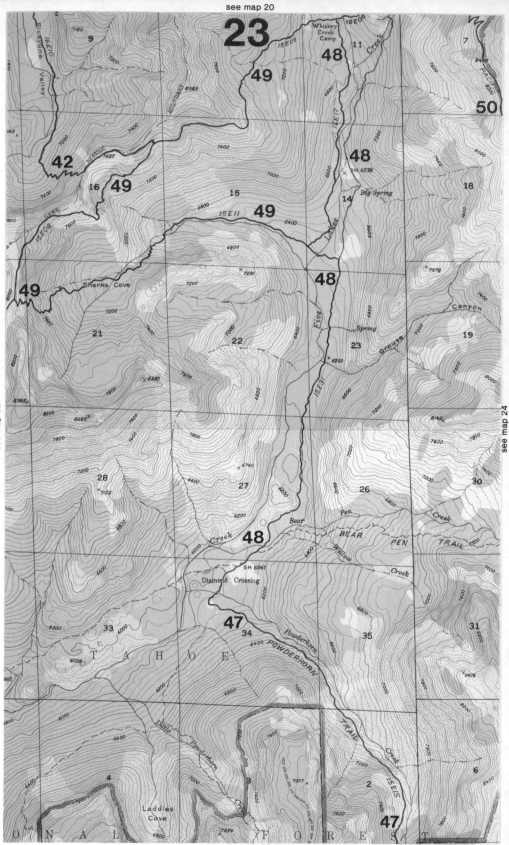

see map 22

see map 24

see map 21

**24**

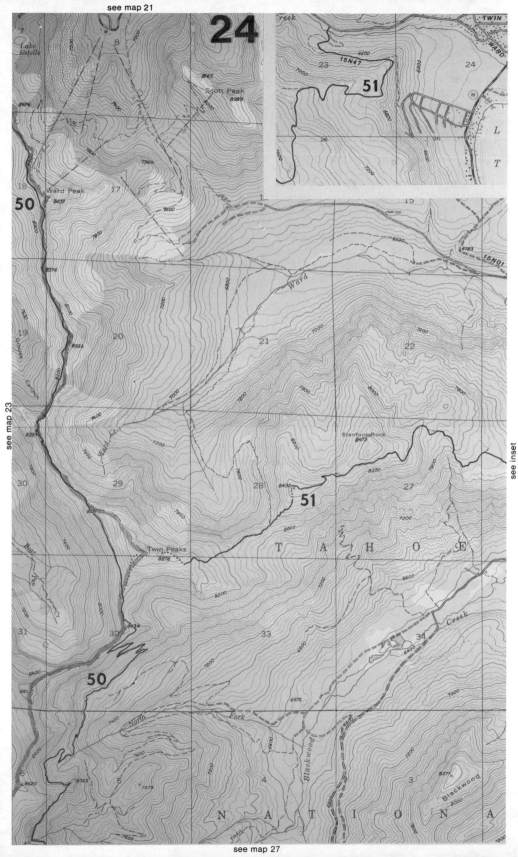

see map 23

see inset

see map 27

Trail 15E11, heading down a shallow gully, switchbacks down to its trailhead at a bend in a logging road. (To drive to this trailhead, leave Road 96 about ¾ mile east of the junction by French Meadow Reservoir's dam. Take winding Road 48 up to Chipmunk Ridge, then briefly down into South Fork Long Canyon. Just past its creek, about 4½ miles from Road 96 and about 2½ miles before a junction with a road to Hell Hole Reservoir, leave Road 48 for a 6-mile jaunt to the trailhead.) From the trail junction a cattlemen's trail traverses ¼ mile south to a verdant, spring-fed gully, and 60 yards past it is an isolated campsite, beneath mountain hemlocks, in a miniature hanging valley.

From the south end of the long saddle, 3.4 miles along the hike's basic loop, we branch left and make a switchbacking descent east toward Shanks Cove. When we arrive at this almost level cove, which stands apart from most others in the wilderness in that it is completely forested, we cross a rhapsodic creek, then parallel its

cascading course over a winding path down metamorphic bedrock. Where the gradient decreases, we recross the creek, ⅔ mile downstream, and parallel its trout-inhabited waters east through lodgepole forest down to a flat where we meet Five Lakes Creek's west-side trail (Hike 48).

With 2.0 miles remaining, we turn left to complete our loop. We first wind northeast up to a junction, 0.6 mile into our climb, from where a trail continuing right diagonals across nearby Five Lakes Creek over to an unmaintained east-side trail, which is an optional, although 0.6-mile longer, route back to Whiskey Creek Camp. Branching left, we first climb gently, then gear down for a moderate ascent up the crest of a lateral moraine. This we briefly leave to head over to a small meadow by the union of Whiskey and Five Lakes creeks. We then return to the moraine's crest, now quite indistinguishable, and climb ¼ mile to top the moraine at the outskirts of Whiskey Creek Camp. Welcome home.

# 50  Pacific Crest Trail, north to Twin Peaks and beyond

**Distances**  4.9 miles to south ridge of Twin Peaks, 5.3 miles to west summit, 11.8 miles to Five Lakes Trail, 14.4 miles to Five Lakes trailhead (0.4 mile less if you don't visit west summit).

**Low/High Elevations**  7640′ at start / 8878′

**Classification**  Moderate

**Season**  Early July through mid-October

**Maps**  21, 20, 23 and 24.

**Trailhead**  Same as the Hike 46 trailhead.

**Introduction**  Twin Peaks provide good views of Lake Tahoe, and the easiest way to their summits is from Barker Pass, north along the Pacific Crest Trail. Most of the route to the south ridge of the peaks is viewless, so if you want additional views, you can continue north beyond the peaks. That stretch of the Pacific Crest Trail has almost continual, inspiring views. Then you can head northeast up to Five Lakes for a refreshing swim and follow it with an easy downhill hike to the Hike 46 trailhead. A car shuttle is required.

**The Pacific Crest Trail traverses southwest across open slopes toward Twin Peaks**

**Description** From where the Pacific Crest Trail crosses Road 15N03 (F.R. 3) and an adjacent jeep road, we start west, up the southern slopes of Barker Peak, and have views of past and present logging operations in and around the Barker Creek basin, below us. In a short while we top a ridge and view Lake Tahoe to the east and two small volcanic buttes, our immediate goal, to the north. Traversing toward them, we have views southeast, of Barker Peak and, above and left of it, a ridge sweeping up to Ellis Peak. Both are part of the same series of andesitic lava flows. When we reach the two buttes, our southeast panorama now contains metamorphic Dicks Peak, 14 miles away, standing on the skyline above Barker Peak. Our two blocky trailside buttes are climbable, although the author climbed the closer one unroped only with some trepidation. Its twin is an easier scramble, and it offers the hiker additional Tahoe views. Rock climbers, armed with ropes and assorted gear, will find its 280-foot, nearly vertical east face exceptionally challenging.

Leaving the buttes and concomitant views, we descend into a shady forest of mountain hemlock, western white pine and, soon, red fir. Past seasonal springs we reach a nearly level camping area along the headwaters of North Fork Blackwood Creek. Onward, we descend for another ½ mile and then, 3 miles from our trailhead, start a ½-mile traverse north. Having lost about 400 feet of elevation since we left the buttes, we now have to make it up, which we do on a series of switchback legs of varying gradients, almost to the Sierra crest. Just about every hiker will resent this drop and gain (except those camping by the creek), but there is method to the trail's "madness." We round a crest knoll, point 8434, and about 100 yards later, on the north side of an even smaller knoll, see why the trail goes where it does. To the southwest is a knife-edge lava ridgecrest, across which a trail would have been difficult to build and, with snow, deadly to traverse. In this vicinity you have excellent views in almost all directions, so relax and enjoy them before you make a final push to Twin Peaks.

When you're ready to continue, head ¼ mile north along the wilderness-boundary crest to where the trail begins a gently descending traverse. Start cross-country here, initially up Twin Peaks' south ridge. The gradient increases as you approach the base of a lava knoll, and you leave the ridge, veering left (north) and climbing steeply up behind it. You then see the easy, obvious route up to the west summit of Twin Peaks.

Although you barely need to use your hands to reach the west summit, you'll need to use them a lot to reach the east summit. From the saddle separating the two summits, you can cautiously scramble directly up to that summit, though this route may be too intimidating for some folks. You can find easier routes by traversing east along the peak's south slopes. Do note that all routes up to the east summit require caution, since all are fairly steep and loose rocks abound.

Regardless of which summit you climb, the views are quite similar. You'll see, to the north-northwest, a prominent ridge with about five major summits. The central one is unmistakable Needle Peak, with Lyon Peak north of it and Granite Chief south of it. West of this ridge is subdued Mildred Ridge, while east of it is a ridge topped by Tinker Knob. Below it lies closer, spreading Ward Peak, from which the broad, severely glaciated Ward Creek canyon swoops east to Lake Tahoe. You'll note Mt. Rose rising above the lake's north end and the Freel Peak massif rising above its south end. Desolation Wilderness monopolizes the southern horizon, with Mt. Tallac readily identifiable. Finally, if you're on the west summit of Twin Peaks, you'll have a fine view west down into adjacent, deep Bear Pen Creek canyon. From the pointed east summit, which is the solidified conduit of a former volcano, this view is largely obscured by the blocky west summit. When you're ready to descend, retrace your steps if you're returning to your trailhead. If you're continuing north toward Ward Peak and Five Lakes, make a descent more or less down the northwest ridge to a saddle immediately east of a prominent knob, *8521* on Map 24. The Pacific Crest Trail is about 130 yards below the saddle.

But you don't have to climb Twin Peaks to get good views, for plenty abound along the Pacific Crest Trail north of Twin Peaks. This trail traverses below the peaks, regains the crest just beyond knob 8521, and then stays on or very close to it for the next 4 miles. Classic crest views prevail. Early on this crest traverse you see massive, columnar lava flows on the flanks of Powderhorn and Little Powderhorn canyons, to the southwest. These flows dwarf those of the more famous Devils Postpile, south of Yosemite National Park. Beyond peak 8522, which is a remnant of a lava flow perched high above Grouse Canyon, you pass beautiful, trailside hexagonal columns like those at Devils Postpile. As you head north toward Ward Peak, note how the lava flows dip away from deep Ward Creek canyon, to the east. Perhaps about 5 million years ago a sizable volcano stood above the peak, but today all we see are parts of its western flank. Our trail nearly tops Ward Peak, and just northwest of the summit the trail closely approaches the peak's maintenance road. On it you can descend to Alpine Meadows Ski Area.

Past our view of Alpine Meadows, our trail, which has been mostly on volcanic rocks since Barker Pass, completes its crest traverse on older rocks, first metamorphic and then granitic. Beyond the last crest knoll the trail switchbacks 16 times as it descends to Five Lakes Creek.

Those adept at cross-country hiking can leave the trail at the ninth switchback, traverse on a slight descent north for a minute or two, and then arrive on a crest about 100 feet above the westernmost of the Five Lakes. If you adhere to the trail, you'll meet a trail junction about 150 yards beyond Five Lakes Creek. Head about ¾ mile northwest up the trail to a junction with a short, southbound trail that descends to the westernmost lake, which offers fine swimming from mid-July through mid-August. Then follow the first part of Hike 46 in reverse down to Alpine Meadows Road.

# 51    Twin Peaks via Stanford Rock Trail

**Distances**   4.3 miles to Stanford Rock, 5.4 miles to Trail 16E07, 6.3 miles to east Twin Peak, 6.5 miles to west Twin Peak.

**Low/High Elevations**   6440'/8878'

**Classification**   Moderate

**Season**   Early July through mid-October

**Map**   24

**Trailhead**   From the "**Y**" in Tahoe City, drive 2¼ miles south on Highway 89 to William Kent Campground, then about 250 yards farther to the first road west, Twin Peaks Drive. This goes but 0.5 mile over to Ward Creek Boulevard, on which you continue west for 0.9 mile to a creekside turnout on your left—your trailhead— from which an old road drops to the nearby creek. Just 0.4 mile up the main road you'll meet Page ("Paige") Meadows Road 15N01, climbing right, and ¼ mile beyond it is Road 15N02, along which you can start an alternate route up to Twin Peaks.

**Introduction**   This is a longer route than the previous hike to Twin Peaks, and it has about twice as much elevation gain, so why take it? Well, the first 4.9 miles (the bulk of the route) is along an old road that is recommended for mountain-bike use. By using a mountain bike, you can reach the summit in under 2 hours, if you're in shape. But many hikers and bicyclists

prefer to go only up to Stanford Rock, which by itself is a rewarding goal. Indeed, if you're staying at William Kent Campground, you're close enough to the trailhead (1.5 miles away), that you needn't drive to the trailhead. However, the climb to both Twin Peaks and back is a hefty 16 miles, which is nevertheless not a bad dayhike for strong hikers or bicyclists.

**Description**   On an old road, now known as Trail 15N47, we immediately cross Ward Creek, then keep right at an immediate road branch. We climb briefly upslope through a logged area, then climb east at a moderate grade. Just before we cross a crest, we meet a blocked-off route—an old road—that provides access to our route from roads above Highway 89. From the crest we have views of Lake Tahoe as we traverse brushy slopes, but soon we turn west. The road climbs back up to the crest, switchbacks away from and then back to the crest, and then quickly comes to a junction. Here, about 1.8 miles from the trailhead, a minor road continues right, but we keep left, quickly curving south. We have another Tahoe view just before a meadow, then another one after it, where we approach the brink of deep Blackwood Creek canyon. Now we climb easily and shortly northwest to a junction with a minor road, then traverse shortly southwest almost to the brink of

**Lake Tahoe, viewed from Stanford Rock**

a prominent gully. From the brink, atop a lava cliff of "shaley" rock, you have a fine view up Blackwood Creek canyon toward Barker Pass.

Ahead the road is steeper, and you've got to be in good shape to bicycle farther. You climb to the gully's head, where you'll meet a steep shortcut road that eliminates a switchback. Most folks will take the slightly longer route, keeping left, and will quickly rejoin the shorter route just before once again touching the main crest. You now climb moderately-to-steeply 0.3 mile southwest, then 0.1 mile northwest, to where the gradient slackens as the road turns west-southwest. Here, virtually everyone will leave the road and continue about 250 yards west upslope, then will go an equal distance northwest across the top of an ancient lava flow to the brink of a cliff—Stanford Rock. Clockwise, you see, starting in the southwest: Twin Peaks, Ward Peak, Needle Peak and adjacent Granite Chief, Tinker Knob, the top of the Truckee River canyon, and the north half of Lake Tahoe. Stanford Rock would be a good place to practice rock climbing, were it not so far from the trailhead.

To regain the old road, just traverse southwest, keeping left and below this vicinity's highest point (which has poor, tree-blocked views). Back on the road, you descend to a nearby saddle, then make a brief climb west up to a flat-topped ridge where, at its west end, the road dies out. Here, at a fine rest stop, you have an inspiring view of Twin Peaks, just a mile away, plus a panorama of upper Ward Creek canyon. When you're ready to move onward, make an open, slightly descending cross-country traverse 0.1 mile south to where you'll reach the top of a southwest-descending crest. Following it, you'll quickly locate a footpath that winds rather steeply down it to a trail junction immediately east of a saddle.

For a shorter route back—one that doesn't entail climbing back up to Stanford Rock—you can head down Trail 16E07. This descends ⅔ mile north, then ⅓ mile southwest to gentler slopes. You then parallel, for 0.6 mile, a south tributary of Ward Creek over an increasingly steep grade, then abruptly turn northeast, away from it, in the northeast corner of Section 29. At this point you could leave the trail and descend to the nearby creek, then climb about 100 yards up to Road 15N02. Doing so avoids route-

finding problems down-canyon. If you keep to the trail, you'll again parallel the creek and will reach, in ¾ mile, a junction with an abandoned road, which immediately crosses the creek and heads up toward nearby Road 15N02—your second escape route. Ahead the trail deteriorates over the next ½ mile, the second ¼ mile being essentially cross-country. You then cross Ward Creek, its adjacent western branch, and in a few paces reach a junction with Road 15N02. On it you walk almost 1.0 mile east, to a junction with a north-starting road, east from which the road, though rough, is drivable. In 0.5 mile it ends at Ward Creek Boulevard, 4.4 miles from the route's start and ⅔ mile west of your initial trailhead.

Bound for Twin Peaks, you leave the saddle and parallel a crest west-southwest toward the summits. The crest gives way to amorphous, hemlock-clad slopes, which become steeper with elevation. You regain the crest after ⅓ mile, then have a short, steep ascent to the top of a southeast-descending ridge—a volcanic dike. Your goal, east Twin Peak, is congealed lava that formed in the throat of an ancient volcano. Lava, upwelling from below, exerted enough pressure to cause a vertical fracture in the volcano, which was intruded with lava, and much later eroded, revealing this dike.

Your trail basically ends here, in a field of mule ears by the upper end of the dike. However, the route ahead is obvious, though it should be attempted only by competent hikers/mountaineers lacking acrophobia. Others should traverse below the east summit over to the west summit. To reach the east summit, continue up through the field to the crest and follow it to the top. A cliff-edge footpath hugs the precipitous crest, and a fall from it could certainly be fatal. Therefore, don't feel compelled to take this route; you can always traverse west and then scramble up boulders and bedrock to the top. Regardless of how you ascend steep slopes to the summit, use caution, for there is plenty of potential for dislodging rocks. To reach the west peak, you can descend directly to the saddle separating the two peaks. This descent route starts out quite intimidating but quickly becomes easier. The walk up the back of the west peak is a piece of cake. Summit views from both peaks are described near the end of the previous hike.

**Lake Tahoe, view from the Rubicon Trail**

# Ch. 12 Southwest Lake Tahoe Basin

**Introduction**  Lying between Lake Tahoe and Desolation Wilderness is a stretch of Highway 89 terrain, some in private hands, but the rest in Sugar Pine Point, D.L. Bliss and Emerald Bay state parks and in the USFS Lake Tahoe Basin Management Unit's Fallen Leaf Lake recreation area. These public lands are immensely popular during summer, as any would-be camper in search of a campsite can tell you. If you are lucky enough to procure a site, you can spend some time relaxing in or hiking through this area. In winter this area is particularly popular with cross-country skiers.

Sugar Pine Point State Park, the northernmost park, has a fine Lake Tahoe beach along the park's east-side day-use area. Starting from the park's campground, west of Highway 89, is this chapter's first route, Hike 52, which is easily the longest, taking you 7½ miles up to Lost Lake. You'll find swimming at this lake considerably warmer than down at Lake Tahoe, and certainly far less crowded.

D.L. Bliss State Park is very popular, for from its campsites you can walk down to its two beaches: Lester Beach and Calawee Cove Beach. From Calawee Cove, Hike 53 heads south past several miles of shoreline, staying high above Lake Tahoe until it approaches Emerald Point, the mouth of Emerald Bay. Trail users can try rather frigid swimming around here in Lake Tahoe, or swim in its appendage, Emerald Bay, which is usually several degrees warmer.

Emerald Bay State Park, which shares a boundary with D.L. Bliss State Park, also offers a beach route, Hike 54, down to Vikingsholm, at the head of Emerald Bay. Because this route is short, it is very popular, as you can judge from its often overflowing trailhead parking lot. The trail is short enough for you to carry air mattresses, inflatable rafts and beach chairs.

Hike 55, to Cascade Creek Falls, starts immediately south of Emerald Bay State Park. You won't reach a beach, but you'll reach a scenic viewpoint, which is a good spot for a picnic.

East from the Cascade Lake environs lie Lake Tahoe's south-shore beaches: Baldwin, Kiva and Pope. Just south of these lies Fallen Leaf Lake, which is separated from Lake Tahoe by a few low glacial moraines. During some earlier times, this lake was, like Emerald Bay, an appendage of Lake Tahoe. Today, Fallen Leaf Lake nudges out Donner Lake as the Sierra Nevada's second largest *natural* lake. The largest, of course, is Lake Tahoe. The chapter's remaining routes, Hikes 56-58, offer hiking suggestions in this Fallen Leaf Lake area. Most folks, however, will probably spend time relaxing at Tahoe's beaches or boating in either Tahoe or Fallen Leaf.

# 52   General Creek Trail to Duck and Lost Lakes

**Distances**   3.5 miles to Lily Pond, 5.3 miles to uppermost General Creek crossing, 7.3 miles to Duck Lake, 7.5 miles to Lost Lake.

**Low/High Elevations**   6290'/7700'

**Classification**   Easy along creek, moderate to lakes.

**Season**   June through October for creek, mid-July through mid-October for lakes.

**Map**   28

**Trailhead**   From where Highway 50 leaves Highway 89 in South Lake Tahoe, drive 18¼ miles north on 89 to the entrance to General Creek Campground. If you're coming from Tahoe City, drive 9⅓ miles south on 89 to the entrance. Your trail starts from a picnic-area parking lot, which is just east (left) of the campground's entrance station.

**Introduction**   In Sugar Pine Point State Park, lower General Creek is flanked by two trails, giving fishermen many access points to the creek, which is stocked with rainbow, brown and brook trout. Naturalists and hiking addicts may appreciate the trail up to Lily Pond or upper General Creek, but most hikers will not. Backpackers, however, will certainly like Lost Lake, which is one of the Tahoe Sierra's warmer lakes. It even comes with a huge granite slab on which you can sunbathe.

**Description**   From the far (east) end of the picnic area's parking lot you go but a few yards, then branch right (south), departing from an eastbound bike path. Your trail, skirting the perimeter of giant General Creek Campground, soon turns west and stays along the rim of a minor gorge cut by the creek. We pass campsites on our right and trails down to the creek on our left, then leave the rim for a quick junction with a spur trail from campsite 150. If you happen to be camping at or near this site and begin your hike from it, then you can subtract 1.1 miles from all of the above distances.

Now on a closed road we strike a level ¼ mile southwest to a junction with a second closed road, and are confronted with a choice of two equally long routes to upper General Creek, Duck Lake and Lost Lake. The north-bank route is shadier and wetter, and before mid-August can have quite a mosquito problem. However, its vegetation is more diversified, and this route is the shortest way in to Lily Pond.

If you take the north-bank route, you'll hike ¾ mile along your closed road, passing midway along this stretch a glade with ferns and thimble-berries. Just before reaching General Creek, the road dies out in a lupine field, and a trail takes its place. This trail, becoming narrow, rocky and quite winding, goes a shady mile southwest to a junction immediately past a gully. From it you can climb an even poorer trail (at least in 1983) to the south shore of Lily Pond, which, for all but diehard naturalists, is not worth the effort. The terrain is boggy and the mosquitoes ubiquitous. This shallow pond, which tends to dry up in late summer, does indeed nurture Indian pond lilies, and it also supports a healthy crop of tall bul-rushes. Like all of the park's species, these two plants are protected, although Indians formerly ate both. The bulrush in particular was highly desirable. One could eat the green shoots raw, or wait until autumn and make flour from the plant's roots. Its seeds, too, could be crushed and eaten. Furthermore, the stalks were useful for weaving bed mats and similar articles. From the junction with the Lily Pond spur trail the north-bank route turns southeast and winds 100 yards to the south-bank route, the junction lying along the fringe of an aspen grove.

The south-bank route, mostly a road, begins by first crossing General Creek. Immediately downstream from this wet ford you'll find a foot-bridge, so that hikers can keep their feet dry. You then quickly reach a road which, eastward, goes ⅔ mile to the entrance to the park's day-use area. We parallel the usually unseen creek upstream, passing granitic boulders abandoned by a re-treating glacier. Soon we enter a long, thinly forested flat, which offers views of the two huge lateral moraines that border our creek valley. If the valley floor had been 250 feet lower or Lake Tahoe 250 feet higher (as it sometimes was in former times), we'd be passing through another "Emerald Bay." The views disappear after about a mile of southwest hiking as we enter a thick, shady forest and soon bridge General Creek. Beyond it the road rapidly diminishes to a foot-path, which cuts across often soggy soils, reaching the aspen-grove junction about 0.4 mile beyond the creek. (This soggy route may be replaced with a drier route in the near future.)

From this junction we head south on a poor tread, which in ¼ mile improves considerably as the trail turns westward, climbing up to drier terrain. Jeffrey pines, lupines and mule ears now line much of the trail, each species producing a pleasant, though often subtle, aroma. (Walk up to a large pine and stick your nose in a bark furrow. Smell like butterscotch? vanilla?)

Beyond the state-park boundary, we're in for an easy 1¼-mile climb through National Forest lands, which offer the first camping possibilities. We then cross General Creek immediately below a lovely triangular pool and now, briefly on private land, climb a steep, rocky, ducked route to a closed jeep road.

The jeep road, which is just within National Forest land, winds 250 yards west to General Creek and thence back onto private land. We start east, then immediately curve south, crossing the creek from Duck and Lost lakes in 0.8 mile, then recrossing it in an equal distance. About 100 yards before this second crossing, you'll spot a broad crest saddle up to the left. Experienced hikers sometimes take the fast way in to Duck and Lost lakes by leaving the Tahoe-Yosemite Trail (Hike 76) where it first crosses Meeks Creek and then climbing west to the saddle. This cross-country route cuts about 3 miles off the distance to the two lakes, but a thick, almost impenetrable band of brush frustrates some hikers. The brush is least below the south end of the saddle.

About 230 yards past your second creek crossing, you'll come to an old logging spur that drops 100 yards to lodgepole-fringed Duck Lake, which is shallow enough to wade across. The main road curves right, climbing up to a second spur road, this one dropping north 200 yards to beautiful Lost Lake. Although logging

**Lost Lake, view from its peninsula**

is very evident along the main road to these two lakes, a swath of trees ringing each lake was wisely spared the axe. You'll find a large campsite by Lost Lake's knobby south-shore peninsula and more-secluded ones along the path that circles this fine swimming lake.

# 53    Rubicon Trail to Emerald Bay

**Distances**   3.1 miles to Emerald Point, 3.6 miles to boaters' campground, 4.4 miles to Vikingsholm.

**Low/High Elevations**   6230'/6580'

**Classification**   Moderate

**Season**   Late May through mid-September

**Map**   32

**Trailhead**   From where Highway 50 leaves Highway 89 in South Lake Tahoe, drive 11 miles north on 89 to the entrance to D.L. Bliss State Park. If you're coming from Tahoe City, drive 16½ miles south on 89. Drive down to the

park road's end, 2.4 miles down from Highway 89. Halfway down this road, just 0.2 mile past the entrance station, a 100-yard path heads east from a small parking area. This is an alternative trailhead.

**Introduction**   Lester and Calawee Cove beaches are the prime attractions for the hundreds of campers who nightly crowd the park's campground complex. A few campers may visit "balancing rock" along the park's short nature trail, and even fewer hike the Rubicon Trail south to either Emerald Point or to Emerald Bay's Vikingsholm beach. Secluded shorelines await those who are willing to take this scenic trail.

**Description**  A 150-yard, almost level walk from Calawee Cove along the Rubicon Trail takes the hiker to the back side of Rubicon Point. Here you'll see several use trails descending east to Tahoe's shore. One of them descends to the base of Rubicon Point, from which bathers can dive into the lake's chilly water. The lake's shoreline water warms to its maximum in late summer, getting into the low 60s by mid-September, just when the state park is about to shut down. In late May, when the park usually opens, a wet suit is a must. Granitic Rubicon Point has climbing routes that attract rock climbers, but better climbing is found ¼ mile along the trail on the rocks below the lighthouse.

Climbing toward that structure, we leave the back side of Rubicon Point as we ascend shady, steepening slopes. Fortunately, a protective railing is present on the steeper slopes, for a slip here could easily be fatal. Just before the trail turns briefly west, you'll spy the old lighthouse, a small wooden structure resembling an outhouse, perched high above the trail. Where the trail bends west, you have dramatic views from atop a precipitous point just east of the trail. The east face of this point plus the nearby overhanging pinnacles collectively offer tough challenges for roped rock climbers. From its back side the point is a safe, easy climb, and you can gaze into Tahoe's deep, deep-blue depths. In 1970 you could see objects clearly as much as 120 feet down, but by 1983 this figure was cut by a third. If this trend continues, you may be able to see only 40 feet down by the turn of the century.

Climbing briefly west, our route passes some trailside pinnacles and immediately meets a spur trail that climbs steeply to the lighthouse. At one time the lighthouse must have commanded quite a view, but today tall conifers prevent such a view, and the stiff hike to this vandalized, windowless structure is bound to be disappointing.

We now climb gently south, heading toward usually unseen Mt. Tallac, the most prominent peak above Tahoe's southwest shore. We see it, and most of Lake Tahoe, from a large trailside boulder found where the trail turns from south to southwest. Continuing onward, we reach the tread of an old road after only a couple of minutes of easy walking. The old road—now a broad path—goes 100 yards west to the park's main road, where you'll find a small parking area. From that alternative trailhead the lighthouse is ⅔ mile away, whereas it is only ⅓ mile from the Rubicon trailhead.

The Rubicon Trail continues from the old road, briefly climbing through a dense forest of relatively young white firs. The firs are so closely packed that little grows beneath them, and here one sees dead remains of many huckleberry oaks that once thrived when sunlight was more abundant. In this viewless, shady forest we start a one-mile descent to Tahoe's shoreline. About ⅓ mile down it you'll notice a fairly recent burn, on your right, where a white-fir forest has been replaced by tobacco brush. Given time, huckleberry oaks will replace the tobacco brush, which will then be overshadowed by light-blocking conifers, leading once again to a shady forest.

A pair of switchbacks marks the approaching end of our descent, and just past them we meet the first of several use trails that descend to the bouldery shoreline. Here, 2 miles from the trailhead, you have your first access to Lake Tahoe since Rubicon Point. In the next ¼ mile you pass about half a dozen access trails, then climb briefly to a rhapsodic, spring-fed creeklet, the only lasting trailside flow between our trailhead and Emerald Bay. A short, moderate climb takes us to a point from which we can gaze down into the intensely blue lake. With brief switchbacks the trail drops from the point, almost touches the shoreline, and climbs a low rise to tiny, tranquil Bonnie Bay, ideal for swimming (if indeed the lake's cold water can ever be considered ideal).

**Bonnie Bay**

From the shallow entrance to Emerald Bay the 1955 rockslide stands out well on the flank of north Maggies Peak

**The Vikingsholm**

About 150 yards southeast from the bay, the trail forks. The main branch—termed the Bypass Trail—climbs over a low terminal moraine, first south and then southwest, to reach the northwest corner of Emerald Bay in just over ¼ mile. A less-used, sometimes vague tread starts east to a small cove, then parallels Tahoe's shore ⅓ mile over to Emerald Point, from where it parallels the bay's north shore ½ mile over to the main trail. The mouth of Emerald Bay is extremely shallow, so much so that when Lake Tahoe reaches its lowest level, usually in mid-September, one can boulder-hop halfway across the bay's mouth, getting a spectacular view up-bay of the rugged glaciated scenery. Had the last glacier occupying Emerald Bay left just a bit more debris, we'd see "Emerald Lake," like similar Cascade and Fallen Leaf lakes south of it. Emerald Point is a good vantage spot from which to study the two enormous moraines that flank the bay. These are deposits left by glaciers of the last two, and perhaps three, ice episodes. Above the bay's far end is a huge scar—the results of a December 26, 1955, rockslide that was triggered by the construction of Highway 89 across a steep, potentially unstable slope.

Where the Emerald Point trail rejoins the Bypass Trail, the bay is easily accessible, and the shallow water is fine for late-summer swimming. Now hiking southwest on the Rubicon Trail, we walk along the shoreline for 0.2 mile to an enormous, decapitated white fir that "sprouts" a young fir from a massive, horizontal branch. Along a short "avenue of the giants" we climb past notable representatives of white fir, Jeffrey pine, incense-cedar and sugar pine. On a slope carpeted with bracken ferns our trail levels and

we pass some of the tallest willows to be found in the Sierra Nevada. You'll recognize these 40-foot-high Scouler willows by their pale gray, aspen-like bark.

Leaving the willows behind, we descend 100 yards to an old road, cross it, and immediately reach the shore of Emerald Bay. About 3½ miles from our trailhead, we skirt along the fringe of the Emerald Bay boaters' campground, reaching its public pier in 150 yards. This spacious campground is also open to hikers. Our trail continues to hug the shoreline, departing briefly from it to climb behind Parson Rock, about ½ mile past the public pier. A use trail goes out to Parson Rock, giving the avid photographer one of the best views of Emerald Bay. Swimmers, usually walking northwest from the Vikingsholm beach ¼ mile away, find Parson Rock a nice hunk of granite to dive from. You can expect the water temperature to be about 65° or less—usually less. Past Parson Rock the shoreline trail heads over to popular Vikingsholm beach, described in Hike 54.

# 54     Vikingsholm Trail to Emerald Bay

**Distances**   0.8 mile to Emerald Bay, west shore, 0.9 mile to Vikingsholm, 1.1 miles to Eagle Falls

**Low/High Elevations**   6230'/6630'

**Classification**   Easy

**Season**   Late May through mid-September

**Map**   32

**Trailhead**   From where Highway 50 leaves Highway 89 in South Lake Tahoe, drive 9 miles north on 89 to a large parking area, on your right. This area is just ¼ mile past the Eagle Falls Picnic Area parking-lot entrance. Coming from Tahoe City, drive 18½ miles south on 89. Lock your car, for thefts are all too common here.

**Introduction**   Lake Tahoe beaches attract throngs of sunbathers, and the beach on the west shore of Emerald Bay is no exception. However, because it is the only major Tahoe beach you have to hike to, it is somewhat less congested than other public beaches. Limited trailhead parking, which is usually overflowing on summer weekends, also restricts the number of Emerald Bay visitors. Most Tahoe visitors would agree that this bay is the most scenic stretch of shoreline to be found along all of mammoth Lake Tahoe.

**Description**   The route is simple—you follow a closed road down to Emerald Bay. Near the start of this road you can walk out to some nearby rocks and study all of Emerald Bay as well as Eagle Falls and much of the deep canyon southwest above you. Huge glaciers repeatedly descended this canyon, scooping out the bay and leaving towering piles of debris—lateral moraines—behind when they melted. The glaciers were at least as tall as the moraines they left, and therefore may have been close to 1000 feet thick. Glacier-resistant Fannette Island captivates most people's attention, for this hunk of

bedrock pokes out of Emerald Bay like some Pacific volcano. Volcano it is not, though its granitic rock does resemble Lake Tahoe's volcanic rocks in chemical composition.

Before making your 400-foot descent to Emerald Bay, be sure to leave your pets behind—and not in the car where they might expire in the hot summer heat. The closed road drops ⅔ mile to a paved road, just beyond which you'll meet the first of two paths dropping to nearby Emerald Bay. If you stay on the closed road 200 yards past the second path, you'll arrive at the back side of Vikingsholm. Here, at its back side, two paths start west, quickly merging for a 300-yard climb to an Eagle Falls viewpoint. The cool, lush vegetation behind Vikingsholm gives way to brush-covered slabs moments before you reach Eagle Falls.

Eagle Falls are roaring when Emerald Bay State Park opens in late May, and they continue to do so well into July. Swimmers will find the bay's water chilly until early August, when it climbs into the low 60s, where it stays till mid-September, when the park generally closes. Perhaps the two weeks after Labor Day are best, for the crowds have diminished and Lake Tahoe has dropped by several feet. This drop creates a sandy beach along the Vikingsholm area that is not enjoyed by midsummer visitors. In September, however, you may not get to visit Vikingsholm unless you're there on a weekend. It is usually open daily during the height of summer tourism, from July 1 through Labor Day, and the small fee for the guided tour is well worth the price.

The Vikingsholm area is for day-use only. However, about ¾ mile northeast of it is a camp open to boaters and also to hikers. You reach it by the shoreline Rubicon Trail, which is described, north to south, in Hike 53.

# 55     Cascade Creek Fall Trail

**Distance**   0.7 mile, one way

**Low/High Elevations**   6800'/6910'

**Classification**   Easy

**Season**   Mid-June through mid-October

**Map**   32

**Trailhead**   See the Hike 77 trailhead.

**Introduction**   Cascade Lake, which unfortunately is mostly on private land, is confined between two giant, 500-foot-high lateral moraines. You get fine views of this lake as you're switchbacking on Highway 89 up or down the lake's western moraine, and you'll see a voluminous waterfall plummeting toward the lake. This fall, like Emerald Bay's well signed Eagle Falls, is easily approached by a little-known trail. The fall and the southwest shore of Cascade Lake are on National Forest land.

**Description** From the trailhead parking area immediately above Bayview Campground, you head 110 yards southeast (left) over to a brushy crest, then 150 yards southwest along it. From the crest you now have a ½-mile footpath across steep slopes to the brink of the fall.

Because all but the start of the path is across either brushy or rocky slopes, you have almost continual views of Cascade Lake and Lake Tahoe. Your descending, brushy traverse turns into a climb up rocky slabs, upon which the trail dies out. To reach the brink of the falls is easy, but be careful as you approach it, since a slip over the brink would certainly be fatal. This spot is a fine one for a picnic, since the views rival those from the brink of Eagle Falls, above Emerald Bay, and here, you don't have the crowds. Photographers take note: don't hike before mid-morning, or else most of your shots will be into the sun.

# 56      Lake Tahoe Visitors Center Trails

**Distances** Smokey's Trail: 0.1 mile; Forest Tree Trail: 0.2 mile; Rainbow Trail: 0.6 mile; Trail of the Washoe: 0.9 mile; Lake of the Sky Trail: 1.0 mile; Tallac Historic Trail: 1.3 miles.

**Low/High Elevations** All trails lie between 6235 and 6300 feet. All but the Trail of the Washoe are essentially level.

**Classification** Very easy

**Season** Late May through late October

**Map** 32

**Trailheads** The first five trails begin at the Lake Tahoe Visitors Center, whose paved access road leaves Highway 89 only 150 yards west of the Fallen Leaf Road. This southbound road, in turn, lies 3.1 miles west of the South Lake Tahoe Y. Opposite this road is a northbound one, which quickly splits, the left fork going to a parking lot for Tallac Point visitors, the right fork going to a parking lot for Kiva Beach and Tallac Historic Trail users.

**Introduction** A plethora of foot, bike and horse trails lace the Fallen Leaf/South Shore Tahoe/Camp Richardson area. Hike 56 covers only six of these, which basically are nature trails for hikers only. If you're staying in this area for a spell, you may want to take one or more of them.

**Descriptions Smokey's Trail** This extremely short trail, starting immediately south of the Visitors Center, shows you how to set up a safe campfire. Young children may be interested in this trail. Certainly, they should learn proper campfire procedures.

**Forest Tree Trail** A broad path just east of the Visitors Center curves northwest over to adjacent Lake of the Sky Amphitheater. You go but 30 yards on it, then branch right onto the Forest Tree Trail, for a short loop through a fairly open Jeffrey-pine forest that is understoried with bitterbrush and sagebrush. The former blooms in early summer, producing a cinnamon odor. The latter blooms in late summer, but its leaves always produce a subtle odor. Squeeze one of its light-gray-green leaves and smell your fingers. The Jeffrey pine also produces an odor, which is noticeable on hot days. Stick your nose in a bark furrow and smell the tree's "butterscotch" resin, an aroma lacking in the superficially similar ponderosa pine.

**Rainbow Trail** Easily the Visitors Center's most popular route, this trail begins just past the center. It loops around a grassy, willowy marshland, which is quite a change from the nearby Jeffrey-pine forest. Midway along this popular trail is the Stream Profile Chamber, a partly sunken viewing room. Through its plate-glass

**Trout viewed from Stream Profile Chamber**

**Wildflower Plate 12. Tahoe Basin flowers.**
1 Macloskey's violet (white), 2 mountain dogbane, or Indian hemp (white to pink), 3 vari-leaved phacelia (dusty white to greenish brown), 4 narrow-leaved lotus (yellow top, white bottom), 5 gumweed (yellow), 6 meadow goldenrod (golden yellow), 7 large-flowered collomia (salmon), 8 Oregon checker (pink), 9 giant red paintbrush (rose-red).

windows you can view and photograph several
species of trout that swim in a pool fed by a
channel diverted from Taylor Creek. For best
photographic results, visit this site in mid-day,
since you'll be shooting into the sun in the early
morning and into shadow in late afternoon. A
signed shortcut path near the end of the loop trail
heads over to the Visitors Center's parking lot.

**Trail of the Washoe**   Starting from the southwest corner of the parking lot, this trail heads
south to Highway 89, crosses it, climbs briefly
southwest, then starts a loop along Taylor
Creek. Signs mention how the local Indians used
various plants. The forest along the loop is
largely one of white firs.

**Lake of the Sky Trail**   Like the Forest Tree
Trail, this one starts by the amphitheater. From
that open structure it continues north to Tallac
Point, with many Tahoe views, including one to
the west of the large lateral moraines hiding
Cascade Lake and Emerald Bay. From the point
you head ¼ mile east along Kiva Beach, then
branch right and walk south to your trailhead.
About ⅓ of the way, you'll cross a parking lot,
which also serves as a trailhead. Signs along this
trail deal with water quality, geology and wildlife.

**Tallac Historic Trail**   This route starts from
the Kiva Beach parking lot's north end, traverses
¼ mile west to the previous route, and then
heads north briefly to Kiva Beach. You then
walk ½ mile east along the beach, taking in the
Tallac Museum and wandering among some old
estates. The museum is only open for the
summer season, during which you can take a

**Fallen Leaf Lake, from the Mt. Tallac Trail**

guided tour of the estates. After exploring the
historic buildings, head back to the parking lot,
which is about 200 yards southwest from the
museum.

   Starting from the Visitors Center, you can
put together a scenic and historic 2.0-mile route.
Follow Lake of the Sky Trail north to Tallac
Point, next head east to the museum and the
estates, from the museum head southwest, cross
the Kiva parking lot and continue southwest to
your trailhead.

# 57                Fallen Leaf Lake Trails

**Distances**   Variable, but the "Moraine Trail"
   loop is 1.1 miles.
**Low/High Elevations**   6360'/6410'
**Classification**   Very easy
**Season**   Late May through late October
**Map**   32
**Trailheads**   For the Fallen Leaf Lake trail
system there are several possible trailheads,
although only two will be mentioned. From the
South Lake Tahoe **Y**, drive 3.1 miles west to
southbound Fallen Leaf Road. Take it about ½
mile to the entrance to Fallen Leaf Campground. By its entrance station you'll see a
detailed map of the campground's layout. Part

of the Fallen Leaf Lake trail system, a part
formerly known as the Moraine Trail, begins at
a small parking area opposite campsite 74 and
ends at site 85. This loop route provides
campers with lake access. Noncampers are
urged to use a trailhead ¼ mile south of the
campground's entrance on the Fallen Leaf
Road. From there a trail heads 0.4 mile west,
mostly along the campground's south edge, over
to the loop route.

**Introduction**   The Fallen Leaf Campground
and its associated trail system offer a diverse
array of trees, shrubs and wildflowers, especially the latter, of which there are dozens of

species. In the campground's main meadow, for example, you can find tasty Sierra onion growing side by side with its toxic relative, death camas. The author spent a half day in the Fallen Leaf vicinity identifying as many species as he could before having to move on to another botanical area. A small fraction of this area's flowers appears on Plate 12, while most of the others appear on Plates 1–8.

**Description**   Most campers take a loop trail, formerly known as the Moraine Trail, to reach the north shore of giant Fallen Leaf Lake; they really aren't interested in flowers. At the lake one can swim and sunbathe, though the heaviest use probably is by fishermen. They can fish from the shore or a boat, but they aren't allowed to do so from the lake's dam. From the dam's west end other trails strike north, west and south. The last route goes ½ mile to Sawmill Cove, where you'll see a huge stone fireplace. This is all that remains of a fancy home built for Anita Baldwin, who incidentally commissioned the lake's dam for her own use. She had hoped to install an electric generator to supply power to her estate.

From the dam the "Moraine Trail" traverses a shady ⅓ mile east along Fallen Leaf Lake's north shore, coming to a trail that cuts north through a gap in the lake's low moraine. This is a shortcut route back to the campground. Then, in a couple of minutes, you leave the lake view as you fork left, cut through a second gap, and walk over to nearby site 85. From the north side of the gap a horse trail curves east over to Fallen Leaf Road, to the trailhead ¼ mile south of the campground's entrance. From here another trail, one of several, heads over to the Camp Richardson horse stables.

# 58   Fallen Leaf Lake to Angora Lakes

**Distance**   1.6 miles to Upper Angora Lake
**Low/High Elevations**   6420'/7470'
**Classification**   Moderate
**Season**   Early July through mid-October
**Map**   35
**Trailheads**   From the South Lake Tahoe **Y**, where Highway 50 turns northeast toward Nevada, drive northwest 3.1 miles on Highway 89 to Fallen Leaf Road, on the left. Take it south past Fallen Leaf Campground and, 2.0 miles from the highway, reach Tahoe Mountain Road. If you're interested in the shortest route to the Angora Lakes, turn left here and follow the road 0.4 mile to a fork. Angle right and drive 1.8 miles up Angora Ridge Road to Angora Fire Lookout (great views), then 1.0 mile south to the Angora Lakes parking lot. From there the Fallen Leaf-

**Upper Angora Lake attracts summer-weekend crowds**

Angora trail to the site of Fallen Leaf Resort heads northwest over an obvious saddle just above the lot's upper end. Start your hike on a trail that begins at the south end of this lot or take the closed road that parallels the trail.

To reach the trailhead for the following route description, take Fallen Leaf Road 4.8 miles from its Highway 89 junction, just past the site of former Fallen Leaf Lodge, to where a major

**Cooling off in Upper Angora Lake**

road branches right, across the lake's inlet creek. No parking in this vicinity.

**Introduction**  If you're staying in the vicinity, for example at Stanford Sierra Camp, then this trail offers an exercise route to Upper Angora Lake. Those interested in just visiting the lake should drive to the Angora Ridge Road trailhead, which will cut their hiking distance in half. However, on summer weekends, this lot is overflowing, despite the relatively poor nature of the road to it, for South Lake Tahoe is itself overflowing, lapping right up to the National Forest boundary. If you want to visit Upper Angora Lake, do so on a week day, not a weekend.

**Description**  Just opposite a major road branching north toward Stanford Sierra Camp is a driveway. Your trail begins 5 yards west of it, starting south between two houses, then making a steep climb, generally southeast, through a shady forest. You pass several verdant oases of lush vegetation before you top out at a saddle, from which you descend southeast to the nearby Angora Lakes parking lot and join a crowd of people.

From the southeast end of the lot take either a closed road or use trails up to Lower Angora Lake, with private summer homes, then continue on the road to Upper Angora Lake. Here you can rent boats from Angora Lakes Resort, which also rents cabins, but these are booked *looooong* in advance. You can also buy snacks at the resort's small store, or bask at an adjacent beach. The author can't recall another Tahoe Sierra lake with such an attractive beach, which is part of the magnet that lures weekend crowds. The other part is an assortment of diving rocks, above the lake's far shore. Swimmers reach them by traversing the talus of the east shore. For super-high dives, up to 50+ feet, try the cliffs west of these, but be careful—there have been too many accidents. The Angora Lakes, and Angora Peak west of them, were named for the herds of Angora goats that were pastured nearby by Nathan Gilmore, an early stockman who discovered Glen Alpine Springs.

**An unnamed tarn lies below the northwest face of Pyramid Peak**

# Ch. 13    Desolation Wilderness, west side

**Introduction**    This book's star attraction is compact Desolation Wilderness, which is certainly northern California's most accessible wilderness It's just a 3½-hour drive from the San Francisco Bay Area, a 2-hour drive from Sacramento, and a few minutes' drive from South Lake Tahoe. This 100-square-mile roadless area stands as an island of "primitive solitude" hemmed in on all sides by civilization's demands. Logging operations press close to its western and northern borders, while South Lake Tahoe's burgeoning populace, to the east, looks to the wilderness with land-hungry eyes. On the south the wilderness is bounded by Highway 50 and its resort homes, which prevent union with the *de facto* wilderness lands south of the highway.

Compact it is. Averaging 12½ miles long by 8 miles wide, this wilderness can be traversed in any direction by a veteran hiker in a day or less. Because it is so compact and readily accessible, it is too crowded to be considered a wilderness in the strict sense of the word. Although the Wilderness Act stipulates that wilderness areas should be pristine havens for solitude, don't expect to find any unless you get off the beaten path—and this requires extra effort plus a good route-finding sense. And pristine it's not: dozens of lakes have low dams, several hundred cattle invade the west side in late summer, and too often visitors leave visible traces of their presence. Although the Forest Service limits the number of backpackers to 700 per day, they place no limit on the number of day hikers. Wilderness permits are required for both types of visitors, and those caught without them are usually cited (*see Chapter 3's section on Wilderness Permits*). With all these visitors treading the trails and splashing or fishing in the lakes, Desolation Wilderness is neither desolate nor wild; rather, it's best viewed as a mountain playland, an extension of the Lake Tahoe recreation scene.

And what attracts hikers to this readily accessible, triple-crested wilderness? Its Crystal Range, which is the prominent, granitic, light-gray crest you see when driving east up Highway 50, averages only 9500 feet in elevation, and the two crests east of it are even lower—hardly a match for central California's High Sierra. But where else can you find 130 lakes, about 90 of them named, packed into 100 square miles of mountain scenery?

To describe the whole wilderness and the trails leading into it would make a very large chapter. Consequently, the area has been divided into two parts, Chapter 13, covering trails west of the Sierra crest, and Chapter 14, covering those east of the crest. In each chapter the routes are arranged from north to south. In Chapter 13 some routes never enter the wilderness: Hikes 59, 61, 62 and 70. None of these require wilderness permits, but all are inferior to Desolation Wilderness trails in terms of scenery.

# 59    Loon Lake to Bugle and McKinstry Lakes

**Distances**   3.8 miles to Bugle Lake, 4.8 miles to McKinstry Lake, 11.2 miles for total trip to both.

**Low/High Elevations**   6150'/7060'

**Classification**   Moderate

**Season**   Late June through mid-October

**Maps**   26 and 25.

**Trailhead**   See the Hike 60 trailhead description.

**Introduction**   By early August both Bugle Lake and McKinstry Lake are accessible by off-road vehicles, so if you plan on a quiet, relaxing visit to these rather ordinary lakes, go before the end of July—during, unfortunately, the height of mosquito season. Cross-country side trips to Guide Peak and McKinstry Peak make the hike worthwhile, ORVs or no ORVs. And for the ultimate Tahoe Sierra wilderness experience, one can descend to the Rubicon River and follow it upstream, hiking across a virgin terrain barely tainted by the hand of man.

**Description**   Fifty yards beyond the parking area our road crosses the dam's overflow channel and becomes a ducked jeep route over large, barren, glacier-polished slabs that bear glacial striations in a west-southwest orientation—the direction the glacier flowed. The ducks guide us down to the outlet creek and into a swampy lodgepole forest, through which the jeep road remains boggy and mosquito-ridden until mid-July. In addition to finding the usual lodgepole-associated flowers, the midseason hiker will likely spot the Leichtlin's camas, a six-petaled, blue-violet tulip, whose bulbs Indians roasted to give this nourishing food a pleasant vanilla flavor.

At the edge of the forested flat our jeep road, heading north-northeast, meets the Wentworth Jeep Trail at the point where this level "trail" curves northward and starts to climb. About ½ mile west on it is the Wentworth Springs Campground, rather shoddy, and in another ½ mile are the run-down accouterments of Wentworth Springs. Rust-tainted soda springs, with their bubbling water, are seen along the roadside just beyond the east side of this desolate settlement.

From our jeep road junction we immediately start a northward climb, steep at times, up the now-almost-unusable jeep road. Jeep usage eroded the road down to the bedrock so that plenty of one- and two-foot-high steps exist,

making the route treacherous for jeeps and motorcycles but not for hikers. Just beyond a seasonal creek crossing, the gradient eases and we curve northeast up an obviously glaciated, open slope with a few junipers, across which we can look south to the Loon Lake dam. The route levels off, and we enter a lodgepole forest and soon reach a junction with another jeep road just 40 yards short of refreshing Ellis Creek.

Up this road we tread northwest, almost immediately crossing one of the creek's tributaries. By the time we come to a fork on a small ridge, 0.9 mile farther, lodgepoles become subordinate to red firs. The McKinstry Lake jeep road branches northwest up to the lake and beyond, but most folks will head up to Bugle Lake. They angle left (southwest) and climb this little used road up to a morainal saddle, then make a short descent to Bugle Lake's brushy shore. Continuing along the path, you can traverse this island-dotted lake's north shore and find several good campsites under red firs near its west end. Hikers who enjoy panoramic views can cross the lake's outlet creek, at its west end, and climb an easy, scrubby slope to a summit immediately south of the lake, from where the Loon Lake Reservoir/Wentworth Springs area unfolds before them.

Those bound for McKinstry Lake or beyond climb northwest from the Bugle Lake jeep-road junction. You quickly reach a jump-across tributary of Ellis Creek, then climb steeply up a minor ridge, only to descend its other side steeply to an open, sandy flat sandwiched between Ellis Creek and the base of granitic, conical, aptly named Guide Peak. Several suitable campsites are found along this 100-yard-long flat.

Leaving the flat, we climb an increasingly steep grade north through a forest of red fir, lodgepole and western white pine in upper Ellis Creek canyon, and then, just below a saddle ahead, veer west to a ridge crossing north of and above a second saddle. For excellent panoramas of the Rubicon River country you can hike cross-country up to the first saddle, briefly east to a higher one, and then southeast up to Guide Peak.

The jeep road now winds westward down to a boggy flat and crosses several branches of the outlet creek from McKinstry Lake, 200 yards upstream. Forty yards north of the last ford you arrive at a junction, from where you walk 300 yards west along a jeep road to adequate campsites along the northeast shore of lodgepole-fringed McKinstry Lake. This shallow lake, with a small, turfy, lodgepoled island, is certainly more liable to have mosquitoes than Bugle Lake. However, it does make a good base camp for a 1-mile, 1000-foot, cross-country ascent to the top of McKinstry Peak. Standing 3300 feet above the east end of Hell Hole Reservoir, this awe-inspiring summit is the highest point on the lip of the glaciated Rubicon River canyon. As little as 12,000 years ago the Red Cliffs, below the summit, supported hanging glaciers that fed into the huge Rubicon River glacier. This trunk glacier, reaching a length of up to 25 miles, was roughly 1000 feet thick, which was enough volume to provide roughly 3000 cubic feet of ice for every man, woman and child in the country. That's a lot of ice cubes!

From the summit you see the Tahoe Sierra's three major rock types: the Red Cliffs are metamorphic rocks, the lands to the south and east are mostly granitic rocks, and the ridges and summits to the north—in the Granite Chief area—are volcanic rocks. Note how the forest cover varies with each rock type, as does the topography, or "lay of the land."

A final hiking option is open to those taking Hike 59. Rather than walking briefly west to McKinstry Lake, you can head northeast from the previously mentioned junction. You parallel a creek, which soon curves north, then northwest, greatly increasing its gradient, as does the road. Where Hell Hole Reservoir comes into view, the jeep road narrows to become the McKinstry Trail, which makes a traverse west before curving north and dropping very steeply to a crossing of the creek you've been parallel-

ing. Along this descent, light-gray granitic rocks contrast vividly with reddish-brown metamorphics of McKinstry Peak and the Red Cliffs. The trail down to this crossing isn't too obvious, but about 100 yards before the crossing, the trail passes just 5 yards west of a huge, 5-foot-diameter Jeffrey pine—the largest tree around.

From the crossing our ducked route heads downstream about 50 yards, makes a traversing arc northeast across an open slope, and then descends to a creek. Beyond it we cross a boulder field and reach the main creek, about 1 mile from the last jeep-road junction. This creek emanates from Little McKinstry Meadow, which is perched in a glaciated, hanging valley below Guide Peak. The meadow and its environs offer the backpacker a degree of solitude seldom found anywhere in the entire Sierra Nevada. From a low crest near the meadow you have views down at the Rubicon River and Barker Creek, each incising along a major linear fracture in the granitic terrain.

Ahead, the McKinstry Trail soon becomes overgrown with brush. Expert pathfinders may be able to follow the trail all the way down to the Rubicon River, but the isolated camping down at it won't justify the hot, steep climb back up your route. However, you could hike up along the Rubicon River, reaching the Wentworth Jeep Trail in about 7 miles. Such an excursion, not done by the author, would be through what is probably the most isolated, human-free landscape in the entire Tahoe Sierra. Be forewarned that much of the Rubicon is seasonally diverted to Loon Lake, so after the snowmelt creeks have ceased flowing, the river at times can be little more than a trickle.

# 60    Loon Lake Trail to Camper Flat

**Distances**   4.1 miles to Pleasant Campground by Loon Lake, 4.5 miles to Spider Lake, 5.3 miles to Lake Winifred, 6.1 miles to Buck Island Lake, 6.7 miles to Rockbound Lake, 8.1 miles to Fox Lake, 8.2 miles to Rubicon Reservoir, 11.6 miles to AAA Camp, 13.4 miles to McConnell Lake Trail, 13.5 miles to Camper Flat, 13.7 miles to Blakely Trail to Lake Schmidell.

**Low/High Elevations**   6410'/7210'

**Classification**   Moderate

**Season**   Late June through mid-October

**Maps**   29, 26, 30 and 31

**Trailhead**   Be sure to get a wilderness permit if you plan to go to Rockbound Lake or beyond. From the Highway 49 junction in Placerville, drive 22 miles east up Highway 50 to its bridge across the South Fork American River and in 100 yards reach the Crystal Basin Recreation Area turnoff, Ice House Road, on your left. (Westbound drivers: this junction is about 27 miles west from Echo Summit.)

Your road, paved all the way to the trailhead, climbs 9 miles to Ice House Resort. Farther north, you pass the Crystal Basin Ranger Station as well as spur roads to lakes and to good, popular campgrounds. After a 13-mile winding course from the resort you reach the Loon Lake Road, branching right, which you follow 4½ miles to a **Y.** Branch right and go 0.4 mile to a parking lot, generally used by boating enthusiasts, then continue past it 0.3 mile to a second parking lot, used by swimmers and hikers alike.

Had you branched left at the **Y,** as one does to reach Hike 59's trailhead, you'd drive 3¼ miles to a junction near the end of Loon Lake's second dam. Here, you fork left and drive 0.2 mile down a road that ends in a parking area by the base of that dam.

**Introduction**  For easy hiking in Desolation Wilderness, you can't beat this route. The 13½-mile route has only minor ups and downs and, if you hike to its end, you'll gain only 800 feet in elevation. In late June and early July, when most of the Desolation Wilderness lakes are still frozen or just thawing, the seven lakes along this route provide good fishing and brisk, but enjoyable, swimming.

**Description**  From the east side of the trailhead parking lot our route, the Loon Lake Trail, immediately crosses the Loon Lake Campground road and switchbacks quickly up to a closed road. You follow this northeast for 200 yards to the trail's resumption at a point where the road begins to climb east. The trail starts north, then traverses northeast and generally parallels the lake's visible shoreline, usually about 100 yards distant. About ½ mile beyond the closed road the trail almost touches the lake, and then it climbs quickly to a gargantuan, 15-foot-high boulder perched on a trailside granitic outcrop. This is one of the largest glacier-transported boulders you'll see anywhere in the Sierra

Nevada. The smaller, "giant size" boulders nearby were also glacier transported.

Beyond these boulders the trail soon bends east-northeast for a mile-long, fir-and-pine shaded traverse past seasonal creeklets. Along this undulating stretch you'll get your first glimpse of Brown Mountain, about ½ mile east, which is a remnant of a relatively youthful basalt flow. Enormous glaciers removed most of this area's volcanic rocks, and they even topped Brown Mountain, as evidenced by the granitic rocks they left behind on its summit.

About 2½ miles from the trailhead we climb to a ridge, whose northwest extension almost divides the lake in two. Before 1967, when the new dam was completed, this ridge separated Pleasant Lake from Loon Lake. As we make an eastward descent, we can obtain good views northwest of Guide Peak's barren summit looming above the Pleasant Lake lobe, and views east toward a saddle, between two unnamed peaks, in which lies Hidden Lake.

After an eastward traverse toward that saddle, we momentarily turn south into a gully to cross its creek, then turn north and gradually descend to a closed road that terminates at the east arm of Loon Lake. We make a short climb north up the road to a roadcut blasted out of bedrock, exposing a thick, light-colored vein, or dike. From it we can look southwest down the lake to its dam and the hills beyond. At the shoreline below us is a cove along which are some campsites used by boaters. In ¼ mile our road reaches a gully and begins a moderate climb west. Here a sign indicates a 0.4-mile-long spur trail to Pleasant Campground. Just before

**Pyramidal Guide Peak stands above Loon Lake's north lobe**

one reaches the actual campground, one has to leave the gully and cross northwest over a low ridge. Boaters are the main users of this campground, which is complete with tables, stoves and an outhouse.

On the closed road, hikers continuing onward first climb northwest to a ridge, then follow it east up to a broad saddle, exchanging views of the Loon Lake terrain for those of the gentle Sierra crest. Northeast below us we see a ducked route down to a seasonal lily-pad pond not far below. By heading east from its shoreline, you would reach, in about 200 yards, fair-to-good campsites on the westernmost arm of sprawling Spider Lake. Just ¼ mile farther along the road we reach another ducked route, which leads northeast down to now-visible Spider Lake, arriving at a fair campsite above its shallow south arm. This second of several routes to Spider Lake begins just as you reach a long, straight stretch of road. Moments before reaching this vicinity, you could have followed a ducked route southwest ½ mile up to the Hidden Lake saddle—although the slope up to it is so open that you need not follow any ducked route. We now continue on our road, first gently down, then gently up to a second broad saddle, from which an easy ⅓-mile cross-country jaunt southwest takes one over a low ridge and down to secluded campsites beside tranquil Lake Winifred.

From the start of the cross-country route leaving the broad saddle, our road east is blocked, in 60 yards, by a large tree purposely felled to discourage motorized traffic. Now our feet ache as we make a long, steady, one-mile descent, crossing a seasonal, cascading creek just before reaching a trail intersection 50 yards from shallow, rocky Buck Island Lake. During most of the summer the lake's level is low and its shoreline unattractive. Little water flows out from its dammed outlet; rather, the water flows through a tunnel to slightly lower Loon Lake, which, like Rockbound and Rubicon reservoirs upstream, is part of Sacramento's hydroelectric system. After Labor Day, Loon Lake loses much of its water to reservoirs closer to the city, dropping 30-35 feet by early October.

Since camping at Buck Island Lake is more appealing to marmots than to humans, it's best to move on from the trail intersection, hiking southeast on a ¼-mile trail to a bend in a road that ascends south from nearby Buck Island Lake. Now back on the closed road, start up as it bends east to climb quickly into Desolation Wilderness and over to nearby Rockbound Lake. With the addition of a low dam, this lake has been deepened, making it appealing in early summer, before the water line drops. As your road curves above this lake, look for small campsites under sparse tree cover by its south shore.

Near the lake's inlet our sunny road dips into forest cover to quickly reach Highland Lake creek. Look for logs to cross this wide, attractive creek, then continue 300 yards east to the "new Rubicon River," up to 15 yards wide, which gushes from a tunnel outlet 150 yards upstream. Rather than wade this fast, knee-deep river, you can cross it upstream, beyond a cable-slung, water-gauge trolley. You'll see a trail crossing over the tunnel. The closed road then climbs to a saddle overlooking Fox Lake, lying 250 yards north. As you start down from the saddle, you can leave the road and make a quick, fairly easy cross-country descent to this tempting lake. On a small island—a peninsula in late summer— several lodgepoles grow beside two large, dark erratic boulders, which were left behind by the last glacier that scoured this river canyon. Glacial striations, oriented north-northwest, mark the direction of its flow.

From the saddle the road descends ¼ mile to a trail junction above the northwest lobe of Rubicon Reservoir. Here, water empties into a ¼-mile-long tunnel, diverting water away from the Rubicon River and into Rockbound Lake. Now back on trail we hike south, paralleling the west shore of shallow Rubicon Reservoir, which turns into an unattractive mud-and-boulder flat late in summer. We leave this reservoir as the trail curves east, climbs ¼ mile up to two stagnant ponds on a large bench, and then, after a momentary descent, climbs ½ mile south to a ford of wide Rubicon River, which can be torrential in early season. When the water is low enough, you can keep your feet dry by boulder-hopping about 60 yards downstream.

If you'd like to visit Lake Zitella, you can take a cross-country shortcut route up to it. Rather than ford the Rubicon, climb more-or-less south-southwest up slopes until you reach the lake's outlet creek, on your left, then take the route of least resistance up along it to the lake.

From the ford, where the northwest-flowing Rubicon turns abruptly north-northeast, you start south along low-angle exfoliation slabs and in 300 yards come to a long, shallow river pool. Just past it you nearly touch the river again, then soon curve east for a ⅓-mile climb up-river to a lodgepole flat, saturated with bracken ferns. Arcing south across the flat, the trail goes to nearby Phipps Creek, crossing it at the south end of a shallow, wide pool. Now, in a ¼-mile segment, the trail makes a brief, steep climb, then winds south to where ducks mark a 200-

yard traverse west to lodgepole-shaded "AAA Camp," perched on a bench above the Rubicon. Here the river cascades into a 10-foot-deep pool. Studying Map 30, you might notice that the Rubicon here and elsewhere is quite straight, and where it does make a major deviation, it usually does so at right angles to the canyon. The river's angular course is controlled by long fractures in the granitic bedrock called *joints*. The largest of these, the master joints, trend north-northwest, and along them the ancestral Rubicon River was able to incise a channel. The north-south leg of Phipps Creek and a similar leg in the creek one mile north of it lie along the mid part of such a master joint, this one stretching 5 miles north-northwest from Camper Flat.

With the Camper Flat area as this hike's goal, we wind southward from the AAA Camp junction. Along this undulating stretch the master joint lies about 100 yards east of the trail. About ½ mile past the junction you climb southwest to a crest saddle, then drop along a somewhat brushy gully to the nearby river. For ⅓ mile you parallel it up-canyon, noting several large, shallow pools. At a lodgepole thicket where the river bends from east to northwest, you ford it or, if you're lucky, log-cross it at a narrow constriction 25 yards down-river. In this area the trail can be hard to find due to hikers striking paths up and down the river looking for a dry crossing. If you're on the right track, which starts southeast, you'll reach the north edge of a stagnant pond in about 80 yards. Just ¼ mile past it the trail reaches the Rubicon. Following it gently up-canyon, you pass two of its large, emerald-green pools, the second one at the base of a small cascade.

## Lake Winifred

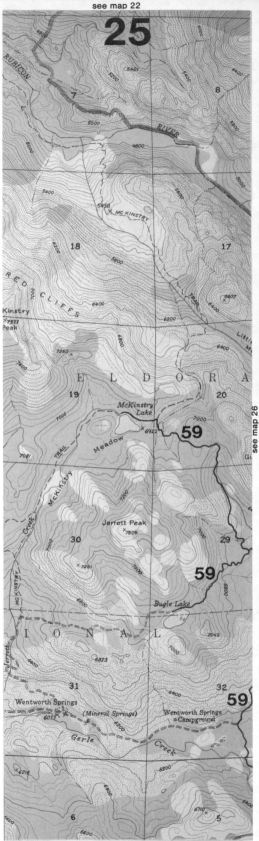

see map 22

see map 26

see map 29 inset

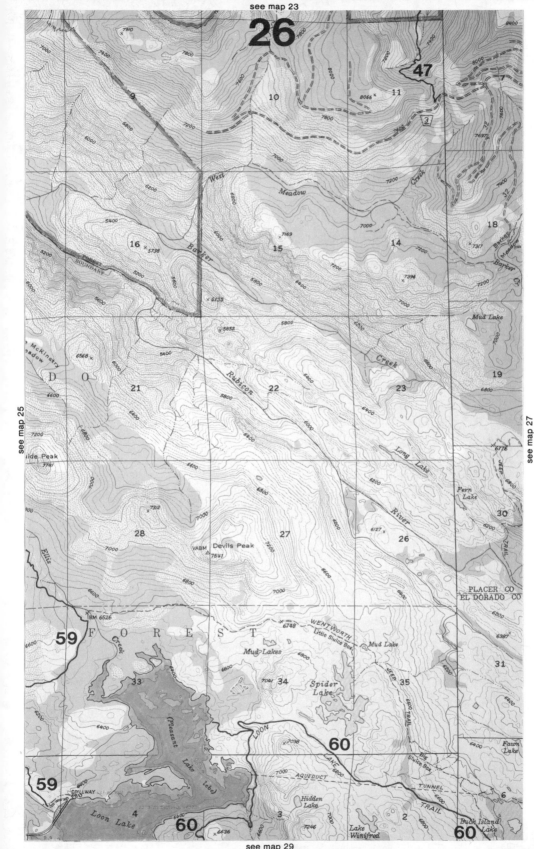

see map 25

see map 27

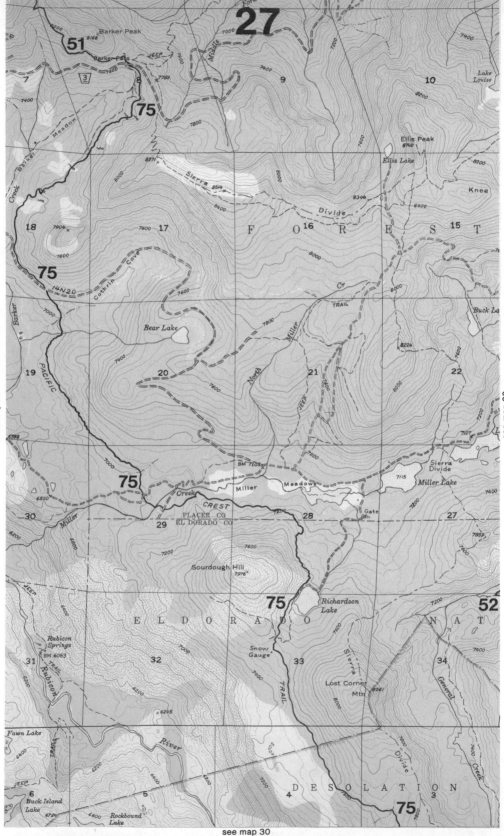

**27**

51

7

75

Barker Peak

Barker Pass

*8166*

*7782*

*3*

JEEP

Middle Fork

7000

7400

7400

9

7600

10

Lake Louise

7400

8200

Ellis Peak
*8740*

Ellis Lake

Knee

8200

7400

7600

Sierra

*8544*

Divide

8344

8400

8400

6400

75

8271

8000

8000

F    O    R    E    S    T

18    *7904* ×    7400    17

7600

16

15

7600

14N20

Cothrin Cove

75

Barker Creek Meadow

Barker

7000

7600

Cr

TRAIL

8000

Buck La

Bear Lake

7400

North

7800

Miller

8224

7600

19

PACIFIC

7400

20

7600

21

22

8000

JEEP

*6798*

7000

Sierra Divide

7127

7200

6820

BM 7103

7115

Miller Lake

7400

75

Creek

Miller

Meadows

CREST

30

Miller

6820

6200

PLACER CO
EL DORADO CO

29

28

Gate

27

*7859*

7600

7200

7600

7600

Sourdough Hill
*7976*

75

Richardson Lake

7200

52

E    L    D    O    R    A    D    O

N    A    T

7200

7400

JEEP

Rubicon Springs
BM 6063

6400

7000

32

Snow Gauge

33

Lost Corner Mtn
*8261*

34

General

7400

31

Rubicon

6200

TRAIL

7400

6200

TRAIL

Sierra

8000

6245

7200

Fawn Lake
6400

River

Divide

7600

7400

Creek

JEEP

6400

6200

6200

7200

75

6

Buck Island Lake
*6724*

5

Rockbound Lake

6400

4

D    E    S    O    L    A    T    I    O    N

3

7600

75

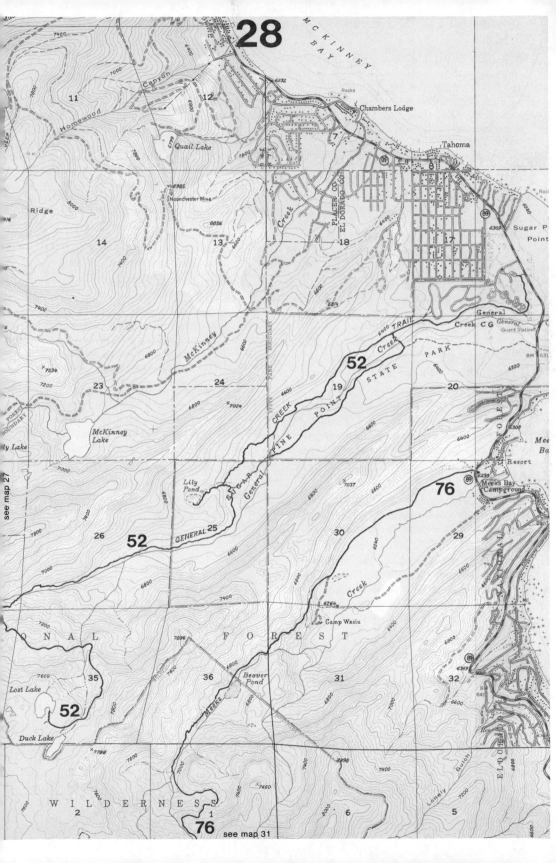

**28**

MCKINNEY BAY

Homewood

Canyon

11

12

Quail Lake

Chambers Lodge

Tahoma

7

Rocks

Noonchester Mine

Ridge

14

13

18

17

Sugar P
Point

Creek

PLACER CO
EL DORADO CO

89

General
Creek CG

General
Guard Station

McKinney

23

24

19

52

STATE

PARK

20

McKinney
Lake

see map 27

Lily
Pond

26

52

GENERAL

25

30

76

29

Meeks Bay
Campground

Meeks
Bay

Resort

89

Camp Wasiu

Creek

6264

NATIONAL

FOREST

35

36

Beaver
Pond

31

32

Lost Lake

52

Meeks

Duck Lake

WILDERNESS

2

1

6

5

76

see map 31

After a few minutes' walk past the second pool, you meet the McConnell Lake Trail, which climbs first to the 4-Q Lakes. If you've got a couple of days to spare, you might make the 4-Q, Horseshoe, McConnell, Leland, Schmidell lakes loop and perhaps even take in Lake Zitella and Highland Lake. All these lakes, which are usually mosquito-ridden and chilly before early August, are described in Hike 65.

Just 70 yards past the McConnell Lake Trail our trail meets Lake Schmidell creek. If it is too high and wide to jump across, look upstream for a log crossing. Past its east bank we slog through a damp meadow, usually very alive with vibrant wildflowers and pesky mosquitoes, then arrive at a spacious campsite at Camper Flat. Here you'll find a good Rubicon River swimming hole that begs you to linger. Shortly beyond this area you'll note a short spur trail going west a few yards to a cold, seeping, rust-stained mineral spring. In 70 more level yards you meet the Blakely Trail, this hike's end. From here you can ascend southwest up this trail to Lake Schmidell (Hike 65), south up-canyon to Lake Aloha (Hike 66), or east up to the Velma Lakes (last part of Hike 66, in reverse). This last option begins from another trail junction 100 yards south of the Blakely Trail junction. No camping is allowed along this 100-yard stretch or along a 100-yard stretch south of that junction.

# 61    Wrights Lake Trails

**Distances**  Variable, but all short
**Low/High Elevations**  6900'/7100'
**Classification**  Very easy
**Season**  Early July through mid-October
**Map**  33
**Trailhead**  See the Hike 64 trailhead description.

**Introduction**  A number of short trails, some official and some *de facto,* lie close to Wrights Lake. For campers and summer residents, these provide access to Wrights and Beauty lakes. Fishermen certainly use the trails around Wrights Lake, but they avoid barren Beauty Lake. Wildflower lovers, bird watchers and joggers all may appreciate this area's network of trails and closed roads.

**Description  Wrights Lake**  Basically, a fishermen's trail rings Wrights Lake. From the west side of the lake's dam, one can skirt north through a picnic area, then pass west-shore and north-shore summer homes before reaching a bridge across the lake's inlet. From the east side of the lake's dam, one has a more isolated shoreline route. This fishermen's trail closely hugs the shoreline and provides a number of fishing and bathing sites before reaching another cluster of summer homes. (Despite its large size, Wrights Lake is mostly less than 6 feet deep, making it one of the Tahoe Sierra's warmer lakes, excellent for swimming. Due to the shallow depth, the lake all but freezes solid each winter and must be restocked each spring to keep the crowds of fishermen happy.)

From the inlet-creek bridge you can make two triangular loops, each just over a mile long.

From the northwest side of the bridge you can head ⅓ mile north to the Twin Lakes Trail. One loop goes ⅓ mile east on this trail, leaves it, then winds almost ½ mile southeast back to the bridge. The other loop, less soggy, curves southwest along a road, whose first half is closed to motor vehicles. About 300 yards beyond a gate, you reach a north-shore road, which you take east. From its turnaround a well-used trail heads over to the bridge.

**Beauty Lake**  Five trails converge on Beauty Lake, so it receives intense use. These trails will be identified from west to east. First, Dark Lake summer residents can start up the Barrett Lake Trail, which is an old jeep road opened in midsummer to motor vehicles. In ⅓ mile, at a junction immediately before a pond, they turn right and take a path that vaults a low granitic ridge hiding Beauty Lake.

The second trail, easily the most popular, is the first part of a main route into Desolation Wilderness. Signed for Twin Lakes and Willow Flat, this trail leaves the Dark Lake road where it curves right and starts a moderate descent. For most of its ⅔-mile length to Beauty Lake this trail stays atop a broad, glaciated bedrock ridge.

The third route, up an old trail, is the steepest, though shortest, of the lot. Near Wrights Lake's north corner two roads converge, and the old trail starts less than 100 yards west on the upper road, the trail climbing up a gully.

From the north shore of Beauty Lake the main eastbound trail quickly forks into routes four and five: the Twin Lakes and Willow Flat trails. Both top a granitic ridge before descending to a moist, flat-floored valley.

# 62                Wrights Lake to Pearl Lake

**Distance** 4.7 miles, one way
**Low/High Elevations** 6860'/7350'
**Classification** Moderate
**Season** Mid-July through mid-October
**Map** 33
**Trailhead** Same as the Hike 64 trailhead.

**Introduction** Isolated from other Silver Creek lakes is lightly visited Pearl Lake, which lies at the base of geologically interesting, instructive, exfoliating granitic slabs.

**Description** Our initial trail, closed to motor vehicles, makes a brief climb to a broad, glaciated bedrock ridge and winds north atop it ½ mile to tree-ringed Beauty Lake. Large granitic boulders, left by the last major glacier in this area, form miniature islands that add charm to this peaceful lake. From here an old trail descends south-southeast ⅓ mile to summer homes by the northwest corner of Wrights Lake. After strolling 70 yards north along Beauty Lake's west shore, we leave the main trail to branch northwest over a nearby gap in a low moraine ridge, and then descend 250 easy yards west to the Barrett Lake Trail. Here we're about one mile from our trailhead but only ⅓ mile from the Barrett Lake trailhead at Dark Lake. On summer weekends as many as a dozen drivers pack their vehicles in the tiny parking area by the lake's north corner, then trudge up the steep, rutted jeep road to this junction.

Exchanging footpath for jeep road that is open to ORV's on August 1, we start north,

approach the east edge of a quiet pond in 15 yards, make a long, partly shady descent north, muddy in places, down to a seasonal creek, then angle northwest a few yards to a fair campsite, shaded by red firs and lodgepoles, on the east bank of Jones Fork Silver Creek. Where the road crosses the creek the ford can be as wide as 15 yards, but by walking upstream far enough you'll be able to cross this large creek on boulders.

Our road leaves the creekside and the forest cover, climbs northwest, and offers a view of Rockbound Pass and the adjacent Crystal Range. Soon we reach a wet meadow, rich with corn lilies, shooting stars, bistort and brodiaea. Here, in Mortimer Flat, the road splits. Since Pearl Lake is your destination, take the left fork. This Pearl Lake Jeep Trail first climbs ¾ mile through a viewless forest to a broad, equally viewless saddle, then descends north ¼ mile to the northeast edge of a meadow. Where the road turns west to start a climb, a faint path, the Red Peak (Rockbound) Stock Driveway, starts northeast for an insane, wildly fluctuating 1.5-mile climb to the Barrett Lake Trail.

Our short climb ends atop a morainal ridge rich in granitic boulders. Beyond its crest lies the private property of the Henningson Ranch, so we stay on the road and descend it to a ford of alder-choked Big Silver Creek, which drains the Pearl Lake basin. Beyond the creek we walk about 100 yards west, then follow a spur road northeast ½ mile up a moraine to Pearl Lake. Like almost every lake in the Wrights Lake area,

**Exfoliation slabs above Pearl Lake**

as well as those in adjacent Desolation Wilderness, this lake has a low dam, here built to stabilize summer streamflow and to provide a better year-round habitat for fish.

On the south shore is a fair campsite overlooking the lake's shallow waters, which in the morning peacefully reflect the somber, exfoliating slabs above the northeast shore. To surpass this show of *exfoliation,* one would have to visit Yosemite. These slabs, composed of granodiorite, are exfoliating—peeling off like onion layers—because they are out of equilibrium with the surface environment. When this rock originally cooled to a solid state, about 100 million years ago, it was buried under approximately five miles of rock, at which depth the pressure

was about 2200 atmospheres, or roughly 16 tons per square inch. The rock exposed at the earth's surface today is exposed to only *one* atmosphere of pressure, 14.7 pounds per square inch; hence the crystals in it tend to expand and break apart in this new "vacuum" they are exposed to. Because of this tendency to "unload," these rock slabs would gradually peel off even without the aid of any crustal movements to shake them or any weathering processes to etch away at them.

Although Pearl Lake's water is semistagnant, obtaining fresh water is no problem, for just to the south, below the recessional moraine that makes up the lake's natural dam, is a spring-fed creek. You need ask for nothing more.

# 63  Wrights Lake to Barrett, Lawrence and Top Lakes

**Distances**   5.9 miles to Barrett Lake, 6.3 miles to Lawrence and Lost lakes, 6.7 miles to Lake No. 5, 6.8 miles to Lake No. 9, 6.9 miles to Top Lake, 7.3 miles to Lake No. 4, 7.6 miles to Lake No. 3.

**Low/High Elevations**   6860'/8270'

**Classification**   Moderate

**Season**   Mid-July through mid-October

**Maps**   33 and 30.

**Trailhead**   Same as the Hike 64 trailhead.

**Introduction**   The Barrett Lake Trail—a jeep road—provides access to an area along the west border of Desolation Wilderness that has over a dozen lakes and ponds. This hike describes routes to eight lakes, from justifiably popular Barrett Lake to lightly visited Lake No. 9. Just above Barrett Lake is Lawrence Lake, which one old-timer called "the most beautiful lake in the whole area." Above it is Top Lake, a unique, split-level lake. And geologically interesting Lake No. 3 provides the start of a novel cross-country route into Lake Schmidell and the lakes north of it.

**Description**   The previous hike describes the first 2.6 miles to a junction in Mortimer Flat. Keeping to the Barrett Lake Trail, we head up a little canyon above the flat, curve north up to a low ridge, and then cross a trickling creeklet before reaching an open slab from which we obtain a panorama of the Crystal Range to the east and southeast. From this vantage point the huge Wrights Lake and Lyons Creek moraines

are very obvious as moraines, whereas close up, their forest cover and their minor irregularities tend to camouflage their shape. On this open slab our road divides, only to rejoin in a hundred yards, and then it climbs to a marshy, forested flat, curves east across it and turns northward up a ridge. This we eventually cross, and then climb steeply up to a saddle and the intersection of a ridgecrest trail, the Red Peak (Rockbound) Stock Driveway. Cattle are still being grazed today in Desolation Wilderness, and one of the routes by which they are led in and out is this trail. Looking gentle and safe where we see it, this driveway becomes, one mile east, a steep, potentially treacherous route.

From this ridge we make a descent, steep in places, to a logged-over meadow now being invaded by young lodgepoles. Just past the turn of the century, this plot was sold by the Barrett family to the University of California at Davis, which set up an experimental station here and tried to improve the local herds through selective breeding. From this site we climb, steeply in places, to a broad saddle. After a short, sunny, gravelly descent we reach the swift Barrett Lake outlet creek, a 5-yard boulderhop. Now we follow a gully that in places becomes a low chute, and in ¼ mile reach an enormous, flat campsite, under shady red firs, along most of the west shore of Barrett Lake. This site would hold a whole Boy Scout troop with room to spare, and its coves and diving rocks, together with its shallow rock-slab pools below the little dam would keep all the kids active and content.

**Top Lake has a naturally terraced east end**

Beyond Barrett Lake, you take the Red Peak Trail, which begins as a horse trail, first climbing steeply 0.1 mile to the wilderness boundary, then steeply up another 0.1 mile to a trail junction by the cascading Lawrence Lake outlet creek. Branching right and easing off, our trail now approaches a fair campsite near the northwest end of the waist-high Lawrence Lake dam. Cross the dam and take a footpath past a small rock island to the outlet creek of Top Lake, which announces itself 150 yards before entering the beautiful, symmetrical lake by cascading 50 feet down a glistening rock slab mantled with a coat of black fungi. To the east is the higher but less spectacular cascade of the outlet creek of Lake No. 9. A ½-mile walk up either creek will get you to isolated campsites at these lakes.

A side trip to Top Lake is particularly rewarding. Perched at the lip of a cirque, it seems to sit on top of the world, and the backpacker who sets up his camp here sees panoramic sunsets that are hard to match anywhere. The most amazing aspect of the lake, however, is its naturally terraced east end, at which the water is ponded up as much as 2 feet higher than at the west shore. Thick clumps of grass and heather are progressively invading the lake, building dikes and trapping sediments. More vegetation grows upon them and ponds up the water level.

For more lake hunting, return to the Red Peak Trail junction. If you were to contour ¼ mile southwest from it, you'd reach a bench holding shallow Lost Lake, probably the least visited of the Red Peak lakes. Keeping to the trail, climb steeply north 0.2 mile to a forested ridge, then make a short descent to a meadow in which you pass three snowmelt ponds, all on

your right. Flowing from the last of these, as well as from the soggy meadow, is a small creek we must cross before it enters Lake No. 5. This lake is a haunt of spotted sandpipers, who build their nests in the dense grass along the water's edge. If you want to camp by this serene lake, do so on the west bank, a dry, rocky moraine from which you obtain tree-framed views down the glaciated slopes to the west.

Beyond the lake we climb to a saddle, where our trail turns abruptly right. The ducked path straight ahead leads 0.2 mile northwest down to unappealing, semistagnant Lake No. 4. Our faint, ducked trail climbs north-northeast up an open, bedrock slope to a narrow ridge. Many hikers have trouble on this stretch, taking a faint, often ducked path climbing north-north*west* up the slope and into brush. The correct route goes through a shallow gap in the narrow ridge and continues 50 yards beyond it to a junction.

From here the Red Peak Trail drops northwest 1½ miles—very steeply at times—to the west edge of the *Fallen Leaf Lake* 15' quadrangle (the west edge of Map 30), crossing Lake No. 3's creek at this point. It then continues another 1½ miles down to the west boundary of Desolation Wilderness and heads west ½ mile across Eldorado National Forest land before reaching Van Vleck Ranch property—off limits to the public.

With Lake No. 3 as the last goal on this hike's agenda, we leave the Red Peak Trail just beyond the narrow ridge and hike northeast through a swampy meadow, head between a rock pile on the left and the main rock slope on the right, and curve northward up to another wet, spongy meadow through which flows the tiny outlet creek from Lake No. 3. Small though it is, this creek nevertheless supports 10-inch trout.

Across the creek we head northwest toward the base of a moraine, 30 yards west of the creek's cascade. Now it's just a short climb up to Lake No. 3, whose relative isolation from Wrights Lake rewards one with unspoiled lakeside campsites beneath a cover of mountain hemlock and lodgepole and western white pine. Those wishing to spend a few more days in the wilderness might start a cross-country hike north-northeast, climbing 500 feet to a shallow saddle in the Crystal Range. From this saddle, between Silver and Red peaks, you can descend an equal distance to the Leland Lakes, where you intersect the Hike 65 loop.

# 64 Wrights Lake to Lakes Lois and Schmidell

**Distances** 4.6 miles to Maud Lake, 5.9 miles to Rockbound Pass, 6.2 miles to Lake Doris, 7.3 miles to Lake Lois, 8.6 miles to Lake Schmidell.

**Low/High Elevations** 6960'/8530'

**Classification** Strenuous

**Season** Late July through mid-October

**Maps** 33 and 30

**Trailhead** From the Highway 49 junction in Placerville, drive 31 miles east up Highway 50 to Kyburz, your last stop for food and gas, and then, after 5 more miles, reach the Wrights Lake Road, on your left. (Westbound drivers: this junction is 13 miles west from Echo Summit.) Drive 4.1 miles up this road to an obvious spur road branching right 150 yards before Lyons Creek. For Hike 71, park here, or farther up this rutted, 0.4-mile-long spur road. For all other hikes, continue 3.9 miles up the Wrights Lake Road to a large trailhead parking area, on the right. Park in it. Just 0.2 mile past it you'll find the Wrights Lake Ranger Station, on your left, the Wrights Lake Campground road, branching right, and a west-shore road, with a picnic area, continuing ahead. To reach the trailhead, branch left (northwest) immediately past the ranger station (where you can get wilderness permits *when* the ranger is in). You'll pass an old-campground road in 140 yards and reach the obvious trailhead in another 280 yards. If you were to continue ⅓ mile farther, you would reach Dark Lake.

There are at least five *other* trailheads in the Wrights Lake area that you could start from, and each would give you a different distance to a given point. But since the Forest Service wants you to start from this particular trailhead, the mileages for Hikes 62-69 are measured from it. Keep in mind, however, that the *round-trip* distance from the parking area to this trailhead adds 0.9 mile to your hike. There is essentially no parking space at the trailhead.

**Introduction** Some visitors will want to make only a 9.2-mile day hike to Maud Lake and back. Unfortunately, when too many people linger at Maud Lake, it is likely to metamorphose to "Mud Lake." It's probably the most popular trailside lake reached from Wrights Lake. Sturdy day hikers can perspire up to Rockbound Pass for well-earned vistas before returning on their 11.8-mile route. If you go beyond the pass, you'll probably want to make your trek a backpack trip. Weekend backpackers usually venture only as far as Lakes Lois or Schmidell, leaving the more-distant lakes to those with more time (Hike 65).

**Description** Start at the main trailhead and make an easy ridge traverse to Beauty Lake. You curve around its west and north shores to a gap and, just east up from it, meet a trail fork. Keep left here and climb northeast to a nearby ridge gap, which harbors a few fine red firs and one huge Jeffrey pine. It's a shame that when this section of trail was built in the late 1970s, the trail crew didn't extend it north along the ridge. Instead, it drops ¼ mile to a junction with the old Rockbound Pass Trail. On this trail, which is also called the Willow Flat Trail, we climb—begrudgingly if one has a heavy pack—0.6 mile north to regain the ridge. Our trail crosses this ridge, then climbs along northwest-facing slopes before dropping abruptly to a junction in a small, shady flat. The Tyler Lake Trail (next route) heads east, but we head north.

Our heavily used tread immediately crosses two snow-fed, short-lived creeklets, then climbs moderately-to-steeply ½ mile north through a thinning forest to a stagnant pond atop a saddle. Now just within the wilderness, our trail makes an equally long and steep descent across brushy slabs to a boulder crossing of Jones Fork Silver Creek 1¼ miles below Maud Lake. Beyond the crossing, our route—lined with rocks—ascends a largely barren, low-angle, glacially polished slab upon which rest numerous erratic boulders left behind by the last retreating glacier. Along the massive slab's sparse fractures grow junipers, lodgepoles and other plants that can get a roothold.

We now cross a low, minor ridge, parallel it north, and enter the thicket of Willow Flat, which in addition to a dense stand of willows has plenty of bracken ferns, corn lilies and aspens. A short, bouldery, creekside ascent gets us to a shady lodgepole flat, where we jump across the creek just below its slide down a polished ramp. One might camp here, and certainly people do, but all the passing traffic would make this otherwise good site objectionable. Immediately south of it—and north of Willow Flat—is a highly fractured granodiorite knoll that is good exercise for those who enjoy short, roped climbs.

From the site we continue our shady ascent 200 yards to within several yards of the forest's abrupt north edge, where, if you look closely, you'll detect a faint, blazed and ducked lateral trail. This seldom used path springs from one brushy granite bench to the next on a ½-mile ascent west to a pine-shaded saddle. It then descends ¼ mile, quickly passing a wisp of a pond before reaching a campsite near the northeast tip of a chest-deep lakelet. Should you camp here, you can expect to have this ordinary lakelet all to yourself—and perhaps a million mosquitoes. From the lakelet the path climbs ⅔ mile to a saddle intersection with the Red Peak (Rockbound) Stock Driveway, the last 200 yards to it being quite vague. In just under ½ mile the path drops to the Barrett Lake Trail (Hike 63).

Climbing toward Maud Lake, the Rockbound Pass Trail leaves the lateral-trail junction—and forest shade—behind as it switchbacks up a barren slope, traverses northeast above the Silver Creek gorge, and then makes a short descent to a pond immediately below Maud Lake.

Campsites abound on the low, rocky benches surrounding Maud Lake. Many of them are illegally within 100 feet of the shoreline, but there are still enough legal ones to accommodate several dozen campers—the typical number of weekend backpackers. Look for fair-to-good campsites west of the trail and also above the northeast and south shores. With heavy use, the lake's water isn't as clear as it used to be. Packers have clouded the situation by making this a rest stop for their dozens of horses. Its water should be treated before drinking. Evidently one irate backpacker found the semiclear water objectionable, for someone removed the *a* in a *Maud Lake* sign, thus giving it a more

appropriate name. Swimmers who venture out in this lake's relatively warm, shallow water can attest to the muddy character of the lake's bottom.

No one forgets his first climb over Rockbound Pass. Of this steep, 900-foot climb from Maud Lake, one often hears "It was very grueling" or "I just about died." However, one retired couple, laden down with heavy backpacks, thought the climb wasn't bad at all. The ascent is psychologically defeating only because you almost always see the pass looming up before you, and because its dwarf trees make it look higher and farther away than it is.

The Rockbound Pass Trail was built around 1918, after an early heavy October snow storm of the previous year almost decimated a herd of cattle then grazing in and above Rockbound Valley. Joe Minghetti, a hired hand on the Blakely Ranch but formerly a Swiss stone mason, was commissioned by the Forest Service to build the trail so that there would be an escape route for the cattle when they had to be quickly evacuated. The trail was not to exceed 15 degrees in grade, but as the backpacker soon finds out, it does.

Our climb from Maud Lake starts out through a sloping, spring-water-saturated meadow—boggy for most of the summer—and then climbs steeply up slopes abundant in huckleberry oak, western serviceberry and wildflowers. The trail's switchbacks—short and steep—are characteristic of old, pre-recreation-trail design standards, when trails were made as steep as the traffic would allow. After the last set of switchbacks we reach a small flat with several large junipers growing on and near it. From this welcome rest spot we can absorb the view of the tarns below, Maud Lake in the middle distance and Wrights Lake beyond.

Also evident are three granitic plutons, each formed separately—almost certainly at different times—miles below the earth's surface. Each of these light-density molten masses worked its way up through existing rock until it finally cooled to form a solid mass, a pluton. On the opposite canyon wall, from north to south, the three plutons are orange, dark gray and light gray, and their respective compositions are granite, diorite-gabbro and probably granodiorite.

Beyond the junipers it is almost a stroll up to sometimes windy Rockbound Pass, with its weather-beaten dwarfed mountain hemlocks and lodgepole and whitebark pines. Snowbound through late July, our trail from this pass switchbacks northeast down toward Lake Doris, passing both red and white heather along the way.

**Fishing at trout-stocked Lake Lois**

Among the hemlocks above the north shore is a fair campsite. After briefly touching this shallow lake's east shore—painted yellow with buttercups and marsh marigolds—our trail climbs a few feet, then makes a brief descent to a signed junction, from where the Rockbound Pass Trail continues northeast down to Rockbound Valley, 1½ miles distant.

Our trail, the Blakely Trail, descends northwest, immediately crosses Lake Doris' outlet, makes a scenic traverse with panoramas to the east, passes just above one pond and then two more on a low, broad saddle, and reaches an east finger of metamorphic-rock-bound Lake Lois. Its rocky cliffs and benches of varying hues are marine sediments that were metamorphosed in part when the neighboring granitic plutons welled up and intruded them. These metasediments, about 200 million years old, are also found in Rockbound Valley, and grade upward and eastward into the slightly younger metavolcanics of the Mt. Tallac area.

Popular Lake Lois and its neighbor one mile northwest, Lake Schmidell, both bear the brunt of weekend backpackers. On each you'll find many used sites that are within 100 feet of the shore, and very few sites that are more than 100 feet away. Lake Lois' southeast corner, although only 50°F in mid-August, attracts some backpackers who like to do some brisk high diving—up to 20 or more feet—into its very deep water. Those who just like to swim will find its isolated east finger 10 degrees warmer.

Paralleling the east finger, our rocky trail winds over to the outlet creek, crosses its low dam, heads briefly west along the north shore, and then climbs to a ridge, where we meet the Red Peak (Rockbound) Stock Driveway. This old stock trail climbs 1¼ miles to a high, but shallow, gap on the Crystal Range crest. It then descends just over 2 miles—absurdly steep over one 400-foot drop—to the previously mentioned saddle where it intersects a lateral trail from Willow Flat. Past it the stock driveway traverses an easy ½ mile to an intersection with the Barrett Lake Trail (Hike 63), then oscillates wildly along a 1½-mile course to the Pearl Lake Jeep Trail (Hike 62). This occasionally very scenic route back to Wrights Lake is best left to stout-hearted mountain men (and women) who want to take "the route less traveled by."

From the Red Peak Stock Driveway junction ⅓ mile north of Lake Lois we make a fairly steep descent through an open forest, almost touching a small creek before we come to a junction not far from Lake Schmidell. To reach this lake's campsites you could hike northeast 200 yards down a trail to a pond, then 250 yards northwest up a spur to the lake's dammed outlet creek. An easier way to the campsites, which are perched on a hemlock-and-lodgepole bench above the lake's southeast shore, is to walk due north 100 yards from the junction. If you find Schmidell too crowded for your taste, you can strike out for other lakes, which are described in the next hike.

# 65     Wrights Lake to Horseshoe Lake, Lake Zitella and Highland Lake

**Distances** 9.8 miles to lower Leland Lake, 10.6 miles to McConnell Lake, 11.8 miles to Horseshoe Lake, 12.0 miles to 4-Q Lakes via Camper Flat, 12.3 miles to Lake Zitella, 13.5 miles to Highland Lake, 13.9 miles to 4-Q Lakes via McConnell Lake.

**Low/High Elevations** 6960'/8530'

**Classification** Strenuous

**Season** Late July through early October

**Maps** 33, 30 and 31

**Trailhead** Same as the Hike 64 trailhead.

**Introduction** This backpack trip is an extension of the preceding hike, offered to those who are willing to put forth the effort to visit less used lakes in one of the more remote parts of Desolation Wilderness. From Rockbound Pass onward, the trip averages about one lake per mile and gives backpackers plenty of opportunities to select a campsite. Those fortunate enough to have the time to visit every lake mentioned in this hike will log about 30 miles, and should allow at least four days to properly savor the route's many delights.

**Description** The preceding hike describes the 8.6-mile route past Maud Lake, Lake Doris and Lake Lois to Lake Schmidell. Just above Schmidell is a junction, which marks the start of a 9.6-mile loop that, clockwise, visits the Leland Lakes, McConnell Lake, Horseshoe Lake and its Highland Lake Trail junction, 4-Q Lakes, Camper Flat and Lake Schmidell. Clockwise, the first part of this loop reaches the Highland Lake Trail junction in only 3½ miles, which is certainly the shorter and the more scenic way to it. However, before describing this route, we will first describe the alternative, 6-mile, counterclockwise route to it.

This generally viewless, lightly used route first drops 200 yards to the pond below the Lake Schmidell outlet, staying on the main trail as it makes an eastward, heather-lined descent—muddy and mosquito-ridden through mid-August—to a crossing of the outlet creek. Immediately beyond this it reaches a lateral trail for those traveling to upper Rockbound Valley, Mosquito Pass and Lake Aloha (Hike 66). Beyond this junction you make an equally long, but drier, descent to a second stream crossing, then in ⅓ mile reach a junction on a bench above the Rubicon River. One hundred yards south of this junction a trail fords the Rubicon and then

climbs east to Middle Velma Lake (the route on which Hike 66 returns).

Start north along the Rubicon and in 70 yards pass a short spur trail west to a cold, rusty, seeping mineral spring. After a few minutes' winding walk north, you reach broad, level Camper Flat, where beside a good Rubicon swimming hole is an old campsite. Bearing westward through a lush meadow, you reach your last crossing of Lake Schmidell's outlet creek. Look for logs upstream on which you can cross it and reach in 70 yards the McConnell Lake Trail. Ahead, the Rubicon River Trail goes 13.4 miles to the Loon Lake trailhead (Hike 60), becoming the Loon Lake Trail midway to it.

On the McConnell Lake Trail you climb past several stagnant ponds before you see the first small lake of the 4-Q Lakes, this one about 40 yards northwest of the trail. Only ¼ mile beyond it is the second 4-Q Lake, across which you must "walk on water." Two peninsulas almost cut the lake in half, and you cross the shallow, 40-foot strait via rocks and/or logs. Beyond the lake crossing the trail curves over to the west shore of this lake, touches upon the north shore of adjacent lake number three, and then makes a brief climb to a stagnant, bush-fringed pond, where you often do have to walk on the water to follow the trail. Most hikers keep their feet dry by going around and above the pond's west edge, and then relocate the trail, which climbs a few paces west before descending southwest to the fourth lake, which is the best of these shallow lakes. When camping near any of these "4 Quiescent Lakes," treat your drinking water.

From the north end of the fourth lake the ducked route makes a moderate descent north down a joint-controlled gully and through red-fir stands, then eases its pleasant, creekside descent through alternating lodgepole-pine stands and huckleberry-oak-scrub fields. Nearing the end of this 1.4-mile descent, we find ourselves more often than not walking along glaciated granodiorite slabs. Watch carefully for ducks (trail markers). Our trail crosses the creek just 20 yards above a narrow chute you can jump across. Anywhere in this vicinity you can find rocky campsites whose hardness is more than compensated for by their isolation and by the nearby views north down Rockbound Valley.

Now climbing west, you must religiously follow the ducks if you want to minimize your effort. The faint trail climbs steeply up a slope, staying about 100-200 yards north of the outlet creek from Horseshoe Lake. The route reaches a ridge above that lake, and then you follow ducks for about 50 yards west down to the Highland Lake Trail junction, where you meet the shorter, preferred route to it.

This 3½-mile route begins at the junction above Lake Schmidell, from which you traverse southwest to a cascading creek, boulder-hop it, and make a scenic though exhausting ascent to a shallow saddle on the granodiorite ridge above the Lake Schmidell talus slopes. The two Leland Lakes quickly come into view as we make an equally steep descent north toward the upper lake. Rather than skirt this lake's grassy east shore, the trail now swings northeast a bit, dips through a boggy meadow, and then descends to the southeast corner of lower Leland Lake. Since all its lakeshore campsites are now off limits, you might look for alternative sites on tiny, grassy flats among the boulders and slabs between the two lakes.

Leaving the lower lake above us, we descend along its cheerful, frolicking outlet creek, cross it in a forested flat, and continue briefly northwest to the forest's edge. Watching for ducks—both the rock kind and in late season the live ones—we follow a faint path that arcs around the west shore of a knee-deep pond called McConnell Lake. Leaving its soggy meadow of grass and heather behind, we reach a low ridge, on which the trail becomes indistinct for a few yards among the brush, then improves as it descends an open slope northwest to the base of an imposing granodiorite wall, which should provide challenging ascents to all types of mountaineers and rock climbers. A prominent low-angle waterfall glides down the middle of this wall, and just after crossing its creek on level ground, we run into route-finding problems. Watch for ducks that mark the route up and down a low slab. Then just beyond it, where the trail climbs over another low slab to a gully with a trickling creek, pay close attention to where the trail actually crosses the creek. Beyond the creek we contour east 100 yards, descend sightly to another short traverse, this one northeast, then top a low, rocky ridge and follow four short, steep switchbacks down to an alluvial flat on which lies shallow, rock-island-speckled Horseshoe Lake. Traversing above the shore to a point just above its northeast corner, we reach a junction from which the Highland Lake Trail climbs northwest up a huckleberry-oak-filled gully. Should you choose to follow the faint trail to 4-Q Lakes, look for ducks standing out against the skyline on the ridge immediately east of you.

We climb steeply up the gully, diagonal left up more open slabs, and take a glance back at photogenic Horseshoe Lake, with the Crystal Range for a dramatic backdrop. Notice how the trees on the granitic slopes beyond the lake are concentrated along *master joints,* which are major fracture lines in this otherwise very resistant rock. Our 200-foot ascent tops out at a saddle, from which our route ahead to seductive Lake Zitella descends ¼ mile to this shallow lake's outlet creek. Just before crossing the out-

**Vegetation grows along linear master joints above Rockbound Valley**

**Red Peak (right) stands high above Horseshoe Lake**

**Icy, rockbound Highland Lake**

let, look northeast across Rockbound Valley. If the master joints above Horseshoe Lake weren't obvious to you, then you need a more impressive example. The master joints on the opposite canyon wall are unmistakably clear.

Now that you're at shallow, slightly cloudy Lake Zitella, you might wonder what's so seductive about it. Feel its water temperature; it is the warmest cirque lake—rising into the low 70s—in the entire Desolation Wilderness, and so is an excellent swimming hole, with plenty of shoreline slabs and rock islands to bask upon. Fishing isn't great, though, unless you like yellow-legged frogs, which are abundant. In between swims, climbers might want to explore the easy Class 5 climbing routes on a large, low-angle, exfoliating cliff above the lake's west shore.

Those seeking isolation can now begin an arduous route to Highland Lake. The northwest-bound trail climbing from Lake Zitella's north shore is simple enough, but from the saddle above it, the trail makes an extremely steep descent—almost an uncontrolled slide at times—down a gully. Despite its steepness, it is not very exposed and not very dangerous. This steep route exists because a cliff prevents a traverse west. At the base of the cliff our route turns west and begins to climb. At this point you can take an obvious, open, cross-country route—spread out below you—down to Rubicon Reservoir and from there either follow Hike 60 in reverse out to Loon Lake or follow it up the Rubicon River and back to Lake Schmidell.

Watch for ducks that mark our open rock-slab ascent to a crossing of Highland Lake creek at the lip of a cirque, then traverse 150 yards southwest to the northeast shore of an unnamed lakelet. From it our trail makes a winding, ducked ascent in the same direction up to a ridge 70 yards north of a tiny, photogenic lake, whose waters are constantly being aerated by several cascades splashing into it. After a momentary descent, we make a short, steep ascent to a shelf, which we follow south to icy, rockbound, rainbow-trout-stocked Highland Lake, which has some small campsites nearby that are fair at best.

# 66 Wrights Lake to Lake Aloha and Velma Lakes

**Distances** 8.6 miles to Lake Schmidell, 11.3 miles to Clyde Lake by shortest route, 13.1 miles to Middle Velma Lake, 15.1 miles to Clyde Lake by Hike 66 route, 16.5 miles to Pacific Crest Trail at Lake Aloha, 39.4 miles for complete semiloop trip, 40.5 miles total with side trips to Clyde, Gilmore and Dicks lakes.

**Low/High Elevations** 6960'/9380'

**Classification** Strenuous

**Season** Late July through early October

**Maps** 33, 30, 31, 34 and 35

**Trailhead** Same as the Hike 64 trailhead.

**Introduction** This lengthy hike explores the heart of Desolation Wilderness. In the process of traversing the Sierra Nevada highlands, you'll cross three mountain passes, each usually snowy through late July (sometimes longer), and will visit a dozen lakes, of which only Clyde Lake is not heavily visited. To avoid possible crowds at the other lakes, start your hike on Monday and end it on Friday. With so much scenery to embrace, you won't want to hike this route in any less time.

**Description** As in Hike 64, climb to Rockbound Pass, then descend briefly to Lake Doris and its nearby trail junction. Here, if you continue down the Rockbound Pass Trail to Rockbound Valley and China Flat (which is 8¼ miles from your trailhead), you'll shave almost 4 miles off the described route. To maximize your exposure to lakes, our hike, which begins with the last part of Hike 64, follows the Blakely Trail past Lake Lois and down to Lake Schmidell. Plan to spend your first and last nights at either lake.

From the junction of the Schmidell Lake spur trail, you then continue down the Blakely Trail, immediately passing a trailside pond. Your trail, likely to be muddy and mosquito-ridden through mid-August, descends eastward to Schmidell's creek, crosses it, and immediately reaches an important junction. Here you'll begin and end a lengthy loop, which is 20¼ miles long if you don't make any side trips.

Branch right onto the Schmidell Trail, which immediately recrosses the creek, winds downstream, and then climbs ¼ mile southeast to a minor ridge. From it a lightly used trail veers left, descending to the Rubicon River Trail, but we continue ahead, ½ mile south down to it.

Now along the floor of 8-mile-long Rockbound Valley, we cross several branches of the Lake Lois outlet creek, then meander southward upcanyon. After many minor twists and turns, our trail crosses the Lake Doris outlet creek, then in ¼ mile we join company with those descending the shortcut route, the Rockbound Pass Trail.

In a couple of minutes our southbound trek presents us with the first of three Rubicon River fords, this one up to 15 yards wide. Look downstream for a log crossing or be prepared to get your feet wet. Just 300 yards south of it you enter large, shady-but-open China Flat, which is an ideal base camp for the complete fisherman. It is also the logical first-night camp for those who have taken the shortcut route.

Onward, we continue south ¼ mile, head southwest through a meadow, and reach the Rubicon's lodgepole-lined east bank. The river here is wide, and therefore quite shallow, and if you ran fast and lightly enough, you'd barely get your boots wet. However, with a heavy pack the probable reality is a wet ford. Along the west bank you ascend gently south, crossing many creeks as you parallel the Rubicon, which is largely unseen due to the thick, lush vegetation. Hidden campsites as well as hidden fishing holes await the inquiring backpacker. One mile from the second Rubicon ford, we come to the third, where the river is up to 7 yards wide. To keep your feet dry, go a few yards downstream and cross a narrower stretch via large boulders. By the east bank you'll find the last good campsite until the north shore of Lake Aloha.

You now climb south through an open forest of red fir, mountain hemlock, western white pine and lodgepole pine, reaching, in just under a mile, a spur trail. This strikes 100 yards east to swampy Jacks Meadow, which is currently being invaded by willows, heather and mosquitoes. One-third mile farther, we hit another spur, this one descending ¼ mile down a large-block talus slope to Clyde Lake. Although lower and smaller than upcoming Lake Aloha, this cirque lake is much colder, usually reflecting a snowfield across its protected waters until well into August. The steep walls above three of its sides perpetuate a sense of chill in this glacier-carved head of Rockbound Valley. In addition to the steep trail and the bleak environment, a lack of good campsites is another argument for not visiting the lake. It does, however, have some positive features: it is often good for the seeker of solitude, and it is stocked with rainbow and golden trout.

From a seasonal creek by the start of the Clyde Lake spur trail the Rubicon River Trail climbs out of forest cover and up past seeps with ferns, columbines, larkspurs, monk's hoods and corn lilies. With unrestricted views north down Rockbound Valley we tread up the rock-blasted trail, and at the west edge of broad Mosquito Pass reach a crude stone windbreak, which serves as an emergency shelter.

On the far side of the pass we make a short, switchbacking descent through a sparse stand of mountain hemlocks, entering expansive, glacier-resistant Desolation Valley, whose flat floor is now occupied by Lake Aloha. This shallow lake, created to supply hydroelectric power to the people of Sacramento, is easily the largest lake in Desolation Wilderness—at least before late summer. After Labor Day, it can shrink appreciably, to only a fraction of its maximum size.

From where the switchbacks end we quickly come to a long, grassy flat, which has suitable campsites. About 7½ miles from Lake Schmidell this flat makes a scenic second night's stop. After a ½-mile traverse east along Lake Aloha's picturesque north shore (before September, that is!), you reach the lake's northeast corner, and meet the very popular Pacific Crest Trail. We'll hike north about 10 miles along it, and for this entire stretch, the "PCT" coincides with the unofficial Tahoe-Yosemite Trail, or "TYT," the two splitting into separate routes about a mile north of Middle Velma Lake. All the lakes and camps along this stretch are heavily used.

From the northeast corner of Lake Aloha, which has a 2-foot-high retaining wall to prevent it from spilling over the actual Sierra Nevada crest into Heather Lake, our PCT descends east, giving us views of the Freel Peak massif, lording it over Lake Tahoe's south shore. A switchback takes us to a delicate 20-foot-high waterfall just above deep Heather Lake's north-west shore, ¾ mile below Lake Aloha. Near a large red fir and the fall's creek is an adequate campsite. Our trail leaves Heather Lake at its low dam, climbs a low, barren ridge, and descends to a cove on the southwest shore of heather-ringed Susie Lake. On a weekend several dozen backpackers may be seen camped at poor, tiny campsites along this easily accessible, dark-shored lake below the towering, rusty, metamorphic shoulder of Jacks Peak. The best campsites are on a small bench 70 yards down the lake's outlet creek. We cross the outlet creek, follow the rocky trail over a low ridge, pass two stagnant ponds, and descend to a flowery, swampy meadow, where the trail forks. A well used trail to the Fallen Leaf Lake area branches southeast across the meadow. This route, Hike 83, is the quickest way in to our hike's 20¼-mile loop. Other reasonably short routes to it begin at Echo Lake (Hike 87), Bay View Campground (Hike 78) and Emerald Bay (Hike 77).

The PCT, now all uphill 3.4 miles to Dicks Pass, first switchbacks ½ mile northeast up to an intersection with a second trail southeast down to the Fallen Leaf Lake area. Northwest, this trail goes to Half Moon and Alta Morris lakes (Hike 82). Beyond this intersection the PCT

**Many islanded Lake Aloha, from trail above its north shore**

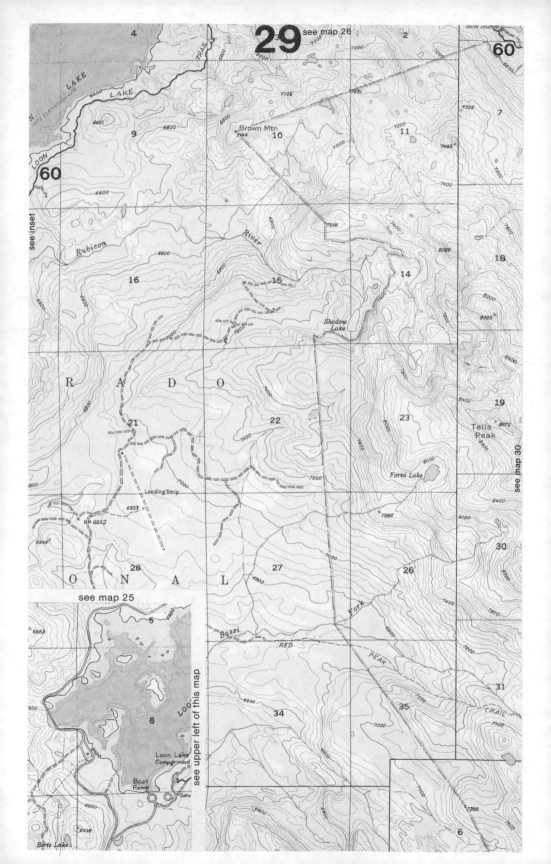

60

60

see inset

see map 30

see map 25

see upper left of this map

Brown Mtn

Rubicon

River

Shadow
Lake

Tells
Peak

Forni Lake

Landing Strip

BM 6812

Loon Lakes
Campground

Boat
Ramp

Gate

Berts Lake

Bassi

RED

FORK

PEAK

TRAIL

R A D O

O N A L

4
3
2
7
9
10
11
18
16
15
14
19
21
22
23
30
28
27
26
31
5
8
34
35
6

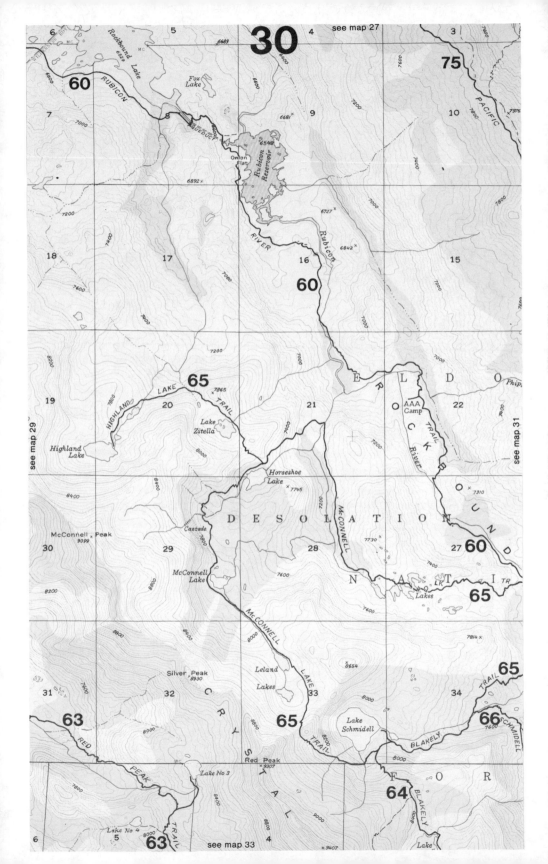

# 30

60

75

6

5

4

3

7

8

9

10

18

17

16

15

19

20

65

21

AAA
Camp

22

Highland
Lake

Lake
Zitella

Horseshoe
Lake × 7745

D E S O L A T I O N

Phip

McConnell × Peak
9099

30

29

Cascade

28

27 60

McConnell
Lake

LK
Lakes

65

N A T I

TR

31

32

Silver Peak
8930

Leland
Lakes

33

34

65

63

RED

Lake
Schmidell

BLAKELY

66

Red Peak
9307

Lake No 3

64

6

5 Lake No 4

63

4

× 9407

Lake

Rockbound
Lake

Fox
Lake

RUBICON

AQUEDUCT

Onion
Flat

Rubicon
Reservoir

RIVER

Rubicon

6689

6681

6727 ×

6842 ×

6892 ×

7865

McCONNELL

R O C K

B O U N D

R I V E R

C R Y S T A L

TRAIL

PEAK

TRAIL

HIGHLAND LAKE TRAIL

McCONNELL LAKE TRAIL

BLAKELY TRAIL

SCHMIDELL

F O R

7310

7730

7814 ×

8654

6548

PACIFIC

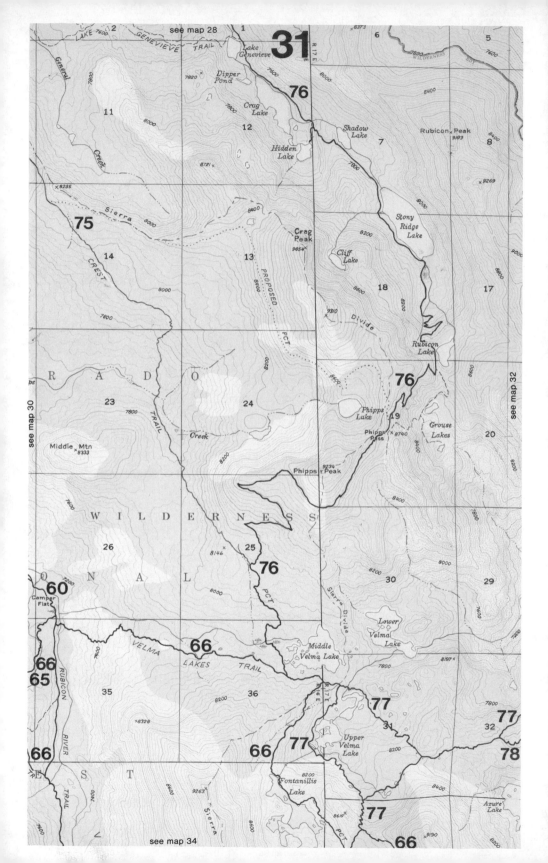

see map 28

# 31

see map 30

see map 32

see map 34

Lake Genevieve

LAKE GENEVIEVE TRAIL

Dipper Pond

Crag Lake

Hidden Lake

Shadow Lake

Rubicon Peak
9193

Stony Ridge Lake

Crag Peak
9054

Cliff Lake

Rubicon Lake

PROPOSED PCT

Divide

Phipps Lake

Grouse Lakes

Phipps Pass
8740

Phipps Peak
9234

Middle Mtn
8333

Creek

WILDERNESS

CREST TRAIL

Sierra Divide

Lower Velma Lake

Camper Flat

VELMA LAKES TRAIL

Middle Velma Lake

RUBICON RIVER

Upper Velma Lake

Fontanillis Lake

Azure Lake

General Creek

Sierra

Sierra

11 12 7 6 5 8

75 14 13 18 17

23 24 19 20

26 25 30 29

60 35 36 31 32

66 65 66 66 66 77 77 78 77

76 76 76 77

8235 8721 9269 8373 9310 8146 8328 9263 8197 8619 9190

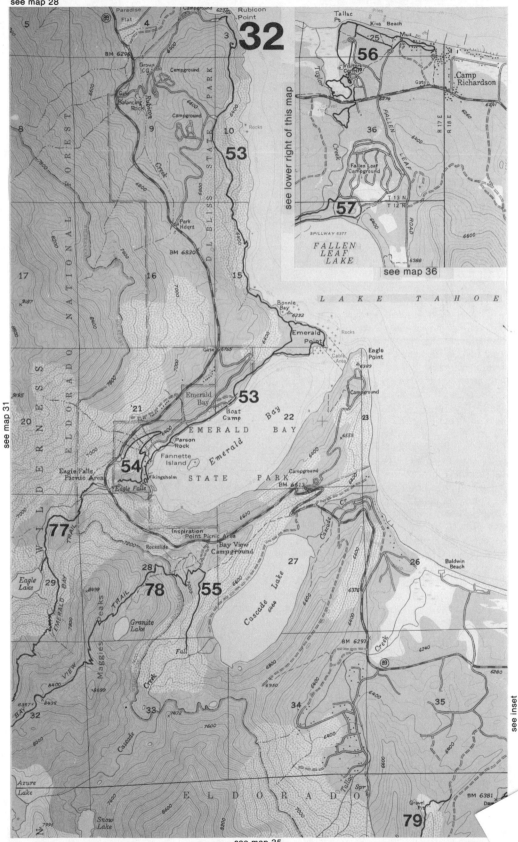

see map 28

Paradise
Flat

Rubicon
Point

**32**

Tallac
Pt

Piles

Kiva Beach

Muz

**56**

Camp
Richardson

4

Campground

6237

3

see lower right of this map

Tiglor

25

6279

Gate

R 17 E

R 18 E

6241

6560

BM 6296

Group
CG

Campground

6

Gate
Balancing
Rock

Rubicon

10

Campground

9

53

Rocks

Creek

36

Fallen Leaf
Campground

D L BLISS STATE PARK

Creek

FALLEN LEAF

ROAD

6400

6600

57

T 13 N
T 12 N

Park
Hdqrs

8

Creek

6600

17

16

BM 6830

15

SPILLWAY 6377

6388

see map 36

FALLEN
LEAF
LAKE

9187

Bonnie
Bay
6232

L A K E   T A H O E

Emerald
Point

Rocks

Eagle
Point
6389

Gate 6755

Cable
Area

Campground

20

21

Emerald
Bay

53

Boat
Camp

Bay

22

23

9195

EMERALD    BAY

6555

54

Parson
Rock

Emerald

Fannette
Island

Eagle Falls
Picnic Area

Vikingsholm

STATE    PARK

Campground
BM 6613

Eagle Falls

77

Inspiration
Point Picnic Area

Bay View
Campground

Cascade
Creek

26

Baldwin
Beach

Rockslide

6376

Eagle
Lake

29

28

78

55

27

Cascade

Lake

BM 6297

6240

6280

Granite
Lake

Fall

Creek

6950

34

35

33

7472

Azure
Lake

32

8357

8435

8699

ELDORADO

Tallac

Spr

Gravel
Pit

BM 6381

see inset

Snow
Lake

7998

79

see map 35

see map 31

switchbacks up past junipers to a junction with Trail 17E09, which leads ¼ mile to good campsites above the south and east shores of orbicular Gilmore Lake. This lateral (Hike 81) then continues 1¾ miles up to Mt. Tallac's summit, which gives you perhaps the best view of Lake Tahoe you'll ever see.

As we start west up toward Dicks Pass, we get a peek through the lodgepole forest at Gilmore Lake, and then we ascend steadily northwest, climbing high above the pale-brown metavolcanic-rock basin that holds Half Moon and Alta Morris lakes. Lake Aloha plus Susie and Heather lakes also appear. Lodgepoles, mountain hemlocks and western white pines are soon joined by whitebark pines, the harbinger of timberline, as we approach a saddle east of Dicks Peak. From it, a faint but fairly popular unofficial trail heads up a ridge to the rusty peak's summit.

Rather than descend north from the saddle, our trail climbs ¼ mile east up alongside the ridgecrest in order to bypass the steep slopes and long-lasting snowfields that lie north of the saddle. Our trail reaches Dicks Pass, an almost level area on the ridge where clusters of dwarfed, wind-trimmed conifers serve as windbreaks or shelters for those who want to camp overnight here to experience the glorious sunrise lighting the richly hued metamorphic massif to the west. Lingering snowpatches usually provide campers with a water source. Here, on the highest trail pass in Desolation Wilderness, we get far-ranging views both north and south.

Ducks guide us across Dicks Pass, the boundary between metamorphic rocks to the south and granitic rocks to the north, and then we descend on hemlock-lined switchbacks, rich in thick gravel from the deeply weathered bedrock. After descending northwest to a rocky saddle, 1.7 miles beyond the pass, we reach a junction. Hike 78, from Highway 89's Bay View Campground, climbs up to meet us here. We descend south 0.2 mile to a spur trail, which in turn descends 100 yards to a shoreline trail that leads you to popular campsites along the north shore and east peninsula of Dicks Lake.

From the Dicks Lake spur-trail junction we follow the PCT northwest down to a large tarn with a good campsite. Soon we descend a gully to a small cove on Fontanillis Lake's east shore and parallel this shore northwest to the outlet creek. Campsites are fair to poor around this trout-stocked lake.

To leave this rockbound lake, we cross the outlet creek, make a brief climb north to a shady lateral moraine, and then descend part way along its crest before curving left, jumping an

**Dicks Lake, from saddle near Dicks Pass**

intermorainal creek and descending a slightly older lateral moraine to a trail junction above the south shore of Middle Velma Lake. Hike 77, from Eagle Falls Picnic Area on Highway 89 above Lake Tahoe's Emerald Bay, joins us here. Only 70 yards west on this trail we get a good view of Middle Velma Lake, and here you'll probably want to descend to campsites by the lake's shore, which are about the best you'll find north of Dicks Pass. On weekends this lakeshore is crowded, since it is readily accessible from Emerald Bay and many hikers have discovered it has inviting water. You can swim out to and dive from the lake's rock-slab islands, which are also good for sunbathing.

Westward, the PCT reaches, only 35 yards beyond a minor creek, a trail junction at which we leave the PCT/TYT. On the Velma Lakes Trail, we head west through a dense forest, which thins as we lose altitude. After about 1½ miles, where the trail jogs from northwest to southwest, we find a short spur trail, which departs north to a quiet pool at the base of a rock slab. We next make an open descent southwest, with views up and down Rockbound Valley, cross an alder-bordered creeklet in ¼ mile, then conclude our descent in thickening forest cover, reaching the broad Rubicon River in ½ mile. Camping would be good here were it not illegal.

Across the Rubicon, which can be a substantial wade before late July, you meet the Rubicon River Trail. Hike 100 yards north on it to a junction with the Blakely Trail, located near the south margin of Camper Flat. Hike a winding, shady 1.2 miles up this trail to complete your 20+ mile loop, then another mile up to Lake Schmidell, for your last night's stay in the wilderness. The next day—Friday, if you're on schedule—retrace 8.6 miles out to your trailhead. Most of this distance is downhill, and since you've got a lighter pack, you'll probably reach the trailhead about noon.

# 67  Wrights Lake to Gertrude and Tyler Lakes

**Distances**  4.3 miles to Gertrude Lake, 4.6 miles to Tyler Lake.

**Low/High Elevations**  6960'/8220'

**Classification**  Moderate

**Season**  Mid-July through mid-October

**Map**  33

**Trailhead**  Same as the Hike 64 trailhead.

**Introduction**  Two photogenic subalpine lakes climax this moderate hike. Despite their easy accessibility, they remain relatively unvisited because most hikers prefer lower, closer lakes or else backpack into the lakes beyond Rockbound Pass. If you're in good shape, this route is not a difficult day hike.

**Description**  The first 2⅓ miles coincide with the first part of the Rockbound Pass Trail (Hike 64), which is also known as the Willow Flat Trail. This stretch is described in the first paragraph of that route. From where these two routes split, in a small, shady flat, we follow the Tyler Lake Trail 2 miles to its end at, surprisingly, Gertrude Lake.

Climbing east above the flat, we first quickly enter Desolation Wilderness as we follow this ducked trail up slabs and a gully to a viewpoint, from where we can trace the outlet streams of Umpa and Twin Lakes flowing, and sometimes cascading, over open, glaciated slabs on their way down to Wrights Lake. Our trail makes an unexpected 20-foot drop, then climbs north steeply up a brush-lined gully to a forested, shallow saddle on a ridge. From here you could go cross-country to Twin Lakes by climbing up-

ridge about 100 feet elevation and then traversing east past Umpa Lake to a shallow, rocky saddle which lies directly above Lower Twin Lake's west shore.

The Tyler Lake Trail leaves the forested saddle, parallels an ephemeral creeklet, and then climbs steeply north above it, becoming faint before reaching another ridge. Immediately after dropping north to a shallow ridge saddle, it enters a hemlock forest, then passes a small, ankle-deep pond, makes a short traverse northeast, and later, at a blazed lodgepole pine, heads north straight downslope 80 yards before curving northeast again. Blazes and ducks guide our traverse across numerous snow-fed creeklets, and then we make a steep, bouldery ascent to a short, signed spur trail, which descends a willow-choked gully 125 yards to Tyler's grave. Tyler, a local ranch hand, froze to death in a November 1882 snowstorm while trying to round up cattle in this area. Our destination bears his name.

Along a 0.2 mile ascent bisected by Tyler Lake creek, our trail to Gertrude Lake becomes faint. Short on campsites but long on scenery, this shallow lake has an exquisite balance of shoreline slabs and spaced conifers that please the nature photographer.

To reach cirque-bound Tyler Lake, we backtrack to its streaming creek and follow it up open slabs to the lake. Only a few scattered western white pines and mountain hemlocks provide shade at this timberline, slab-surrounded lake. Nevertheless, the naked beauty of its setting will long remain with you. Look for exposed but legal campsites above its rocky east shore.

# 68  Wrights Lake to Twin and Island Lakes

**Distances**  3.9 miles to Lower Twin Lake, 4.3 miles to Upper Twin Lake and Boomerang Lake, 4.5 miles to Island Lake.

**Low/High Elevations**  6960'/8150'

**Classification**  Moderate

**Season**  Mid-July through mid-October

**Map**  33

**Trailhead**  Same as the Hike 64 trailhead.

**Introduction**  Because these attractive lakes and those of the next hike lie so close to Wrights Lake, they receive heavy use. Therefore, to minimize your impact at these lakes, please make day hikes to them rather than camp over-

night at them. They aren't that hard to hike to, and if you start your walk at the Wrights Lake northeast-corner trailhead, you can subtract 1.2 miles from the above distances. Although the lakes are close together, they are quite different, each having its own special qualities.

**Description**  As in Hike 64, start at the main trailhead and make an easy ridge traverse to Beauty Lake. You curve around its west and north shores to a gap and, just east up from it, meet a trail fork. Keep right here and climb over a nearby ridge, then descend moderately for ⅓ mile to a closed road. Walk 90 yards east on it to a road fork, from which the *old* Rockbound Pass

Trail still begins its way north. The right branch curves south, and after 25 yards along it, you'll come to the Twin Lakes Trail. This trail quickly log-crosses South Fork Silver Creek, then in an equal distance strikes southeast to the north edge of a meadow, in which Ed Wright grazed his dairy cattle from 1850 to 1900.

Beyond the meadow the hiker makes a very brief climb up to a low cliff, on the left, which is topped with an erratic boulder left by a glacier. Just past this cliff we meet a ½-mile spur trail that descends southwest to the inlet of Wrights Lake. There, from the east-shore road's end, you could begin your hike up the spur trail to this junction, shaving 1.2 miles off the distance to your intended goal. The Forest Service, however, bans parking in this limited roadend area, so you might get someone to drop you off there.

From the spur-trail junction the Twin Lakes Trail climbs steadily northeast, often being within hearing distance of the Grouse Lake outlet creek. In early summer one stretch of trail seems more like a creek than a trail. After 0.9 mile of climbing, you reach another junction, from which the Hemlock Lake Trail continues upslope to Grouse, Hemlock and Smith lakes, which are described in the next hike.

To continue on the Twin Lakes Trail, branch left (north) and immediately cross the Grouse Lake outlet creek. Continuing north, we enter Desolation Wilderness in about 100 yards, then bend northeast for a curving ascent moderately up quite open glacier-polished slabs. The trail crosses a minor ridge, then swings east, passing two small ponds along the Twin Lakes outlet

## Lower Twin Lake

creek. Just beyond the second, we must cross a once-narrow creek lined with a thick, spongy mat of vegetation. Heavy trail use has caused collapse along most of its bank, thereby widening the crossing to a running jump. A sturdy log placed across the creek would stop, if not reverse, this deteriorating creek environment.

Beyond it, a short climb northeast brings us to Lower Twin Lake, whose outlet creek the trail crosses about 40 yards below its waist-high dam. You'll probably find it more convenient to cross immediately below the dam. Before you cross, however, you might want to stop at the lake's south shore and rest a while or swim and dive from rocks along this fairly deep shore. Anglers will find the lake stocked with rainbow trout. Rainbow were first introduced in 1904 by Joe Minghetti, a local ranch hand, who eventually stocked most of the lakes in the Wrights Lake Recreation Area. Today many of these lakes receive yearly plantings.

Our trail parallels the lake's west shore to a gully at its northwest corner. (An easy cross-country route, rewarding in views, starts west from here, climbs over the low ridge saddle, and descends to Umpa Lake. From the lake, the route traverses west, staying on the bald slope just below the higher, brushy slope, and then descending a ridge to a saddle where you meet the Tyler Lake Trail.) Our faint, rocky trail climbs northeast from the gully, passes through a 10-foot-deep notch, then reaches Boomerang Lake, named for its shape, from whose west shore on the north arm one can dive from 12-foot ledges into the lake's cold, deep water.

After passing between Boomerang Lake and its tiny northeastern relative, we climb above the western end of a small, linear lake, nourished by a snowfield and two narrow cascades from Island Lake. Just above this silver dagger we reach Island Lake, a fairly large, rock-island, timberline lake. Near its shore, small, fair campsites can be found that are the required 100-foot distance from the lake. Although tall, dark-gray diorite-gabbro cirque walls lend a stark beauty to this subalpine lake, it is not as popular as the Twin Lakes, with their border of sparse trees. At Island Lake you may find more California gulls than backpackers.

From the southeast shore of Island Lake you can go cross-country to Upper Twin Lake—2 feet higher than its sibling—by descending southwest to the outlet of the "silver dagger" lake, and then contouring around Upper Twin until you can descend easily to the glacier-polished gentle slabs that separate the twins, on which fair campsites can be found.

# 69    Wrights Lake to Grouse, Hemlock and Smith Lakes

**Distances** 3.3 miles to Grouse Lake, 3.8 miles to Hemlock Lake, 4.2 miles to Smith Lake.

**Low/High Elevations** 6960'/8700'

**Classification** Strenuous

**Season** Mid-July through mid-October

**Maps** 33 and 34

**Trailhead** Same as the Hike 64 trailhead.

**Introduction** Three sparkling subalpine lakes, each with its own special qualities, are the highlights of this trip. From Smith Lake, the highest of the three, you have one of the best views of the Wrights Lake and Crystal Basin recreation areas.

**Description** Follow the previous hike 2½ miles up to where the Hemlock Lake Trail branches right from the Twin Lakes Trail. Here, you've got 60% of the distance to Smith Lake already behind you, but only 30% of the net-elevation gain. About 100 yards up your northeast-climbing trail you enter Desolation Wilderness, following a ducked route up granitic slabs into an open forest and to a gravelly flat. Turning southeast, our trail then starts to climb gradually, but soon it becomes steep, and then very steep, before easing off atop a moraine that dams Grouse Lake. A few glimpses of Wrights Lake, far below, are obtained near the top of this climb.

Rock-lined Grouse Lake, fringed with red heather and Labrador tea, is a very pleasant lake to linger at, particularly after the strenuous climb. Its shallow, clear water invites a swim. Nearby campsites, on sloping ground above its northeast shore, are only fair.

A steep climb north up a low lateral moraine, then another, longer ascent northeast up a rocky slope brings us to tiny Hemlock Lake, named for the mountain hemlocks that border its south shore. Its small size is compensated for by a dramatic exfoliating cliff above its north shore. A fair camp sits above its southeast shore.

Hiking southeast, we make a final ducked climb and reach nearly treeless Smith Lake, which at 8700 feet elevation is almost at timberline. Its steep, confining slopes, most having snowfields that last well into summer, are also detrimental to growth. Nevertheless, a small stand of lodgepole and western white pines does thrive above the lake's northwest shore. From a rocky, emergency bivouac spot near the lake's outlet we can look out over the Wrights and Crystal Basin recreation areas and identify Wrights Lake and Dark Lake below us and Union Valley Reservoir in the distance. This is the only lake from which you can get such expansive views of these two areas.

**Grouse Lake**

# 70    Wrights Lake to Bloodsucker Lake

**Distance** 1.8 miles, one way

**Low/High Elevations** 6910'/7430'

**Classification** Moderate

**Season** Mid-July through mid-October

**Map** 33

**Trailhead** See the Hike 64 trailhead description to the trailhead parking area.

**Introduction** For those who have never seen leeches in real life, this hike can be a real eye-opener. It is also an alternative, though longer, approach to upper Lyons Creek, Lyons Lake, Lake Sylvia and Pyramid Peak, which are all described in the next hike.

**Description** From the Wrights Lake Horse Camp at the south end of the large trailhead parking area, head south about 180 yards on a well-used horse trail, fork left, then log-cross the adjacent South Fork Silver Creek. If you're temporarily residing at the Wrights Lake Campground, start your hike from it by following this creek about ¼ mile downstream until you meet this trail ford. From it you start south along the creek's east bank, then quickly veer up to a blocked-off road, which you meet atop a low crest—a glacial moraine.

On this almost level stretch of closed road we walk ¼ mile east, to where it curves northeast and starts a moderate climb. At this curve you may see a TRAIL sign, the trail veering south and momentarily crossing several alder-lined creeks. Before mid-August, these crossings can be soggy indeed, and you might prefer to keep to the road which, despite some seasonally boggy spots, at least allows you to keep your feet dry. The road to the lake is perfectly obvious, and is the same length—plus or minus a stone's throw—as the trail.

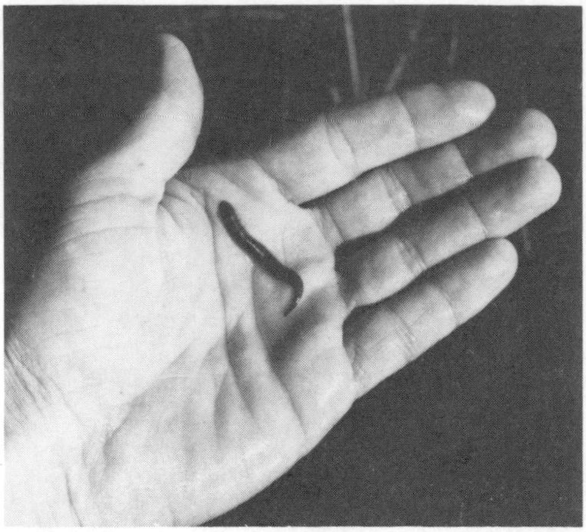

Beyond the creeks the trail commences a moderate-to-steep climb, and you climb 300 feet southeast over a viewless ½-mile route. Where the trail levels off, you arrive at a junction, from which the route to Bloodsucker Lake heads northeast. Ahead, you'd pass, in 200 yards, a shallow, leech-free lakelet, on your right. You'd then cross a broad ridge, make a steep 350-foot descent to Lyons Creek, cross it on rocks a few yards downstream, and climb east-southeast through a sloping meadow to a junction with the Lyons Creek Trail. If you don't visit Bloodsucker Lake, this route to the junction is about ⅔ mile longer, and it contains a lot more climbing, than the Lyons Creek Trail's route to this junction.

However, bound for Bloodsucker Lake, we don't take this route, but rather strike northeast, dropping slightly to a boggy meadow alive with colorful flowers that are at their best, unfortunately, when the mosquitoes are at their worst. After a short climb from the meadow, we're standing on the previously mentioned road, near

**A Bloodsucker Lake leech**

Bloodsucker Lake's southwest shore. Thirty yards southeast on the road is a campsite, although this lake is not conducive to camping, for the knee-deep lake's water is questionable at best.

Blue Mountain, with the Crystal Range as a backdrop, adds to the scenic beauty of the lake, but its main attractions are the bloodsuckers—yes, leeches—up to 3 inches long. (You may have to stir the water a bit to find them.) It seems that the only aquatic species that could serve as hosts for these leeches are yellow-legged frogs, which are sometimes very plentiful. In the absence of frogs, however, the leeches could survive on many of the lake's arthropods, for blood is not essential for their subsistence. Just how the leeches got here in the first place is a puzzling question; none of the other shallow lakes in this guide's area seem to have any. Perhaps one or more were carried up to this lake in relatively recent times by some unsuspecting host, such as a cow.

# 71 Lyons Creek Trail to Lake Sylvia, Lyons Lake and Pyramid Peak

**Distances**   4.5 miles to Lake Sylvia, 4.6 miles to Lyons Lake, 5.9 miles to Pyramid Peak.

**Low/High Elevations**   6710'/8380'; 9983' at summit.

**Classification**   Moderate to lakes, strenuous to summit.

**Season**   Mid-July through mid-October

**Maps**   37 (inset), 33 and 34

**Trailhead**   See the Hike 64 trailhead. Room for several cars at spur road's end.

**Introduction**   The several meadows found along this trail will reward both botanist and photographer. Those who like to frolic or fish in creek pools will find at least three sets of them.

**Wildflower Plate 13. Desolation Wilderness flowers.**
1 Leichtlin's camas (blue-violet to purple), 2 branched Solomon's seal (white), 3 lesser star tulip (white to pale-violet), 4 Newberry's gentian (grayish white), 5 mountain sorrel (brownish red), 6 Jessica's stickseed (blue with white center), 7 one-sided wintergreen (whitish), 8 large-leaved lupine (violet to blue), 9 Bolander's locoweed (pale yellow).

However, most hikers prefer water sports in the two lakes, which by early August warm to acceptable temperatures. Mountaineers often use Lake Sylvia as a base camp for an ascent of dominating Pyramid Peak, which is the highest summit in Desolation Wilderness, beating out Mt. Price and Dicks Peak by less than 10 feet.

**Description**   The above mileages are measured from the trailhead at the end of the 0.4-mile-long spur road. Before August this road may be too rutted and muddy to drive, and then your distance will be a bit greater. From the southeast side of the roadend, Lyons Creek Trail 16E13 climbs gently eastward. Where the trail almost touches the creek, a short spur goes over to a set of shallow pools nestled among granitic slabs. Many seasonal tributaries are passed, as well as several big meadows, before we reach the site of Lyons at the edge of another meadow. In this meadow, as well as others, you're likely to find corn lily, wandering daisy, lupine, common monkey flower, ligusticum, senecio, cinquefoil, paintbrush, brodiaea, shooting star, and alpine lily—to name the more prominent species. Just as our trail climbs east to leave this meadow, a trail to Wrights Lake cuts off west-northwest to Lyons Creek, which is crossed on rocks a few yards downstream. Hike 70, which goes to Bloodsucker Lake, mentions this trail, and you can use it as an alternate route to Lake Sylvia and Lyons Lake. It adds about 1½ miles to your hike, but you get to visit a lake that has some interesting inhabitants.

About midway up the Lyons Creek Trail, just beyond the Desolation Wilderness border, you can take a short spur northwest to a second set of slab pools, deeper than those near the trailhead. More climbing up open, granitic slopes gives you your first view of Pyramid Peak and takes you to a third set of pools, which you discover just before crossing lodgepole-shaded Lyons Creek. Then 200 yards east of the crossing you reach a junction. The branch east quickly reaches and then traverses a 50-yard-long swath of creeks, boggy through late July, then climbs ¼

mile to shallow, placid, trout-inhabited Lake Sylvia. Although this lake lacks impressive views like those found along the trail, it does have some large good campsites, under a canopy of shady conifers, and can be delightfully warm. Camp here if you plan to climb Pyramid Peak; the route to it is described at the end of this hike.

You might also investigate the two upper cirque lakes above and northeast of Lake Sylvia. The wildflower display seen along the cross-country ascent to them is one of the best to be found anywhere in the Sierra Nevada. Indeed, it is a botanist's paradise (see this hike's wild-flower plate and other plates). The two lakes lie in a basin that is nestled below the highest stretch of Desolation Wilderness crest. As a consequence of this topographic barrier, the basin receives a prodigious amount of snow. In an average year the lakes may not become snow-free until August. In some years they never become entirely snow-free.

From either lake you have an unimpaired view of Pyramid Peak and the knife-edge ridge extending north from it. At the north end of this ridge is a prominent point, which faces Pyramid Peak. There is a deep cleft at the base of this point, and it constitutes the hardest of four climbing routes up to the crest—the only one difficult enough to require a rope. A second route—60 feet long—is the shortest, and it goes straight up to a nearly level part of the crest. At its south end the crest gives way to an ascending ridge, which has two high points. On the south side of each is a prominent chimney, routes three and four. The first chimney is 10-20 feet wide, the second is about 5 feet wide. All four routes are very appealing to mountaineers, but all four contain dangerously loose rocks. The author, an experienced mountaineer who soloed one of them and inspected the others, recommends you avoid all four. Too bad, since once you reach the crest, the route to the summit is easy.

If you don't take the side trip up to the two cirque lakes, you might consider visiting Lyons Lake, which, like Lake Sylvia, is a cirque lake.

**A summit panorama, from north to east-southeast. Dicks Peak rises above Aloha's west end, Mt. Tallac rises above its east end. Echo Peak rises above Lake of the Woods and Pyramid Lake. Ralston Peak slopes toward the South Fork American River canyon.**

From the junction east of Lyons Creek the left fork climbs north steeply up an open granitic slope, affording us views of the snowbound lower northwest face of Pyramid Peak. Our steep ascent is quickly over, and we reach scattered hemlocks near the Lyons Lake forebay, which is 3 feet lower than the dammed lake. Small, minimal campsites lie on slopes east of and above this bay, but the Lake Sylvia sites are clearly superior. Lyons Lake, like Sylvia, is fringed with red heather and Labrador tea. Conifers, however, are much more scarce, creating an entirely different atmosphere than at Sylvia. Its cirque encloses a mountaineer's world, with cliffs crowding in all around the lake, daring the climber to escape. Up the granite walls are found long, easy climbs as well as some short, very difficult ones.

But it is Pyramid Peak, and not the Lyons Lake walls, which attracts most mountaineers. How can you ignore the highest peak in Desolation Wilderness when it is standing so alluringly close? To reach its summit from Lake Sylvia, first locate your immediate goal, to the southeast: a shallow notch at the base of the peak's southwest-descending ridge. Traverse along the lake's swampy west shore, then start east along its south shore. You veer up and away from it, climbing a talus slope that can be snowbound through midsummer. Ascend a chute up to the notch. This straightforward climb is easily the most difficult part of the whole ascent route. When snow-free this scramble is quite safe— just be sure you don't sprain an ankle on loose rock. However, when snow is present, it can ice over, and this can make the route dangerous. August is usually the best month for an ascent, for by then the chute is quite safe and the wildflowers both in the chute and on slopes above are at their prime.

**The shallow notch above Lake Sylvia**

From the shallow notch the route to the summit is obvious. Basically, you stay at or close to the ascending ridge, leaving it only when you almost reach the peak's nearly vertical northwest face. From this point the remaining 300 feet of elevation gain is up a "talus slope" composed of large, sometimes giant, granitic blocks. This is not a true talus slope, for the blocks did not tumble down from above; they formed *in situ*. Diagonal east up this slope to the peak's south-descending ridge (along which those on Hike 72 will be ascending). Due to the large blocks here and at the summit, soil is virtually nonexistent, as are alpine wildflowers. Flying insects, however, can be quite plentiful, being wafted up here by the wind.

The summit views are somewhat disappointing, partly because the Desolation Wilderness landscape below you is so desolate. Also, you don't have a good view of Lake Tahoe, for Mt. Tallac hides most of it. Nevertheless, you can peruse a lot of scenery, from Round Top in the south to the Sierra Buttes in the distant north-northwest. And on exceptionally clear days you should be able to see Lassen Peak, just left of the Sierra Buttes, and 133 miles away.

# 72 Horsetail Falls Trail to Lake of the Woods, Lake Aloha and Pyramid Peak

**Distances**   1.3 miles to base of lower Horsetail Fall, 1.8 miles to Avalanche Lake, 2.0 miles to Pitt Lake, 2.4 miles to Ropi Lake, 3.5 miles to Lake of the Woods, 4.9 miles to Lake Aloha, southeast corner, 5.1 miles to Pyramid Peak.

**Low/High Elevations**   6110'/8120'; 9983' at summit.

**Classification**   Strenuous

**Season**   Mid-July through mid-October

**Maps**   37, 34 and 35

**Trailhead**   From the Highway 49 junction in Placerville, drive 40 miles east up Highway 50 to the settlement of Strawberry, where gas and food are available, then drive an additional 1⅔ miles to Twin Bridges, with a store and post office. About 200 yards past it you bridge Pyramid Creek and in 50 yards turn left into a parking area that holds about a dozen cars. (Westbound drivers: this parking area is 6¾ miles west from Echo Summit.)

**Introduction**   Twin Bridges is the USFS-designated official trailhead #5 for entry into Desolation Wilderness, and its unofficial Horsetail Falls Trail is the quickest route to the Desolation Valley lakes. Not only is the trail unofficial, it is, in places, essentially nonexistent. It is also one of the most dangerous routes mentioned in this book. Supposedly a number of hikers have fallen to their deaths trying to follow it. Nevertheless, its trailhead seems to attract overflow crowds of autos every summer weekend, undoubtedly because this route is such a quick way into scenery unsurpassed anywhere in this wilderness.

**Description**   If you need a guidebook to stay on route, you shouldn't be on this sketchy trail. Consequently, the directions for it are intentionally very brief. Also, if you haven't hiked this route, don't hike it alone—you might have to be rescued.

At least two paths start along the west side of Pyramid Creek, soon uniting. You leave the creek only to rejoin it ½ mile later and follow it 250 yards northwest through open forest to a bend, then 160 yards north to the Desolation Wilderness boundary, within a shady fir grove. About ¼ mile past the boundary your first real route-finding problems begin, and if you can't find the trail, turn back; it gets worse ahead. After about 200 yards of climbing up one of two increasingly steep treads, you reach a vantage point from which you can look down-canyon and identify its huge east-wall lateral moraine. You can also study nearby lower Horsetail Fall, roaring as it plunges 100 feet into a churning pool. This vantage point is on ice- and water-polished, gravel-covered, sloping bedrock. In other words, it's very slippery. You could easily lose your footing and plunge on a one-way trip into the lower fall's rocky gorge.

The trail, if you can call it that, veers away from the lower fall and starts steeply west up open slabs. In several places you'll have to use good judgment in route finding. High above the lower fall the route bends north and diagonals up a talus slope before cutting 80 yards east to a small flat just above the brink of upper Horsetail Fall. The view from the flat *almost* justifies this arduous ascent, and from it you can now identify the canyon's west-wall moraine, which isn't nearly so spectacular as its multistage east-wall counterpart. It's hard to believe that a glacier descending Pyramid Creek filled the canyon *at least* to the crest of these 900-foot-high moraines.

With danger behind you, drop briefly north from the small flat, then parallel Pyramid Creek 200 yards up to small but scenic Avalanche Lake. Your route to Ropi Lake is now essentially cross-country. About ¼ mile beyond Avalanche Lake you approach relatively unappealing Pitt Lake, and near its northern end you must make a decision. To get to Lake of the Woods you'll have to cross Pyramid Creek, and this is best done before you reach Ropi Lake—if you want to keep your feet dry. Therefore, start looking for suitable boulders and/or logs on which you can cross the creek.

The main cross-country route stays along the creek's west bank as it climbs ⅓ mile to an old, defunct dam on Ropi Lake. From here many hikers turn west to explore nearby Toem Lake or Gefo Lake, on a bench above it. Some prefer to get to Lake Aloha the fast way, and so climb north cross-country on an easy 1¼-mile jaunt, passing Pyramid and Waca lakes along the way. Others start from Ropi Lake's north shore, climb due north from it or northeast up Pyramid Creek, then follow a chain of lakes 1 mile to Lake Aloha's principal dam.

From the east arm of snag-infested Ropi Lake an official, primitive trail starts a climb to Lake of the Woods. This trail ascends east-northeast ⅓ mile up a joint-controlled gully, crosses a tiny, seasonally boggy flat, then continues on an easier grade ¼ mile east to Lake of the Woods' outlet creek. This it follows 200 yards upstream to a crossing that can be hard to find for those *descending* this trail. From the crossing you head east past the south edge of an adjacent small, stagnant pond, then immediately turn north to begin a ½-mile climb to a low ridge damming extremely popular Lake of the Woods. This lake's shores abound with campsites, the better, more private ones being found along its west shore. Should you camp here, make sure your camp is *at least* 100 feet from the shore; 200+ feet is even better.

At the lake's northwest corner, which is nearly a mile by trail from its outlet, a sketchy, minor trail starts a climb northwest, reaching the popular trail to Lake Aloha in less than ½ mile. Just 60 yards down it you reach a junction above a southeast arm of shallow, sprawling Lake Aloha. From here a *de facto* trail branches left and embarks on a ¾-mile course over to the lake's 20-foot-high dam, with a justifiably popular, island-dotted, swimming area.

If Pyramid Peak is your goal, make a climb west from Ropi Lake up past Toem Lake to Gefo Lake. From it several routes are possible, for the slopes are not too steep. You can diagonal due south up to roughly the 8600-foot crest; you can climb west up either side of the Gefo Lake inlet creek; or you can head due north to Pyramid Lake, go west up its inlet creek, and then traverse south. All these routes end up on the nearly level southeast ridge of Pyramid Peak. From it you diagonal west up to the peak's south flank, then climb straight to the bouldery summit, which is mentioned in the last part of Hike 71.

**Left: Pyramid Peak above Ropi Lake**

# 73     Ralston Peak Trail to Ralston Peak

**Distance**   4.6 miles, one way
**Low/High Elevations**   6500'/9235'
**Classification**   Strenuous
**Season**   Early July through mid-October
**Maps**   37 and 35
**Trailhead**   From Twin Bridges, mentioned in Hike 72's trailhead description, drive just 1¼ miles up Highway 50 to Camp Sacramento, on your right, and Sayles Flat roadside rest area, on your left. Park at the rest area, for there is no room at the trailhead. (Westbound drivers: this rest area is 5¾ miles west from Echo Summit.)

**Introduction**   You'll command excellent views, both nearby and far-reaching, from the summit of Ralston Peak. From it you can study the different characteristics of Desolation Wilderness, the river canyons to the west, the Carson Range to the northeast, and the Freel Peak area to the east. By inference from the Mt. Tallac erosion surface, you can also mentally visualize what the Desolation Wilderness looked like before the Ice Age.

You can reach Ralston's summit by the excessively steep Ralston Peak Trail or by the moderately graded Pacific Crest Trail (Hike 86) from Echo Lake. The "PCT" route is about 2¼ miles longer, but its trailhead is about 1000 feet higher, which means you have a lot less effort. Furthermore, you can cut 2½ miles off the PCT route by taking the Echo Lakes water taxi, thereby making it the shorter and much easier of the two routes. Only seasoned botanists or hikers hell-bent for punishment will want to take the grueling Ralston Peak Trail.

**Description**   From the rest area walk northeast up an old, paved road, and after 200 yards reach the parking lot of an unpretentious chapel. Immediately beyond the lot the road curves right and abruptly ends. You'll find the trailhead at this curve, and the hike's mileage is measured from this point.

The trail begins by switchbacking up through a white-fir forest that shades the slopes of a giant lateral moraine. Midway to a viewpoint atop this moraine we cross a closed road, which serves to mark a short stretch of easier climbing.

The trail almost tops the level crest of the moraine but chooses instead to parallel it for about 200 yards before actually reaching it. From this spot you can gaze northwest at pointed Pyramid Peak, which stands high above 900-foot-deep, glaciated Pyramid Creek canyon below you. To the southwest you see the nearly vertical west face of Lovers Leap, Highway 50's most popular climbing area. Along the stretch of trail just before and after this viewpoint you may see one or more faint trails climbing up to yours. These start from a Seventh Day Adventist Camp in Pinecrest.

Now we have a steep-to-very-steep 1350-foot climb ahead of us up weathered granitic rock largely vegetated with huckleberry oak, manzanita and some chinquapin. A 60-yard-long spur trail west to a disappointing view from a shallow ridge saddle marks the 500-foot point. Continued steep climbing up short switchbacks for 450 more feet brings us to an eastward traverse, along which we pass a trickling spring. A few more short, steep switchbacks are negotiated, and then the gradient eases as we climb to a prominent spur ridge, covered with an open stand of red fir and western white pine. From it a brief initial descent speeds us on our way along a ⅓ mile northwest traverse across a meadowy slope. Some of the more conspicuous flowers you're likely to see here are Bolander's locoweed, eriogonum, streptanthus, lupine, phlox, pussy paws and paintbrush.

Just after our traverse turns into a moderate climb, we encounter two small but profuse springs, each with its associated cluster of corn lilies—telltale indicators that water is nearby. Beyond them a steep, ducked ascent brings us up to a generally open ridge, but with clusters of mountain hemlocks, and from it we can look northwest down at Lake of the Woods, below us, and beyond at island-dotted Lake Aloha, which has as a backdrop the metamorphic masses of Jacks and Dicks peaks. Pyramid Peak is the prominent granitic guardian above Aloha's southwest shore.

From this ridge the trail descends a short, steep north slope to a small, boggy meadow, and then traverses north to a signed junction among mountain hemlocks, from which a spur trail climbs southwest to Ralston Peak. See Hike 74 for the northward description of the main trail. Rather than descend the north slope, which is usually snowbound well into August, follow the gentle ridge eastward to the ridgecrest, along which you should be able to locate the faint, ducked trail up it to the ice-fractured quartz-monzonite summit rocks of Ralston Peak. At its foot lie three cirque lakes: Tamarack, Ralston and Cagwin, and to their east and below them lie moraine-dammed Upper and Lower Echo lakes. Above the canyon beyond them are the granitic summits of the Freel Peak massif, mostly unglaciated, the closest and tallest peak being Freel Peak.

Perhaps the most instructive view from our summit is the view north toward Fallen Leaf Lake, barely visible, and Lake Tahoe, immediately beyond it. Our view is framed by the

**Tallac bench and Lake Tahoe in background, Ralston and Tamarack lakes in foreground**

metamorphic mass of Mt. Tallac, on the left, and the granitic mass of Echo Peak, on the right. From our vantage point, the lower southeast slope of Mt. Tallac *appears* to be almost level, and it forms a conspicuous bench from which canyon walls drop steeply to Fallen Leaf Lake. The deep canyon was carved out during glacial times, whereas the "bench," or gentle slope, above it existed before those times. Three million years ago, before the Ice Age, Desolation Wilderness appeared much more rounded and subdued, like this bench on Mt. Tallac or the unglaciated west side of the Carson Range visible above the east shore of Lake Tahoe.

# 74     Ralston Peak Trail to Lake of the Woods and Ropi Lake

**Distances**   5.7 miles to Lake of the Woods, 7.4 miles to Ropi Lake.

**Low/High Elevations**   6500'/8870'

**Classification**   Strenuous

**Season**   Mid-July through mid-October

**Maps**   37 and 35

**Trailhead**   Same as the Hike 73 trailhead.

**Introduction**   Justifiably popular Lake of the Woods, with its islands, coves, bays and good campsites, is a fine subalpine lake for pure relaxation, and it is stocked with brook trout. Ropi Lake, below and beyond it, serves as a base camp for forays up and down Pyramid Creek as well as for an ascent of Pyramid Peak—the highest and most dominating peak of the Crystal Range. Its ascent is described at the end of Hike 72.

Since all these attractions are more easily reached by Hikes 72 and 87, Hike 74 is only for those who want to take in Ralston Peak's summit views. Doing so will add 1.3 miles to the total length of the hike.

**Description**   From the ridge overlooking Lake of the Woods (mentioned in Hike 73) follow the trail down the short, steep north slope, which is usually buried under snow through early August. The trail may be temporarily lost in a small subalpine meadow, boggy from the snowmelt, but it can be located in a stand of hemlocks and pines occupied by Clark nutcrackers. These large, gray, vociferous cousins of the lower-elevation jays feed primarily on pine-cone seeds, which at this elevation would be those of the thin-barked five-needled whitebark pine. From this conifer stand a signed spur trail climbs ⅔ mile southeast to the summit of Ralston Peak.

A northward descent takes us down a gully toward a bench on which there is a pond, with plenty of water-loving wildflowers on the gentle slope above it. We then curve around a flat to a smaller pond, on a saddle, and then start a climb northward up a low knoll. Near its top we obtain a pine-filtered view east of the Echo Lakes and of the Sierra beyond. Then we descend to another saddle, where we meet a trail to Haypress Meadows. This lateral descends ⅓ mile east before reaching a junction with the Pacific Crest Trail. If we were to continue north from this saddle, we would reach, in ¼ mile, a second junction with the Pacific Crest Trail (see Hike 87).

Since we're going to Lake of the Woods, we turn left and follow a lateral westward steeply down to the northeast shore, obtaining enticing views of the lake as we descend. In its last few yards before reaching a small peninsula, the trail ramifies into several paths that link up with a shoreline trail. A ¼-mile contour west gets you to a sloping campsite at the northwest corner, from where several ducked trails climb toward Lake Aloha. (The correct route climbs only 80 yards north—the others continue on—then angles west to a gully and switchbacks up it to the west sides of small ponds atop a broad saddle.) Beyond the sloping campsite, the shore trail heads south 300 yards to "land's end" on a rocky, forested peninsula that separates the warm, island-cluttered west arm from the main lake body. Several good-to-excellent campsites are on this large peninsula, and fair-to-good campsites are near the arm and south of it near the west shore.

Our trail to Ropi Lake contours the wetter, more forested east shore and descends to a forested flat where it's easy to get lost by following false ducks too far south. When you reach the flat, you should head west along the south edge of a small, stagnant pond, then immediately cross Lake of the Woods' outlet creek and follow it south. The creek curves westward, as does our faint, ducked trail, and we reach a tiny, swampy flat at the base of a small peak ¼ mile south of Lake of the Woods that serves as a constant landmark.

From the flat we hike west along the peak's south slope down a joint-controlled gully that has red "blazes" painted on rocks. Immediately beyond the gully we arrive at the southeast arm of shallow, snag-infested Ropi Lake. Campsites can be found near its rocky, sinuous shore, and although they and the lake aren't the best, they serve as a base for further exploration of the lakes in this basin. Pyramid Peak can be climbed by many ways, the easiest route being up its southeast spur.

Below Ropi Lake are several ponds and small lakes. Avalanche Lake sits farthest downstream, atop a lip from which plunges upper Horsetail Fall. From this lip a ducked route (mentioned in Hike 72) descends a steep slope to Twin Bridges, along Highway 50. Don't take it unless you are an experienced mountaineer. You could slip over a cliff and into the Pyramid Creek gorge. At least several people have died trying to negotiate this route. (It is a reasonably safe route if you *first* ascend it, so that you'll know where the dropoffs are and how to avoid them.)

Dark, metamorphic Dicks Peak looms above granite-lined Middle Velma Lake

# Ch. 14    Desolation Wilderness, east side

**Introduction**    Since the introduction to Chapter 13 describes Desolation Wilderness in some depth, there is no need to repeat that information here. Be aware, however, that to enter the wilderness you'll need a wilderness permit—the how, when, where and why of it being mentioned early in Chapter 3.

The east side of Desolation Wilderness differs from the west side in at least two ways: 1) the routes tend to be more popular, and 2) about half of them have Lake Tahoe views. The latter, however, is not the cause of the former; these routes are more popular simply because their trailheads are more accessible. It would be very subjective to say that the east-side scenery is better than its counterpart; the author rates both equal.

As in Chapter 13 this chapter's hikes are arranged from north to south. The first route, Hike 75, is a very long, almost viewless way in to the heart of Desolation Wilderness. Furthermore, it has a particularly bad stretch which should have been rerouted some time ago, but wasn't. Strike two. The only redeeming factor that precludes it from being omitted is that it is part of the popular Pacific Crest National Scenic Trail. The stretch of PCNST that constitutes Hike 75 is not scenic, although it has the potential to be so if it is relocated closer to the crest and up to Phipps Pass.

Hike 84 is another questionable hike, not due to lack of scenery, but rather to its severity. This exceptionally scenic route to the summit of Echo Peak is certainly the harder of two routes; Hike 85 is definitely easier, if less scenic. Other than Hikes 75 and 84, the chapter's other hikes are highly recommended.

# 75    Pacific Crest Trail, Barker Pass to Richardson and Velma Lakes

**Distances**    6.2 miles to Richardson Lake, 13.8 miles to Tahoe-Yosemite Trail, 14.9 miles to Middle Velma Lake.

**Low/High Elevations**    6960'/8140'

**Classification**    Moderate

**Season**    Mid-July through early October

**Maps**    27, 30 and 31

**Trailhead**    See the Hike 47 trailhead.

**Introduction**    This route, although not difficult, is certainly the long way in to Desolation Wilderness. You reach its north boundary about 1 mile beyond Richardson Lake, this lake being a worthy goal. By starting from a Barker Creek camp, you can reach this lake in 4.3 nearly effortless miles.

Through at least 1984 the 4.4-mile stretch of trail from the General Creek Trail junction south to the Tahoe-Yosemite Trail junction ranked as one of the worst stretches along the entire tri-state Pacific Crest Trail. If and when this stretch is relocated closer to the crest, then this back-door route to the heart of Desolation Wilderness will merit serious consideration—but not before.

**Description**    For the long way in to Richardson Lake start where Road 15N03 (Forest Route 3) crosses the Pacific Crest Trail, in the Barker Pass environs. On the "PCT" you curve south, staying above an old jeep road that once climbed over the original Barker Pass. Soon you begin to meet springs and creeklets, some active throughout the summer. For 1½ miles you make a

**Metamorphic Dicks and Jacks peaks and the granitic, snowy Crystal Range**

winding traverse southwest, generally through forest, but sometimes across meadow. Near the end of your gently descending traverse you cross a sloping meadow whose north edge is demarcated by a spring-fed creek. Just ¼ mile past this meadow you come within a stone's throw of the Bear Lake road (14N20) and then parallel it ⅓ mile before crossing it. Bear Lake, although shallow, is pleasant enough. Unfortunately for hikers, it is readily attainable by ORV's, which drive about 2 miles up the Bear Lake road to the lake's north shore.

You can cut 1.9 miles off your hike by starting from a Barker Creek camp. Reach it by first driving 1.3 miles west along Forest Route 3 to Road 32, a major logging road, and following that 2.4 miles down to Barker Creek. Here on Forest Service land, you'll find abundant camping space frequented by car campers—an appropriate trailhead. By driving an additional 0.5 mile, to where the PCT crosses Road 14N20, you'll have to hike only 3.8 miles to reach Richardson Lake. In the early 1980s this stretch of road was quite rough, although it is adequate for pickups.

Just ⅓ mile past Bear Lake Road 14N20 the PCT crosses Bear Lake's reliable outlet creek, and then traverses 1½ miles through viewless forest to a crossing of the McKinney-Rubicon Springs jeep road. Beyond it you quickly reach usually flowing Miller Creek, of very questionable purity, then in 100 yards cross a lightly used road. Your remaining, winding 1¾ miles to Richardson Lake are through a forest that is so dense you could lose your bearings. Many hikers are unaware they are circling Sourdough

Hill, for one feels he is wandering aimlessly. At last you come upon Richardson Lake, whose surrounding lands were acquired by the Forest Service in the mid'80s, but not until the former owner did some rather extensive logging. So, while not scenic, the lake does offer fishing and swimming, plus camping along the north shore.

From the lake the PCT south first parallels a jeep road ½ mile up to a forested saddle, then in 200 yards passes close to a snow-depth indicator, standing in a small meadow just below the trail. After about a ½-mile traverse you reach a large, flat, bedrock bench which, just west of the trail, is almost devoid of trees. The isolationist will find plenty of open space for usually dry, relatively mosquito-free camping. Along the west edge of this bench you have command over many miles of glaciated Rubicon River canyon scenery. Although you're standing ¼ mile above the canyon floor, your vantage spot once lay under glacier ice as recently as 12,000 years ago.

Ahead lies mosquito land—*prime* mosquito land, particularly when you duck into a shallow, soggy bowl. Fortunately, just after you climb out of it you reach a short, dry, open stretch and can take a breather, beside a few junipers, knowing you won't inhale mosquitoes if you do so. Here you have some more views of Rubicon River country plus metamorphic Dicks and Jacks peaks and granitic Crystal Range. In a couple of minutes you pass a monstrous trailside Jeffrey pine, armed with threatening, pendulous limbs, then you stroll ½ mile farther, mostly close to a broad, fairly level crest, to a junction with the General Creek Trail. This descends, sometimes too steeply, just over ½ mile to a junction with the Lake Genevieve Trail, which, eastward, finds its namesake in 1½ miles. There you'd meet the Tahoe-Yosemite Trail (next hike). Downstream, the General Creek Trail falls into abandonment, not tying into its lower section, Hike 52, which takes one out to Highway 89 in Sugar Pine Point State Park.

South from the General Creek Trail junction the next 4.4 erratic miles of Pacific Crest Trail are best left to the mosquitoes. On Map 31 is the author's proposed route to circumvent this highly undesirable stretch. This proposed route begins at the old route's high point, from where you can follow a 40-yard spur trail southwest to some rocks. There you'll see Rubicon, Rockbound and Buck Island reservoirs. (This point is 0.9 mile south of the General Creek Trail junction.)

The proposed route stays close to the crest, sometimes on it, climbing east about 1½ miles to a shallow lakelet. From it the barely climbing route traverses south a similar distance to Phipps Lake, with possible camping, then circles up and out of the lake's cirque, tying into the Tahoe-Yosemite Trail near Phipps Pass. With views of Lake Tahoe, your climb certainly has a climactic ending. Although this route climbs to an appreciably higher elevation than does the old route, your effort is about the same, since the latter does some excessive climbing and dropping.

Whether you take the old route or go cross-country on the author's scenic proposed route, once you meet the TYT, you follow it down to Middle Velma Lake. Beyond this lake, follow, in reverse, the description of the last part of Hike 77.

# 76   Tahoe-Yosemite Trail, Meeks Bay to Velma Lakes

**Distances**   4.6 miles to Lake Genevieve, 4.9 miles to Crag Lake, 5.7 miles to Hidden Lake, 5.9 miles to Shadow Lake, 6.3 miles to Stony Ridge Lake, 8.1 miles to Rubicon Lake, 9.1 miles to Phipps Pass, 13.0 miles to Middle Velma Lake.

**Low/High Elevations**   6238'/8880'

**Classification**   Moderate

**Season**   Late July through mid-October

**Maps**   28 and 31

**Trailhead**   From where Highway 50 leaves Highway 89 in South Lake Tahoe, drive 3.2 miles northwest on Highway 89 to the Lake Tahoe Visitors Center. Get your wilderness permit here, then continue 13¼ miles to a closed road just 230 yards past the Meeks Bay Campground entrance. If you're driving from Tahoe City, follow Highway 89 2.2 miles to the William Kent Visitor Center, get your wilderness permit, and continue 8¾ miles to the trailhead, just 250 yards past Meeks Bay Resort. Park where you can find space anywhere along the highway.

**Introduction**   This relatively easy backpack route takes the hiker along the northernmost part of the unofficial Tahoe-Yosemite Trail, which happens to be very enjoyable because along it you pass one lake right after another. Those who choose to finish by taking Hike 77 or 78 in reverse down to Highway 89 can, hopefully by 1985, take a bus back to their trailhead, for by

then the transit system expects to be operating a loop that totally circles Lake Tahoe.

**Description**   Our route starts west along a closed road at the north edge of Meeks Bay Stables. The road is supposedly closed to all vehicles, but there seems to be some use along it and the side roads branching from it. A horse trail from the stables parallels the road, crossing and recrossing it. After passing two forks going left, our 1⅓-mile-long road—lined with white fir, incense-cedar and lodgepole, ponderosa and sugar pines—enters Forest Service land.

Near the upper end of a grassy swamp, on the left, we reach the signed trailhead for the Tahoe-Yosemite Trail, on our right. The road continues ⅓ mile to the now defunct Camp Wasiu. On trail, we climb moderately for ⅓ mile up the huge lateral moraine the road was following, and meet a spur trail that descends southeast to the camp. One hundred yards later we pass a dripping trailside spring, and then continue up a now gentler trail to flower-lined Meeks Creek. Here we find ranger's buttons, asters, monkey flowers, thimbleberries and bracken ferns as well as the inevitable alders and willows that try to monopolize its waters.

Our ascent now becomes almost negligible as we progress southwest, paralleling the usually unseen creek along a large, mostly forested flat. We hike along the south edges of three dry meadows that sprout variable amounts of lupine and mule ears, and offer potential campsites along their border. Beyond the last one we parallel the creek up a moderate ascent that has two older trail segments along it, both branching left but quickly rejoining the TYT. Where we reach a second forested flat, we also reach a third trail segment, this one branching right and dying out upstream.

In this higher, forested valley, the more alpine red fir, Jeffrey pine and western white pine have replaced their less alpine look-alikes: white fir, ponderosa pine and sugar pine. Incense-cedar was the first to go, but a somewhat similar tree, the juniper, will be seen on exposed rocky benches above. Lodgepole pine— an inhabitant of several vegetational, climatic and edaphic zones—remains with us.

We angle south gently down to a quickly reached large campsite beside Meeks Creek, find suitable rocks on which to cross the creek, and climb a moderately ascending path as it arcs east into a shady, moist, red-fir-forested cove rich in vine maple, currant, thimbleberry and fireweed. Then, winding southwest up the cove's south slope, we soon arrive at a much drier, more open ridge, a good resting spot from which we can just barely see Lake Tahoe. Climbing again, we have a short, pleasant stretch beside cascading Meeks Creek as we hike up to warm, shallow Lake Genevieve, lowest of the Tallant Lakes.

In 1895, California's Fish Commission authorized the stocking of these lakes with Great Lakes Mackinaw fingerlings. When fully grown, these trout top 30 pounds. They migrated down Meeks Creek into Lake Tahoe, grew, and were eventually blamed by Tahoe fishermen with destroying Tahoe's native cutthrout trout. Since all large trout are known to cannibalize smaller trout, the Mackinaws weren't the only culprits. Besides, commercial fishing had been going on unrestricted for decades, first to feed the mining populations in western Nevada's silver mines, then later to supply more distant markets, and very little effort had been put into restocking the lake. (In like manner, the forests were mowed down to provide timber for mines, fuel and mining buildings, and then the denuded slopes were abandoned.) Today you'll have to go to the Angora Lakes (Hike 58) to catch cutthroats; Tahoe has Mackinaw, rainbow and brown trout and Kokanee salmon, but no cutthroat trout. The Tallant Lakes have Mackinaw, rainbow, brown and brook trout.

Along Lake Genevieve's northeast shore you'll see old blazes that mark a narrow trail striking northwest toward the lake's outlet. This

**Crag Peak rises high above Crag Lake**

trail heads over to the Pacific Crest Trail. There are campsites around this lake, some even with a good view of domineering Crag Peak, but since most of them are within 100 feet of the lake, we move onward upstream and quickly reach larger, more appealing Crag Lake, from which Crag Peak rises in all its granitic glory. Like Lake Genevieve downstream and Stony Ridge Lake upstream, Crag Lake has a low dam, so you can expect its water to fluctuate slightly. Good trailside campsites are found along much of its northeast shore, and those willing to make the extra effort will find more secluded campsites on a granitic bench midway along the lake's southwest shore.

After a pleasant stay, continue your TYT trek southeast, climbing up to a boulder-hop ford of Meeks Creek, and then encounter an unsigned trail junction on a ridge just beyond it. This side trail descends to shallow Hidden Lake, nestled at the foot of Crag Peak. Climbers wishing to attempt one or more of the very difficult Class 5 routes up the 400-foot northeast cliff of Crag Peak can reach it by following the glacial trough that curves up to it from the south end of this lake.

From the Hidden Lake trail junction, we climb up the ridge, a lateral moraine, and then curve east to another ridge, this one being a recessional moraine that has dammed diminishing Shadow Lake, below us. The eventual fate of all lakes is extinction, and Shadow Lake is well on its way. Sediments have filled it to such an extent that pond lilies have invaded the upper half of the lake. Close behind them in the marshy water are hydrophytic grasses and wildflowers. Pursuing them on mucky soil are currants and alders. In time the lower half will become a meadow, while the upper half will be sprouting lodgepole pines and mountain hemlocks. Eventually almost all traces of the lake will disappear under the floor of a red fir and western white pine forest. But before that will happen, a glacier may well be advancing down the Tallant Lakes canyon, obliterating all the vegetation in its path.

Leaving this swampy lake behind, we hike along a moderately graded trail that momentarily becomes steeper as it climbs alongside Meeks Creek, whose water is tumbling in cascades and rapids down a granitic gorge. Above the gorge we reach Stony Ridge Lake, largest of the Tallant Lakes. Here, the best campsite of many available may be the one above its north end, just across the low dam. Our trail contours the long, southwest shoreline, briefly crosses some mafic rock, and fords several creeks, which are bordered by yampah, larkspur, columbine, common monkey flower and other wildflowers. The dark, mafic bedrock is similar to granitic bedrock in that it was intruded from below up into overlying rocks that have since been eroded. It differs in that it is much richer in iron and magnesium—hence the darker color.

At the lake's southwest corner we cross and immediately recross the lake's inlet creek, proceed south along the west edge of a boggy

meadow, and then, near an impressive, low-angle cliff of granodiorite, start up a series of well-graded switchbacks, bounded by two tributaries. After almost reaching a steep, churning cascade, we turn onto the last switchback, climb southwest, and get hemlock-framed views below of Stony Ridge Lake and its damp meadow. We soon curve south into a little, willow-lined creek cove, bordered by steep, vertical-jointed cliffs. Now a short climb southeast past a tiny tarn takes us to Rubicon Lake's west shore. Dammed by a ridge of resistant bedrock, beautiful Rubicon Lake is the highest of the Tallant Lakes, which, because they form a line of "beads" along the creek that connects them, are called *paternoster lakes,* after their resemblance to beads on a rosary. Fairly close to the water is a good campsite under mountain hemlocks and lodgepole pines. A large decaying log near the camp serves as home and food for large, black carpenter ants and other invertebrates as well as home for golden-mantled ground squirrels, who may find your pack their most enjoyable source of food. Don't spoil them on processed food.

The lake's water is a bit nippy, reaching only into the low 60s, but a tempting rock just off the west shore beckons one to jump into the cold, clear water. After you climb out to bask atop this rock, you can peer over its edge and see 10-inch trout swimming lazily below you.

Above the lake's south end we reach an abandoned trail that descends to the Grouse Lakes, which are a bit stagnant, and then 15 yards beyond the junction we top a saddle. Our trail then switchbacks up to a granodiorite outlier, just beyond which we can look back at it

**A brave jump into Rubicon Lake's cold, clear water**

and see how joints—the fractures in the bedrock—really control its angular shape. We pass a small gully, snowbound as late as early August, then reach a switchback. Before climbing any farther, you might stop, rest under a juniper or a western white pine, and enjoy the view in the southeast. Looking beyond the north end of Fallen Leaf Lake, we see Tahoe Mountain immediately above it, and from its slopes a long, level ridge—debris left by glaciers—extends southward. Although this ridge, a glacial moraine, towers 900 feet above the lake, that doesn't mean the morainal deposits are 900 feet deep; if we were to tunnel into it, we would surely find granitic bedrock underlying these *surficial* sediments.

A switchback leg north takes us higher up the joint-controlled rocks, and then our trail climbs moderately southward and crosses a gully just before skirting above Phipps Pass, the shallow saddle on your left. Just beyond the pass the trail almost tops a crest on your right, and from it you could descend 320 feet down a steep slope to cold, circular Phipps Lake.

The route ahead, except for a few trivial gains, is all downhill. After almost cresting the ridge, our trail traverses granitic slabs and boulders along the southeast slope of Phipps Peak, named after General William Phipps, who settled along his ("the General's") creek near Sugar Pine Point. We encounter a spring, then swing around to the peak's open south slope, from which we can see the Velma Lakes in the gray, granitic basin below us, and the rusty, metamorphic summit of Dicks Peak towering above it. The contact between the two rock types is clearly evident.

On the TYT we curve northwest, re-enter an open forest of mountain hemlocks and lodgepole, western white and whitebark pines, pass some scolding Clark nutcrackers flying from tree to tree, and then come within 30 yards of a ridge. Here we get poor, hemlock-blocked views northward. Our route now descends southwest, almost reaching the ridge again, then traces three long, well-graded switchback legs down to a junction with the Pacific Crest Trail. Along this descent we thrice cross a trickling creek and we pass many large red firs. Some of the older firs, now in the process of decay, have had their rotting trunks excavated by busy pine martens—larger cousins of the weasel—who chase down ground squirrels, which might also nest in these rotting trunks.

At the junction, we're only about a mile from and 200 feet above Middle Velma Lake, and we head down to this swimmer's paradise. The trail makes a moderate, generally viewless, descent to the lake's outlet creek, which all too often gets hikers' feet wet. The acres of soggy soil found in this forested flat prove to be a great breeding ground for mosquitoes. Before August you'll want to scamper south along the trail to evade the needling critters. This hike ends at the southwest shore of Middle Velma Lake. Most hikers prefer to camp above the lake's south shore, which you can reach by continuing ¼ mile east from a junction with the westbound Velma Lakes Trail (see last part of Hike 66).

If you don't want to make a round trip, Hike 77 or 78 (in reverse) will get you back to Highway 89 in fewer miles.

# 77    Emerald Bay Trail to Eagle and Velma Lakes

**Distances**   1.0 mile to Eagle Lake, 4.3 miles to Dicks Lake, 4.4 miles to Middle Velma Lake, 4.5 miles to Upper Velma Lake, 4.9 miles to Fontanillis Lake via Dicks Lake, 5.2 miles to Fontanillis Lake via Middle Velma Lake.

**Low/High Elevations**   6580'/8500'

**Classification**   Strenuous

**Season**   Mid-July through mid-October

**Maps**   32, 31 and 34

**Trailhead**   From where Highway 50 leaves Highway 89 in South Lake Tahoe, drive 3.2 miles northwest on Highway 89 to the Lake

Tahoe Visitor Center. Get your wilderness permit here, then continue 5.6 miles to the fairly large parking lot of Eagle Falls Picnic Area, its entrance being immediately past Eagle Creek. If you're driving from Tahoe City, follow Highway 89 south 2.2 miles to the William Kent Visitor Center, get your wilderness permit, and then continue 16½ miles to Eagle Falls Picnic Area. Lock your car, for thefts are all too common here.

For Hikes 55 and 78, which use the same trailhead, drive to the Bay View Campground. This is along Highway 89 about one mile south of the Eagle Falls trailhead. Just above the upper end of the campground is parking for about three dozen cars. Don't park in the campground's sites.

**Introduction**   Despite its difficulty, the trail up Eagle Creek canyon is one of the most popular in the Lake Tahoe region, for it takes you, in a few hours' time, to the Dicks Lake-Velma Lakes area. By making a loop through this area you pass at least five lakes and one lakelet, all good for swimming or camping by.

Both the Emerald Bay Trail and the next route, the Bay View Trail, provide access to this lakebound area. Which one should you choose? If you're on horseback, there is no choice, for horses aren't allowed on the Emerald Bay Trail. To its debit the Bay View Trail is ¼ mile longer and has perhaps about 100 feet of additional elevation gain. But to its credit this trail has a better tread and, while fairly steep, is certainly better graded. It also has better views, and its off-highway trailhead is probably less likely to attract thieves. Along either route day hikers can reach a fine lake after only about a mile of walking.                                      **Eagle Lake**

**Description**   From the west end of the parking lot the Emerald Bay Trail, which doubles as the Eagle Lake Trail, makes a short, brushy climb up-canyon, climbs past a vertical cliff, then crosses Eagle Creek, which drains Eagle Lake and the Upper and Lower Velma Lakes. Due to fortuitous circumstances Middle Velma Lake drains west, down to the Rubicon River, whose water ultimately reaches—if not usurped by Sacramento—the Pacific Ocean. In contrast, Eagle Creek, which is tumultuous in early season, flows into Lake Tahoe, whose water should reach the Washoe Indians' Pyramid Lake—but more likely is usurped by Reno. In September 1983 a much needed sturdy steel bridge was placed across this creek.

From it the trail cuts across the foot of a blocky talus slope, climbs up to a bench, and enters Desolation Wilderness as it swings west to a second bench. From this bench we can gaze northeast down at Emerald Bay and out to the Carson Range above Tahoe. Beyond the bench we cross a small lodgepole flat, round a low headwall, and parallel Eagle Lake's outlet creek. Shortly we reach another flat, shaded by white firs and Jeffrey pines. We now make a brief ascent, see the creek's rapids, and catch a glimpse of Eagle Lake as we reach a well-used spur trail that goes 200 yards over bedrock to the lake.

Hemmed in by granitic cliffs, this picturesque lake is a good area for climbers, who can establish a base camp above the north shore. Nonclimbers will find a photogenic lake to relax at, to fish in or to photograph.

Beyond this lake the Emerald Bay Trail climbs steeply up to a saddle and a junction with the Bay View Trail. On this strenuous climb, aromatic tobacco brush, drab huckleberry oak, and needle-tipped snow bush dominate the vegetation, and these can be rough if you're hiking in shorts. Starting up it, we first pass under the towering cliff of North Maggies Peak—a challenge to rock climbers—then arrive at a gully, shaded by pines and firs, which has a small creek trickling down it. Short, steep switchbacks guide us up the gully's west side, and as the gradient eases, an old branch of trail climbs west out of the forest cover, but our route switchbacks southeast one more time before curving west and rejoining the old route. From the reunion you follow ducks up a barren slab to a small lodgepole flat, whose west side the trail traverses for 50 yards before it climbs south-southwest up to and through a clump of alders, arriving at the base of an outcrop. After an initial 30-yard climb west along this base, our trail, which can be indistinct over the last ¼ mile, becomes obvious, and we climb steeply south up a slope and then traverse to a rocky bench on the west ridge of South Maggies Peak. These two similar, pointed peaks, popular conversation pieces for 19th century Lake Tahoe boaters, were not named for Maggie, but rather for part of her anatomy. Back in those days, however, the two peaks' names were more explicit.

A short, steep switchback leg takes us down from the bench, and then we make a traverse high above a large pond being overgrown with grass and lily pads. Along the trail we find, in an alder thicket, a trickling spring, which is our last dependable fresh water until we reach the Velma Lakes area, about 2 miles farther.

Beyond the spring we switchback up to an ephemeral creek, cross it, and climb a gradually easing slope to a saddle on which we meet the Bay View Trail. From here we traverse west, pass two crest-bound ponds, and then engage a ½-mile traverse past brush and bedrock almost to a saddle. Here, close to an ankle-deep, 10-yard-long seasonal pond, we reach a junction.

From it the trail to Dicks Lake first traverses ½ mile southwest, passing four more ponds—these larger—before reaching a lakelet worthy of a lunch break or a refreshing swim. Just 250 yards past the lakelet this trail reaches the top end of the Upper Velma Lake trail, which descends ½ mile northwest to the south tip of

that lake, then continues ¾ mile north to this hike's main trail. If Dicks Lake is on your mind, then climb a steep ¼ mile south to a crest junction with the Pacific Crest/Tahoe-Yosemite trail, which you can then take ¼ mile south down to a spur trail that drops 100 yards to the northwest shore of Dicks Lake. Popular campsites lie along the lake's north shore and its east peninsula. Beyond this lake's spur trail the PCT/TYT descends past a large tarn, with a good campsite, then traverses along Fontanillis Lake's east shore. Campsites here are only poor-to-fair, although better, more isolated ones may be found near the two lakes just west of Fontanillis Lake.

Our route, Hike 77, takes the most popular tread—the one to Middle Velma Lake. We leave the junction by the ankle-deep pond as we climb northwest 50 yards to a slightly larger pond atop a broad saddle, and then descend a convoluted ¾ mile to a shallow, unnamed Velma lake ringed with illegally close campsites. When you reach its wide outlet creek, you may have to walk just upstream to find a dry crossing. If you were to hike downstream 0.4 mile cross-country, preferably along the creek's west bank, you would reach Lower Velma Lake. This receives a lot less use than its trailside sisters and, being bedrock-bound, it has fewer mosquitoes.

From the outlet creek our trail climbs 100 yards to a junction with the Upper Velma Lake trail. You can reach this lake's north end by hiking ⅓ mile south along this trail. Upper

**Swimmers at Middle Velma Lake**

**Lightly used Lower Velma Lake spreads out below Phipps Peak**

Velma Lake's "claim to fame" is its "lake within a lake," actually, just a grassy, semistagnant pond on the lake's island.

Only 180 yards past the Upper Velma trail junction our westbound course meets the Pacific Crest/Tahoe-Yosemite trail, which climbs one mile to Fontanillis Lake and an additional mile to Dicks Lake. We take the PCT/TYT about 100 yards northwest, to where it curves west. Here you'll see Middle Velma Lake, and you can leave the trail for a quick descent to it. On weekends this lakeshore is crowded, for it has inviting water that tempts hikers to swim out to, dive from, or sunbathe on one or more of the lake's rock-slab islands. Rainbow trout also lure fishermen to this sprawling lake.

# 78 Bay View Trail to Granite, Dicks, Fontanillis and Velma Lakes

**Distances** 1.1 miles to Granite Lake, 2.7 miles to Emerald Bay Trail.

**Low/High Elevations** 6910'/8440'

**Classification** Strenuous

**Season** Mid-July through mid-October

**Maps** 32, 31 and 34

**Trailhead** and **Introduction** See the previous hike's trailhead and introduction.

**Description** From the trailhead, you climb moderately through a dense white-fir forest with a chinquapin understory, then switchback up to a sharp bend in a jeep road. You could have hiked southwest up this very steep road to reach this bend, but the effort wouldn't have been worth it. From the bend you immediately enter Desolation Wilderness as you follow the closed jeep road northwest up to the top of a ridge of weathered granodiorite bedrock. By walking a few paces north you'll obtain a tree-framed view of Emerald Bay, its bedrock Fannette Island, and Lake Tahoe.

Your route ahead is now a trail that climbs southeast along Granite Lake's trickling, alder-lined outlet creek. Also along it you may find water-loving wildflowers such as Bolander's yampah, or olaski, as the Miwok Indians called it, who ate the roots of this wild carrot. Don't pick this plant because first, it is illegal to do so, and second, there are some poisonous wild carrots that closely resemble it.

The sensuous aroma of tobacco brush heralds your approach to clear, moderately large Granite Lake. You'll appreciate the relatively warm water—up to 70°F—of this moraine-dammed lake. There are no large campsites, but small ones lie along its east and north shores. However, due to its proximity to Highway 89, the lake should be day-use only.

With about 800 feet under your belt and 700 feet left to climb—most of it quite steep—resume your trudge up the no-nonsense Bay View Trail. Halfway up this stretch, at a short switchback leg, you have an excellent view of Granite Lake, moraine-bound Emerald Bay, and Lake Tahoe. You also see moraine-bound Cascade Lake which, were it a little lower, would be another "Emerald Bay."

To get an even better view of the Lake Tahoe scenery, leave your vantage point and traverse over to the nearby ridge. If you've got a backpack, leave it at the ridge and make a rocky, brushy traverse north along its crest to North Maggies Peak, point 8499 on the map. A 200-foot-climb, involving some use of hands, gets you to the top. The sublime view is so over-powering it almost knocks you off the summit. Only Mt. Tallac's view (Hikes 79 and 81) can rival it, but attaining that summit requires twice the hiking effort. You see not only most of Lake Tahoe, but also a goodly part of Desolation Wilderness. You can make a visual east-west traverse of the wilderness, identifying, one above the other: Lower Velma Lake, Middle Velma Lake, Lake Schmidell and Red Peak.

Back on the trail the last part of your climb can be snowbound well through July in a typical year. Your trail gradient abates as you cross just above the south end of the ridge connecting North and South Maggies peaks. A fairly open traverse ensues, along which you have fair views across the Echo Creek canyon. After ⅓ mile you commence a winding, usually gentle descent along a ridge down to the Emerald Bay Trail junction. Along this part you'll glimpse isolated Azure and Snow lakes, these nourished by essentially perennial snowfields. From the junction you have the same options as in the previous hike—read the second half of its trail description.

# 79      Mt. Tallac Trail to Mt. Tallac

**Distances**   1.7 miles to Floating Island Lake, 2.5 miles to Cathedral Lake, 4.6 miles to Mt. Tallac.

**Low/High Elevations**   6480'/9735'

**Classification**   Strenuous

**Season**   Mid-July through mid-October

**Maps**   32 and 35

**Trailhead**   From where Highway 50 leaves Highway 89 in South Lake Tahoe, drive 3.2 miles northwest on Highway 89 to the Lake Tahoe Visitor Center. If you're going to Floating Island Lake or beyond, you'll need a wilderness permit, which you can get here. Westward, you bridge Taylor Creek in ¼ mile, then reach a signed intersection in ½ mile. Most folks drive ½ mile north to Baldwin Beach, but on a paved road you head south, branching left in 0.4 mile, then keeping right at a quickly reached second fork. Now on a gravel road, you drive ½ mile to a parking area with space for at least a dozen vehicles.

**Introduction**   Like Hike 81, this one takes you to Mt. Tallac's summit, but it does so in fewer, and therefore steeper, miles. Two small lakes— one of them unique—are passed along your way up this route, which undoubtedly has more views but fewer campsites than does Hike 81.

Actually, the first 1.2-mile stretch constitutes a route unto itself, for you climb to the crest of a giant lateral moraine, then hike ½ mile south along it, receiving exceptional views of Fallen Leaf Lake and the southern Lake Tahoe Basin. This largely open day hike is typically snow-free by late May or early June.

**Description**   You start among Jeffrey pines and sagebrush, climb 120 yards up an old road to a blocked-off fork, veer right, and reach an old gravel pit. The gape left here offers a glimpse of the structure of a glacial moraine, which is largely composed of unsorted boulders in a gravel matrix. Beyond the pit we're now on a trail, climbing south up a shallow gully that lies between two lateral moraines. The east one was left by the last glacier to occupy the basin now filled by Fallen Leaf Lake. The west one probably was deposited by the same glacier, only earlier in its history. A larger, considerably older moraine lies unseen west of it, this one terminating at about the 6400-foot elevation, just south of the major bend in Highway 89. We'll be crossing it near Floating Island Lake.

Starting toward that lake, we make a moderate climb south, the gradient rapidly reducing to gentle. In ⅓ mile we crest the moraine, which is largely cloaked in huckleberry oaks and greenleaf manzanitas, on its east slopes and in white firs and Jeffrey pines on its west slopes. Our first views are stunning, but better ones lie ahead as we traverse south.

After a ½-mile walk we drop away from the crest, being saturated with views. We enter another intermorainal gully, then make a rocky ascent across the earlier moraine, the ascent yielding to a brief traverse into a red-fir forest. Under deep shade we make a short, steep climb south up almost useless switchbacks, then level off just inside the Desolation Wilderness boundary by the north end of Floating Island Lake.

In 1890 this unique lake was noted as having a 20-foot-diameter floating mat of grass and shrubs, whence the name. In 1979 there were four floating, grassy mats, and more mats were ready to slough off from the lake's soggy northwest shore. It's a mystery why the mats slough off at this lake and not at any other, for in all other respects Floating Island Lake seems quite ordinary. Anyway, mats do slough off here, gradually enlarging the lake while replacing older mats that break up. Therefore chances are very good that you'll see at least one island floating in the lake. Conifers ring this lake, denying the backpacker space to set up a legal campsite, so it's best to head on to Cathedral Lake.

Climbing toward it, you leave Floating Island Lake and parallel its inlet creek to a nearby gap. From it an essentially cross-country route— formerly a trail—traverses south 0.2 mile to a trail from Fallen Leaf Lake. From the gap we continue southwest up our trail, lined with wildflowers, currant, western serviceberry, sagebrush and other shrubs we've seen, and soon come to a saddle immediately west of a little rocky knoll. From its juniper-covered summit, free of mosquitoes, we can relax and take in a panorama that includes most of Lake Tahoe, some of Fallen Leaf Lake, and beyond it the granitic summits of the Freel Peak massif.

Mt. Tallac's summit area is now visible, and it beckons us onward, so we make a brief descent to Cathedral Creek, cross it, and meet the Cathedral Lake Trail, which ascends from Fallen Leaf Lake. This drops—excessively so in one stretch—a full mile to a junction about 130 feet above the lake's west shore. From there a trail heads ⅓ mile south to the private grounds of Stanford Sierra Camp, while in the other direction it heads ⅔ mile north to the Fallen Leaf Tract of summer homes.

Just a few minutes' hiking past the Cathedral Lake Trail junction, we reach Cathedral Lake. Named for its proximity to Cathedral Peak, which is not a peak but rather a cliff on Tallac's southeast ridge, this shallow lake, with a few trout, is a disappointment. Still, its water is better than that of Floating Island Lake, though its camping prospects are almost as bleak.

After climbing very steeply west 200 feet above this lake, we reach a trail segment with fresh, cold water running along it. Bordered with common monkey flower, stickseed, tall larkspur, fireweed, thimbleberry and other hydrophytic wildflowers, this short stretch is an excellent place to take a lunch break, since it may be your last dependable source of water. Beyond it our trail climbs steadily and steeply up the sloping floor of a cirque toward its headwall, which usually has snowfields well into August. Several trails, formed on talus through continual use, try to avoid most of the snow. The correct route has a switchback leg that climbs south up to the ridge and tops it at a point immediately west of where the trail curves from southeast to east. Standing atop it, we get great views east, south and west— a taste of what's to come.

We leave the edge of the ridge as we hike northwest up an increasingly steep trail bordered by currant, gooseberry, snow bush, spiraea and sagebrush. Scattered clumps of western white, lodgepole and whitebark pines speckle the slope. Near the 9000-foot level, the brush diminishes and wildflowers become more predominant. Finally we reach a junction with the larger, more evident trail from Gilmore Lake (see Hike 81). Enjoying a breather while taking in a view of many lakes below, we can identify circular Gilmore Lake in its cirque southwest of us, Susie Lake on a bench beyond it, and Lake Aloha along the east base of the granitic Crystal Range.

There being now only 400 vertical feet to climb to the summit, we start with more determination than ever, climbing north steeply up an increasingly faint though ducked trail, or up one of its parallel branches. Midway to the summit this trail cuts east up to a weatherbeaten clump of conifers, which makes a good wind-protected emergency shelter, but it is no place to sit out a lightning storm. You shouldn't attempt to climb to this summit—or any summit—if a storm is impending.

We now follow a rocky route, first northeast to the brink of a dangerously steep avalanche chute, then diagonally northwest for the last few steps to the pointed summit. Most panoramas from any high summit are spectacular, and those from dark, metamorphic Mt. Tallac certainly are. Because it stands so close to Lake Tahoe, it provides us with a view of almost the entire lake. Standing above Tahoe's northeast end is ande-

**Lake Tahoe and Fallen Leaf Lake. See title page for another summit view.**

site-capped Mt. Rose, which at 10,776 feet is the basin's third highest peak. Along the east shore rise the granitic western slopes of the Carson Range, which remain unglaciated because they lie within a rain shadow cast by the Sierra crest above Tahoe's westen shore. Today the western crest receives 70–90 inches of precipitation annually, whereas the eastern crest receives only about 30–40 inches.

Along the lake's south shore are the readily visible Tahoe Keys, which together with the high rises stand out in this basin as a monument to man's economic exploitation of a unique, fault-dropped, high-mountain lake basin. Southeast of this shore rise Freel Peak (10,881') and Jobs Sister (10,823'), ranking first and second among the basin's peaks. In the distance to the southeast is the 10,000-foot-high ridge near Carson Pass. To the south rises granitic Echo Peak, and beyond it Ralston Peak, the unseen Echo Lakes lying between them. West of Ralston Peak is Pyramid Peak, the high point and south end of the Crystal Range.

Of much interest are the huge, linear, lateral moraines that border Emerald Bay, Cascade Lake and Fallen Leaf Lake. Towering up to 900 feet above their basins, the heights of these moraines indicate the minimum thickness of the glacier that filled the basins. Since each of these glaciers also scoured its basin and made it deeper, it is likely, in the case of the Fallen Leaf glacier, that the glacier was at least ¼ mile thick. (Today, Fallen Leaf Lake has a maximum depth of 418 feet.) The Tahoe basin must have been an extremely impressive sight 15,000 years ago. At times, equally large glaciers from Squaw Valley, and from Pole Creek north of it, dammed Tahoe's northwest outlet and raised the lake's level by as much as 600 feet. Then these glacial-ice dams broke, creating catastrophic floods. Take your time at the summit, crowded on weekends, and try to visualize the evolving landscape of this majestic basin. Up here with all the hikers you might find a far marmot freeloading off their luncheon leftovers. Other fauna include a variety of insects wafted up here by updrafts.

**Pyramid Peak caps the Crystal Range; Gilmore Lake lies in the foreground**

# 80    Glen Alpine Trail to Grass Lake

**Distance**   2.3 miles, one way
**Low/High Elevations**   6560'/7240'
**Classification**   Easy
**Season**   Early July through mid-October
**Map**   35

**Trailhead**   Hikes 80-84 start near Glen Alpine Creek, and since all of them enter Desolation Wilderness, you'll need a wilderness permit. The most convenient place to get one is at the Lake Tahoe Visitor Center, whose entrance is on Highway 89 just 150 yards west of Fallen Leaf Road. (This road is 3.1 miles northwest on Highway 89 from the South Lake Tahoe **Y**, the signaled intersection where Highway 50 branches northeast from Highway 89.)   With permit in hand, drive 4.5 miles south on Fallen Leaf Road to the site of former Fallen Leaf Lodge. Continue 0.3 mile to where the road forks, the right branch swinging north across Glen Alpine Creek to Stanford Sierra Camp, the left branch paralleling the creek up-canyon. Hike 84 begins at a post 0.4 mile up the left branch, this spot being just 300 yards before the road bridges the cascading creek. Hikes 80–83 begin from a gate ⅓ mile beyond the bridge. Parking is limited between the south shore of Fallen Leaf Lake and the gate. Park where you can find a spot that doesn't block this road which, beyond the bridge, is narrow and rocky.

**Introduction**   An easy day hike, this route leads to a rockbound lake with a dramatic cascade on the cliffs beyond it. Its fairly warm water is just right for a midsummer afternoon swim. Being so close to the trailhead, the lake has developed notable vegetation, sanitation and soil problems due to overuse. Therefore, if you feel you absolutely must camp at Grass Lake, do so with minimum impact (no fires; carry out all wastes).

**Description**   From the gate follow the closed road past private residences as it more or less parallels Glen Alpine Creek westward to where the trail begins at a DESOLATION WILDERNESS sign just beyond Glen Alpine Springs. Nathan Gilmore discovered these iron-rich mineral springs while looking for his stray cattle in 1863. They were then gushing about 200 gallons an hour. In the late 1870s Gilmore began bottling the carbonated water, which soon achieved a reputation, and he developed Glen Alpine Springs into a very popular resort.

Start up the Glen Alpine Trail, which climbs southeast about 200 yards before climbing west up a rocky, joint-controlled gully. We make a switchback south out of our gully, curve around a low ridge, and walk west again to a small, waist-deep pool with a tiny fall splashing into it. Just beyond this cool bathtub, on a flat immediately before the trail bends northeast as it starts a switchbacking climb, we arrive at a signed junction with the Grass Lake Trail. From here, head a few yards west, jump across the Gilmore Lake outlet creek, which is the actual Desolation Wilderness boundary, and then follow the trail southwest up a brushy slope, inhabited by mountain quail, to reach a grassy pond that is an overflow of Glen Alpine Creek. The best spot to cross this creek is at some rapids below the pond, where water flows east down a small, granitic, 20-foot-high **V** gorge.

Beyond this crossing our trail winds almost up to the audible outlet creek of Lake Lucille. An older trail still climbs southwest to it before curving northwest to Grass Lake, but our trail curves north, passes northwest through a **V** trough, and then curves southwest and descends through another one. Joint control certainly expresses itself in this granodiorite bedrock. Just beyond the second trough our newer trail meets the older trail, and 100 yards farther we are at the southeast corner of shallow Grass Lake. The trail continues for 0.2 mile to a shallow bay, passing several campsites located too close to the shoreline to be legal. We then reach a campsite just east of the bay on a bench covered with fir and pine.

East of this are some open metavolcanic rocks, below which is the lake's deepest water. Here, an 8-foot-high rock bench makes an ideal platform for diving into the lake's fairly clear water, which warms up into the mid-60s. These brown rocks contrast strongly with the gray, joint-controlled granitic rocks that dam the lake's east end.

Fishing is poor because the lake is relatively small and is heavily fished. However, what may be lost in the way of a fish dinner is made up for by the lovely lakeside surroundings, including a silvery cascade from Susie Lake that plunges down the cliff northwest of us.

# 81   Glen Alpine Trail to Gilmore Lake and Mt. Tallac

**Distances**   3.9 miles to Gilmore Lake, 5.7 miles to Mt. Tallac.

**Low/High Elevations**   6560'/9735'

**Classification**   Moderate to lake, strenuous to summit.

**Season**   Early July through mid-October

**Map**   35

**Trailhead**   Same as the Hike 80 trailhead.

**Introduction**   Of all the significant peaks you can climb by trail, Mt. Tallac is the closest one to the shore of Lake Tahoe. Consequently, your view of the lake is truly exceptional, and it is highlighted by the dramatic topography of the prodigous lateral moraines that border Emerald Bay, Cascade Lake and Fallen Leaf Lake. Gilmore Lake, along your ascent route, is an ideal spot to rest or camp before making the final wildflower-bedecked push to the summit.

**Description**   As in Hike 80 start at the closed gate, walk 0.8 mile up the road to a DESOLATION WILDERNESS sign, and then hike up the Glen Alpine Trail to a small flat just above a splashing, trailside pool. Above this flat and its Grass Lake Trail junction, we switchback north up a brushy, open-forested granitic slope, where frisky golden-mantled ground squirrels scamper about. Re-entering forest shade, we soon come to an alder-lined, step-across creeklet, then continue upward and onward to Gilmore Lake's outlet creek. Just 30 yards beyond its crossing, we reach a signed trail fork. Both forks climb to the Pacific Crest/Tahoe Yosemite trail. Those on Hike 83 fork left, those on Hikes 81 and 82 fork right. Taking the right fork, we make a ¼-mile ascent up a rocky path, climbing steadily above a shallow tarn below us to a juniper-flat intersection with the PCT/TYT.

From here the next hike continues straight ahead to Half Moon and Alta Morris lakes, but your trail switchbacks north up a ½-mile segment of the PCT/TYT. Along this open ascent past large, rusty-barked junipers, you can look south to shallow Grass Lake and southwest to sparsely-tree-lined Susie Lake. Just before the trail comes alongside Gilmore Lake's cascading outlet creek, you catch a glimpse of granite-lined Lake Aloha in the southwest. Veering slightly away from the creek, we reach an almost level junction in an open lodgepole forest.

Here the PCT/TYT turns west and continues its climb to Dicks Pass (see the last part of Hike

66). We, however, head north, upstream, and cross the outlet creek just before reaching Gilmore Lake. In the entire Sierra there is hardly a lake more circular than this one, and it is amazing that it doesn't bear the name *Round Lake,* especially when you consider how many noncircular lakes in the Sierra do bear this name. Instead, it was named to honor Nathan Gilmore, a local settler from 1863 onward, and who in 1877 stocked this lake with 20 black bass. Now it has a population of rainbow, brook and lake trout. Please don't camp at the lake's overused southeast shore; rather, use fine, lodgepole-shaded campsites *above* the lake's south and east shores.

From the southeast shore our trail climbs steeply, first northeast and then north, heading up through a rapidly thinning forest of lodgepole and whitebark pines and crossing three flower-lined creeklets. As the last of the snow is melting, these creeklets and associated seeps can be densely speckled yellow with a myriad of buttercups, which are shown on Plate 14. Other wildflowers which appear on this plate can also be plentiful, but the smaller ones—the lewisia and steer's head in particular—are easily overlooked. Interested botanists will also want to consult Plates 11, 13, 15, 16 and 17, all dealing with high-elevation wildflowers.

Our path becomes drier as we hike to within 150 yards of a 9000-foot-high saddle, then switchback east up the grass- and sagebrush-lined trail. About 200 feet below the summit we meet the Mt. Tallac Trail, which has climbed past Floating Island and Cascade lakes (Hike 79). The last part of that hike describes the final ascent plus the views you'll see from the summit.

**Gilmore Lake and Mt. Tallac**

**Wildflower Plate 14. Desolation Wilderness flowers, continued.**
1 Three-leaved lewisia (white with pink stripes), 2 western spring beauty (white to pale-pink), 3 steer's head (pale pink), 4 Sierra saxifrage (whitish with yellow center), 5 water-plantain buttercup (yellow), 6 rosy sedum (burgundy red), 7 shaggy hawkweed (yellow), 8 hawksbeard (yellow), 9 Douglas' catchfly (white to lavender).

# 82     Glen Alpine Trail to Half Moon and Alta Morris Lakes

**Distances**   4.5 miles to Half Moon Lake, 5.2 miles to Alta Morris Lake.

**Low/High Elevations**   6560'/8150'

**Classification**   Moderate

**Season**   Late July through mid-October

**Maps**   35 and 34

**Trailhead**   Same as the Hike 80 trailhead.

**Introduction**   Situated on the corrugated bedrock floor of an immense cirque, these two lakes see relatively little use despite their accessibility; they are bypassed for lakes in more demure settings along the highly popular Pacific Crest/Tahoe-Yosemite trail. Within this cirque basin you're almost guaranteed to find a suitable, isolated campsite.

**Description**   Follow the first paragraph of the previous hike up to the PCT/TYT, from where you continue straight ahead. The trail starts a contour northwest as a narrow footpath, then becomes more distinct as it arcs west across a small, forested bowl. Leaving the bowl, we climb to a low ridge and see Susie Lake, nestled in her metamorphic bed. On the skyline, granitic Pyramid Peak stands at the south end of a long, snowy stretch of the Crystal Range. Leaving this viewpoint, we descend slightly into a shallow gully, go up it, cross a low ridge bordering it, and then traverse a lodgepole flat and a mucky-banked creeklet flowing through it. With mud falling from our boots, we climb up the southwest slope of yet another gully and soon approach a chest-deep pond, on the left, which has drinkable water and at times an aquatic garter snake or two. After passing two smaller ponds on our right, which support pond lilies and other aquatic vegetation, we come to a grass-lined pond with a campsite on its northeast shore. Since this site is within 100 feet of the shoreline, it is off limits to camping, so if you

want to camp in this vicinity, try above the south or west shores.

From a low ridge immediately beyond the last pond, we see clear, blue, appropriately named Half Moon Lake, which occupies almost the entire width of the huge cirque carved out between Jacks Peak and Dicks Pass. Not only is this the largest cirque in Desolation Wilderness, but it is also the deepest, and the lake is hemmed in on three sides by a dark wall of steep rock that averages ¼ mile high.

The trail makes an undulating traverse across the meadowy talus slope of metamorphic rock that borders the lake's north and west shores. In some places the trail is boggy; in others it is indistinct and somewhat overgrown with willows. Eventually you'll reach a fairly large campsite, nestled under western white pines and mountain hemlocks, on a bench above the northwest shore of Alta Morris Lake. This lake, perhaps the most scenic cirque lake in Desolation Wilderness, rests above the southwest corner of Half Moon Lake, and it can be approached by a more direct, drier, cross-country route.

Starting this route when you first see Half Moon Lake, head west and stay on the rocky bench above its south shore. On the map this route looks almost level, but in reality you ascend and descend across a number of small, glacier-cut gullies. Midway across your washboard traverse you'll cross Half Moon's outlet creek, which cascades into a clear, linear, grassy-bottomed lake—nice for swimming in or camping nearby. Continuing west toward the dark rusty-brown metasediments that buttress Jacks Peak, we walk across buff-colored metavolcanic bedrock that contrasts strongly with them. Soon we reach one or more small, semi-stagnant ponds and, just beyond them, the northeast bench above Alta Morris Lake.

# 83   Glen Alpine Trail to Susie and Heather Lakes and Lake Aloha

**Distances**   3.8 miles to Susie Lake, 4.9 miles to Heather Lake, 5.8 miles to Lake Aloha.

**Low/High Elevations**   6560'/8120'

**Classification**   Moderate

**Season**   Mid-July through mid-October

**Maps**   35 and 34

**Trailhead**   Same as the Hike 80 trailhead.

**Introduction**   This route takes you up to large, shallow Lake Aloha, which is probably the most popular lake in Desolation Wilderness. By arriving at its scenic northeast shore, however, you avoid most of its backpackers, who generally camp at its south shore. Susie Lake, two thirds of the way up to Aloha, is a favorite lake of many backpackers, and for late-season excursions it is a well chosen goal, because much of Aloha dries up after Labor Day. Before then, both Susie and Heather lakes may be too crowded—at least on weekends—to suit your fancy.

**Description**  Follow part of the first paragraph of Hike 81 up to a fork, from where two trails begin a climb to the Pacific Crest/Tahoe-Yosemite trail. You take the left fork, which makes an initial climb west, traverses through a lodgepole forest past four lily-pad ponds, and then descends westward to meet the PCT/TYT. Here, at the upper end of a boggy (and buggy) meadow, you can identify a variety of wildflowers.

Ahead, we pass two stagnant ponds, climb over a low ridge, and find bedrock-rimmed Susie Lake lying before us. Precious little flat space for camping is to be found here, although on a weekend several dozen backpackers may try to do so. Head south along the lake's shore, cross the outlet creek, and find a spur trail. This descends 70 yards along the creek to a small bench, which has suitable campsites. Your route then rounds the lake to a cove along its southwest shore, from which it leaves the multihued environs for a short climb over a barren ridge to Heather Lake.

After you skirt Heather Lake's north shore, you'll find an adequate campsite near a large red fir by an inlet creek. We cross this creek, climb a bit to a switchback by the creek's 20-foot-high

waterfall, then with a bit m[...] the northeast corner of Lak[...] the PCT/TYT heads south[...] con River Trail (part of H[...] Along the latter you'll find[...] sunrise views across the lake—before mid-September, that is. After then, you won't see the sun's rays playing on the water, but rather will see a desolate lake bottom, for every late summer, Desolation Valley is resurrected, in a ghastly form, as the lake is drained to fill other reservoirs lying closer to Sacramento. This draw-down does allow, however, cross-country routes across the lake where midsummer hikers would have to walk on water. The more conventional route along the lake's northeast shore is described, in the reverse direction, in Hike 87.

**Heather Lake and the Crystal Range**

**Susie Lake and Dicks Peak**

# Tamarack Trail to Triangle Lake and Echo Peak

istances 2.7 miles to Triangle Lake, 3.6 miles to Echo Peak, 7.0 miles for entire loop.

**Low/High Elevations** 6640′/8895′

**Classification** Strenuous

**Season** Mid-July through mid-October

**Map** 35

**Trailhead** See the Hike 80 trailhead description.

**Introduction** Almost every ascent to a mountain's summit provides the climber with far-ranging, panoramic views. This hike up a primitive trail to the Echo Peak ridge and summit area certainly is no exception, but in addition it routes your return trip past Upper Angora Lake, which is an ideal relaxing site after your arduous climb. The Tamarack Trail is definitely the hard way up to Triangle Lake and Echo Peak. However, for summer residents or visitors in the Fallen Leaf Lake area, it is an appropriate route, for one does not have to drive all the way up to the Echo Lake trailhead. For these people, a hike part way up the trail may be rewarding. The wildflowers along the ascent in midsummer are so abundant that the amateur botanist may feel fulfilled even if he or she never makes it to the top.

In early summer the Tamarack Trail may be too dangerous. Before mid-July, start from the Echo Lakes trailhead and follow Hike 85 up to the Triangle Lake saddle and then east to Echo Peak. Hike 84's descent route is safe, but it is so steep that few would want to climb up it. It is, however, the shortest way to the top, only 2.0 miles from the Angora Lakes parking lot (see Hike 57's trailhead directions).

**Description** Starting on metamorphic bedrock with granitic boulders transported here by a glacier, our trail enters an open forest of white fir and lodgepole and Jeffrey pine, with a rich substory of aspen, alder, willow, vine maple, tobacco brush, currant and spiraea. Beyond a low knoll we get a view of Mt. Tallac's dark back side, then enter a shady forest where we see white thimbleberry (with pink berries in late season), red columbine, purple monkshood and the green fronds of bracken fern. Less common is pine drops, and rare is snow plant, both being red saprophytes that live off decaying organic matter. Two large white firs mark the start of a steep ascent, but thirst on this climb can be slaked at a number of creeklets, each with its refreshing water plus its own population of water-loving plants.

Our grade eases and the forest opens as we approach a second knoll, from which we can look west-northwest at the two brownish-red metamorphic summits of Jacks and Dicks peaks. Perched nearby us is a huge, 20-foot-high orange-and-gray boulder of metamorphic rock in contact with the granitic rock that intruded the metamorphic rock just over 100 million years ago. Beyond it we are soon climbing up steep switchbacks through an overwhelming amount of vegetation. Finally emerging from this jungle, we make a short traverse west to a relatively barren flat on which a few hardy junipers survive. From here we see most of Fallen Leaf Lake and part of Tahoe beyond it. Now also visible are the summit rocks of rusty Mt. Tallac. Just above this flat is an exposed campsite, relatively close to a long-lasting snowfield, and both are just within the Desolation Wilderness boundary.

A short, climbing traverse west brings us to a dangerous creek we must jump across; should you slip, you're likely to go over the brink of a very steep cascade—a one-way trip. Short, steep switchbacks up a path gloriously lined with wildflowers take us to a safe recrossing of the creek and to some good rocks to stop at and rest, from which we can photograph the magnificent canyon and lateral moraines north of us.

Refreshed, we climb steeply up the wild-flowered east bank of the creek, cross it after a 250-foot climb, and then continue up an increasingly easy grade that eventually levels off. Here we see a panorama from Tahoe, in the north, past Tallac, Dicks and Jacks summits to barely showing Pyramid Peak, in the west-southwest. The forest is now an open one of juniper, western white pine and mountain hemlock, and on the grassy slopes grow sagebrush and a diverse array of showy and nonshowy wildflowers. If you are quiet you might observe a chicken-sized, chunky blue grouse nibbling away on berries or pine needles. An easy stroll now takes us down to a flat saddle with a trail intersection. To the north, the trail descends to Triangle Lake; south, it descends to the Echo Lakes (see next hike for more details).

To climb Echo Peak, we retrace our steps 85 yards east to a rockpile, from where a faint, unmaintained trail continues east while the main trail we came up curves left. Fallen trees make the trail hard to follow in a few places, but the slope's topography and vegetation are so amenable to cross-country travel that you need not stick to the trail. From the junction, the trail soon turns northeast and then climbs steadily through an open forest that now includes whitebark pine; then, as it approaches the rocky northeast ridge of Echo Peak, it fades into nothingness.

Here it behooves you to walk 130 yards north to the brink of the ridge, from where you not only see everything you might have seen from the Angora Fire Lookout (Hike 57), but also have a better perspective of it all. Very conspicuous is Mt. Tallac's preglacial, almost flat erosion surface, which has remained little changed over the past few million years except that glaciers have cut a deep canyon into it. Before these ice-rivers came, the gentle part of the southeast slope of Mt. Tallac descended almost to the spur one mile northwest of Echo Peak. Glaciers cut back into both of these rounded peaks, sculpting out steep, ragged faces, and successive glaciers cut back up the Glen Alpine Creek canyon, deepening it by 1300 feet and steepening its sides considerably.

An easy, ducked path southeast takes us to granitic, potholed Echo Peak, which provides us with an additional panorama, this one of the Crystal Range to the south and west. On the southeast horizon near Carson Pass stand Stevens and Red Lake peaks, respectively 10,059 and 10,063 feet, with hulking Round Top, to their right, overtopping them at 10,381 feet. Like just about every other Tahoe peak visited by people, ours has its resident golden-mantled ground squirrels to inspect you or your pack (should you leave it for a moment).

To descend to Upper Angora Lake, follow a ducked trail northeast down through grus, which is largely a surface accumulation of feldspar and quartz crystals that have broken off weathered granitic rock after the dark minerals disintegrated and freed them. The trail descends a very steep, minor northeast ridge of Echo Peak, and then continues down a gully so rich in grus that you can almost ski down it. Large backpacks are definitely not recommended on this very steep descent. Several short-switchback routes descend northeast down this gully and merge on a flat 300 feet above the lake.

From the flat we descend northwest very steeply down another gully to Upper Angora Lake's southeast corner. Here you can traverse west to a rock slab above the south shore, from which you can high-dive into water that is incredibly deep for a lake this size. Lower diving points are available for the more cautious, but so too are very high rocks for any "Acapulco" diver. However, be careful; there have been too many accidents.

The trail from the southeast shore consists of merely a traverse across a large-block talus slope to the lake's outlet. You then walk northwest to Angora Lakes Resort, with a small store for refreshments, then descend a closed road, following in reverse Hike 58's description down to Fallen Leaf Lake. From it you hike southwest 0.4 mile up its road back to your trailhead.

# 85 Echo Lake to Tamarack and Triangle Lakes and Echo Peak

**Distances**  3.8 miles to Tamarack Lake, 4.2 miles to Ralston and Cagwin lakes, 4.2 miles to Triangle Lake via northbound trail, 5.2 miles to Echo Peak via northbound trail, 5.5 miles to Triangle Lake via eastbound trail, 6.5 miles to Echo Peak via eastbound trail.

**Low/High Elevations**  7420'/8895'

**Classification**  Moderate

**Season**  Early July through mid-October

**Maps**  36 and 35

**Trailhead**  From the Highway 49 junction in Placerville, drive 46 miles east up Highway 50 to Echo Lakes road, on your left, which is just 280 yards before Little Norway. (Westbound drivers: this road is 1¼ miles west from Echo Summit. Get your permits at the Lake Tahoe Basin Management Unit office complex, which is located on the left side of Highway 89 0.3 mile northwest from the South Lake Tahoe **Y**.)

The Echo Lakes road climbs 0.6 mile east to a junction, then angles sharply left and climbs 0.9 mile to a trailhead parking lot above Echo Lake Resort. Park here, not down at the resort. The southbound Pacific Crest/Tahoe-Yosemite trail starts from the east side of the parking lot; the northbound PCT/TYT (Hikes 85-87) starts from Lower Echo Lake's dam. To reach this north trailhead, follow the road ⅓ mile down to Echo Lake Resort, or take a short, steep trail, which starts opposite the south trailhead, and descends northwest to the resort. The above mileages are based from the north trailhead, not from the parking lot.

**Introduction**  The trail from Lower Echo Lake to Lake Aloha is probably the most heavily used one in this wilderness. Its popularity is due in part to its accessibility—just off Highway 50— and to the elevation of its trailhead, which at

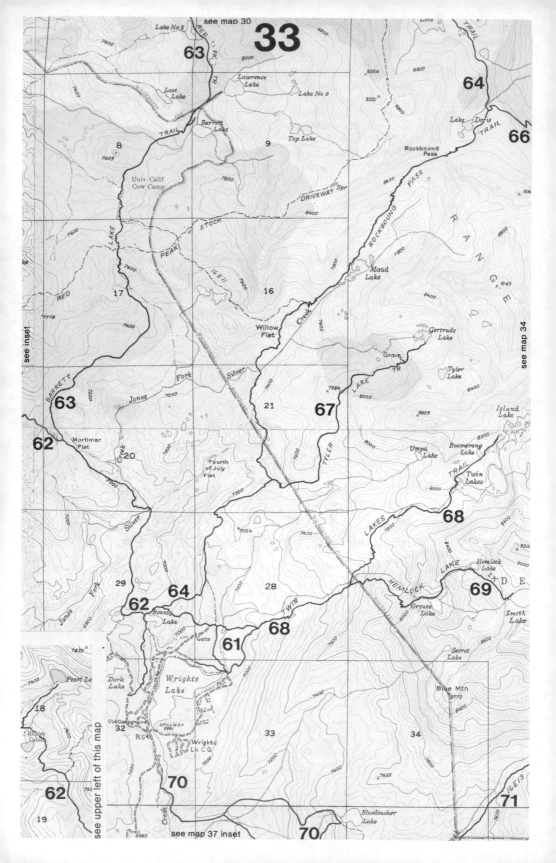

**33**

**63**

**64**

**66**

Lake No 5

Lake No 9

Lawrence
Lake

Lost
Lake

Top Lake

Barrett
Lake

Lake Doris

Rockbound
Pass

8
7609

9354
9331

9 904

Univ Calif
Cow Camp

DRIVEWAY Spr

ROCKBOUND PASS

RANGE
9163

17

16

Maud
Lake

Gertrude
Lake

Willow
Flat

Grave
TR

Tyler
Lake

see inset

see map 34

Barrett

Jones    Fork    Silver

**63**

7984

LAKE

**67**

Island
Lake

**62**

Mortimer
Flat

20

Fourth
of July
Flat

8925

Umpa
Lake

Boomerang
Lake

TRAIL

Twin
Lakes

TYLER

LAKES

**68**

9316

Silver

7254

HEMLOCK LAKE

Hemlock
Lake

29

28

Grouse
Lake

**69**

**62**  **64**

Beauty
Lake

TWIN

**68**

Smith
Lake

**61**

Gate

Secret
Lake

Pearl La

Dark
Lake

Wrights
Lake

Blue Mtn
8772

18

Old Campground    SPILLWAY
6941

32    RS

Wrights
Lk CG

33

34

Rulley
Cabin

**62**

**70**

7655

19

Bloodsucker
Lake

**71**

16E13

see upper left of this map

see map 37 inset  **70**

**70**

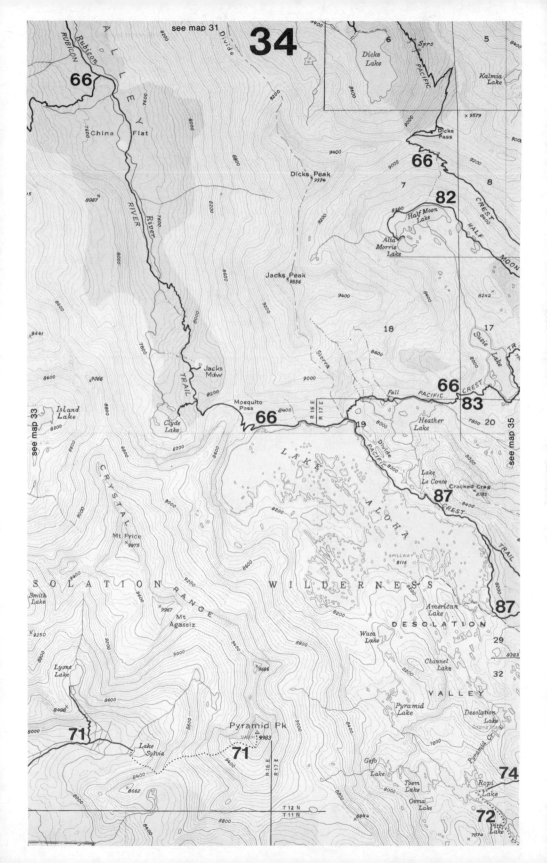

see map 31

**34**

see map 33

see map 35

66

66

China Flat

Dicks Lake

Spr

Dicks Pass

66

82

Dicks Peak
9974

Half Moon Lake

Alta Morris Lake

Jacks Peak
9856

Susie Lake

66

83

Fall

Heather Lake

Jacks Mdw

Sierra

Mosquito Pass

66

Clyde Lake

Island Lake

Lake Le Conte

Cracked Crag

LAKE

ALOHA

87

CRYSTAL

RANGE

SPILLWAY

Mt Price

WILDERNESS

DESOLATION

American Lake

87

ISOLATION

Smith Lake

Mt Agassiz

Waca Lake

Channel Lake

Lyons Lake

Pyramid Lake

VALLEY

Desolation Lake

71

Pyramid Pk

Lake Sylvia

71

Gefo Lake

Toem Lake

Ropi Lake

74

Osma Lake

72

Pitti Lake

T 12 N
T 11 N

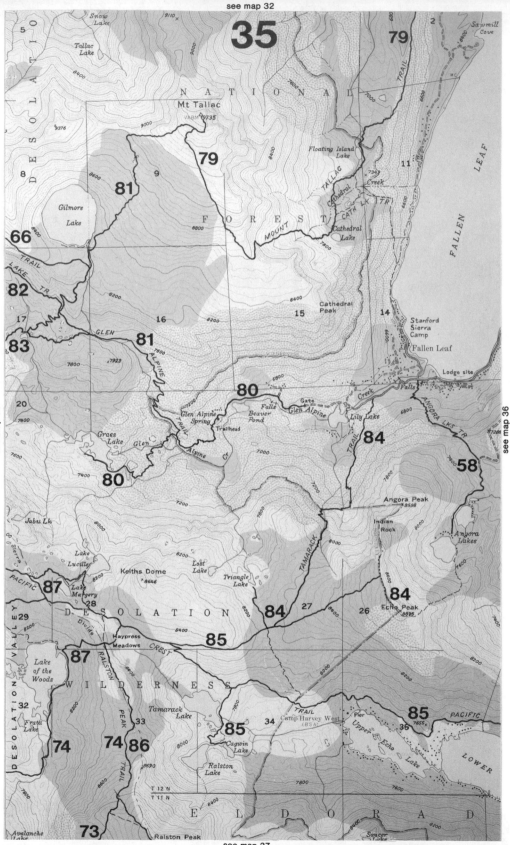

**35**

see map 34

see map 36

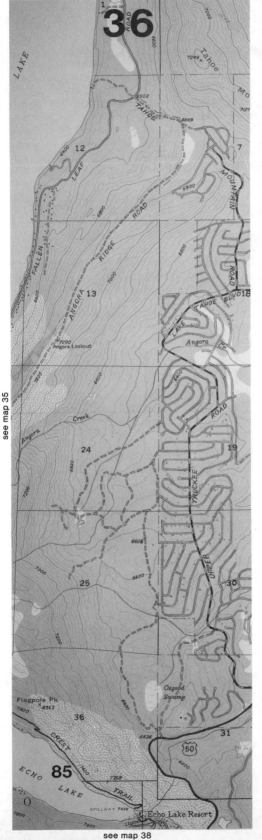

see map 32 inset

see map 35

see map 38

7420 feet is the highest trailhead for Desolation Wilderness. Consequently the hiker has that much less elevation to gain. Hikers who take the Echo Lakes water taxi can subtract 2.5 miles from the above mileages and from those of Hikes 86 and 87.

**Description** To save 5.0 miles of round-trip hiking, for $1 or so per mile, take the Echo Lakes water taxi, operated by Echo Lake Resort. Since P.G.& E. owns the top 12 feet of the lake (because they've dammed it that high), they have the right to lower the water by that amount, and by mid-September they usually do so. Then the lake reverts to its natural, upper-lower pair of lakes, and the water taxi goes only to the peninsula separating the two lakes. You'll still save 3.4 miles, round trip.

The signed trail is the Tahoe-Yosemite Trail, which starts near Meeks Bay, on Lake Tahoe, and extends south to Tuolumne Meadows in Yosemite National Park. The Pacific Crest Trail, extending from the Canadian to the Mexican border, coincides with the TYT through most of Desolation Wilderness, the two splitting about a mile north of Middle Velma Lake. Cross Lower Echo Lake's dam, make an initial climb east, and then head west on this sparsely timbered rollercoaster.

The trail traverses below some prominent granodiorite cliffs, on which you might see a rock climber struggling up the cracks. Beyond this slope the trail switchbacks twice and climbs high above lakeshore summer homes. Scattered Jeffrey pines give way to thick groves of lodgepoles as we descend toward the lake's north shore. We then traverse to a rusty, granitic knoll, round it to forested slopes above Upper Echo Lake, and continue westward. The tree cover is thick enough to blot out any possible view of the public pier at which the water taxis land, and several short trails down to the lake add to the confusion. If you've taken the taxi, you'll know which trail to take back. The proper trail should be signed, and it descends 90 yards to a public telephone near the pier. Phone the resort's water taxi if you want a ride back.

Beyond the pier's trail you climb a rocky tread up open slopes of slightly metamorphosed quartz monzonite and quickly reach a cryptic junction with a faint northbound trail. This is the fast way to Triangle Lake and Echo Peak, steeply climbing ¾ mile to a saddle, from which you then can descend ⅓ mile to the lake. For the route to and the sights from Echo Peak, read the second half of Hike 84. This cryptic junction with the northbound trail can be easily missed. It lies just 20 yards past a small bend which has conspicuous junipers growing on it and 70 yards before you enter an obvious, small, shady grove of lodgepoles. The dark inclusions you've been seeing in the rocks over the last stretch are clusters of high-melting-point crystals, which are the first ones to solidify in the molten, cooling mass of a newly forming pluton.

The next junction, with the trail to the Ralston Peak basin lakes, is more obvious. Only 0.6 mile past the Triangle Lake lateral, our main trail rounds a bend and passes through a dynamited, 5-foot-high trail cut, then in 40 yards reaches a trail junction. From here the PCT continues to climb, and a ducked trail descends south over barren bedrock to Tamarack Lake, largest of the Ralston Peak basin lakes and, like the other two, fringed with mountain hemlock and lodgepole and western white pine. From the south tip of this shallow lake you can head south on a ducked route directly over a low ridge and descend to the north shore of moderately deep Cagwin Lake, lined with red heather and Labrador tea. Or, from Tamarack Lake you can follow a primitive trail southwest over the west end of the ridge and down to deep Ralston Lake, which is totally surrounded by steep slopes. Because these three lakes are so close to the trailhead, they are heavily used, and the Forest Service discourages camping at them.

From the Ralston Peak basin lakes trail junction, the Pacific Crest Trail climbs to a tiny creek in a gully, which is a good place to rest after your moderate climb. Rather than shortcut up the gully, as too many careless hikers have done, follow two switchbacks up to a bench, from where you see a lateral trail traversing east across a slope predominantly colored with paintbrush and sagebrush.

To reach Triangle Lake by a nearly effortless route, take this eastbound lateral trail. On it you pass occasional junipers and view the changing perspective of the Ralston Peak basin lakes below and the peak above. Then make a brief climb to a ridge and instantly a panorama explodes into view. To the east you get an aerial view of both Echo Lakes and the Sierra beyond; to the west looms Pyramid Peak above Haypress Meadows; to the south we have a detailed inspection of the basin lakes below us; and to the north we even see a bit of Lake Tahoe beyond Angora Peak. Stunned by the sudden shock of this grandstand panorama, we meander with new thoughts and vivid emotions northeast down to a flat saddle, where we intersect a lateral that leads ⅓ mile down to Triangle Lake, this trail first having climbed north from the PCT.

**An Echo Lakes panorama, from the eastbound lateral trail**

**Indian Rock, Fallen Leaf Lake, Lake Tahoe and the Carson Range**

Descending this lateral northward, first through a meadow and then across ducked quartz-monzonite bedrock above the lake's south shore, you obtain an excellent inspection of the gentle part of Mt. Tallac's southeast slope, which escaped glaciation. Much of Desolation Wilderness was a rolling topography with similar slopes before wave after wave of glaciers began to dig out lake basins. After 40 yards down the jagged bedrock, drop a few yards east to a creeklet and follow a faint, duff trail down to the shallow, grassy south end of Triangle Lake. From good diving rocks above the lake's northwest shore one can look down into the water and perhaps see some trout swimming lazily in this deep arm. Small, fair campsites can be found in nooks among the ice-fractured rocks above the lake. Its water is of questionable purity, so you might consider treating it before drinking it. The same applies to its inlet creek.

Those who want to climb Echo Peak, one mile east of the flat saddle above Triangle Lake, follow a trail 85 yards east-northeast to a pile of rocks, from where the Tamarack Trail descends northeast. You continue east-northeast on a faint trail, following the description of the last part of Hike 84, which also mentions summit views.

# 86     Echo Lake to Ralston Peak

**Distance**   6.9 miles, one way
**Low/High Elevations**   7420'/9235'
**Classification**   Moderate
**Season**   Mid-July through mid-October
**Maps**   36, 35 and 37
**Trailhead**   Same as the Hike 85 trailhead.

**Introduction**   See the Hike 73 introduction.

**Description**   Follow Hike 85 up to the eastbound lateral trail to Triangle Lake. Just ⅓ mile beyond this lateral you meet the Lake of the Woods Trail, which you take past Haypress Meadows, climbing ¼ mile southwest to a ridgecrest intersection of the Ralston Peak Trail. While most hikers continue down to Lake of the Woods, you stick to the crest. Your rocky route, an old one, climbs south over a ridge knoll rather than around it. Oh well, at least by doing so you get views of Tamarack, Ralston, Cagwin and Echo lakes to the east, and Lake of the Woods, Lake Aloha and a gaggle of Desolation Valley lakes to the west.

From a saddle with a seasonal pond, you traverse quickly past a more permanent one, then climb, steeply at times, up through a hemlock forest. Before August this ascent can be quite snowy. About 1⅓ miles from the Lake of the Woods Trail you enter a small subalpine meadow, in which the trail can be easily lost. A snowfield, often lasting into August, lies above the boggy meadow's south side, and it can obscure the route. You climb south, steeply up a slope, to a generally open ridge that nevertheless has clusters of mountain hemlocks. If you continue south any farther, you'll be descending Hike 73. Rather, follow the last part of that route ⅔ mile east up to the summit of Ralston Peak. Observe that while its north and east slopes have been greatly steepened by glaciers, its southwest slope, which was never glaciated, has changed very little in the last 3 million years.

# cho Lake to Lake of the Woods and Lake Aloha

miles to Lake Margery, 5.2
miles to Lucille, 5.3 miles to Lake of the Woods, 5.8 miles to Lake Aloha, southeast corner, 6.1 miles to Lake Aloha, east shore, 6.7 miles to Lake LeConte, 7.0 miles to Ropi Lake, 7.5 miles to Lake Aloha, northeast corner, 9.3 miles to Clyde Lake.

**Low/High Elevations**   7420'/8430'

**Classification**   Moderate

**Season**   Mid-July through mid-October

**Maps**   36, 35 and 34

**Trailhead**   Same as the Hike 85 trailhead.

**Introduction**   Most backpackers starting from Echo Lake set either Lake Aloha or Lake of the Woods as their primary goal. If they take the Echo Lakes water taxi, they can subtract 2.5 miles from the above mileages. Then, only lightly visited Clyde Lake, on the far side of Mosquito Pass, is more than 5¼ miles (or a couple of hours) away. And there are over a dozen lakes—mostly between Lake Aloha and Ropi Lake—that can be reached by easy cross-country hiking. Furthermore, this hike's main thoroughfare is part of the Pacific Crest and Tahoe-Yosemite trails. No wonder the Echo Lake trailhead is so busy. While most hikers won't proceed past Lake Aloha, those on the PCT/TYT do. Since the PCT goes on to the Canadian border—certainly beyond the scope of this book—you might be more prudent to take the TYT, which ends at Lake Tahoe's Meeks Bay.

**Description**   Follow Hike 85 up to the eastbound lateral trail to Triangle Lake. Just ⅓ mile beyond this lateral you reach the Lake of the Woods Trail. If you're bound for that lake or any of the Desolation Valley lakes except Lake Aloha, fork left here. You skirt past Haypress Meadows and in ¼ mile have a crest intersection of the Ralston Peak Trail (Hike 86).

Most hikers prefer to skip Ralston Peak and descend west from the crest intersection, arriving at the northeast shore of Lake of the Woods in 0.4 mile. This lake competes with Lake Aloha in popularity, and by late summer it probably attracts more backpackers. That's because Lake Aloha almost dries up by then, while Lake of the Woods drops only a foot or two. Campsites almost completely girdle Lake of the Woods, threatening to choke its essence. Camp away from the shoreline, preferably at least 200 feet from it. The best sites are above the west shore.

From the lake's south end a trail descends 1.1 miles to Ropi Lake. This lake, other nearby lakes, and the routes to them are described at the end of Hike 74. From Lake of the Woods' northwest corner several ducked "trails" climb toward Lake Aloha. The correct route to it climbs only 80 yards north, then angles west up to a gully, which it climbs to a nearby saddle; then it descends ¼ mile to the Lake Aloha Trail. The lake's southeast corner is just beyond.

About 300 yards past the Lake of the Woods Trail, our hike's main thoroughfare—the Pacific Crest Trail—reaches the north end of the Ralston Peak Trail. This climbs 0.2 mile south to the crest intersection of the Lake of the Woods Trail. Just 150 yards farther on the PCT, we reach the popular, ⅓-mile-long Lake Lucille Trail, forking right. This descends 150 yards to a trailside pond, from which you can head cross-country 200 yards northwest to the east shore of Lake Margery. If you keep to the sometimes soggy trail, you'll reach Lake Lucille in ¼ mile. At its northwest shore you'll find a small peninsula, almost an island, which is a good relaxing spot for lunch.

Enriched with food and thought, and perhaps a view from the end of this lake down upon Fallen Leaf Lake and Lake Tahoe, you can follow the Lake Margery Trail up the northwest side of that lake's outlet creek. Pausing at this shallow, rocky lake, you may see backpackers traversing high above it on the Pacific Crest expressway. Like Lake Lucille, Lake Margery has very limited camping potential if you camp a legal 100+ feet away from its shore.

If you keep to the Pacific Crest Trail, you'll log just over ½ mile between the Lake Lucille and Lake Margery trail junctions. About ⅓ mile west along this stretch you'll meet the Lake Aloha Trail, which many hikers take ½ mile west down to the southeast corner of Lake Aloha. Approaching this corner, you'll pass the Lake of the Woods lateral—a narrow tread—just 60 yards before another lateral branches left. This one winds ¾ mile over to Lake Aloha's 20-foot-high-dam, at a popular swimming area when there's water in this reservoir. The great bulk of Lake Aloha is less than 10 feet deep, and after Labor Day the lake's water level drops sufficiently to create a desolate wilderness. Lake Aloha owes its existence (and Desolation Valley owes its demise) directly to P.G.& E. and indirectly to California's burgeoning population.

**Pond lilies in placid Cagwin Lake**

If you're a purist and want to adhere to the PCT/TYT all the way to Lake Aloha, then continue northwest from the Lake Margery Trail, which starts its eastward course from the south tip of the westernmost of three shallow, nearly attached ponds. After 0.6 mile you'll reach a trail junction above the east shore of Lake Aloha. You can find good, legal camps between this junction and the one by the southeast corner, a 0.6-mile hike south along the east-shore trail.

The next trail stretch starts out ugly, for you'll pass hundreds of dead lodgepole snags that once grew in Desolation Valley before it became Lake Aloha. The lake is so shallow, one wonders if it holds enough water to justify its existence. When the lake drops just 5 feet, you can wade across it in several places. At its height the lake is a swimmer's paradise, for there are hundreds of rock islands you can reach. Should you want to swim in it, come here in the first three weeks of August, when the water is warm enough and the lake is full.

Soon our trail—the PCT or TYT, depending on your preference—takes us alongside a fairly clear, chest-deep, large pond, on our left, which like Aloha, warms up to the mid-sixties in mid-summer. Walking 150 yards beyond it, we reach a gully, up which our trail seems to head. A snowbank, lasting through July, can obscure the correct route, which makes a brief climb south-west before traversing northwest again. Had you gone straight ahead on an abandoned trail, you would have reached chilly, rockbound Lake LeConte, stocked with rainbow trout. This diversion would have provided you with a view of two high summits, Jacks and Dicks peaks. Jacks Peak, the closer one, is equally divided between brown metasedimentary rocks north of the summit and gray granitic rocks south of it.

Continuing northwest just above Lake Aloha, we now traverse along a nicer, snag-free section of lake, and then reach its northeast corner, which has a two-foot-high retaining wall to prevent the lake from spilling over into Heather Lake, below us to the east. Climbing just a few yards beyond the wall, we meet a junction, from where the PCT/TYT descends first north and then east to Heather Lake. Here, at the north-east corner of Lake Aloha, Hike 87 ends. Note that although you are surrounded by mountains, you are actually standing on the actual crest of the Sierra Nevada, which runs along the dam. East, water flows down to Lake Tahoe, then out to Nevada. West, water drains from Lake Aloha out to the Pacific Ocean.

If you plan to continue onward, then consult the last half of Hike 66, which first climbs past Clyde Lake and over Mosquito Pass to your junction, then continues past Heather, Susie and other lakes to Middle Velma Lake, which is about 17¼ miles from your trailhead. Meeks Bay is another 13 miles farther, and you achieve that objective by following Hike 76 in reverse. By traversing west from your junction, you can find additional campsites above the north shore of Lake Aloha. This is your last chance to sample the lake's water sports—before mid-September that is. After that, the water bids "aloha" to the basin, leaving a desolate environment of bathtub-ring rocks and cracked-mud floor.

Round Top (left) and The Sisters, from Trail 17E47 one-half mile below Round Top Lake

# Ch. 15  Dardanelles Roadless Area and northern Mokelumne Wilderness

**Introduction**  Highway 50 is a dividing line between two obviously different land-scapes: granitic Desolation Wilderness, to the north, and volcanic lands, to the south. In this chapter we investigate the latter. Along most of this landscape's trails the hiker is confronted with dark, volcanic cliffs, ridges and peaks—some very impressive. Who would forget a campsite view of towering volcanic palisades above Round Lake's east shore, or a lake-hopping hike along the base of Round Top, the eroded core of a former volcano?

But although the hiker is left with the distinct impression that this landscape is largely volcanic, it's not. It is largely granitic. Our impression is due to the fact that the light granitic bedrock is almost everywhere overlain by dark, volcanic rocks. The area's streams, avalanches and former glaciers have covered much of the granitic basin lands with a veneer of volcanic sediments, thereby hiding much of the granitic bedrock. Furthermore, these sediments decompose to soils that usually produce luxuriant forests, so the hiker, surrounded by trees, doesn't really notice the geology. And, it might be added, because the hiker typically is struggling uphill toward a lake, he couldn't care less. However, when he reaches the lake, he can relax and enjoy the views, which usually include volcanic cliffs, ridges or peaks. And if he is enjoying views of such ridges and peaks, he sees more of them. The granitic nature of the basin lands escapes notice, for a green forest mantle enshrouds them.

The observant hiker, however, might notice one interesting feature about this seem-ingly volcanic landscape: every single lake in it lies in a *granitic* basin. You see none in a volcanic basin, although Round Lake superficially appears to be one. For a glacier to excavate a basin, the bedrock must be highly fractured. Granitic bedrock can vary from solid to highly fractured. Where it is solid, glaciers hardly abrade it; where it is highly fractured, glaciers quarry deeply into it. Volcanic bedrock, on the other hand, is in our area composed of relatively horizontal, less resistant beds of volcanic sediments and flows. Glaciers, flowing over such beds, plane them away, one layer after the other.

This chapter's first seven routes, Hikes 88-94, deal with trails in the Dardanelles Roadless Area. This "proto wilderness" is roughly triangular in shape, its north edge extending from Lovers Leap east to Echo Summit, and beyond to Luther Pass. The two other sides converge on Carson Pass. Hikes 88-90 are unappealing to most hikers (other than botanists), the first two providing very long routes in to Showers Lake. Hike 90, the Hawley Grade Trail, is basically for history buffs. The remaining Dardanelles Roadless Area routes are deservedly popular, taking you to Dardanelles, Round, Meiss and Showers lakes, each in a unique setting.

Hike 95, the Lake Margaret Trail, doesn't fit well into any category. Instead, it appears to be a transplant from Desolation Wilderness set apart in its own space. The trail is easy and the lake is enjoyable.

The last four routes, Hikes 96–99, enter a northern, 1984 addition to Mokelumne Wilderness. This addition is dominated by the eroded ruins of an extinct volcano, Round Top. From it a high, volcanic crest extends west, and the author has drawn the Tahoe Sierra's southern boundary along this crest, although Hike 98 does extend beyond it, down past Fourth of July Lake and then east up Summit City Creek canyon. For most hikers the braking descent to this lake coupled with the rigorous ascent from it do not justify a visit.

Three Mokelumne Wilderness lakes do justify a visit: Winnemucca, Round Top and Emigrant lakes. Frog Lake, which you pass along Hikes 98 and 99, has frogs and about enough water to wash the trail dust from your legs. All four are subalpine, and therefore too chilly for enjoyable swimming. Their average elevation is 8945 feet. Compare that to the average elevation of the four highest *peaks* in Granite Chief Wilderness—8954 feet.

The northern part of Mokelumne Wilderness is quite spectacular, being perhaps the most photogenic area in the Tahoe Sierra. In botanical terms, it is also spectacular, having, mile for mile, the greatest number of species. This is particularly true along the chapter's last hike, whose chief attribute is its flora.

If you plan to spend the night in the wilderness during a period lasting from about the Memorial Day weekend through all of September, then you'll need a wilderness permit— see pages 17 and 18 for details. Day hikers don't need permits.

# 88   Sayles Canyon and Bryan Meadow Trails

**Distances**   4.3 miles to Pacific Crest Trail via Bryan Meadow, 5.0 miles to PCT via Sayles Canyon, 8.5 miles to Showers Lake via Sayles Canyon, 8.7 miles to Showers Lake via Bryan Meadow, 10.2 miles for complete Sayles Canyon/Bryan Meadow semiloop trip.

**Low/High Elevations**   6880'/8700' to PCT; 8990' to Showers Lake

**Classification**   Moderate

**Season**   Mid-July through mid-October

**Maps**   37 and 38

**Trailhead**   Drive up Highway 50 to the Sierra Ski Ranch turnoff, which is 3.1 miles west of Echo Summit. Drive 1.4 miles up this paved road to a junction with a graded road, branching right. Take this road 2.0 miles, traversing a ski area before reaching the trailhead at road's end. At times this road may be closed, though you can still hike along it. However, few people would, since it adds 4 miles to your total hiking distance.

**Introduction**   There are at least 10 trail routes in to Showers Lake. Sayles Canyon Trail 17E14 and Bryan Meadow Trail 17E13 are the two longest and, in the author's estimation, the least scenic. Therefore, these trails, which climb appreciably, will appeal to only a select few: equestrians, who let their horses do the walking; and botanists, who may hike only part way.

**Description**   From the upper end of the parking loop the Sayles Canyon Trail climbs initially through a shady forest. You then ascend a bouldery, rocky tread southeast to scrub-vegetated granodiorite slopes and, before curving east around a low glacial moraine, can glance back and see Pyramid Peak towering above barely visible Horsetail Falls. Curving east between the moraine and a creeklet alongside it, we quickly reach a junction with the Bryan Meadow Trail, 0.6 mile from the trailhead. We'll be returning down it.

After crossing the creeklet, we soon reach an alder-lined Sayles Canyon creek tributary descending from Bryan Meadow. Rather than ford the shallow creek where the trail does, you can veer east 20 yards upstream to a boulderhop crossing. Here, under lodgepoles, you'll find a nice, flat campsite near the creek's north bank.

Beyond the ford our well-maintained, verdant pathway climbs southeast up the stepped canyon floor, at times almost touching Sayles Canyon creek. We pass some large boulders—up to 20 feet high—then traverse through a meadow largely overgrown with willows, alders and corn lilies before we ford lushly vegetated Sayles Canyon creek. Then we tread a progressively easier trail east up to the northwest corner of grassy Round Meadow. Here, the trail can be vague. Near the meadow's north edge it starts out along the south side of a clump of willows, then heads east-southeast to a quick crossing of trout-inhabited upper Sayles Canyon creek, and then diagonals east-northeast toward some corn lilies and some girdled, dead lodgepoles. Beyond them it reaches slopes at the forest's edge, from which the trail upward is well blazed and also ducked. Mosquitoes, abundant through mid-August, make this damp meadow an undesirable camping area in early and mid season.

On a trail that is bouldery at first, we ascend moderately through a forest of red firs and lodgepole pines, parallel eastward a linear corn-lily meadow, climb steeply north, and make a long, relatively gentle uphill traverse southeast before curving east up to a saddle. Here we encounter the Pacific Crest Trail, which also coincides for some distance with the unofficial Tahoe-Yosemite Trail. Hike 89 continues south from this junction for 3½ miles, reaching Showers Lake's east-shore campsites.

Tracing the Pacific Crest Trail northward, we climb to a low summit, with weathered boul-ders but no views, gradually descend through an open forest of mountain hemlock and lodgepole pine, cross a mucky slough that annually sprouts a magenta field of blazing, ephemeral shooting stars, and reach a trail junction at Bryan Meadow's upper east end. Here the Pacific Crest Trail turns east.

An old trail once cut straight down Bryan Meadow, and we can follow it 50 yards west down to a small, poor campsite in a cluster of lodgepoles. A newer trail heads north a short distance, curves west to a gully, and then parallels the north edge of Bryan Meadow. In a number of spots we walk along the meadow's thick soils, rich in humus and clay. Both hold a lot of water. The clay is derived from micas that have been weathered and eroded from the adjacent granodiorite slopes. Beyond the meadow our trail traverses a slope while paralleling Bryan Meadow's creek, below us. The trail here is drier, for the slope has a typical cover of *grus*—the chunky, residual quartz and feldspar crystals that are left behind after most of the micas and other dark minerals decompose and are carried away. At this elevation, ice wedging hastens the formation of grus. We descend a ridgecrest, switchback down its more forested north slope, ford several branches of a creek and then curve westward as we descend to a fairly large, forested flat. At the west end, the creek tumbles down a steeper slope while our trail switchbacks down to a sloping meadow. Just west of it, we encounter a wretched motorcycle trail up which cyclists drive, sometimes to Bryan Meadow and beyond, even though they are prohibited from doing so. At the junction our trail forks left and descends via short and long switchback legs through more open forest back down to the Sayles Canyon Trail, on which we retrace our steps to the trailhead.

# 89    Pacific Crest Trail, Highway 50 south to Showers Lake

**Distances**   1.0 mile to Benwood Meadow, 3.9 miles to Bryan Meadow Trail, 4.8 miles to Sayles Canyon Trail, 6.4 miles to Trail 17E16, 8.3 miles to Showers Lake.

**Low/High Elevations**   7380'/8990'

**Classification**   Moderate

**Season**   Mid-July through mid-October

**Maps**   38 and 40

**Trailheads**   Drive up Highway 50 nearly to Echo Summit. The Pacific Crest trailhead is near the start of the Echo Summit Ski Area's Road 1N03, which you'll find 0.3 mile west of Echo Summit. After 100 yards along it you'll find parking for about a dozen vehicles.

For the alternate trailhead, drive 200 yards east of signed Echo Summit, turn south on a

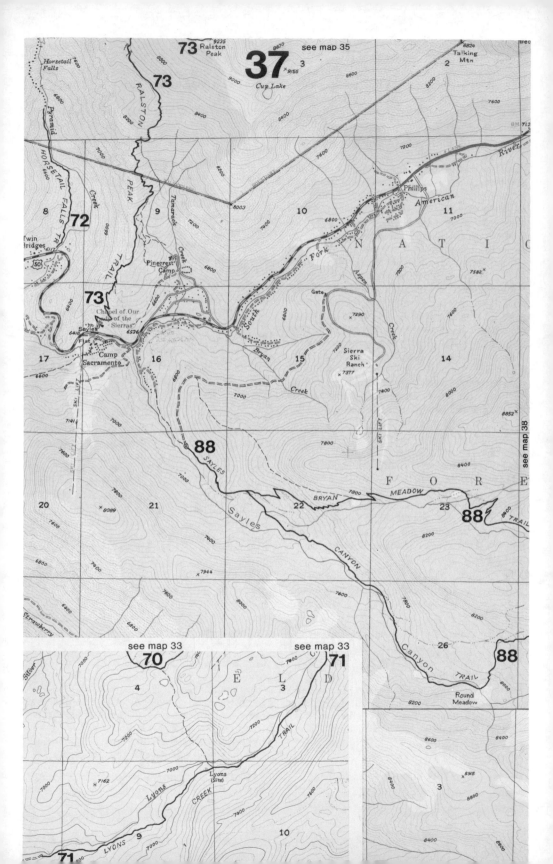

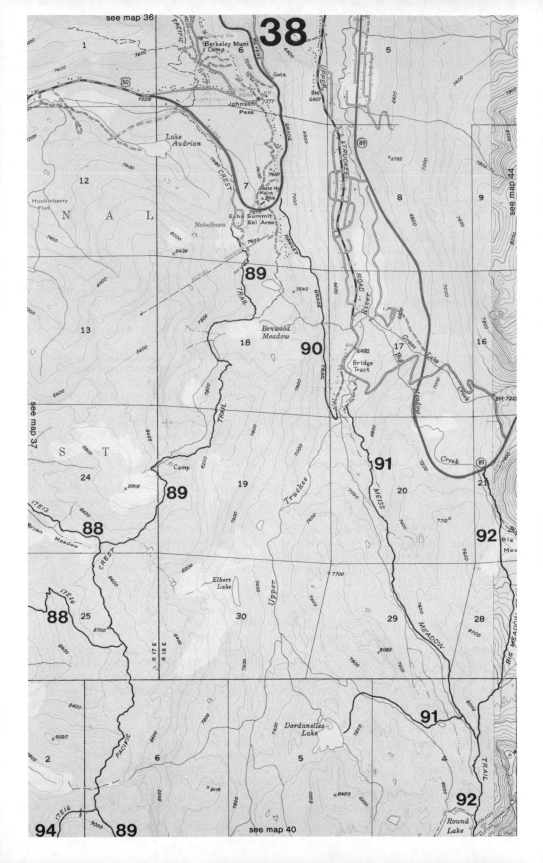

see map 36

**38**

see map 44

Berkeley Muni Camp

Casino Sta

MEYERS

6

5

1

7600

7400

7800

7800

50

7200

Echo Portal

Johnson Pass

Gate

BM 7377

BM 6407

UPPER

TRUCKEE

6600

6400

7600

7800

8

9

7800

89

6795

7000

Lake Audrian

7600

CREST

LAKE

State Hwy Maint Sta

7487

7000

8000

8439

Echo Summit Ski Area

Nebelhorn

7990

HAWLEY

7377

7000

12

N         A         L

Huckleberry Flat

7400

13

7800

TRAIL

7600

AERIAL

TRAM

7800

7600

**89**

7542

GRADE

6600

ROAD

RIVER

7000

7800

6800

7600

16

17

Benwood Meadow

18

**90**

BM 6492

Bridge Tract

Grass Lake

7000

Big

Creek

BM 7222

8600

8600

7800

7600

TRAIL

see map 37

S         T

8600

8905

Camp

8200

Camp

24

19

Truckee

7000

7600

**91**

MEISS

20

7712

89

Creek

7200

**23**

17E13

8600

Bryan Meadow

**88**

CREST

8200

8600

Elbert Lake

30

Upper

7400

7600

7700

29

MEADOW

7600

**92**

Big Mea

25

17E14

**88**

8700

8400

R 17 E   R 18 E

8200

8600

7400

8085

7600

8000

28

BIG MEADOW

8600

7800

7800

Dardanelles Lake

7800

7810

**91**

8600

PACIFIC

8600

6

5

4

9020

8600

2

8000

TRAIL

7600

8402

8200

8000

**92**

8119

8000

**94**

17E16

9000

**89**

see map 40

Round Lake

EL DORADO CO ALPINE CO

narrow spur road and follow it ⅓ mile to its end, with parking for several vehicles.

**Introduction**  Like the previous hike this route is another long way in to Showers Lake, and like that route this one appeals to equestrians and botanists. The route's greatest users, however, tend to be neither, but rather long-distance hikers doing part or all of either the Pacific Crest Trail or the unofficial Tahoe-Yosemite Trail. From the heart of Desolation Wilderness south to the Carson Pass area, these two famous trails share the same tread.

**Description**  Walk along the Echo Summit Ski Area's road to its fairly large parking area. Here, at the base of several ski runs, you'll see the facility's lodge, just east of the parking area. From the lodge's south side a service road climbs south. With these features identified you can plan your route, for in 1983 the Pacific Crest Trail wasn't too obvious, and it may be hard to follow for several more years until it is rerouted around the ski area instead of through it.

From the south edge of the parking area, climb about 120 yards south to the "start" of the PCT, near some red firs, which goes but 90 yards southeast to the road climbing south from the lodge. Here the road bends southeast and you walk 65 yards along it before branching right. On trail you go but 110 yards, crossing a creeklet just before reaching the road, which winds south up a 25-yard-wide ski run. You diagonal about 80 yards up this run to its east side, and on your piecemeal trail hike 150 yards up alongside the run. From where the trail ends you continue 35 yards up the ski run to find the trail's resumption. At this point the ski run and its road turn southwest and climb more steeply. For most hikers it's probably easiest to start their hike from the lodge and follow the road ⅓ mile up to this bend. At last on hopefully permanent trail you traverse just under ½ mile south, almost to the northeast edge of Benwood Meadow, where you'll meet an older trail coming from the alternate trailhead.

This trail, 0.3 mile shorter than the main route, begins from a small flat just west of a cluster of summer homes. It winds southward along a boulder-lined path atop a mammoth moraine that towers up to 1100 feet above the Upper Truckee River's canyon floor. Soon the trail descends past a lily-pad pond, to the west, and crosses its southeast-flowing outlet creek. The pond resembles so many others one sees in the glaciated High Sierra, but it is quite distinct in its mode of origin. Instead of being dammed behind a recessional moraine, as most are, this pond was dammed between two lateral moraines. The huge Upper Truckee canyon lateral moraine blocked the creek's drainage eastward and another lateral moraine extending east from the north edge of Benwood Meadow blocked its drainage southward, thereby ponding up the creek. On the low Benwood Meadow moraine you traverse southwest and, just after spying the meadow, join the Pacific Crest/Tahoe-Yosemite Trail. The meadow is a popular goal among botanists, for it is readily accessible, and it contains a diverse array of native species. Botanizing is best from about mid-July through mid-August, when mosquitoes are—unfortunately—plentiful.

The PCT fortunately avoids this fragile environment, circling around its west edge on somewhat drier, forested terrain. You then climb a brushy, rocky slope, cross a creek feeding the unseen meadow, and climb to a nearby switchback. Continuing briefly west, you get your first view north of Lake Tahoe. Turning south you climb ¼ mile to a shallow gap, having several more lake views along this moderate ascent. You next climb slopes up through an open forest, the terrain characterized by granitic outcrops and giant boulders.

About ½ mile past the gap you reach a crest saddle, which poses your route's best view—one of the Upper Truckee River basin. Murky Round Lake, at the base of a volcanic palisade, is one of the most identifiable features. Just right of it and about a mile closer to you is Dardanelles Lake, which is nestled at the foot of a granitic cliff. Rising between the two lakes is flat-topped Red Lake Peak, which at 10,063 feet, nudges out Stevens Peak by 4 feet to be the basin rim's highest point. Stevens is above and just left of Round Lake. Note how thick the volcanic deposits are in this area, roughly 2000 feet from Stevens Peak down to the Round Lake environs. These flows, which are mostly highly fractured andesite-lava flows, were deposited over a lengthy period, from about 26 to 5 million years ago. One of the last eruptions came from the site of Stevens Peak, which today is the remnants of an andesite-lava dome. In the ensuing 5 million years, the Upper Truckee River basin was created, owing its origin to stream erosion, glaciation, down-faulting and mass wasting.

Before moving on, note two more landmarks, both to the south-southeast. The first is the basin rim's low point, a saddle above the river's headwaters. Through this saddle the Pacific Crest Trail climbs south, bound for the Mexican border. Just right and beyond the saddle is Round Top, the glacier-gouged remains of an ancient volcano, which at 10,381 feet is the highest peak between Highways 88 and 4. Showers Lake, due south on a high, granitic bench, is unseen.

Beyond the viewpoint you skirt along the base of some intimidating granitic cliffs as you climb moderately southeast. Just past them you reach the jump-across Benwood Meadow creek and above its west side can spy a small flat above the east bank. This is the site of "Six Pack Camp," in which you can pack six campers.

Ahead, we climb rather steeply southwest to a lovely cove beneath a conspicuous dark cliff of volcanic rocks. The contact between them and the underlying granodiorite marks where the earth's surface was when they solidified on it perhaps 5 million years ago. As you can tell by the deep Upper Truckee canyon east of you, a lot of erosion has taken place since then.

We cross a sparkling creeklet that drains from the melting snowfield clinging to the upper slopes, then begin a reasonable ascent southeast to the gentle volcanic summit's forested east shoulder. We then descend southwest on volcanic soils which, due to the porosity of their rocky particles, are much drier. Flowers of mule ears and lupines, both with unmistakable scents, thrive in these soils. We get a brief view of peaks to the southeast but then submerge under the forest's cover once again as we descend, sometimes steeply, on granitic soils to a ravine with a tiny creeklet.

A short, easy climb west now takes us to a thickly cloaked saddle above Bryan Meadow, which has fair-to-poor campsites along its fringe. Descending about 200 yards to the meadow's east edge, we reach a trail junction from which the Bryan Meadow Trail (Hike 88) curves north and our Pacific Crest Trail turns south. After climbing 100 feet in elevation in that direction, we can see Pyramid Peak, *the* prominent summit of the granitic Crystal Range, on the northwest skyline. Through an open forest of mountain hemlock and lodgepole pine we now complete our easy climb to a low, viewless summit, then momentarily drop to a crest-saddle junction with the Sayles Canyon Trail (Hike 88).

From the saddle our trail south meanders along the broad crest for about ½ mile, then crosses a seasonally soggy, small meadow with a snowmelt creeklet. A rocky ascent of 300 feet gives way to a descent of 100 feet to a shallow crest gap. From it a faint, discontinuous path strikes east 250 yards down a linear meadow to a camp with a fine view, just beyond the meadow's far end. To the west, a similar tread descends 330 yards to the upper edge of a large meadow, then angles at 330° for 130 yards to a cow camp among a cluster of lodgepoles. Both camps usually have water nearby through July.

Climbing 0.2 mile from the gap, we reach a near-crest junction with Trail 17E16. This route eventually descends to Schneider's Cow Camp, and is described in Hike 94. Our route traverses southeast for ⅓ mile, then drops steeply, but briefly, south into a broad, severely glaciated basin. With volcanic flows and sediments above us and granitic bedrock below, we make an undulating traverse across the basin, always staying close to the contact between these two rock formations.

While hiking this stretch, you might observe how the rock types differ in kinds and abundance of plants, in soil production, and in the shape of the landscape. You might also note that volcanic rock formations tend to have more streams and springs while granitic ones have more lakes.

Our glaciated basin traverse takes us just beneath a precarious, overhanging volcanic point, beyond which we descend quickly to a fork. Here the old, abandoned trail skirts southeast across willowy slopes that lie south of Showers Lake. For equestrians, this shortcut route is okay, but for hikers, the mire of mud negates the time saved.

The newer trail heads northeast through a gap in a linear wall of granite that hides Showers Lake—a stone's throw from us. Due to the obtrusive bedrock, the trail was built to drop steeply down the lake's outlet creek, only to climb equally steeply up its other side to the lakeshore and our goal, campsites shaded by hemlocks, western white pines and lodgepole pines. However, it's easier to leave the trail and cross the dam at the outlet. If you camp here before early August, be prepared for abundant mosquitoes.

# 90      Hawley Grade Trail

**Distance**  1.9 miles to Highway 50
**Low/High Elevations**  6520'/7370'
**Classification**  Easy

**Season**  Late June through late October
**Map**  38
**Trailhead**  From where Highway 89 branches

south from southwest-climbing Highway 50, drive southwest ⅓ mile on 50 to privately owned Tahoe Pines Campground. Immediately past it and immediately before a KOA Campground, turn south and drive 3¾ miles up gently climbing Upper Truckee Road. Just before this road bridges the Upper Truckee River, you branch right on a spur road, 12N13A, to some Bridge Tract summer homes. The hike begins at the boulder-blocked end of this road. Park at a turnout 200 yards before these boulders. Space for several vehicles.

**Introduction**  Along the Hawley Grade you relive a bit of California's history by hiking up the first wagon road to be built across the central Sierra. The Hawley's Grade was a short-lived but key link in a trans-Sierra route to Hangtown and Sacramento. By 1850 Hangtown—today's Placerville—had become the unofficial capital of northern California's gold-mining region, and two years later a route of sorts was built from it to Johnson Pass—¾ mile north of today's Echo Summit—whence it dropped into Lake Valley. Drop it did, so steeply in fact that block and tackle had to be used to haul westbound wagons up it. An alternative grade had to be found.

A route over Luther Pass, to the east, was surveyed in the winter of 1854 for the purpose of providing a wagon road to Sacramento and Hangtown that would be better than Johnson Pass and also shorter and easier than the primitive Carson Pass route. That spring, Asa Hawley established a trading post in upper Lake Valley near a part of the Upper Truckee canyon's wall that quickly became known as Hawley's Hill. Construction soon began on a grade that would be gentle enough to safely accommodate wagons. Financed by private interests, this route—Hawley's Grade—was completed in 1857, making it the first conventional wagon road to cross the central Sierra. Combined with the recently constructed Luther Pass segment, this grade fast became *the* route to take. In 1858 El Dorado and Sacramento counties improved western segments of this largely-one-lane toll road, making it far superior to the higher, longer-snowbound Carson Pass route to the south.

Timing couldn't have been better, for in 1859 silver was discovered in the Comstock Lode at Virginia Town, today's Virginia City. Traffic was reversed on this road as a flood of miners from California's gold fields scrambled east over this toll road to try their luck at or near Virginia Town. Alas, even as Hawley's Grade was constructed to channel westbound miners and pio-

neers into California's Mother Lode country faster than was possible along the Carson Grade, so too were plans made to convey miners and others east to the Comstock by a faster route. By the summer of 1860, a wagon-and-stage toll road—abandoned today—had been constructed down Meyer's Grade, then east to climb over Daggett Pass, situated above Tahoe's southeast shore. Hawley's Grade, briefly a shortcut that siphoned traffic from the Carson Pass route, now became the longer, unprofitable toll road.

**Description**  From the boulders that today block the road, we start our hike up this historic grade by walking south about 100 yards, to where the road bends sharply and commences its climb to Echo Summit. From this bend, if you choose, you can first follow a good trail 50 yards south to the tumbling waters of the Upper Truckee River. The road quickly reduces to a trail and we soon encounter a tangle of alders, bushes and wildflowers that take advantage of the preponderance of springs and creeklets in this area. Beyond them we're on a narrow road again with more spacious vegetation. Scattered Jeffrey pines and other conifers break the monotony of the slope's mantle of huckleberry oak, and in shady spots bracken fern, thimbleberry and Indian hemp add variety. In October the leaves of this diminutive hemp turn a bright yellow, making the plant one of the more conspicuous species. After the first fall frost, Indians would collect its stems in order to make string which would be used for basket weaving and for bowstrings.

Midway along the ascent we reach our first good view north, then enter a gully down which a creek from Benwood Meadow and a pond north of it falls and cascades toward us, splashing on the large boulders we must cross. Although our path across this gully is partly washed out, we have little difficulty crossing, and from its north side we can look back and see the tall volcanic cliffs that loom above Round Lake. Soon we get a glimpse of Lake Tahoe and spy trucks climbing up Highway 50's present Meyer's Grade. We can also see how growth along Tahoe's south shore is spreading southward, gradually transforming the forested valley below us into a suburb of South Lake Tahoe. This valley could house thousands of new residents, but crystal-clear, deep-blue Lake Tahoe could not withstand the added sewage they would contribute. Tahoe-basin residents therefore export their treated sewage to other drainage systems rather than see their lake undergo eutrophication and lose its purity and its brilliant color.

Our views of Tahoe improve as we climb steadily north, but soon we veer west into a forest of white fir and Jeffrey pine and lose the views. Replacing them are the undesirable noise from traffic on Highway 50, which we're rapidly approaching, and the highly desirable aroma of a spread of tobacco brush. You can follow Hawley's Grade all the way to Highway 50's embankment, but most hikers will want to retrace their gentle route back to its trailhead.

# 91    Meiss Meadow Trail to Dardanelles Lake

**Distances**    3.6 miles to Round Lake, 4.0 miles to Dardanelles Lake.

**Low/High Elevations**    6520'/7820'

**Classification**    Moderate

**Season**    Mid-July through mid-October

**Map**    38

**Trailhead**    See Hike 90's directions to a bridge over the Upper Truckee River. Drive across the bridge and immediately turn right on a second spur road, 12N13B, which you take for ¼ mile, passing more Bridge Tract summer homes before you come to a trailhead near the road's end. Parking for several cars about 35 yards before road's gate.

**Introduction**    Since Hike 92 gets you to Round Lake in 0.9 mile less and to Dardanelles Lake in 0.5 mile less, many hikers will skip Hike 91. However, the Hike 92 trailhead may be overflowing on weekends, and you may be forced to take this less-used route. For sure, auto vandalism is relatively high at the Hike 92 trailhead and is certainly low at the Hike 91 trailhead, which is an added plus for Hike 91. Though longer and starting lower, this peaceful hike does have favorable attributes. It usually stays within earshot of a spring-fed stream, and wildflowers are more abundant along it than along Hike 92. And you won't see cattle, which you often do on Hike 92.

**Description**    This trail starts in a shady forest whose floor and slopes are adorned with a variety of colorful wildflowers, most of which appear on the botany chapter's wildflower plates.

*Dardanelles Lake and point 8402*

The trail starts to climb immediately, and quickly reaches the large boulders of a talus slope, which it traverses, and then it climbs steeply through the forest up to a more open, minor ridge. Here we contour toward a trickling creek, and then make a steep ascent alongside it to a crossing of it just before topping a not-too-evident second minor ridge. The third rise turns out to be shorter and less steep than the first two.

The trail eases as we approach a gurgling tributary of the Upper Truckee River. We make a relaxing stroll up along this alder- and willow-lined creek, but then must climb moderately again as we reach a section of rapids. Eventually our steady ascent comes to a junction in a predominantly red-fir stand of conifers that also includes Jeffrey, western white and lodgepole pines. The main trail continues south-southeast 0.2 mile gently up to a union with the more popular Big Meadow Trail (**Hike 92**) this junction lying ⅔ mile below Round Lake.

Since Dardanelles Lake is our goal, we veer southwest and descend 30 steep yards toward the creek we've been paralleling. Here, you may notice a strange, 10-foot-high boulder, which differs markedly from any granitic boulder we've seen downstream. This boulder broke off from the impressive palisade of volcanic rocks that towers above Round Lake. The cluster of smaller volcanic rocks that make up the large boulder we see is just a biopsy of one of the large volcanic flows we will see on Hike 92.

After perhaps a pleasant lunch stop, we jump across the spring-fed creek, which receives its water from subterranean channels that flow through the volcanic rocks downstream from Round Lake, ⅔ mile south of us. The trail then makes a traverse across a broad, low slope, first passing a second Round Lake creek, larger than the first, and then a lily-pad pond. After a quick descent, the trail reaches the lake's third Round Lake creek, the one that leaves a dam at the lake's northwest corner and tumbles down a narrow, curving canyon. At one point these outlet creeks are almost a mile apart, before they finally merge 200 yards upstream from our trailhead.

Our creekside journey downstream soon takes us past an aged patriarch—a 7-foot-diameter juniper—then past many creekside willow thickets to a ford of this creek. We tread across some low, glacially polished granodiorite slabs, and then climb south-southwest on a ducked trail up a straight, easy, joint-controlled gully leading to rock slabs above the east shore of Dardanelles Lake. From its south shore rise the steep granodiorite cliffs of point 8402, which, for climbers, are the reward of this long ascent. Nonclimbers will have to admit that the cliffs do add to the beauty of this shallow lake, which in midsummer warms up to 70° or more, making it ideal for swimming; fishermen can try to catch a tasty brook-trout dinner. Late in the summer the lake's water becomes slightly cloudy. Fair-to-good campsites are scattered among junipers and lodgepoles on slabs bordering the east and northwest shores.

# 92    Big Meadow Trail to Round, Dardanelles and Meiss Lakes

**Distances**   0.5 mile to Big Meadow, 2.7 miles to Round Lake, 3.5 miles to Dardanelles Lake, 4.9 miles to Meiss Lake.

**Low/High Elevations**   7200'/8070' to Round Lake

**Classification**   Moderate

**Season**   Early July through mid-October

**Maps**   38 and 40

**Trailhead**   From Echo Summit, Highway 50 drops into the Lake Tahoe Basin, reaching a junction with Highway 89 in 4.0 miles. Drive 5.2 miles south up this highway to a signed trailhead, 3.5 miles before Luther Pass, on your right, about 100 yards beyond a notable creek. A turnout, opposite the trailhead, holds about a dozen cars. On weekends this turnout is usually packed with cars, which unfortunately invite theft. Although odds are your car won't be vandalized, you can always take the Hike 91 route instead. To reach its trailhead, drive 1.2 miles back down Highway 89 to the Upper Truckee Road and descend it one mile to a spur road, on your left, which leads ¼ mile to that hike's trailhead.

**Introduction**   Because it has volcanic and granitic soils in various stages of development, the Upper Truckee River's uppermost basin supports approximately 300 species of plants and a correspondingly diverse assemblage of invertebrates. The Big Meadow Trail is the most popular trail into this lake-dotted, volcanic-rimmed basin, which offers climbers some interesting routes. Most hikers go to Round Lake, the basin's largest lake, which lies little more than an hour's hike away.

**Description** From the trailhead you make an initial ascent south toward Big Meadow Creek, jog east, and then pant southeast up an increasingly steep slope of weathered, glacier-deposited granitic boulders. Near the top of the climb you pass through a stock gate and may spy a lateral trail just before you arrive at the north end of grassy, appropriately named Big Meadow. The lateral, bound for Scotts Lake, takes 2½ miles to reach it. Most of this lake lies on private land. Just within the north fringe of Big Meadow, beyond a clump of willows, our trail curves slightly right (southwest) and fords trout-inhabited, jump-across Big Meadow Creek.

Beyond the creek crossing, our path turns south again and we head toward a conspicuous wooden post along this very flat traverse before we enter forest cover again, in a cluster of mature lodgepoles that trespass into the southeast corner of the meadow. Now our path winds south up the lodgepole-covered slope, which also is cloaked with clusters of red firs in some places and with open patches of aromatic mule ears and sagebrush in others. Near the top of our climb the grade eases off and the trail swings southwest, passes through a barbed-wire fence, and leaves meadow-grazing cattle behind to begin a moderate descent from a broad, forested saddle.

On a fairly steep slope of volcanic rubble that we descend, the trees aren't as densely packed as were those along our ascent, so we can survey the basin we are about to enter. At the base of a prominent granitic cliff one mile west lies shallow, unseen Dardanelles Lake; above and beyond both stands a volcanic ridge, usually decked with snowfields and composed of many flows that are discernible by the naked eye. At the base of the massive volcanic cliffs ahead of us lies our unseen destination, Round Lake.

After passing some fine specimens of Jeffrey pine, whose deeply furrowed bark emits a butterscotch odor that permeates the warm air, we meet the Meiss Meadow Trail, which has climbed up a tributary of the Upper Truckee River. A gentle 0.2-mile descent along its aspen-covered banks will take you to a junction from where a 1.2-mile trail to Dardanelles Lake branches west (**Hike 92**). We continue south, climbing

up, down and around on hummocky terrain of volcanic mudflow deposits and blocks. Our trail, now over fine-grained volcanic soils, is considerably dustier than the coarser-grained granitic soils we started on.

Arriving at Round Lake, we see it is different from all the other lakes of the Tahoe Sierra. The lake is brownish-green in color, and this may be due to super-fine volcanic particles held in suspension, which are derived from mudflow sediments. Since you'll probably not want to drink this water, hike 170 yards along the lodgepole- and cottonwood-lined east shore and obtain water from a trickling creek. Fair campsites are scattered about the north half of the lake, the south half being too vegetated and swampy. From the northeast corner follow a narrow path west past Jeffrey pines, junipers, sagebrush, mule ears and buckwheat to a small campsite on a granitic bench just west of the head-high dam. Beneath red firs and lodgepole pines you can experience superb sunsets that light the towering volcanic palisade east of you with color. Just east of this campsite is a small cove in which one could enjoy a refreshing swim or could fish for some of the lake's cutthroat trout.

If you want to hike up to shallow, boulder-dotted Meiss Lake, you can reach it from Round Lake by at least two routes. The first is to start from the northwest campsites and follow an unofficial path south along the west shore of Round Lake. At this lake's southwest corner you'll find more campsites, these shaded by lodgepoles growing on a flat bench above the lake. From this bench a faint trail climbs south almost a mile to Meiss Lake. The second way to Meiss Lake is to hike south from Round Lake on the Meiss Meadow Trail. After one mile you reach a meadowy area with a conspicuous, entrenched creek. Leave the trail just before it crosses this creek and go cross-country ½ mile west to Meiss Lake. This second route is preferable if you are carrying a heavy pack, for its terrain is easier than the first. Just 2.3 miles from Round Lake, the Meiss Meadow Trail reaches the Pacific Crest/Tahoe-Yosemite trail in Meiss Meadow (see Hike 93).

Meiss Lake is one of the warmest lakes in the Tahoe area, for it is very shallow. Indeed, you can wade across it. If you use the lake's campsites, which are along its west shore, expect an occasional cow and, until early August, hordes of mosquitoes.

Near a creeklet dropping to Round Lake's northeast shore, the Meiss Meadow Trail passes an enormous block that, like so many around us here, has broken off from the vertical-to-over-

**The Dardanelles, which are a row of volcanic cliffs, tower over Round Lake**

hanging cliffs above us. (See the geology chapter's "Tahoe Sierra volcanism" for the origin of this volcanic rock.) Climbers who like to go "bouldering" will find this an ideal block to climb on. Since some routes are overhanging and others are as long as 40 feet, and since the flat-sided handholds aren't always secure, you should use a top rope. More daring climbers may want to try the potentially dangerous deep fissures on the vertical cliffs above.

# 93 Pacific Crest Trail, Carson Pass north to Showers Lake

**Distances**  4.0 miles to Meiss Lake, 5.0 miles to Round Lake, 5.1 miles to Showers Lake.

**Low/High Elevations**  8350'/8790'

**Classification**  Moderate

**Season**  Mid-July through early October

**Maps**  41 and 40

**Trailhead**  Drive up Highway 88 to a curve with a parking lot, just 0.2 mile west of the parking area at Carson Pass. This pass is about 100 miles from Highway 99 in Stockton and about 20 miles from Highway 50 in the Lake Tahoe Basin.

**Introduction**  This walk along the Pacific Crest/Tahoe-Yosemite trail presents the hiker with a very scenic route to Showers Lake, the highest lake in the Upper Truckee River basin. The lake is a worthy goal in itself, but even if it were not, the hike to it across a glaciated volcanic landscape would justify the effort. The country traversed along this hike is among the Sierra's best for subalpine botanizing. Side trips include visits to Meiss and Round lakes, plus a cross-country jaunt up to Red Lake Peak, which has both exceptional views and wildflowers.

**Description**  From the trailhead at the northwest corner of the parking lot, first climb southwest and then round a ridge to make an undulating traverse northwest past junipers and occasional aspens to a gullied bowl. Both tree species release subtle scents, though these usually go unnoticed by the hurried hiker; they are often masked by the stronger scents produced here by mule ears and sagebrush. After winding in and out of several gullies, you follow short switchbacks north, then traverse west to a junction with the old Meiss Meadow Trail. Starting opposite a Woods Lake road junction 0.9 mile west of Carson Pass, this trail climbs very steeply to this junction in 0.5 mile, versus 1.3 miles for the leisurely PCT/TYT.

In 110 yards your north-climbing trail tops a pond-blessed saddle, which is a good place to rest and admire the view to the south, dominated by Round Top (10,381') and flanked on the east by Elephants Back (9585'). In early season the saddle's pond looks quite fresh, but with time, horses and cattle muddy its water. Don't drink the water regardless of how clear it looks.

The saddle is the logical spot to start a cross-country excursion up to Red Lake Peak. Work east up an ascending ridge, then veer north when the gradient gets too steep. Tackle the peak anywhere along its lengthy west flank. The summit abounds in resplendent vistas, which encompass three major basins: Upper Truckee River, to the west; West Fork Carson River, to the east; and Caples Creek (which feeds into the Silver Fork American River), to the southwest. The relatively gentle slopes below the peak's summit rival those of Mt. Rose and Stevens and Freel peaks in diversity of alpine cushion plants. However, the soils they grow in are incoherent and therefore readily erodible. So whether you're botanizing or just up here for the lofty views, take care not to disturb these diminutive plants.

From the pond-blessed saddle, you make an easy traverse ⅓ mile north along jeep tracks to a junction. There you angle left and descend tracks to a campsite by a jump-across ford of the infant Upper Truckee River. We now have an easy descent northwest, then pass through a gate, recross the river, pass through a second gate and in a moment reach a trail fork. From here, near cabins in the large meadow, the Meiss Meadow Trail heads 2.3 miles to the northeast corner of large, slightly cloudy Round Lake (see Hike 92). You can follow this trail over a low, broad ridge, reaching a lodgepole-fringed meadow in 0.5 mile. From it you can then leave the trail and head cross-country 0.6 mile northwest down

gentle slopes to the southeast shore of shallow, warm Meiss Lake.

Our main trail continues northwest, passing another set of northbound tracks in ¼ mile—these leading to the meadow south of Meiss Lake. Just before we meet our third river ford, we see that lake, and immediately before the ford a faint trail provides the hiker with an easy ½-mile meadow traverse to Meiss Lake. The cow-dotted meadow, however, is often damp, if not downright boggy, particularly near the south end of the lake, and until early August this wet environment nurses a multitude of mosquitoes. Before mid-August take the earlier trail-plus-cross-country route to Meiss Lake. From mid-August through mid-September this chest-deep lake is ideal for swimming or just plain relaxing.

After jumping across the Upper Truckee River for the last time, we continue northwest along a meadow's edge and, just before crossing a shallow gap, see a faint trail, on our left, which comes 2.1 miles from Schneider's Cow Camp (Hike 94). Just beyond the gap we descend north to a pond, and resume our lodgepole-and-meadow traverse. Our jeep tracks soon curve left up an increasingly steep slope on which they narrow to a trail. Nearing a crest, this trail is joined by an abortive set of jeep tracks. We then cross this broad crest and, as we start a descent to nearby Showers Lake, we see a second trail from Schneider's Cow Camp, 2.0 miles distant (also Hike 94). Momentarily we reach campsites along the east shore of granite-bound Showers Lake. An old trail may still be seen traversing northwest across willowy slopes south of the lake, but the slopes are very muddy and the trail should be avoided. If you continue north past the lake, follow Hike 89, which is described in the reverse direction.

**Shallow, warm Meiss Lake and Stevens Peak's broad 9700' outlier**

# 94 Schneider's Cow Camp to Showers and Meiss Lakes

**Distances** 2.1 miles to Showers Lake, 2.9 miles to Meiss Lake, 5.7 miles to Showers Lake via alternate long route.

**Low/High Elevations** 8340'/9200'

**Classification** Strenuous along main route

**Season** Late July through mid-October

**Maps** 40 and 38

**Trailhead** From Highway 99 in Stockton, drive about 96 miles northeast up Highway 88 to Caples Lake Resort, above the north shore of Caples Lake. Continue 0.9 mile past the resort to a paved road, on your left, signed for Caples Lake Maintenance Station. (Westbound drivers: this road is 3.0 miles west of Carson Pass.) Take this road ¼ mile to the maintenance station, and immediately past it turn right and drive up a graded road. Before August it can be muddy in several places, mostly in the first ½ mile. After 1¼ dusty or muddy miles you pass Schneider Camping Area (no tap water), on your left, then continue 0.4 mile to a gate and a road fork. Park here.

**Introduction** The shortest trails to Showers and Meiss lakes start from Schneider's Cow Camp. Ironically, these steep trails haven't gotten much use in the past. The trail to Showers has a short section along which you get one of the most expansive views to be seen from any trail in the Tahoe Sierra.

**Description** From the fork in the road by Schneider's Cow Camp, you can start two routes to Showers Lake. The longer route starts up the road you drove in on, which quickly becomes a jeep road. The shorter route, which will be described first, starts by the east side of the road fork. This trail climbs 230 yards east to a barbed-wire gate, then climbs at a gradually steepening pace through cow country. Lodgepole stands give way to open spaces, which seasonally abound with many species of wildflowers. You leave most of the cows behind as you switchback steeply up to a crest saddle, passing a few whitebark pines before reaching it.

Only 1.1 miles from the trailhead this view-blessed saddle is a worthy goal in itself. And for even better views you can go cross-country along the crest, either ¼ mile northwest to peak 9325 or, preferably, ½ mile southeast to peak 9422. From the saddle you see Meiss and Round lakes to the northeast, and above them see the volcanic palisades of the Upper Truckee

River canyon. To the left of these cliffs stands the Freel Peak massif, with Freel Peak, at 10,881 feet, lording it above all other peaks of the Tahoe Basin rim. The view to the southwest reveals the volcanic palisades above Kirkwood Creek but Caples Lake and Round Top remain hidden.

From the saddle you gently climb a brief 85 yards to a junction. From it a trail drops 0.9 mile east to the Pacific Crest Trail (which here also happens to be the Tahoe-Yosemite Trail). It is generally easy to follow, but the last 200 yards to the PCT/TYT can be vague, bearing 110°. If you take this short trail, you won't have any trouble finding the PCT, but study this locale so you can find your trail if you plan to return along it after following the last part of Hike 93 to Showers Lake. On the PCT this "junction" is about 180 yards south of a pond and 360 yards northwest of an Upper Truckee River ford. From the east side of that ford you can follow a faint, often wet trail ½ mile north to Meiss Lake (see Hike 93).

Back at the junction just beyond the crest saddle, the left trail climbs briefly and then descends, usually at a moderate grade. Before Showers Lake comes into view, stop and admire the astounding views, which are among the best in the whole Tahoe area. You can see from 10,776-foot Mt. Rose, above the north shore of Lake Tahoe, southward to 11,398-foot White Mountain, about 4 miles north of Sonora Pass. This 70-mile panorama includes, northeast to southeast: granitic Freel Peak, relatively close Stevens and Red Lake peaks, and very distant Highland and Arnot peaks—all above 10,000 feet. Lower prominences rising above the end of the Upper Truckee River basin are Reynolds Peak, the Nipple, peak 9381 and, on the far right, broad-topped Elephants Back.

Your panoramic views continue until you reach a cluster of mountain hemlocks, by which you have the first view of your goal, Showers Lake. Distant Mt. Tallac, in eastern Desolation Wilderness, stands above this lake, and to its left stand the two summits of Dicks and Jacks peaks, in the heart of that wilderness. The isolated peak west of them is Pyramid Peak, the sentinel guarding the southwest border of the wilderness.

The short descent to Showers Lake is rubbly and excessively steep. It's bad enough when dry, but after a storm, or when snow-patched in early season, you'll really slip and slide down this trail

**Red Lake Peak (left), Elephants Back (far right) and the Upper Truckee River basin**

segment, so be careful. The steep descent moderates just before you reach the PCT/TYT, along which you have only a couple minutes' walk to campsites along the east shore of subalpine Showers Lake. If you camp here before early August, be prepared for lots of hungry mosquitoes. This lake is one of the cooler lakes to be found in the Tahoe area, and most people will find swimming in it acceptable only in August, a couple weeks after nearby snow patches have melted.

If you have a heavy pack or are on horseback, you won't want to make the steep descent to Showers Lake. For variety, hikers might plan to take the longer route to the lake, and then, with lighter packs, climb out via the shorter route just described. From Schneider's Cow Camp the longer route starts northwest up a jeep road, quickly passes a gate, and almost ½ mile from the start crosses a seasonal creek. About 40 yards past it you come to a trail, which you ascend steeply north. The trail rapidly swings left, and on an easier grade you climb west with

### Showers Lake

views south to Caples Lake and Round Top mountain.

About one mile from this route's start the trail bends north, enters forest shade, and climbs to a nearby early-season creeklet. You cross it, parallel it upstream, climb to a subordinate crest, and then drop to a small flat. Staying close to the contact between volcanic rocks above and granitic ones below, you traverse north-northwest for ½ mile, passing two closely spaced springs midway to a trail fork. From here the older trail goes left, descending ¼ mile to a broad ridge, on which it dies out. The newer trail, our route, briefly climbs north, then traverses east below the slopes of Little Round Top. Along this traverse you'll get a couple of views of Pyramid, Jacks and Dicks peaks. From a reliable creek the trail angles north and contours 0.4 mile to an enormous trailside mountain hemlock, on your left—among the largest you'll find anywhere. About 90 yards past it you enter lands of the *Fallen Leaf Lake* 15' quadrangle (Map 38) and momentarily receive additional views of the three Desolation Wilderness peaks seen earlier. Our Trail 17E16 then curves east, drops to a spring-fed creeklet, and reaches the PCT/TYT in 200 yards. From here you follow Hike 89 south 1.9 miles to campsites along the east shore of Showers Lake.

If you're not quite ready to join the weekend crowd at Showers Lake, then descend about 300 yards north on the PCT to a saddle. From it a faint, discontinuous path strikes east 250 yards down a linear meadow to a camp with a fine view, just beyond the meadow's far end. To the west a similar tread descends 330 yards to the upper end of a large meadow, then angles at 330° for 130 yards to a cow camp among a cluster of lodgepoles. Both camps are lightly visited, at least by humans.

# 95                     Lake Margaret Trail

**Distance**   2.3 miles, one way
**Low/High Elevations**   7480'/7740'
**Classification**   Easy
**Season**   Mid-July through mid-October
**Map**   39

**Trailhead**   This is located along a short loop road that is on the north side of Highway 88. Eastbound drivers find it 0.5 mile east of Kirkwood Meadows road; westbound drivers find it 0.2 mile west of the base of Caples Lake's west dam. Parking for about 10 vehicles.

**Introduction**   Lake Margaret Trail 17E46 takes the hiker, in about an hour's time, to a lovely lake in a granitic, hemmed-in setting. For rock climbers this lake is an ideal place for a base camp. In the entire Tahoe Sierra you won't find another backcountry lake with such an abundance of good climbing routes up solid rock.

**Description**   After a minute's walk northwest along a minor, rather open ridge, you turn right and drop to a small, damp flat. This can be prolific in both wildflowers and mosquitoes, and more of these environments lie ahead. You exit to a dry bench, then wind down to the south fork of Caples Creek, which you either log-cross or rock-hop, at least before late summer, by when the creek bed is typically dry. Heading north, you skirt the base of a granitic knoll, ignore a trail heading east along its north base, then in a swampy meadow cross the major north fork of Caples Creek. In 1983 you crossed on a broad bridge, but this structure showed signs of impending collapse. The creek, draining Caples Lake and the watershed above it, could be a very wet ford without a bridge.

**Granite-bound Lake Margaret**

Northward, you immediately pass the east edge of a low granitic outcrop, which has been polished and striated by one or more west-trending glaciers. From it you jog momentarily northeast, then climb a brushy ¼ mile to a narrow pass. Here it's worth your time and effort to scramble east up some smooth granitic slopes, just above the trail, for a 360° view. If you site on a 300° bearing, which is roughly the course of your unseen path, you'll see a broad, low gap, about a mile beyond unseen Lake Margaret. Although this gap in the canyon wall stands about 800 feet above the Caples Creek canyon floor, it nevertheless was too low to contain a major glacier advancing down-canyon. At least one, and probably more, glaciers spilled north through this gap into the Strawberry Creek drainage, burying the gap under at least 200 feet of ice. From your vantage point the views to the south are the most impressive, particularly of the gaping Kirkwood Meadows canyon, whose steep-sided walls reveal layer after layer of volcanic sediments and flows.

Back on the trail you skirt past a minor pond, then just north of and above it start down a ducked route across bedrock to a larger grass-lined pond. You quickly cross its seasonal outlet creek, only to recross it about 200 yards downstream. In a minute you approach a more substantial creek, follow it a bit downstream, veer away, and then log-cross it just after rejoining it. You continue 150 yards downstream, heading toward an overhanging cliff, then switchback and climb steeply up brushy slabs, skirt through a shallow notch, and behold tranquil Lake Margaret. From its south corner a *de facto* trail circles around the lake's east and north shores, ending near the lake's outlet. The author prefers the shorter, rougher cross-country route above the west shore to reach this outlet.

You'll find two campsites—one quite spacious—near the east shore, two more near the northwest shore. Swimming is recommended, for the lake's small bedrock islands are tempting goals, and from the lake's southeast shore, you can dive from heights up to 10 feet. The lake is surrounded by slabs and cliffs, which offer rock climbers many possible routes, generally about 50 feet long. However, one cliff, 300 yards above the northeast shore, requires a full-length rope. Nonclimbers can scramble up easy routes to one of the lake's adjacent knolls and witness a Sierran sunrise or sunset.

# 96                   Emigrant Lake Trail

**Distances** 2.2 miles to Caples Lake's south end, 4.2 miles to Emigrant Lake.

**Low/High Elevations** 7770'/8600'

**Classification** Moderate

**Season** Mid-July through mid-October

**Maps** 39, 40 and 42

**Trailhead** Along Highway 88, at the base of Caples Lake's *western* dam, which is 4¾ miles west of Carson Pass.

**Introduction** Another writer lauded Emigrant Lake as one of the most beautiful in the area. Perhaps this is why it is so popular. Of all the Chapter 15 backcountry lakes visited by the author, he found only Round Lake to be more popular. Visiting Emigrant Lake on an unseasonably cold midsummer weekday, he found this lake, which is set in a deep, stark, often snowy and windswept cirque, a chilling experience. However, the slopes above the lake's east shore were resplendent with wildflowers which, in the author's prejudiced view, mitigated the otherwise bleak setting.

**Description** The first 2¼ miles of Emigrant Lake Trail 17E18 are extremely easy, for the trail never goes more than 50 feet higher than the lake's shore. Many fishermen hike only along this stretch, dropping to one or more small coves along the adjacent shore to try for trout. Our shoreline route, through a generally shady forest, certainly contrasts with the open forest along the lake's north shore. Our shore is more luxuriant because of all its mineral-rich sediments which were derived from the largely unseen volcanic cliffs and slopes above us.

After only about ¼ mile into your route you pass a snowmelt creeklet that drops over a 10-foot cliff. Note here that the cliff is composed of *stratified* volcanic sediments—ones that were laid down by a stream. When we look at an array of volcanic sediments, such as the giant palisades in the distance above Caples Lake Resort, we tend to think these layers were laid down rapidly, due to eruption after continual eruption. Actually, the volcanic rocks in the Chapter 15 area were laid down, as lava flows or their sedimentary derivatives, over at least 20 million years, and during the vast amount of that time, erosion, not eruption, was the basic element transfiguring the landscape.

When you reach an open area strewn with granitic boulders, you'll be midway along your shoreline trek. Near the far edge of this opening

you may see an old EMIGRANT ROAD sign, although all evidences of its tread are absent. A few aspens herald forest cover, under which you walk a mile to near the south tip of Caples Lake. An 80-yard path goes out to the water's edge, at which you'll have some nice views plus some shoreline slabs for sunbathing or fishing.

Alongside the lake, the trail has served as the Mokelumne Wilderness boundary, but now you enter the wilderness proper as you leave the lake's south tip. After a couple of minutes you pass through a small meadow, which grows a crop of corn lilies and arrowhead senecios, and here you enter prime mosquito country. Through July you can expect their humming

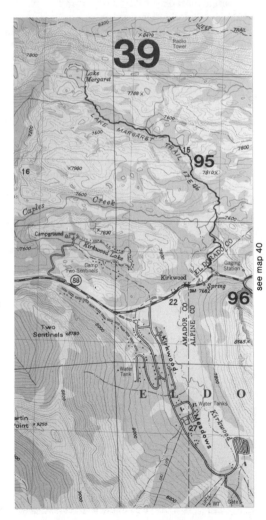

chorus to serenade you all the way up Emigrant Creek. About 0.6 mile past the meadow you come to a junction with a trail that climbs a steep ¼ mile southwest up to a Kirkwood Meadows ski-lift-maintenance road. From the south end of that road one could continue south on a trail into the heart of the wilderness, but that subalpine landscape, the location of many minilakes, is largely beyond the scope of this book. (The Silver Lake area offers easier routes into this region.)

Just 0.1 mile past the junction and a little over 3 miles from the trailhead we rock-hop Emigrant creek and discover a noticeable increase in trail gradient, in mountain hemlocks and, before August, in snow patches. Switchbacks keep the gradient within reason and, just beyond a cascading distributary from Emigrant creek, we're treated to northward views. These disappear as we climb westward to Emigrant creek proper, up which our trail's finale is an easy if marshy stroll. The trail dies out along

**Chilly, windswept Emigrant Lake**

Emigrant Lake's brushy east shore. Instead of hiking onward, cross the creek just below the lake's outlet and head past an assortment of camps to the conspicuous peninsula. From it you can fish or sunbathe (which is necessary after a frigid dip) and, weather permitting, have a fine spot for just soaking up the scenery.

# 97 Woods Lake to Round Top Lake and Round Top Summit

**Distances** 1.4 miles to Winnemucca Lake by Trail 18E06, 2.1 miles to Round Top Lake by Trail 17E47, 2.3 miles to Round Top Lake by Trail 18E06.

**Low/High Elevations** 8210'/9410'; 10,381' to summit.

**Classification** Moderate to lakes, strenuous at summit.

**Season** Late July through early October

**Maps** 40, 41, 42 and 43

**Trailhead** Drive up Highway 88 toward Carson Pass. Eastbound drivers leave this highway just 1.2 miles after they pass a junction with a road to the Caples Lake Maintenance Station, the road and junction both above Caples Lake's northeast shore. If you miss the Woods Lake turnoff, you have a second chance 0.9 mile later. This is the turnoff westbound drivers take, which is 0.9 mile west of Carson Pass. Eastbound drivers traverse a gravel road (the *old* Highway 88) 0.8 mile to another junction, while westbound drivers descend 0.5 mile to it.

Both then drive almost 0.2 mile south to a trailhead parking area that is immediately before Woods Creek. If you are going in for two or more days, park here and hike ⅓ mile up an east-bank trail to Woods Lake Trail 18E06. If you're

day hiking, you can drive 0.4 mile up the road and park in the lakeside picnic area. Trail 18E06 begins 50 yards north of and before the start of the picnic area's loop road.

For Trail 17E47 follow the same procedure. To reach its trailhead hike about 90 yards north from the Woods Lake Trail 18E06 trailhead to the start of the one-way Woods Lake Campground road. Walk west 0.2 mile up to campsite 13, on your right. The trailhead is a few yards past it, on your left.

All of the above mileages are calculated from the start of Woods Lake Trail 18E06. If you are beginning from the start of Trail 17E47 (no parking here), then subtract 0.2 mile. If you hike up the east-bank trail to Trail 18E06, add 0.3 mile. If you hike from the same parking area up to the start of Trail 17E47, add 0.2 mile. This assumes you walk ¼ mile up the Woods Lake Road to the north end of the campground's one-way road, then go 320 yards up it.

**Introduction** Two of the Tahoe Sierra's most photogenic lakes lie only an hour's hike away: Lake Winnemucca via Trail 18E06 and Round Top Lake via Trail 17E47. From the latter you can climb, with a lot of effort, to the Round Top summit in another hour. This peak, surpassed in height only by Mt. Rose and the Freel Peak

**Snow-robed Round Top and whitebark-pine-bordered Winnemucca Lake**

massif, offers unsurpassed didactic views for tens of miles in every direction. Because the features along this hike are so readily accessible, you should day hike rather than backpack to them. The lakes, which do attract campers, are both near timberline, and consequently they have fragile environments that can't withstand the impact of heavy use. Under no condition should equestrians camp at them.

**Description**  From Woods Lake you can make a 4.4-mile loop to Winnemucca and Round Top lakes by starting up either Trail 18E06 or Trail 17E47. By taking in Round Top peak, you add 2.0 miles to your loop. The advantage of a loop is that you of course get to see more terrain. The author prefers ascending Trail 18E06 since it is better graded.

Woods Lake Trail 18E06 begins by heading 50 yards east to Woods Creek, down whose east bank runs a cutoff trail to the trail from the Woods Creek parking area. Climbing southeast, we meet this 0.4-mile trail after a minute's walk, then continue in the same direction, having a glimpse or two of Woods Lake, seen through hemlocks, lodgepoles and western white pines. About ½ mile from our trailhead we hike along a creeklet and its attendant wildflower garden, then reach an old arrastra, which is a circular floor of stones about 10 feet across. Usually a mule would drag a large stone round and round it, the stone pulverizing smaller, ore-laden stones, enabling a miner to extract the gold and silver.

Beyond this historic artifact the forest thins appreciably, the ground cover transforming to one of sagebrush and wildflowers. Along this ⅔-mile open stretch up to Winnemucca Lake, a botanist can have a field day, identifying dozens of wildflowers. This hike's Plate 15 has a fraction of this area's wildflowers. For additional high-elevation species, consult Plates 11, 13, 14, 16 and 17.

Our moderately climbing path, which has paralleled the lake's outlet creek at a short distance, enters Mokelumne Wilderness about ⅓ mile before ending at a junction with Tahoe-Yosemite Trail 17E01. Here, by the lake, you'll see broad, rounded Elephants Back, about a mile to the northeast. From its easily attainable summit, straddling the Sierra Nevada crest, you have excellent views to the east and west, plus one commendable view southwest of dark, solemn Round Top.

Westbound on the TYT we cross the lake's outlet in 70 yards, the outlet's gravelly, saturated soil seasonally highlighted with diminutive mountain monkey flowers and alpine shooting stars. Climbing west, all but late-season hikers are likely to encounter snowfields. The open route, however, is quite obvious, and in ⅔ mile we crest a shallow gap in a granitic ridge. Notice up here—the high point if you don't climb Elephants Back or Round Top—how the freezing winter winds have cropped the whitebark pines down to shrublike stature. Their asymmetrical growth reveals the direction of the prominent winds. You now have an easy descent 300 yards

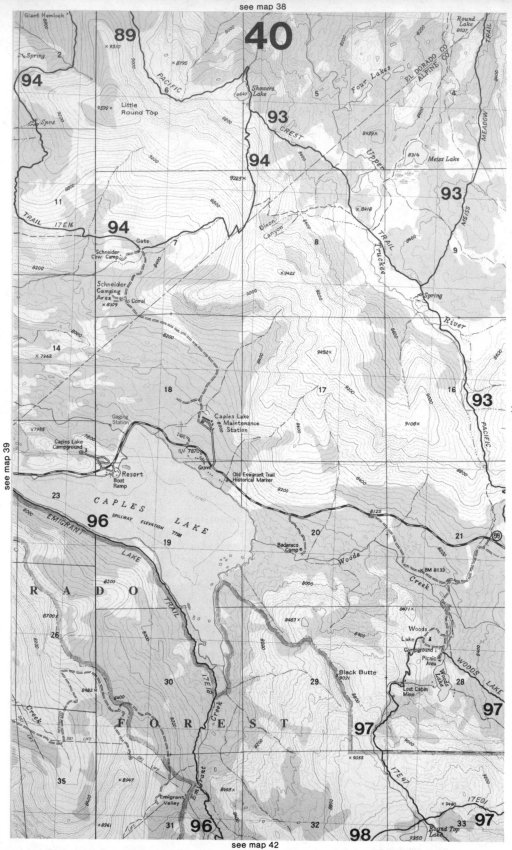

see map 38

89

40

94

93

94

Giant Hemlock

Spring

94

PACIFIC

Little
Round Top

Showers
Lake

Four Lakes

Round
Lake

EL DORADO CO
ALPINE CO

MEADOW

TRAIL

4

Spring

Sprs

CREST

Meiss Lake

Upper

93

11

TRAIL 17E16

94

Gate

Schneider
Cow Camp

Schneider
Camping
Area

Corral

Dixon
Canyon

8

Truckee

TRAIL

9

MEISS

River

Spring

14

18

17

16

Gaging
Station

Caples Lake
Maintenance
Station

Caples Lake
Campground

Resort
Boat
Ramp

Grave

Old Emigrant Trail
Historical Marker

93

PACIFIC

see map 41

see map 39

23

96

EMIGRANT

LAKE

CAPLES

LAKE

SPILLWAY ELEVATION 7798

19

20

21

Badaraco
Camp

Woods

Creek

BM 8133

R A D O

26

TRAIL

17E18

30

Creek

SKI

SKI LIFT

F O R E S T

29

Black Butte

Woods
Lake

Campground

Picnic
Area

Lost Cabin
Mine

28

WOODS

LAKE

97

97

35

Emigrant
Valley

31

96

Emigrant

Creek

32

97

33

Round Top
Lake

98

17E47

17E01

see map 42

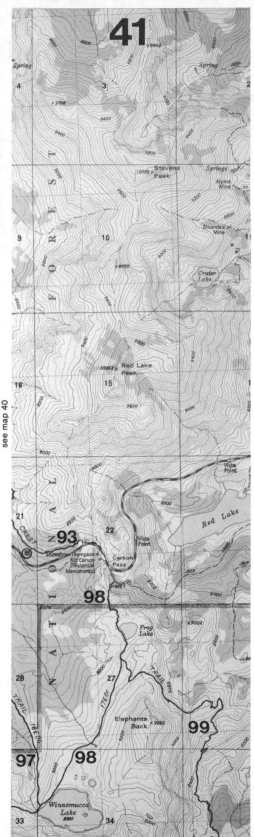

to Round Top Trail 17E47, which intersects the TYT by the northeast corner of Round Top Lake. With clusters of whitebark pines adorning its northwest shore, the lake is relatively wind-free, and is a fine spot for a lunch break. However, if you plan to climb Round Top, then eat lightly.

To climb Round Top, which you should attempt only in good weather, you should have brought along several items: dark glasses, a cap or hat, and a windbreaker. The first two are very useful in protecting your sensitive eyes from the intense ultraviolet radiation you'll receive on this exposed climb. If you are taking color photos, bring along a polarizing filter; if black and white photos, a red filter.

Starting southeast from the lake, you're almost bound to see some sturdy green gentians, which can grow to chest height by late season. Some botanists know this plant by other names: giant frasera, deer's tongue and monument plant. After 0.4 mile of climbing up a narrow tread, your underfooting switches from granitic to volcanic and your gradient switches from steep to *very* steep. You're now in the alpine realm, though alpine wildflowers are relatively scarce due to the rubbly nature of the steep slopes. The rubble is just enough to make us backslide on our ascent, but not deep enough to comprise a scree slope. Consequently, on your way down, instead of "skiing" down the rubble you'll have to cautiously pick your way.

Before August, snow can cover most of the upper trail, which appears to be heading for the broad saddle separating Round Top from the East Sister. Actually, the trail dies out before the saddle and you climb cross-country not to the saddle, but left of it, to a small but obvious notch in Round Top's descending ridge. Once on the ridge you climb up its back side, staying close to the crest, until you reach a false summit. For most hikers this is far enough. The true summit, only a few feet higher, blocks your views to the east, but then, that direction is the least photogenic.

Between the two summits is a small, steep-sided cleft, which perhaps separates the brave from the wise. Were it not for the rubbly nature, the descent into this minor cleft would be quite safe. As matters stand, if you slip on the loose rock, you could find yourself plunging down a steepening slope and into an avalanche chute—almost certain death. From the cleft, don't tackle the true summit head-on, but instead descend a few yards south before taking a curving route of least resistance northeast to the small summit.

**Wildflower Plate 15. Subalpine flowers.**
1 Woolly senecio (yellow), 2 California Jacob's ladder (violet to pale-blue with white center), 3 alpine paintbrush (dull-yellow to purple-green), 4 mountain monkey flower (yellow), 5 Lewis' monkey flower (pink), 6 showy penstemon (red-violet to blue), 7 western blue flax, 8 green gentian (pale green flowers and stem), 9 mountain lungwort (blue or pink).

see map 40

**42**

96

98

97

Round
Top

Thimble
Peak
9805

Emigrant
Lake
8590

10045

The Sisters 10153

2

8200

Covered Wagon
Peak 9565

8800

Fourth of July
Peak
9536

9400

9600

6

9200

9795

5

4

Emigrant
Peak
9763

9607

Corrie
Lochan

8164

Fourth of July
Lake

17 E 01

7800

9002

Scout Carson
Lake

9250

9000

9607

8000

8600

**98**

see map 43

1

7

M O K E L U M N E       W I L D E R N E S S

7200

7200

8600

9

Meadow

Ridge

8600

Horse

Canyon

7800

Summit

City

8600

Squaw

9100

8408

8200

9434

14

Martell Flat

8200

7800

9006

9056

see map 41

9016

99

**43**

Round Top
9038

9842

9400

8600

8600

West

Fork

9600

9200

Foresdale

Divide

8800

9442

8800

9374

PACIFIC

8600

3

9000

8600

9600

18 E 07

1

8600

Lost
Lakes 8772

**98**

7800

8600

Creek

18 E 21

CREST

City

8600

8800

9

Summit

10

Spring

8902

8600

8800

8800

see map 42

M O K E L U M N E   W I L D E R N E S S

E L   D O R A D O

9626

Devils

Corral

11

8600

Upper
Blue Lake
Campground

LINE 12

8400

TRAIL

7800

8600

ROAD

8200

Creek

8600

*Upper Blue Lake*

SPILLWAY ELEVATION 8136

Damsite C.G.

Boat
Ramp

9600

9400

9545

9200

8200

13

Middle Cre

Middle

**Summit panorama. Black Butte partly hides Caples Lake. Pyramid Peak is on horizon above them. Jacks and Dicks peaks are east of it and Mt. Tallac is on far-right horizon.**

The author found this ascent from the cleft considerably less intimidating than the descent into it.

From the summit you have, on a clear day, an extremely far-ranging 360° view. If you look due east along Round Top's descending ridgecrest, you'll see 9415' Markleeville Peak, 5½ miles away, which lies 1½ miles north of 9065' Jeff Davis Peak—a miniature Devils Tower that challenges the best of climbers. (If you've got a Markleeville 15' quad map, then subtract 75 feet. This is quite some discrepancy. Usually the peak elevations in the newer 7½' quads agree to within several feet of the elevations of the older 15' quads.)

Scanning counterclockwise, you next see, above Winnemucca Lake, domelike 10,023' Hawkins Peak—what's left of the throat of an ancient volcano. Above 9585' Elephants Back, you barely see the top of 9118' Pickett Peak. The latter is, like your summit, the core of an ancient volcano, while the former is a dome of andesite lava. Carson Pass is the broad, obvious gash in the Sierra crest, beyond which lies spacious Hope Valley. Sierra-crest glaciers coalesced to form a mammoth glacier that flowed north down this valley and, unable to make a sharp turn east down the West Carson Canyon, part of the glacier continued to plow 1½ miles straight ahead, climbing about 400 feet in the process. This huge glacier, which received some of its impetus from Round Top's north-slope glaciers, was thick enough to spill west

over Luther Pass. Hope Valley, therefore, was buried under about 800 feet of glacier ice (see the geology chapter's glacier map).

Above Hope Valley stands 10,881' Freel Peak and its entourage of 10,000+' peaks. In the distant past the South Fork American River, which today has its headwaters just west of Highway 50's Echo Summit, probably had its headwaters on the upper slopes of this massif. But that was at least 4 million years ago, before lands east of the Sierra crest began to sink along faults. Hope Valley is one fault-formed basin, but of course you'll spot a larger one, the one holding Lake Tahoe. Part of this basin—and most of its appendage, the Upper Truckee River basin—can be seen to the north. On clear days you can see a high peak north of the lake's east shore. This is 10,776' Mt. Rose, a respectable 46 miles away. Scanning westward, you'll readily identify pointed 9735' Mt. Tallac above Tahoe's west shore and, above the east shore of Caples Lake, 9983' Pyramid Peak, which is steeper-sloped than Tallac. Between the two lies the bulk of Desolation Wilderness.

Closer to us beneath that high country lies the broad Caples Creek basin which, from about 50 to 30 million years ago, was a granitic landscape of rolling hills and valleys. But ensuing eruptions interred this gentle landscape in a volcanic sepulcher, and there it lay countless millenia, awaiting resurrection. With the advent of glaciation, the granitic land began to reappear, as wave after wave of glistening white glaciers stripped

**Panorama, continued. Upper Truckee River basin and Lake Tahoe are in distance on left. Freel Peak massif is in distance on right, Hope Valley is below it, and Carson Pass lies closer to us.**

away the dark volcanic blankets. These glaciers were truly monumental. The latest ones filled the Caples Creek basin almost rim to rim, entombing the floor under as much as ¼ mile of glacier ice. In a 2½-mile-wide cascade, they crevassed eastward down upon the equally giant Hope Valley glacier. In the Carson Pass area the glaciers have been thick enough at times to spill over into the Upper Truckee River basin, this basin itself the breeding ground for enormous, north-flowing glaciers that spilled west over Echo Summit into the South Fork American River drainage. Westward, down the Caples Creek basin, the giant glaciers spilled north into this same drainage, overflowing a low pass you see above the north shore of Caples Lake. During one of these glacial displays your summit, surrounded in a sea of ice, must have presented a viewer with a scene of indescribable beauty.

Returning momentarily to present time, we continue our counterclockwise scan. A sinuous volcanic ridge, to the west, separates the Caples Creek basin from the granite-walled Summit City Creek canyon. Averaging about 2000-2500 feet in depth, it is about twice as deep as the Caples Creek basin. Something interesting has happened here. Until rather recently, geologically speaking, this canyon was the route of a major, west-flowing river. But then, with nascent faulting of eastern lands about 4 million years ago, the river was beheaded (as were many other Tahoe Sierran streams and rivers). The canyon

was already quite deep back then, perhaps 1000-1500 feet below our vantage point, but with its headwaters gone, an inconsequential amount of canyon cutting took place over the ensuing 2 million years.

The story was quite different for the last 2 million years, for over most of that time glaciers marched down-canyon, deepening it by 500-1000 feet. These arose in part from hanging side canyons, such as the cirque that today holds Fourth of July Lake (unseen from the summit). However, the driving force to power such glaciers was a *mer de glace*—a sea of glacial ice— such as the one which buried the broad, relatively flat Blue Lakes area to the southeast. From this 8-mile-long, trans-Sierra crest plateau, glaciers flowed in all directions: north down the West Fork Carson River drainage (Hope Valley), northeast down the East Fork Carson River drainage (Charity and Pleasant valleys), south *through* southwest into the North Fork Mokelumne River canyon (in effect, a 10-mile-wide glacier), and west over a "minor" ridge into the Summit City Creek canyon. (Where glaciers are concerned, a ridge of several hundred feet is hardly an impediment.)

And there was another *mer de glace* nourishing the Summit City Creek canyon glacier. This one covered about 60 square miles of rolling uplands from the volcanic peaks above unseen Silver Lake south to 9332' Mokelumne Peak, and 10 miles away to the southwest. From this peak, which easily stands over 4000 feet above the floor of the canyon, the east edge of the *mer de glace* stretched 8 miles north, to 9763' Emigrant Peak, which is 2 miles to our west-southwest. This 8-mile stretch of glacier ice flowed into the canyon, filling it perhaps to the rim, possibly a bit higher. Now that's awesome!

If you've been reading the foregoing, lengthy discourse while on the summit, then the sun must be getting pretty low in the western sky. Hurry on back your route to Round Top Lake, from where you decide what course to follow. You can backtrack, you can head over to Fourth of July or Emigrant lake (Hike 97), or you can continue straight ahead down Trail 17E47.

By and large, Trail 17E47 is a joy to descend. Its fairly steady grade averages 11%, which is steep enough to propel us forward effortlessly but not so steep as to require a braking, knee-knocking effort. Hikers ascending this trail will find it a bit too steep, particularly up here in this rarefied air. We start an open, scenic descent northwest, usually staying a short distance from Round Top Lake's outlet creek. Black Butte, at first insignificant, grows formidable as we approach it. Above it stands the roof of the Crystal Range, topped by Pyramid Peak. Backward glances aren't bad either. If anything, they're more impressive, particularly in mid- or late afternoon, when Round Top and The Sisters cast photogenic shadows on their north-slope snowfields.

After ¾ mile you make a short, steep descent and turn northeast, entering a mountain-hemlock forest that lies just north of the Mokelumne Wilderness boundary. Hemlocks have a propensity to sustain snowfields, so don't be surprised to find snow here in August. This snow can cover the bend in the trail and even our adjacent creek, particularly in early season, leading unsuspecting hikers astray.

A ¼-mile, sometimes steep and rocky descent through the hemlock forest gets you down to a second right-angle bend. Here, where the trail turns northwest, you'll find a good-sized camp, on a small flat. A snowmelt creeklet provides water through most of the summer. Of all the campsites you may see along Hike 97, this is the only one which is suitable for equestrians.

In 130 yards we reach the start of a jeep road, which will be our route over the next ¾ mile. On our right is an old mine shack, "landscaped" with red elderberries. This bush, with foul-smelling leaves, produces a myriad of red berries in late season, but unlike the tart but tasty berries of its lower-elevation cousin, the blue elderberry, these berries are mildly poisonous.

On the road we quickly reach a creekside meadow, which is backdropped by now hulking Black Butte. While the butte appears large, it is but a petty remnant of the extensive volcanic sediments that once buried the Caples Creek basin. Just past the meadow, Round Top Lake's creek has all but destroyed our jeep road. Next we briefly enter forest shade and descend steeply to Lost Cabin Mine, which we reach immediately after crossing the creek. This mine was worked on and off from perhaps the 1860s or '70s until 1962, producing a recorded 132 troy ounces of gold, 375 ounces of silver, 917 pounds of copper and 3,832 pounds of lead. All this came from 196 tons of ore extracted from some faulted quartz veins.

From the mine you have an uneventful, winding, somewhat open descent ½ mile down to Woods Lake Campground. If you're parked at the lake's picnic area, turn right and walk 0.2 mile to the main road, then head south on it. If you're parked by the overnighters' trailhead, turn left and walk 320 yards to the main road, then head north on it.

# 98    Tahoe-Yosemite Trail, Carson Pass south to Fourth of July Lake

**Distances**   0.5 mile to Frog Lake, 2.0 miles to Winnemucca Lake, 2.9 miles to Round Top Lake, 4.7 miles to Fourth of July Lake, 4.9 miles to Emigrant Lake.

**Low/High Elevations**   8560' at trailhead; 8170' at Fourth of July Lake; 7440' at Summit City Canyon junction/9410'

**Classification**   Moderate

**Season**   Late July through early October

**Maps**   41, 40, 42 and 43

**Trailhead**   On Highway 88, drive up to signed Carson Pass, which is about 100 miles from Highway 99 in Stockton and about 20 miles from Highway 50 in the Lake Tahoe Basin. At the south end of a long turnout at the pass is the Carson Pass Information Station, which is sometimes open during summer months. When it is, you can get a wilderness permit, which is necessary if you plan to enter Mokelumne Wilderness. See Chapter 3 for more details. The southbound PCT/TYT trailhead (for Hikes 98 and 99) is 90 yards down a spur road, which forks right from the highway about 200 yards southeast of the pass.

**Introduction** Along this route you can visit all four of the scenic backcountry lakes of the upper Caples Creek basin. In addition, you have the opportunity to visit Fourth of July Lake, although the steep drop to it—over 1000 feet—makes it a debatable objective. Also, you'll need a wilderness permit to visit it, which is another negative point.

**Description** In 1983 our route, the Pacific Crest/Tahoe-Yosemite trail, climbed steeply enough to the base of a 200-foot-high granitic headwall, then tackled it head-on, leaving hikers exhausted by the time they got to Frog Lake, only ½ mile from the trailhead. Hopefully, this situation will be remedied by the construction of a new route for a more leisurely climb to Frog Lake. The lake, which lies just within Mokelumne Wilderness, is aptly named, since it's very suitable for frogs, though it also has trout. If you walk over to the Sierra's crest, which is barely above the lake's east shore, you'll get a view north-northeast into fault-dropped Hope Valley. A fault runs, almost literally, right below your feet, heading north down a gully toward Red Lake. During the last 2 million years, glaciers descending from Round Top scraped across your site, joining forces with the Hope Valley glacier, which once plowed uphill onto the gentle slopes at the north end of the valley, below the Freel Peak massif.

Just 250 yards past the lake, Pacific Crest Trail 2000, which has coincided with the old southbound Tahoe-Yosemite Trail 17E01 for the last 35.2 miles, forks off to the left (the next hike). We continue straight ahead, across an open landscape of sagebrush which is sporadically punctuated with clusters of lodgepole and whitebark pines. Snowy-robed Round Top, the ruins of an ancient volcano, acts like a giant lodestone, drawing us ever nearer.

Along this stretch, indeed, for the next 3 miles, you're likely to pass many mountain snowberries. With relatively small, drab leaves, these waist-high shrubs are easily ignored, particularly since most of the time they lack both flowers and berries. The flowers are small, tubular and pinkish—nothing special—but the berries are white, whence the name "snowberry." No other shrub in the Tahoe Sierra produces white berries. While mildly poisonous, they may

nevertheless be sampled by northward migrating black bears, who use the Tahoe-Yosemite Trail. Such bears, tagged in Yosemite National Park, have been found as far north as Desolation Wilderness!

After we do a mile of easy walking, chilly though photogenic Winnemucca Lake comes into view. For an interesting diversion leave the trail at this point, traverse ¼ mile east, passing above the north shore of a sunken pond, then climb northeast a little over ½ mile to the summit of Elephants Back. The views you obtain are second only to those from Round Top (Hike 97), which requires a great deal more effort. You also get your best possible view of the Red Lake-Forestdale Divide fault, mentioned earlier, which more or less runs along the base of your east-facing escarpment.

For secluded camping, try the broad, treeless crest notch above the east shore of Winnemucca Lake. It tends to be windy, but then, so are the popular, cramped sites along the lake's northwest shore. However, from your solitary site you can experience a glorious Sierra sunrise. In this area, above the east shore, you may possibly find some molybdenite, which is a mineral that is disseminated locally in the granitic bedrock. Its crystals are quite small, flat, and colored silvery gray, with a hint of blue. With it you're likely to find another mineral, pyrite, also known as fool's gold.

By Winnemucca Lake's west corner we meet Woods Lake Trail 18E06 and now join Hike 97 for 0.9 mile as it climbs up snowy, granitic slopes to a notch in a timberline divide, then drops to nearby Round Top Lake. Here you meet Trail 17E47, which descends to Woods Lake. It also continues up toward Round Top, whose summit is the apex of Hike 97. This strenuous but superlative side trip is highly recommended.

Continuing along the Tahoe-Yosemite Trail, we make a ¼-mile traverse west above Round Top Lake's north shore, passing several small, windswept campsites among the whitebark pines, then curve south on a ½-mile traverse to a crest divide. From here you can make a cross-country hike to Emigrant Lake. This is easily done by traversing about one mile west to a notch that is immediately southeast of the map's point 9020. From that notch the ⅓-mile, 420-foot drop toward the lake's outlet is perfectly obvious.

For the botanically inclined the descent to Fourth of July Lake is a sheer delight when the wildflowers are blooming. For most others, it is a sheer drop. The grade, averaging 20%, is too

268 CHAPTER 15

steep and often too bouldery; consequently you'll be scrutinizing the underfooting instead of the dozens of trailside wildflower species. Down at the lake, camping space is limited by either too many willows or too steep slopes. The few good sites are along the east shore, between the trail and the lake's outlet creek. Due to heavy usage here, you should, for ecological reasons, consider camping down along Summit City Creek.

Most of the 1.4-mile descent to the canyon floor is across open slopes that are liberally covered with huckleberry oaks, greenleaf manzanitas, snow bushes and bitter cherries—very Sierran. While the brush may be hard on those in hiking shorts, it does permit abundant views up and down the canyon. Within a stone's throw of

**Descending toward Fourth of July Lake**

Summit City Creek you meet a lodgepole-shaded junction. To continue down-canyon along the Tahoe-Yosemite Trail, consult Thomas Winnett's "bible" to that trail. Only 135 miles to Tuolumne Meadows.

Instead of climbing 2.5 miles back up your route, you can climb 3.1 miles up the canyon to the Forestdale Divide. Along Trail 18E07 the ascent is fairly steady, averaging a moderate 9% grade. About 45 yards up this route you'll spy a small camp, on the right, then in 120 yards will come to a junction with Trail 18E21. This heads two miles up the canyon, climbing 1200 feet before topping an "intracanyon" divide, then heads one mile down to Upper Blue Lake, which is about 450 feet below the divide.

Keeping left, you soon leave lodgepoles behind in exchange for red firs and western white pines. About half way up, just a few minutes beyond your climb up a ¼-mile-long switchback, the forest recedes below you and you have your first good views up and down the heavily glaciated canyon. Sierran brush is your almost constant trailside companion over most of the next ¾ mile, interrupted midway by a wildflower garden around a trailside spring. Here, alpine knotweeds grow to head height.

Beyond another switchback sagebrush takes over as the dominant plant life, though as we climb north toward Forestdale Divide wildflowers and open ground become increasingly prominent. After another switchback you cross often snowy slopes and soon intersect the Pacific Crest Trail. Ahead, your trail terminates in 130 yards, where the Blue Lakes Road crosses Forestdale Divide. To return to your trailhead, follow the next hike in reverse.

# 99 Pacific Crest Trail, Carson Pass south to Forestdale Divide

**Distances** 0.5 mile to Frog Lake, 4.6 miles to Forestdale Divide, 9.1 miles to Fourth of July Lake.
**Low/High Elevations** 8240'/9060'
**Classification** Moderate
**Season** Late July through early October
**Maps** 41 and 43
**Trailhead** Same as the Hike 98 trailhead.

**Introduction** Offering trout-poor Frog Lake and several troutless ponds, this route is not a fisherman's favorite. Furthermore, due to con-

straints imposed by the topography, the trail, although well engineered, drops and climbs too much to suit most hikers. Therefore, it is used primarily by long-distance Pacific Crest Trail hikers who, to stay on route, must hike this taxing stretch. But it should also appeal to botanists since, according to the author's determination, it has more wildflower species, mile for mile, than any other trail in the Tahoe Sierra.

**Description** See the previous hike's first paragraph for the route up to Frog Lake, then continue 250 yards to where you diverge left from

**Red Lake Peak looms over the PCT/TYT junction, just south of unseen Frog Lake**

the Tahoe-Yosemite Trail. Southbound on the Pacific Crest Trail you'll hike a full 80 miles before merging again, just inside Yosemite National Park, with the TYT.

Definitely not going that far, we make a meandering ⅓-mile ascent to the Sierra crest, crossing it just north of dome-shaped Elephants Back. You'll note, both on the map and in the field, that the east side of this remnant volcano is considerably steeper than the west side. (This asymmetry is particularly obvious along Hike 93, from the saddle at the head of the Upper Truckee River basin.) The east flank of Elephants Back has been down-faulted, and the resulting escarpment was later accentuated by glacial abrasion.

From the east side of the Sierra crest you can see your goal, the Forestdale Divide, only 1.8 air miles away. Snaking down into and then out of the intervening basin, the Pacific Crest Trail takes 3.6 miles to reach it. On the PCT you start down the eroded fault scarp, descending rather steeply. Before August you may not see any trail at all, for the tread can lie beneath snow. When this field is iced over, the traverse across it is rather touch and go, and you might prefer instead to voluntarily fanny-slide down to a small pond. From it you can walk briefly southeast up to a small fault-line notch, at the base of the escarpment.

Next you walk across a brushy granitic ridge, which is alive with wild buckwheats, sagebrush and other plants that seek dry, gravelly soil. From the ridge's far end, you initiate a moderate descent with multitudinous views. Examining the trailside vegetation along your descent, you'll note one new species after another pop-

ping up to greet you. Once, while hurriedly traversing the 3.6-mile stretch across the basin to beat the setting sun, the author nevertheless noted over 60 wildflower species. Just think how many more you'll find if you've got the time! (Over 500 plant species have been identified in the Carson Pass area.)

Approaching the basin's floor, we first wind among some granitic outcrops, then briefly descend to cross one of Forestdale Creek's snow-fed creeklets. Now the climb begins, first up beside the creeklet, then up a switchbacking ascent to a second one. Your trail levels just before reaching a third creeklet (early-season hikers may pass more). If you were to head just upstream, you'd reach a pond—the first of five in this subalpine basin. Not far beyond the creeklet you'll reach a tiny pond and, off to your right, will see another one, equally small. The second one you circle, then you approach a fourth, somewhat larger, but only knee-deep, and hardly anything to rave about—unless you're a frog. And frogs we can use, for the mosquitoes, as one could predict, are seasonally fierce. Your trail approaches the Blue Lakes Road—here a jeep road—then turns southwest and climbs above the fifth pond, the only one large enough to qualify as a lakelet. You could camp near it if you're prepared to stave off the mosquitoes.

Beyond the ponds you switchback through a thinning subalpine forest, climbing about 200 feet in elevation before you crest the Forestdale Divide. In a couple of minutes you intersect Trail 18E07, which is described at the end of the previous hike. To continue onward along the PCT, consult the author's logically named *Pacific Crest Trail* (Volume 1: California).

**Difficult climbing routes lie up the north face of Jobs Sister**

# Ch. 16     The Carson Range

**Introduction**     For some time during the geologic past the ancestral Tahoe Sierra extended uninterrupted into western Nevada. But roughly 4 million years ago these high lands began to fracture along fault lines, and some land masses began to sink, forming basins. One large basin occupied much of the eastern Tahoe Sierra, but then extensive volcanic eruptions occurred within it, pouring out lava and dividing the basin in two. Today, the southern basin holds Lake Tahoe, and the lake's east shore lies below the central part of the Carson Range.

To most earth scientists the Carson Range may be little more than an appendage of the northern Sierra Nevada. It is, however, respectable in its own right, with dimensions very similar to those of southern California's San Bernardino Mountains. The Carson Range splits from the Sierra Nevada proper at Carson Pass, then arcs gracefully northward past Lake Tahoe, ending indistinctly just south of Interstate 80's borderline town of Verdi, about 57 miles north.

In geology the Carson Range is very similar to its western counterpart, the Sierra Nevada crest. Both are dominated at their north and south ends by volcanic rocks, with mostly granitic rocks in between. But when you compare the granitic Desolation Wilderness landscape with the granitic central Carson Range landscape, you see quite a difference. This is due mainly to the *rain shadow* cast by the high ridges of Desolation Wilderness. Most storms approach the Sierra from the west, and they unleash most of their precipitation—usually snow—as they rise up the western slope, because air cools as it rises, and the colder the air is, the less water vapor it can hold. By the time a storm has worked its way from the Sacramento Valley, near sea level, 9000 feet up to the Sierra crest, its air mass has cooled about 30° Fahrenheit and its water-vapor capacity has been halved. Half of its water vapor has been converted to precipitation. When the storm reaches the Carson Range, it is carrying much less water, and as a result this high country receives only about half the precipitation received by Desolation Wilderness.

How does this precipitation difference affect landscape development? During the Pleistocene epoch, or "Ice Age," snowfields covered the Desolation ridges and were the source of huge glaciers that scoured out canyons east and west of the ridges. With considerably less precipitation than its counterpart, the Carson Range spawned glaciers only at its high-elevation north and south ends. While admirable in size, these glaciers were no match for the giant Sierra crest glaciers.

The central Carson Range was unscathed by glaciers, though during the Pleistocene epoch it probably had some very decent snowfields. Because it was not scoured by glaciers, its soils were not removed. Whereas most of Desolation's soils have formed since the retreat of the last major glaciers, about 10,000-12,000 years ago, evolution of the Carson's soils has not been interrupted for probably more than a million years. Erosion, of course, has stripped away the particular soils that existed then, but the soil cover has continually been replenished by newly weathered fragments of bedrock—the normal situation.

The immediate advantage is that these deep soils hold more water than the new, discontinuous soils of Desolation. Therefore, while most creeks are rapidly drying up in Desolation after the snow melts, the creeks in this area still flow, since abundant water is stored in the deep soil. Furthermore, this soil, being older and better developed, supports more vegetation, and together with the humus that accumulates from dead plants and animals, the vegetation further retards water runoff, thereby permitting the storage of even more water. But there is, of course, a tradeoff: we don't have the great, glaciated scenery. For all practical purposes, when we don't see Lake Tahoe we might imagine ourselves hiking in the southern Sierra Nevada or in southern California's San Bernardino Mountains.

At present this chapter contains only six hikes, of which two were, in 1986, basically cross-country. When premature snow fell in September 1986, the Tahoe Rim Trail had been built from Luther Pass north almost to Armstrong Pass—Hike 100. Also existing is an old trail that climbs southeast to Armstrong Pass—Hike 101—though most folks will find it rather mediocre, although it does offer climbers one of the finest climbing rocks in the Tahoe basin. Beyond the pass, the terrain is more difficult, and the Tahoe Rim Trail may not be built all the way to Highway 207's Daggett Pass until 1988 or '89. Until then, you can hike to Freel Peak, which is the Tahoe Sierra's highest, by Hike 102, or can backpack to it, to other summits, and to Star Lake by Hike 103.

Between Highways 207 and 50 private land may impede the construction of the rim trail there, though as of 1986 the northern half of this trail section, starting from Highway 50's Spooner Summit, had been built. North from the summit 4 miles of the trail had been built, though by late 1987 it should extend all the way to Snow Valley Peak. Although well over 1000 feet lower than the Freel Peak massif and the Mount Rose area, centrally located Snow Valley Peak nevertheless provides equal or better Lake Tahoe views. This chapter offers another route to the peak, one through Lake Tahoe Nevada State Park which is ideal for mountain bicyclists. You can perspire up to the summit, then head down to Marlette Lake for a refreshing swim before commencing a mostly downhill route back to the trailhead. Finally, Hike 105 leads the hiker to the Mt. Rose summit, which is the third highest summit in the Tahoe Sierra, ranking just behind Freel Peak and adjacent Jobs Sister. With luck, both the Mt. Rose and Freel Peak areas will become official wildernesses by about 1990, when—also with luck (and a lot of hard work by volunteers like you and me)—the Tahoe Rim Trail will finally be complete.

# 100    Tahoe Rim Trail to Armstrong Pass

**Distances**   4.1 miles to Freel Meadows, 4.7 miles to Hell Hole view, 7.7 miles to Armstrong Pass.

**Low/High Elevations**   7716'/9420'

**Classification**  Moderate

**Season**   Early July through mid-October

**Maps**   44 and 45

**Trailhead**   Along Highway 89 at the west end of a large, flat meadow which is about 1.8 miles west of Luther Pass and 1.7 miles northeast of the Big Meadow trailhead (Hike 92). In 1986 parking along the highway was limited to several vehicles, but a large trailhead parking area may be built in conjunction with the Tahoe Rim Trail. At present there is spacious parking at a bend just west of the trailhead, along the highway's south side.

**Introduction**   Although the views along this route aren't too frequent or spectacular (except perhaps at the Hell Hole view), the well-graded trail is a pleasant hiking or riding experience. You can camp in the Freel Meadows environs, which is a good place for a base camp from which you can explore the adjacent crest, its flora and fauna, and its views.

The western Freel Meadow

## Description

**Description** After an initial start west you swing north to reach, after only ¼ mile, an alder-lined creeklet. The old Tucker Flat Trail starts up its west bank, climbing, steeply at times, 1.6 miles up to a saddle above Tucker Flat. This is an acceptable route for your return, although the upper half is a knee-knocking descent. It is too steep for an enjoyable ascent.

The better-graded Tahoe Rim Trail takes an extra mile to reach the saddle. From the creeklet it strikes northwest, climbing ¼ mile to a main creek and then, about 200 yards upstream, crossing it. Just before it does, you skirt a small creekside flat, on which you could pitch a fine camp. Ahead, you climb 0.3 mile to a meadowy area. Confronted with steep slopes, you switchback first southwest then north, up to a creeklet that flows beneath giant boulders.

Ahead, you climb briefly but steeply northeast up to a small flat, on which you could camp, then advance a bit north to the east side of a knoll of granitic boulders. Here you have your first good view: southeast through Luther Pass to 10,023′ Hawkins Peak, 7½ miles distant. Its

Freek Peak, Jobs Sister and Jobs Peak, seen from hike's best viewpoint

steep-sided summit, together with that of Pickett Peak below it and 2 miles closer, are volcanic plugs. These plugs were formed in conduits through which former volcanoes had expelled their lava. When the action finally subsided, these conduits became choked with andesitic lava. Over several million years much of each of the two volcanoes was dissected by erosion, exposing the resistant plugs.

Just north of the knoll you pass a red-fir flat on which you could camp, your evening serenaded by mosquitoes from a small, damp meadow just to the northwest. Continuing upward, you climb north past the meadow, on your left, then veer northeast to cross a secondary ridge. Just 200 yards beyond it you reach a viewless saddle on a major ridge. Here, about 1.8 miles from the trailhead, you could set up a dry camp, although snow should be available on nearby north-facing slopes until August.

Staying just southeast of the actual crest, you climb 0.3 mile northeast up gravelly slopes that support clusters of pinemat manzanitas. Their lowly stature belies the extent of their impressive root system, as volunteer trail builders have found out. From a broad, very shallow gap on the crest, the trail climbs up and around peak 9078's southern slopes, offering some views before descending a bit to the previously men-

tioned saddle above Tucker Flat. If you've labored up the Tucker Flat Trail, you'll join us here.

Once again we climb, first winding southeast and then heading east to a ridge near western Freel Meadow. Here we have our first glimpse of Freel Peak, above the meadow, and of Lake Tahoe, beyond Saxon Creek canyon. Rather than head over to the meadow, our trail climbs east above it, ducks into a wildflowered cove cut into a patch of volcanic rock, then descends shortly north to a broad, forested, almost level divide that separates the two meadows.

Next we climb above the eastern meadow's north edge, soon crossing a sloping meadow rich in mule ears, lupines and paintbrushes. The mule ears in particular are very abundant, growing in volcanic soil, their favorite habitat. The patch of volcanic rock here is the second along our route. After crossing the meadow's wisp of a creek, we're back on granitic terrain, traversing southeast. From where the trail bends northeast across bouldery slopes, we have our best view so far. The snowy south end of the Carson Range, capped by Stevens and Red Lake peaks, lies to the south-southwest, while a cluster of 10,000+' peaks lies to the south-southeast. Hawkins Peak, seen earlier, is the closest to us, followed to the right by distant

**Hell Hole canyon, seen from the hike's best viewpoint**

Silver and Highland peaks, each appearing as a double summit, then intermediate-range, pyramidal Raymond Peak.

You'll forget this panorama when you see the one you get from a crest saddle ⅓ mile northeast. Here you have the hike's best view, which includes deep, glaciated Hell Hole canyon in the foreground, Lake Tahoe beyond it, and the Tahoe Sierra's highest summit, 10,881' Freel Peak, above the canyon's east wall. Flanking Freel is the second highest peak, 10,823' Jobs Sister, which is separated by a fairly deep saddle from the fourth highest peak, 10,633' Jobs Peak. You traverse east along the granitic crest about 200 yards before leaving it. From where the trail turns southeast, you can make a steep descent north down an often snowy slope, dropping 400–500 feet to some possible campsites on small flats below the head of Hell Hole canyon.

The Tahoe Rim Trail next traverses southeast across a broad, sloping field of sagebrush, mule ears, angelica and lupine, growing in the route's third patch of volcanic rocks and soil. Now we cross the head of a gully, which is cut into a volcanic mudflow, then resume a granitic traverse. The slopes ahead become increasingly bouldery, so the trail keeps low while swinging north around peak 9587. Just a few minutes north of this summit we regain the crest, and from it see 10,381' Round Top, to the south above the Carson Pass environs, plus the 10,000+' peaks to the south-southeast above unseen Highway 4. From Round Top and the highlands south of it a mammoth glacier once flowed north toward us, this glacier so thick that it spilled west over Luther Pass. The glacier was too thick and rigid to make a sharp right turn down the West Carson canyon, so part of the glacier just plowed northward, uphill, climbing about 400 feet in 1½ miles before finally coming to a halt in the canyon below us (see glacier map on page 32).

Along the nearly level crest we stroll northeast for ¼ mile, our boots squishing into the deep grus as we pass occasional bedrock outcrops. The crest then begins to descend, taking us with it, though soon we curve north, kicking up the deep grus as we descend through an open forest to a crest saddle. Before the advent of massive down-faulting about 4 million years ago, much of the granitic Tahoe Sierra had gentle slopes like the one you descended to the saddle. Be aware that when this descent is snowbound, you could miss the saddle. However, it lies immediately below a fairly substantial bouldery outcrop, one with splotches of dark, mafic (iron-and-magnesium-rich) minerals.

From this viewless saddle the trail went but a short distance in 1986 before ending. It will undoubtedly be completed in 1987, the route winding down a gully, crossing the upper part of a creek, and then recrossing it lower down at a site with some potential nearby camping. It will then climb briefly for about ¼ mile to a trail junction at the west edge of Armstrong Pass. From here you can either retrace your steps or take the next route, old Trail 18E09, down to spring-fed Fountain Place. The terrain stretching 2 miles north from Armstrong Pass offers one of the greatest challenges to Tahoe Rim Trail laborers, but with a lot of effort a trail should go through to Star Lake by late 1988.

# 101    Fountain Place to Armstrong Pass

**Distance**   1.8 miles, one way
**Low/High Elevations**   7830'/8740'
**Classification**   Moderate
**Season**   Mid-July through mid-October
**Map**   45

**Trailhead**   From where Highway 89 joins Highway 50 at the outskirts of Meyers, drive 0.9 mile northeast through Meyers to the signaled Pioneer Trail, which is a paved road. (From where the two highways diverge in South Lake Tahoe, you can drive 4.0 miles south to this road.) On the Pioneer Trail you drive 0.9 mile northeast, then turn east (right) onto Oneidas Street. From its end, in 0.2 mile, you branch northeast onto Road 12N01, which in 0.7 mile first traverses a ridgetop, passes several junctions with dirt roads, then descends northeast to a fork. Go left here and descend about 200 yards to where Road 12N04 branches northwest to the nearby Burrow Pit while our Road 12N01 immediately crosses Saxon Creek. After a 1.8-mile climb we reach a fork and keep left, now on Road 12N01A, which is the main road. In 0.1 mile we cross Trout Creek, then in 0.2 mile cross a cattle guard. Ahead, follow the road to its end, near the edge of a large, sloping meadow.

**Introduction** Once the Tahoe Rim Trail is built, this hike's Trail 18E09 will provide access to it. Most hikers will use the TRT to reach the.Freel Peak/Star Lake environs (Hikes 102 and 103), but a few will seek seclusion by taking the TRT south for some isolated camping. Trail 18E09's primary attraction is a monolithic granitic rock, which the author calls the Fountain Face, which would attract a lot of climbers were it accessible by car.

**Description** In 1859 silver was discovered in Virginia Town's Comstock Lode. In that year Garret Fountain started grazing beef cattle and milk cows along the headwaters of Trout Creek, and he thought that Armstrong Pass might provide a faster route for the miners who were leaving California's Mother Lode in droves and scrambling east, via Luther Pass, to the Comstock Lode. In 1860 he built a way station at what today is known as the Fountain Place, hoping to profit from the passing traffic. Armstrong Pass, however, never became a popular route, for the Comstock Lode mine operators financed the construction of a road over Daggett Pass, 8¼ air miles north of Freel Peak. No buildings remain standing at the Fountain Place today, but the cattle remain.

From the end of Road 12N01A we immediately leave the forest's cover, jump across a creek, and contour south-southeast across a meadow that is being invaded by willows and cows. Cow paths can obscure the real trail as we enter a forest of lodgepoles and aspens; then, in less than 50 yards, we jump across Trout Creek.

For the botanist adept at cross-country navigation, Hell Hole is a highly desirable destination. All others will find it too swampy and mosquito-prone to warrant a visit. From the creek climb cross-country west-southwest 0.6 mile to the low point on a minor ridge, then descend ¼ mile to Hell Hole's creek. From there onward, you're on your own.

If you're bound for Armstrong Pass, you keep to Trail 18E09. From Trout Creek the first 200 yards of route, up to a trickling tributary, can be obscure. After it, however, the trail is usually quite obvious, and we parallel the usually unseen creek as we climb moderately toward the pass.

Midway up our ascent through a forest of red firs and western white pines, we can see, across the canyon, the Fountain Face, a 300-foot-high granitic cliff that is riven with vertical cracks which provide climbers with over one dozen routes ranging from easy to extremely difficult Class 5. The climbing routes are quite clean, for the cliff was scoured by glaciers.

Whitebark pines line our path as we continue upward, and soon its gradient eases as we approach and traverse the southwest edge of a meadow. It then climbs steeply to the west edge of broad, forested Armstrong Pass, where we meet the Tahoe Rim Trail. You can follow it about ¼ mile south to a creek and, hopefully, some campsites, if indeed ones are developed. But for isolated, dry camping, follow the trail about ¾ mile farther, up gravelly slopes to a broad saddle. Camp on the nearly level, open-forested lands just west of the saddle, or perhaps drop ⅔ mile west, cross-country, to a relatively dry flat above and east of the Hell Hole marsh.

**The Fountain Face**

# 102          Fountain Place to Freel Peak

**Distance**  2.6 miles, one way
**Low/High Elevations**  7840'/10,881'
**Classification**  Very strenuous
**Season**  Mid-July through early October
**Map**  45
**Trailhead**  Same as the Hike 101 trailhead.

**Introduction**  In 1983 once you started up the trail proper, your grade averaged 26%, which qualifies this hike as the book's steepest—as well as its highest. It therefore deserves a *very strenuous* rating, and since you climb it in thin air, you had better be in excellent shape. However, once the Tahoe Rim Trail is constructed, the gradient will be considerably less, at least to a 9730-foot-high saddle, and then the effort will lie in the realm of mere mortals. Although Freel Peak is the Tahoe Sierra's highest summit, its views are somewhat disappointing, particularly since during the summer the Lake Tahoe Basin usually tends to be smoggy, and therefore quite hazy.

**Description**  In 1986 the route to Freel Peak was very direct and very steep. If you were in top shape, you could make the 1.7-mile climb to a saddle in about an hour's time, rest a few minutes, then in 45 minutes or less, climb cross-country to the summit. This assumes you are day hiking with a light pack. If and when a trail is built to the saddle, its length may be about 6 or 7 miles, but even with a backpack you'll be able to enjoy that part of the ascent. Anyone planning to climb all the way to Freel Peak's summit should bring along a cap, hat or dark glasses to reduce the intense amount of ultraviolet radiation your eyes will receive above treeline.

From near the edge of the Fountain Place meadow, you branch north on a road, which parallels a creek upstream. In 330 yards you'll pass a road that traverses northwest, and then in about 270 more yards your road ends. Shift into first gear. Botanists usually aren't avid mountain climbers, which is too bad, because there is a wonderful assortment of wildflowers along this very steep ascent. Nonbotanists can pretend they are botanists, stopping often with the pretext of wildflower observation.

As we climb, the lodgepoles give way to sagebrush and occasional aspens and junipers (strange bedfellows), then these give way to an open forest of Jeffrey pines, red firs and western

white pines. Around the 8700-foot level, we reach the base of a cliff, which has some good climbing routes—if anyone's cared to bring along a rope. The granodiorite is coarse and gravelly—really hard on the hands. If you enjoy climbing at Joshua Tree National Monument, in southern California, you'll feel right at home on this cliff.

Our climb, which has been quite steep, now becomes *very* steep. Furthermore, the ascent is up slopes of deep, loose gravel, which is known as grus. For every two steps you take up it, you seem to slide back one. Grus, at least, is nice and soft to sit in, should you try to key out a wildflower or should you want to sit down, get comfortable, and read the next three paragraphs.

Where did all the grus come from? Easy—from the surrounding cliffs and bedrock. Exactly how it decomposed takes a bit more thinking, and the author concluded that there are at least three unseen processes at work. This rock, known as the Freel Peak granodiorite, is the exposed part of a pluton—a body of granitic rock—that solidified beneath other rocks roughly 90 million years ago. It solidified perhaps 3-5 miles below the surface, and therefore did so under tremendous pressure, roughly 1400 to 2300 *tons* per *square foot*. By about 60 million years ago the overlying rocks had been eroded away, exposing the granodiorite at the earth's surface. At the surface the rock's crystals, which had solidified under extreme pressure, are definitely out of equilibrium, since the pressure is only about one ton per square foot. The rock's crystals, being way out of equilibrium, have a tendency to expand and therefore to flake off from bedrock.

A second process makes the first one a bit easier. About 6% of the granodiorite is composed of dark, mafic crystals, rich in iron and magnesium. In some places, such as along Hike 100, you see concentrations of dark crystals, known as inclusions, but on the whole such crystals are randomly distributed. Being rich in iron and magnesium, these crystals are more subject to weathering by percolating water. The resultant "rusting" of these crystals weakens the bedrock, making it easier for crystals to flake off.

The third process is ice wedging. When the temperature drops sufficiently, which it often does up at these elevations, water that has seeped behind crystals and into tiny cracks freezes, and in doing so expands by about 10%

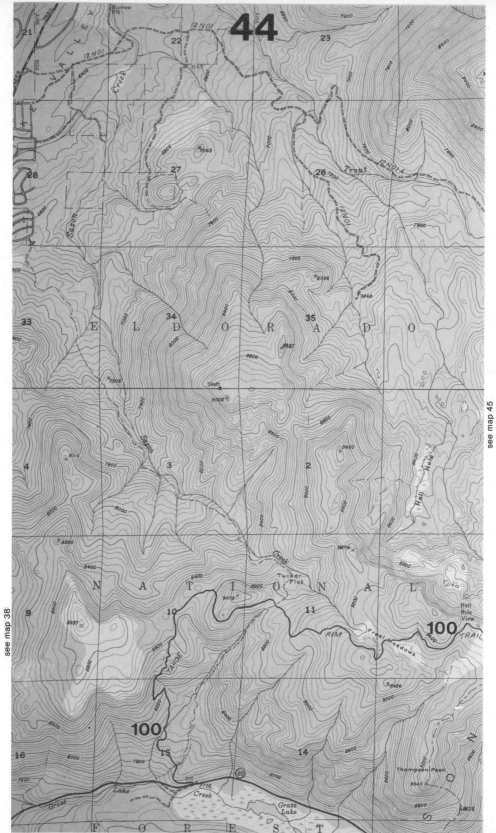

see map 45

see map 38

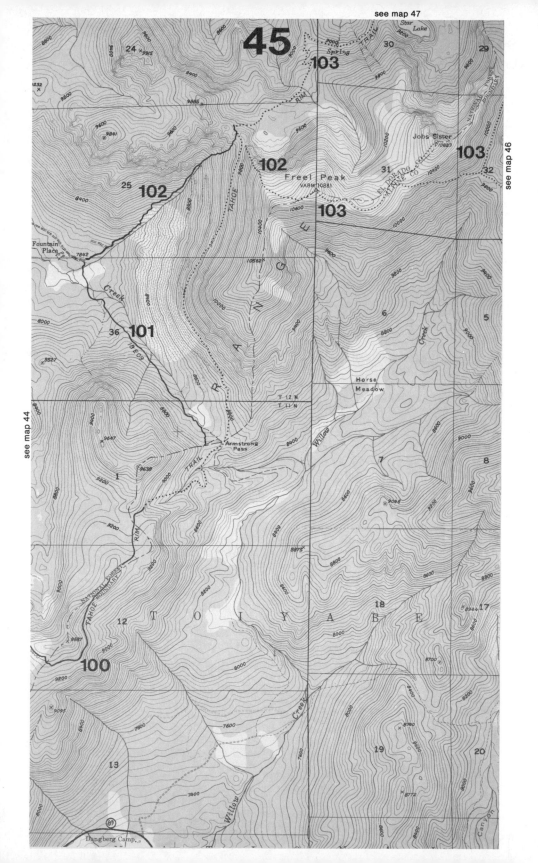
see map 47
see map 46
see map 44

in volume. This expansion gradually splits off loose crystals. Under ideal conditions, when water turns to ice, it can exert a force of 1000 pounds per square inch as it tries to expand. This force is equal to that which you would experience if you could scuba-dive to a depth of 2300 feet, or if you were buried under 800 feet of rock—a very impressive force. The more opportunity water has to repeatedly freeze and thaw, the more it will weather a rock by ice wedging.

Once these three processes have loosened the rock's crystals, gravity, driving rain and howling wind do the rest, keeping the bedrock rather clean and solid. Speaking of rest, it's time to end ours, so get back into first gear and start flailing up the all-too-obvious route. Whitebark pines now appear and quickly take over as the predominant trees.

Around 9000 feet elevation we pass our creek's headwater spring, the last chance for water other than from snowfields one may encounter. This spot is about where two major gullies diverge—one to the north and one to the northeast. Rock climbers take the left gully, climbing about 200 feet in elevation before that gully bifurcates. Up there you'll be surrounded by some impressive *and* intimidating cliffs, which are worth climbing—take your pick (and in winter, your pick-axe).

Nonclimbers take the right gully, slogging up an even deeper mantle of grus than down below. By the 9400-foot elevation the forest has thinned sufficiently for us to sit down again, this time to admire a view to the south-southwest of the broad, gaping Hell Hole canyon, which has been repeatedly abraded by glacial attacks. As we climb higher, the whitebark pines are smaller, which is a sure sign of a more hostile environment. The appearance of alpine wildflowers is another sign. To the northeast, which is the direction we've been climbing, you'll see a saddle. This is not your immediate goal. Instead, you curve north and climb a remaining 200 feet in elevation to a second one, which is so small it barely counts.

If you're still resolved to climb Freel Peak, head southeast over to the slightly higher first saddle and take a well-deserved rest. If you're bound for Star Lake or beyond (Hike 103), or if you've decided Freel Peak is too high and you'd like a much easier summit, then cross the saddle and descend west, rather steeply, to just below and north of a third saddle. The Tahoe Rim Trail, when built, will head north-northwest for a minute's descent, then switch-

back eastward. For summit views leave the trail here, traverse west and slightly up toward a nearby fourth saddle, then climb, in under ¼ mile, moderately to steeply northwest to point 9885. If you simply must see *all* of Lake Tahoe, then scurry over to point 9915, to the northwest, which blocks some of the lake from point 9885.

Regardless of which summit you choose, you have similar views. Both points stand above a steep headwall, past which glaciers from Freel Peak advanced northward down-canyon to flat-floored High Meadows. Glaciers from Jobs Sister advanced northwest, joining them in that locale. Just how many times glaciers flowed down-canyon, one can't say, but likely it was over a dozen. At least one of the earlier glaciers turned west and flowed down Cold Creek canyon to about 6800 feet elevation. During this time, possibly 135,000 to 145,000 years ago, giant glaciers just below Lake Tahoe's outlet may have dammed the Truckee River, raising the lake's level some 600 feet. If we could have viewed the lake back then, we'd see our Cold Creek canyon glacier spalling icebergs into the lake. But it wasn't the only one to do so, for at least 11 other glaciers, all larger than this one, were spalling icebergs into the lake along its west and south shores. Oh, to have a time machine and view such a dazzling sight!

Another instructive view lies to the west-southwest. From either point you see a gentle basin in the foreground, one that sort of hangs there, dropping off on all sides. This is a relict landform, one that might have once been typical over much of the Tahoe Sierra. Far beyond it you see another relict, though somewhat glaciated, landform, the fairly deep canyon of the South Fork American River, which is truncated at Echo Summit. A stream conceived in the gentle basin just below you may have been one of many tributaries that coalesced to form a river that flowed west through what is now today's Echo Summit. But about 4 million years ago, the land between today's two relict landforms began to sink, eventually leading to the creation of the Lake Tahoe Basin.

Anyone still awaiting instructions to the Freel Peak summit will be happy to know I haven't forgotten them. The route, actually, is quite obvious. You first climb southeast more or less up the crest, switchbacking as often as necessary to ease its atrocious grade. Then, at around 10,400 to 10,500 feet, you leave it in order to avoid a rocky crest above you, and you climb east on a slightly easier gradient across some-

The gentle slopes in the foreground may have given rise to a stream that joined others to form a river. This river flowed west through the distant South Fork American River canyon, which you see immediately left of the foreground's high point.

times snowy slopes to the obvious summit. Of course, if the weather is looking threatening, don't even attempt this ascent, for there is no place to hide, should a lightning storm break loose.

Along this rigorous ascent, which is breathtaking due both to a surplus of views and to a shortage of oxygen, you'll note that the whitebark pines have been getting progressively shorter and bushier in stature, dwindling eventually to knee-high specimens. This dwarfed form of trees is called *krummholz,* which is German for "twisted wood."

**A summit view toward South Lake Tahoe**

With all the Tahoe Sierra lands below us, we can make a 360° survey—to the tune of an incessant hum from our summit's microwave relay tower. Like many high peaks outside wilderness areas, this one now serves 20th century man. The views, however, are not blocked. In the south is a ribbon of Highway 88; in the west-southwest beyond Echo Summit is the incised South Fork American River canyon. Unmistakable Pyramid Peak looms above the Echo Lakes to our west. In the northwest the slopes of dark, metamorphic-capped Mt. Tallac descend to Tahoe's shoreline. Above the lake's northeast corner stands volcanic-capped Mt. Rose, whose summit, at 10,766 feet, is third highest in the Tahoe basin, ranking below only Freel Peak and Jobs Sister. Viewing the latter we can identify two parallel, massive quartz veins that paint its west slope white with rocky "snow." Lake Tahoe, of course, is the main feature that captures the eye. This deep, blue gem seems to be too large to be in so high a basin; we almost expect it to overflow into the lower, dry desert to the east.

Atop the summit grow small clumps of whitebark pines, here only knee-high, and above them mountain bluebirds and gray-crowned rosy finches are sometimes seen. The bluebirds dart swiftly after insects wafted up here by updrafts, while the finches pursue ground insects and spiders as well as seeds of alpine plants.

When you are ready to leave, you can retrace your steps, or you can descend to Star Lake, following in reverse the cross-country route described in Hike 103. Under no circumstances should you start a descent north between Freel Peak and Jobs Sister, since the slopes between these two peaks support a fragile community of alpine cushion plants.

# 103 Fountain Place to Star Lake, Jobs Peak, Jobs Sister and Freel Peak

**Distances** 3.9 miles to Star Lake, 7.4 miles to Jobs Sister, 7.5 miles to Jobs Peak, 7.9 miles to Freel Peak.

**Low/High Elevations** 7840'/9730' at Star Lake; 10,881' at Freel Peak.

**Classification** Strenuous

**Season** Mid-July through early October

**Maps** 45, 47 and 46

**Trailhead** Same as the Hike 101 trailhead.

**Introduction** In 1983 the route to Star Lake was 1.7 miles up an extremely steep, unofficial trail followed by 2.2 miles of moderate cross-country. Until the Tahoe Rim Trail is built past it, perhaps in the mid- or late 1980s, the lake will remain quite isolated, which is good for those who want a wilderness experience *sans* people. Once the trail is built, however, the lake will become an extremely popular camping area for rim hikers and a popular staging area for climbers, mountaineers and cross-country hikers who want to explore the Freel Peak-Jobs Sister-Jobs Peak environs.

**Description** The bulk of the Hike 102 route description tells you what to see and expect on a very steep 1.7-mile climb to a saddle. While Freel Peak is best done as a day hike, Star Lake is best as a backpack hike, since it is a logical place for camping. With a backpack you'll probably take three hours to reach the 9730-foot-high saddle, which will be the highest point on your hike unless you decide to climb some adjacent peaks.

As in Hike 102 you pass through this small saddle and descend a bit west, rather steeply, to just below and north of another saddle. The Tahoe Rim Trail, when built, will head north-northwest for a minute's descent to a switchback, from which Hike 102 traverses westward to some viewpoints. If you're not climbing Freel Peak or Jobs Sister, you might head west for some Lake Tahoe views. They'll be the best ones you'll get from near or on the Tahoe Rim Trail until well north of Daggett Pass.

From the switchback, which can lie under snow well into July, you see the steep north slopes of Freel Peak and the gentle west slopes of Jobs Sister. The gentle west slopes appear to make an ideal cross-country route up to either summit. While it may be ideal for hikers to follow, it is not ideal for plants. At least 30

species of alpine wildflowers plus several species each of alpine grasses, sedges and shrubs grow on these slopes in loose, easily eroded gravel. For one species in particular, the alpine senecio, this is the *only* place it grows in *all* of the Sierra Nevada north of Yosemite National Park. Therefore, don't risk uprooting it or other species by slogging up these slopes. For an environmentally sound route to Freel Peak or Jobs Sister, take the cross-country hike, beginning from Star Lake, which is described in the second half of this hike.

From your locale you'll notice a whitish swath on Jobs Sister's gentle slopes. This swath is composed of vein quartz, which has been eroded from two parallel dikes that have intruded the granitic bedrock. With binoculars you should be able to see these two white dikes.

Leaving the switchback, you descend east through an open forest of whitebark pines and mountain hemlocks, the descent often snowy through July, if not longer. In a few minutes you come to the northwest corner of a depression, which would be a lake basin were the area's gravelly deposits not so porous. The route heads briefly north from the corner, then turns northeast and diagonals down across north-facing slopes, crossing the head of a conspicuous gully about 200 yards before reaching a lively creeklet. By its north bank, which is 0.7 mile beyond the high saddle and 1.5 miles before Star Lake, there is plenty of flat space among the whitebark pines to set up a camp.

In 1983 the flagged route first made a north-northeast traverse, followed by a 200-foot-drop in elevation north, then it began a traverse east through a mountain-hemlock forest. The author found this whole stretch too steep and snowy and hopes the Forest Service will change the route. He suggests that from the creeklet the trail should switchback several times, descending north to a shallow saddle at the south end of a conspicuous, north-trending ridge. Along this descent you'll certainly see some vein quartz, eroded from one or more dikes.

The author's proposed route contours east from the shallow saddle, passing immediately above a gushing spring, which is about ¼ mile beyond the saddle. Still contouring, you continue 250 yards farther, and if you're on course, you'll cross a ravine about 20 yards below the point where it breaks into two smaller ones.

**The steep north slopes of Freel Peak (right) and the gentle west slopes of Jobs Sister**

Crossing it can be tricky, particularly if you're carrying a heavy pack, for its steep slopes can be quite loose. With about ⅓ mile left to Star Lake, we make a gently climbing traverse northeast, staying well above a soggy meadow and viewing High Meadows and Lake Tahoe before we arrive at a boulder-and-bedrock ridge. Heading up, down and around this lumpy ridge is not too much of a problem for the cross-country traveler, but building a trail across it is another matter.

Star Lake lies immediately beyond this ridge and is partly dammed by it. It is also partly dammed by a small, man-made dam, which has raised the lake's level by several feet. You can usually cross the lake's vigorous outlet creek just below the dam, using snagged driftwood. In 100 yards you reach a flat area, where people have obviously camped, then 100 yards east you discover a second camping area. For larger sites, climb about ¼ mile northeast to a broad, gentle, but of course waterless divide.

Perched around 9100 feet elevation, Star Lake barely warms up to 60°, and therefore swimming is brisk at best. Lakes lying in high, granitic basins are supposed to be crystal clear, but Star Lake is mysteriously murky. You can see about 5 feet down through the water, which is sufficient to spy a trout or two. Despite the color of the water, it is probably safe to drink, though nowadays, with *Giardia* rampant through the Sierra Nevada, one should always treat the water.

Using the Star Lake environs for a base camp, you can make a number of excursions. The easiest one, shown on Map 47, is a 4½-mile

walk north along the proposed Tahoe Rim Trail. The hardest one is a strenuous, roped climb up the north face of Jobs Sister. At least several routes exist, ranging from challenging to terrifying. Ice wedging has made the rock rough and easy to grasp, which is great for footholds and handholds, but it has also broken rock faces into large, quasi-stable slabs, which could prove dangerous.

Lying between these two extremes are environmentally sound cross-country routes up to Jobs Peak, Jobs Sister and Freel Peak, which are, respectively, 3.6, 3.5 and 3.8 miles from Star Lake. If you assiduously follow the described route, visiting all three peaks, your total

## Jobs Sister and Star Lake

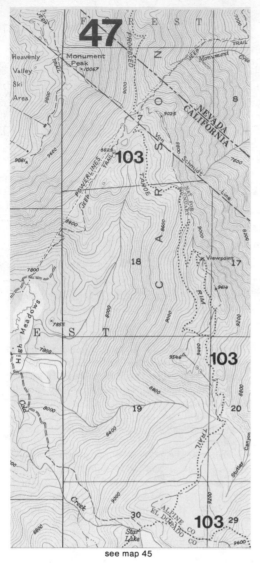

see map 45

The next part of your route is perfectly clear: a 0.8-mile *contour* to the west edge of a broad saddle. To reach the Jobs Peak summit, 1.4 miles away, cross the saddle and climb a ridge-crest almost to peak 10505. (If you go too low, you'll have to diagonal up some slopes of very loose grus.) You then curve northeast and stay close to the crest all the way to the windswept summit. Although the topo map shows your whole route is through a forest, this "forest" is so low that you stand above it, for the whitebark pines are merely low, wind-cropped shrubs.

Carson Valley, with a mosaic of farms and ranches, lies about 6000 feet below, totally exposed for our perusal. Looking across the somewhat glaciated Jobs Canyon, we see the east edge of sprawling Carson City, 22 miles away. Of more interest, at least to the geologically inclined, is the contact between the west edge of the flat-floored Carson Valley and the east base of the steep-sloped Carson Range. The geologically sagacious observer will correctly surmise that a major, north-south fault runs along this angular transformation. But there is more happening here than meets the eye.

The Carson Valley began to form perhaps about 4 million years ago, slowly dropping more or less along today's fault line. During this period, streams cut some fairly deep canyons into the east slopes of the Carson Range and the sediments were deposited, usually in fanlike patterns, at the west edge of the valley. But look at Jobs Canyon, below you to the northwest, and Fay Canyon, below you to the southeast. Both of these moderately glaciated canyons have had more material eroded from them than now exists

round-trip distance will be 11.4 miles. From the lake's campsites walk ¼ mile northeast to the broad, ill defined Carson Range crest, then walk east-southeast along it. Fortunately, the crest becomes fairly well defined by the time you reach the base of some steep slopes. From here you diagonal northeast about 200 yards across these slopes to a gully, which you climb to its head. (This gully is by the lower-right corner of Map 47.) From it you climb 0.4 mile along a 165° bearing, steeply at first, but easing to a moderate ascent before you reach "ridge 9940" (Map 46), a finger of granodiorite perched high above Jobs Canyon, which is cutting down along a fault. Jobs Peak, with its landslide-prone north slopes, stands 1.2 miles southeast across the canyon.

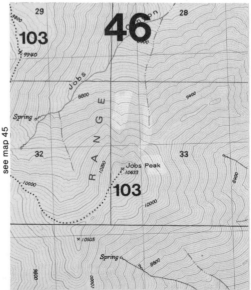

**The climb away from Jobs Peak (background) up toward unseen Jobs Sister**

in their alluvial fans. So where are the rest of the sediments? And, if you look north along the west edge of Carson Valley, you'll see that several miles of it have no alluvial fans at all. Although the canyons that empty into this stretch had little or no glaciation, there should nevertheless be *some* sediments.

A clue to this mystery lies in the course of the Carson River. Note that this braided river flows north along the west side of the valley, not its center. This indicates that the west side of the valley is *still* subsiding, and the river has migrated laterally west. And that observation leads to a solution to the case of the missing sediments. As the west side of the valley sinks, it is filled with incoming sediments from the Carson Range canyons, and these are smoothly distributed by the river, thereby keeping the valley floor level.

From Jobs Peak you have Lake Tahoe views, but such views are much better from Jobs Sister, so return to the west edge of the saddle above Jobs Canyon. If the weather still looks good (no storm clouds a-brewing), then head for your next immediate goal, a treeline saddle, which is 0.8 mile to the west and 630 feet above you. This amounts to a 15% grade, which is quite reasonable when the ground is solid. As you know by now, it isn't. The slope up to it has been extensively weathered by ice wedging, and consequently the route goes through a deep mantle of grus. The climb, however, isn't all that bad, because grasses, shrubs and whitebark pines help hold the loose material in place.

Upon attaining this second saddle, we can see that it is a more inhospitable environment for plants. No grasses, shrubs or trees grow on this broad, barren saddle; whitebark pines on both sides of it, however, form a dense, waist-high thicket. From this saddle we have a choice of routes. Jobs Sister, a 15-minute climb to the northeast, offers better views than any other peak in this area. Its views to the east equal those of Jobs Peak; its views to the north, west and south equal those of Freel Peak; and its deeply glaciated north face is far higher and steeper than that of any nearby peak.

Jobs Sister is also a good summit from which you can get a feeling for the prefaulted, preglaciated Tahoe Sierra landscape. This landscape existed before the Lake Tahoe Basin formed, when streams originating near what is today's crest of the Carson Range flowed west toward the Pacific Ocean. The landscape was gentler back then, having slopes like the long one descending west from your summit. Compare it to your peak's nearly vertical north face, which is the consequence of extensive backcutting by repeated episodes of glaciation.

Most hikers will want to climb Freel Peak, simply because it is the highest peak in the Tahoe Sierra. Leaving the second saddle and its nearby quartz dikes, you can reach a third by skirting around the north or south slopes of an intermediate summit. The south-slope route is less likely to have snow and your passage there is less likely to disturb alpine wildflowers. The author had designed an essentially erosion-free trail route from the 9730-foot saddle, early in your hike, up to Freel Peak and Jobs Sister, then down to Star Lake. But rather than submit it to the Forest Service, he dropped the idea, for it would have adversely affected the wildflowers. To induce hikers to stay on such a trail, it has to be well engineered and well built, so that hikers won't be tempted to cut across alpine fell fields. However, such a trail, even if it is signed "foot traffic only," will nevertheless attract one or more equestrians, and horses, being horses, will munch away at the alpine vegetation.

This must never be allowed to happen. These prostrate "cushion plants" are currently in "exile," relegated, in the Tahoe Sierra, to a few mountaintops. They are patiently waiting for the return of another glacial cycle, like the ones so common in the last two million years. During such a cycle, the temperatures will be cooler, and these plants will expand their range many times over, regaining their former territory. Until then, they are exceedingly vulnerable in their highly erodible, restricted environment, so we must take extra precautions to ensure their survival.

From the third saddle you climb more or less directly up to the Freel Peak summit, as quite a number of other hikers have done. The main landmarks you see from it are mentioned in the

**Prostrate whitebark pines grow on the stark Freel Peak summit**

last part of Hike 103. When you leave, return the way you came, avoiding all temptation (and it is very tempting) to race north down Freel Peak's glaciated canyon or Jobs Sister's west-slope fell fields.

**The Carson Valley, from a viewpoint ¼ mile north of Map 47's peak 9614**

# 104   Lake Tahoe Nevada State Park

**Distances**   4.6 miles to Marlette Lake, 5.3 miles to Snow Valley Peak, 5.9 miles to Marlette Lake's dam, 15.0 miles for complete round trip to both peak and dam.

**Low/High Elevations**   6950'/8157' to Marlette Lake; 9214' to Snow Valley Peak.

**Season**   Late June through late October

**Classification**   Moderate

**Map**   48

**Trailhead**   First, you have to get to the Spooner Lake area, which lies just north of Spooner Junction, where Highways 28 and 50 meet. If you're driving north on 50 from South Lake Tahoe, this junction is 12 miles beyond the California-Nevada border. If you're driving west up Highway 50, this junction is about ¾ mile west of Spooner Summit, which in turn is about 9 miles west of Highway 395. If you're driving south on 28 from the north shore of Lake Tahoe, this junction is 13¼ miles beyond the Highway 431 junction at the western outskirts of Incline Village. You, however, drive only 12¼ miles south to the Spooner Lake Picnic Area entrance, which is just south of the Carson City-Douglas County boundary (technically, the Carson City limits extend all the way west to the middle of Lake Tahoe!). This entrance road is 0.6 mile northwest on Highway 28 from Spooner Junction. You immediately pass an entrance station, then in 0.1 mile, a road right to nearby parking. Use this lot if you're only visiting Spooner Lake, as most visitors do. Otherwise, go a bit farther to a second road right and park along it. This parking loop quickly rejoins the main road, which is blocked to motor traffic beyond this point. The above trail mileages start at a road junction immediately below and west of Spooner Lake's dam. The quickest way to this junction is to start from the parking loop and head about 200 yards northeast downslope. You can also follow the blocked road northwest down to a meadow's edge, then west to the junction—a 0.5-mile trek.

**Introduction**   Lake Tahoe Nevada State Park, extending east from the lake's east shore, had about 25 miles of trail before work was begun on the Tahoe Rim Trail. Once that trail is complete along this part of the Carson Range, perhaps in 1988 or '89, then the author will cover all the trails in the park. In 1986 there were only two really appealing routes in the park, from Spooner Lake to Snow Valley Peak and to Marlette Lake. Both routes are along closed roads, and the one to Marlette Lake is very popular with mountain-bike enthusiasts. When the author mapped the route in 1986, he met only bicyclists—no hikers or equestrians. The road to Snow Valley Peak has a gradient that averages 13.4%, which isn't too bad for hikers, but is a challenge for out-of-shape cyclists. If you plan a trip to the summit, reach it before noon, for afterward you're looking into the sun, and prominent canyons above the lake's west shore become increasingly obscure with lengthening afternoon shadows. Then have a scenic descent to the lake, take a leisurely swim, and finally, after an initial climb, enjoy an easy route back down to your trailhead.

**The state park's greatest attraction is its fine beach at Sand Harbor**

**Description**   From the junction of closed roads immediately below and west of Spooner Lake's dam, we immediately cross the lake's outlet creek, and on Road 15N04 parallel a meadows's edge north. Sagebrush gives way to white firs, lodgepole pines and Jeffrey pines, and soon we see our first aspens, which are very common along this hike though generally sparse throughout most of the Tahoe Sierra. Just 0.6 mile from our starting point, we pass a shelter, on the left, situated near the north end of the meadow. Just a few minutes beyond it we cross North Canyon's aspen lined creek, from which a lightly used road descends toward the meadow.

Our closed road recrosses the minor creek 0.4 mile upstream, then parallels it on a usually gentle grade 0.6 mile farther, to where you'll note a gap in North Canyon's west wall. This gap is seen immediately before the road curves right and you get your first view of treeless Snow Valley Peak. On your ascent, you may have

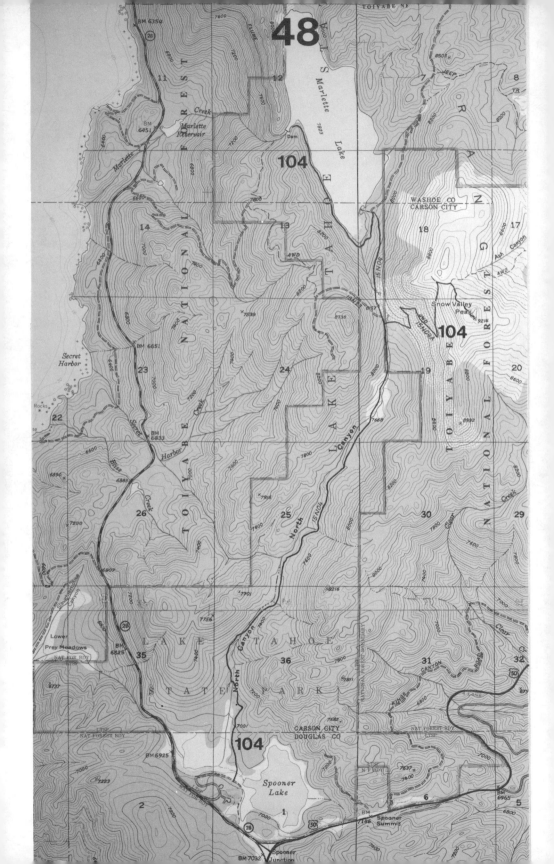

**Wildflower Plate 16. Carson Range flowers.**
1 Silver-leaved phacelia (cream), 2 Recter's rock cress (white to pale-pink), 3 flat-seeded rock cress (white to pink), 4 Copeland's owl clover (pink to red), 5 Nuttall's linanthus (white with yellow center), 6 granite gilia (white to violet), 7 frosty-leaved buckwheat (yellowish), 8 western peony (rusty brown with yellow-and-green center), 9 Brewer's lupine (blue).

**Lake Tahoe and Marlette Lake, from spur road's viewpoint**

noticed that North Canyon's creek seemed rather small, given the size of the canyon. The answer lies here, at the gap. A tributary of Secret Harbor Creek, eroding headward, cut through the canyon's west wall, so that today most of upper North Canyon's drainage flows through the gap, with only a little water flowing south. This is a case of *stream piracy,* or stream capture. Though uncommon in the Sierra Nevada, stream captures are definitely more prevalent than earth scientists realized. But what is exceedingly rare is an stream capture in progress, such as here. The author hasn't seen any captures in progress anywhere else in the entire Sierra Nevada. The ones he's seen have just happened or are about to happen.

Just after we get our first Snow Valley Peak view, the road's first red firs appear, and not much farther, the last white firs disappear. About 0.9 mile past that first view, we come to one of the park's two backcountry campgrounds, which is just above the road. In 1987 or '88, a trail may be built from it east up to the Tahoe Rim Trail. The other backcountry campground is in the upper part of Little Valley, about 5 air miles north. Each has five campsites, with a limit of four persons per site. Campsites must be reserved in advance. For further information and reservations contact park rangers or call park headquarters at (702) 831-0494.

After 0.3 mile we again cross North Canyon's creek, doing so in the south end of a scenic, fairly large meadow. At its north end our road, which has been easy until now, takes on a moderate grade, and this steepens before we reach a junction with Road 15N04A, ⅓ mile beyond the meadow.

If you're game for exceptional views, leave Road 15N04 here, immediately crossing a spring-fed creeklet, which is the only water ahead. Bound for Snow Valley Peak, you switchback up brushy slopes with ever-improving views. Just before you reach a crest saddle, you come to a spur road at the final switchback. Even if you're exhausted, make the effort to

follow it 100 yards up to a viewpoint which, in the author's opinion, equals or exceeds the view from Snow Valley Peak: Marlette Lake spreads naked below you, backdropped by the somber volcanic crests and peaks of the Mt. Rose area, while the northern part of Lake Tahoe evokes wonder at its swirling surface currents.

Once upon the crest saddle, which is just beyond the spur road and 1¼ miles from Road 15N04, you briefly join the Tahoe Rim Trail, which here is an old road climbing rather steeply ⅓ mile southeast to the top of Snow Valley Peak. The summit area, unfortunately, is gently sloped, and its apex is occupied by a microwave relay tower. Thus, to get views in all directions, you'll have to wander about. With good visibility, you can gaze north across nearby terraced slopes to Reno.

If you've brought a Tahoe-area map along, you should be able to identify some of the major features. Clockwise from Reno, you scan the eastern valleys, noting Washoe Lake, Carson City and Carson Valley. From the valley a major canyon—the route of Highway 50— swoops up to the crest of the Carson Range. At its southern end rise the range's highest mass, the Freel Peak massif, with the area's first, second and fourth highest peaks. Scanning westward, you'll note the high, often snowy peaks of Desolation Wilderness, with Tahoe's Emerald Bay lying at their base. Meeks Bay, to the west-southwest, is harder to spot, though it lies at the mouth of the first major canyon north of Emerald Bay. Northward, you'll scan past four major canyons—General Creek, McKinney Creek (lowest gap in the crest), Blackwood Creek (just south of a high point, Twin Peaks) and Ward Creek—before spotting Tahoe's outlet, the Truckee River canyon. Behind the canyon rise the highest lands of Granite Chief Wilderness. From the lake's outlet the Tahoe rim rises, then drops to Brockway Summit, then rises to a culmination at the area's third highest peak, Mt. Rose. About the only prominent feature you don't see is relatively close-by Marlette Lake.

On foot, you can be back to Road 15N04 in a half hour's time. On it you immediately pass abandoned Road 18E23, branching left, then in 220 yards breach a fault-formed 8157' pass. Marlette Lake quickly comes into view, and you pass a number of roadside springs along your ¾-mile long, gentle-to-moderate descent to a junction just above the east shore of Marlette Lake. North, a road first provides lakeside access before it climbs, in 1.2 miles, to another junction. From it a road climbs east, and another one north, each crossing close-by Carson Range crest saddles which in 1987 or '88 should have the tread of the Tahoe Rim Trail.

From the first junction you can head west on a spur road out to a point on Marlette Lake's east shore. However, it is basically shadeless and not terribly scenic, so why not head 1.4 miles over to the lake's dam (an easy traverse on foot or bike). You descend slightly to the lake's south shore where, just south of the lake and your road, you'll see a fish-spawning station. The lake serves as a cutthroat-trout fishery, and fishing is strictly forbidden (yes, rangers drive the roads). Camping too is forbidden.

The road along the lake's southwest shore is nearly level and is fairly shaded with red firs, western white pines and lodgepole pines. However, one possible annoyance to early-season bicyclists is one or more encounters with downed trees. The road ends just before the lake's dam and just beyond a cut through a bouldery bedrock ridge. The toe of the ridge is a fine spot for diving into the lake, which in midsummer warms to the mid and upper 60s.

Marlette Lake is really shallower than one would guess from the way granitic slopes plunge to its west shore. Most of the lake is quite shallow, and its deepest spot, by the dam, is only 52 feet. A dam, just 26 feet high, was constructed back in 1873, ponding up Goodwin Lake. This was quickly raised 11 feet just 3 years later, then in 1959 was raised to its present height. At roughly 350 acres Marlette Lake provides quite a lot of domestic water to Carson City.

# 105     Mt. Rose Trail

**Distance**   5.9 miles, one way
**Low/High Elevations**   8840'/10,776'
**Classification**   Moderate
**Season**   Mid-July through early October
**Map**   49

**Trailhead**   From the Highways 28/431 junction at the west end of Lake Tahoe's Incline Village, drive 8 miles up Mt. Rose Highway 431 to a closed road, on your left. Parking is very limited, so you may have to park by the Mt. Rose Campground, whose entrance is just ¼ mile up the highway. Immediately beyond this entrance the highway crosses the Carson Range at 8924-foot Mt. Rose Summit, then descends 17 miles to Highway 395. This junction on 395 is about 10 miles south of Reno and about 20 miles north of Carson City.

**Introduction**   Mt. Rose is the Tahoe Sierra's third highest peak, its summit being about 100 feet lower than Freel Peak, and about 50 feet lower than the runner up, Jobs Sister (see Hikes 102 and 103). And Mt. Rose is the only 10,000+' peak with a trail all the way to the top. This Mt. Rose Trail is short enough and starts high enough that the summit can be easily climbed and descended in a day. However, don't expect top-notch Lake Tahoe views. The mountain is located north of the Lake Tahoe rim, and hence much of the lake is hidden from view. Furthermore, your view is to the south, so if you try to photograph the lake, odds are you'll be shooting into the sun. Nevertheless, the hike is well worthwhile, and especially so if you're fond of wildflowers. On no other Tahoe Sierra peak can you see such a diverse array of alpine flora.

**Description**   The first 2½ miles of route are an easy climb up closed Road 17N01 to a saddle. We start up toward it through an open forest of lodgepole pines, which tap water in the fairly deep soil of weathered granodiorite our road is built upon. Soon, Lake Tahoe and Desolation Wilderness peaks rise over the ridges southsouthwest of us, while peaks of the Virginia Range—parent of the Comstock Lode—rise above the framed view through Ophir Creek canyon to the southeast. Along our easy walk, the pleasing aromas from sagebrush, mule ears and coyote mint complement our visual experience.

Where our road makes a noticeable curve right, about one mile from the trailhead, its road cut reveals an anatomical vignette of the volcanic rocks we now tread upon. These layered rocks are not horizontal, rather, they slope down

**Wildflower Plate 17. Alpine flowers.**
1 Dwarf cryptantha (white), 2 ballhead ipomopsis (white), 3 Coville's phlox (white to pink), 4 timberline phacelia (white to violet), 5 cushion stenotus (violet rays, which sometimes drop off, with golden disk), 6 cut-leaved daisy (same as 5), 7 Fremont's senecio (yellow), 8 alpine gold (yellow), 9 Davidson's penstemon (red-violet).

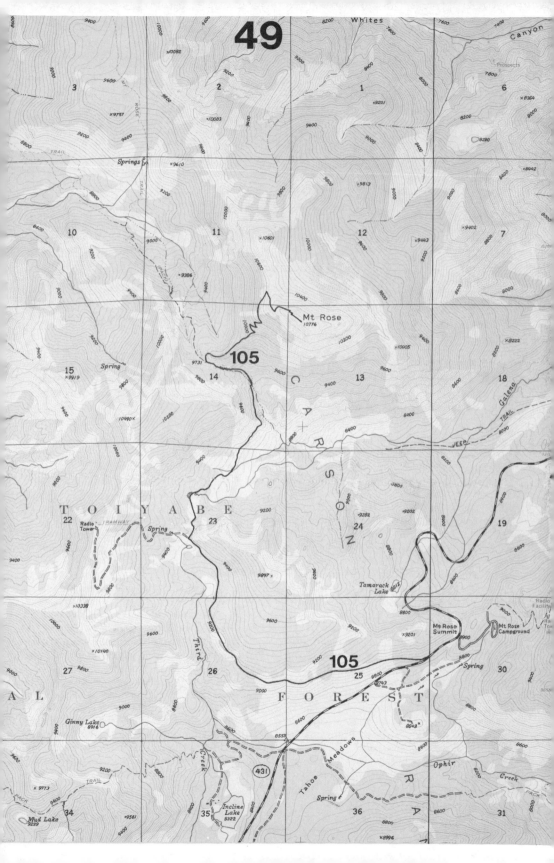

A summit view of the Lake Tahoe Basin. The Freel Peak massif (left) rises above the central Carson Range, while the Desolation Wilderness peaks (right) rise above the lake.

to the east. (Geologists say they *dip* eastward.) A short walk west therefore takes one across increasingly older rocks, probably of early Pliocene age (roughly 5 million years old). From east to west we pass through a purplish volcanic mudflow, then through a buff-colored tuff layer, which is the consolidated product of ash that was explosively ejected from a volcano. Next we pass a brown-gray andesite flow, which rests on weathered granodiorite of Cretaceous age (perhaps 90 million years old). Immediately beyond this small granodiorite exposure we encounter volcanic rocks again.

Our closed road soon curves northwest, leaving behind views of Lake Tahoe and the Incline Lake development, below us. A red-shafted flicker or a Clark's nutcracker might be seen flitting from tree to tree, the flicker in search of bark insects, the nutcracker in search of seeds from lodgepole and whitebark pines. After a ½-mile traverse we approach a meadow, then make a moderate ¼-mile climb to a minor divide that dams a snowmelt pond, which is the mating ground for hoards of treefrogs. Immediately beyond it, our road almost crests a saddle.

We leave this service road and fork north (right), immediately cross over the saddle, and on a minor road descend to a meadow. The road diagonals through it to some trees at its northwest end, and a trail cuts north right through it, to rejoin the road after having saved us a few steps. Near the reunion, a clump of corn lilies signals the presence of a roadside spring emanating from the porous, block-covered, andesitic soil. To the southeast we can look head-on at the fantastically eroded, deeply grooved cliff of easily eroded volcanic mudflows.

Our road descends northeast from the spring, first paralleling overhead powerlines, then bending more northward and crossing a flat with a small, curving ridge at the brink of an east-facing slope. You could camp under the lodgepoles on this flat, which has a convenient creek just north of it. Our road winds steeply down to it in about 200 yards and then terminates.

Continuing from the creek, which is our last source of reliable water, we go north on a trail that traverses a bouldery slope and crosses several seasonal creeklets. Wildflowers abound, particularly lupine, tall larkspur, paintbrush, coyote mint, mule ears, arrowhead senecio and angelica. Shrubs are represented by sagebrush, currant, elderberry and willow. To the east we can look well past the ski lifts and see distant desert ranges. Note the lateral moraines left by the glaciers that descended eastward down-canyon.

The trail climbs moderately northeast, and then at a ridge bends northwest and climbs moderately to steeply up the slope of a deeply incised gully. After gradually leveling off, the trail fords the gully's creek, which usually flows through late August, then it passes a small campsite near the ford and climbs along the northeast bank all the way up to a saddle on which stand some weather-beaten whitebark pines. Descending northwest from it is a faint trail that quickly becomes more prominent as it heads past impressive volcanic cliffs on its way down toward the headwaters of Bronco Creek, along which you can find good, isolated camp-sites. Before this trail fades into oblivion, it gives rise to two other trails that end at roads which are closed to the public.

The more popular Mt. Rose Trail turns northeast, and from about here onward you should watch for alpine vegetation (see this hike's Plate 17 plus Plates 11 and 14-16). Now is the time to put on a hat and/or dark glasses, for the intense ultraviolet radiation up here can cause minor injury to your eyes. Our trail cuts along the crest of a narrow ridge over toward the dark, volcanic hulk of Mt. Rose, from where we get a superb view northwest down the glaciated canyon of Bronco Creek and see large Stampede Reservoir flooding the valleys among some low hills north of Interstate 80. Our views continue to improve as we switchback up the west slope of Mt. Rose, the whitebark pines becoming fewer in number and shorter in stature. We soon see three reservoirs down-canyon from us which, left to right, are Prosser Creek, Boca and Stampede. On September 12, 1966, an earthquake of magnitude 5.4 cracked Prosser Creek Reservoir's dam, demonstrating to the world that the Tahoe area still has some active faults. Lake Tahoe, the Carson Range and Desolation Wilderness come into view to the south. North and just barely below us is an impressive group of granitic "pinnacles," which stand out boldly from the darker andesitic flows above. Along closely spaced vertical joints, or fractures, erosion has worked back, creating deep grooves between narrow arêtes, which have the appearance of pinnacles. Although not too steep, this

granitic complex should offer some interesting Class 3 to 5 climbing routes.

By the time we approach the ridgecrest, we're essentially above treeline, though you may see occasional whitebark pines, cropped by the wind to knee-height. We now see Donner Lake in the west and the unmistakable ribbon of highway called Interstate 80. From the crest an exciting new panorama opens before us in the northeast: Reno and the desert ranges beyond it. Now it's only a few minutes' walk to the summit register atop Mt. Rose.

From the summit we can look due south down the granitic backbone of the Carson Range, which separates the Lake Tahoe Basin from the Nevada desert. Structural geologists would classify the Tahoe basin as part of the westernmost border of the Basin and Range province, which extends across Nevada, for like the basins in that geologic province, the Lake Tahoe Basin is faulted down between two mountain blocks. Geochemists and geomorphologists, on the other hand, would classify the basin as part of the Sierra Nevada, for it is largely granitic rock, and its glaciated, adjacent crests are continuous with similar glaciated crests of the Sierra Nevada.

Botanists would classify the basin as Sierran, but the basin's east ranges have a good share of juniper, sagebrush, mountain mahogany and other high-desert species. As for Mt. Rose, its inhospitable summit supports only the most hardy species, cushion plants.

We see, near the southern part of the Carson Range, Jobs Peak, Jobs Sister and Freel Peak, these ranking fourth, second and first among the Tahoe Sierra's highest peaks. On their summits, as on Mt. Rose, the thickness of the air you breathe is a full one-third less than that at sea level. West of them stand several dark summits of the Carson Pass area. Continuing our clock-wise sweep, we spot pointed Pyramid Peak. Contrasting with it is the dark, metamorphic summit of Mt. Tallac. Turning toward the west-northwest, you'll see the Sierra Buttes, whose sawtooth crest, above Boca Reservoir, is a hefty 42½ miles away. But this distance pales in comparison to the Lassen Peak summit, located above the east shore of Stampede Reservoir and lying a whopping 115 miles away. However, don't expect to see it except on very clear days.

Half Moon Lake spreads out in a deep cirque below Jacks Peak (left) and Dicks Peak (right). View is from a stretch of trail between Gilmore Lake and Dicks Pass.

# Ch. 17        The Tahoe Rim Trail

**Introduction**   Yosemite has its High Sierra Camps loop trail, Mt. Hood has its Timberline loop trail, and hopefully Lake Tahoe will get its long overdue loop trail. In 1983 this proposed Tahoe Rim Trail had one continuous 58-mile segment, most of it being part of the Pacific Crest Trail. It also had many shorter segments of trails, roads and just plain cross-country, many of these segments interrupted by private property. By September 1986 about 25 miles had been added, built by volunteer labor under the leadership of the Tahoe Rim Trail Committee. This group, which heads the Tahoe Rim Trail Association, plans to have 17 miles of trail built in 1987. Until the trail is completed, only certain segments are described and are shown on maps. The distances given below are only approximations and will certainly be changed once the trail is built and its length measured. The completion date will be in 1990, with a lot of effort. Therefore, the author urges all hikers and equestrians interested in this project to get involved. Let's work together high on the Tahoe rim.

# 106        Tahoe Rim Trail

**Distances**   26 miles to Highway 207 near Daggett Pass, 44 miles to Highway 50 near Spooner Summit, 65 miles to Highway 431 in Tahoe Meadows, 82 miles to Highway 267 at Brockway Summit, 100 miles to Highway 89 in Tahoe City, 110 miles to Pacific Crest Trail near Ward Peak, 118 miles to Forest Route 3 at Barker Pass, 156 miles to Highway 50 at Echo Summit Ski Area, 173 miles to starting point on Highway 89 near Luther Pass.

**Low/High Elevations**   6230' in Tahoe City/ 9730' at saddle west of Freel Peak

**Classification**   Moderate

**Season**   Mid-July through early October

**Maps**   44, 45, 47, 48, 49, 24, 27, 30, 31, 34, 35, 36, 38, 40

**Trailhead**   (*Proposed* major trailheads are in parentheses.)
Grass Lake meadow (near Luther Pass): See the Hike 100 trailhead.
(Daggett Pass: Along Highway 207 about ½ mile east of pass, which is 3.1 miles east of Highway 50.)

(Spooner Summit: About 1 mile east of the Hike 105 trailhead.)
(Tahoe Meadows: About 1 mile southwest and below the Hike 106 trailhead.)
(Brockway Summit: At top of Highway 267, about 3¼ miles from Lake Tahoe's Highway 28.)
(Tahoe City: At northwest corner of Lake Tahoe.)
Barker Pass: See the Hike 47 trailhead.
Echo Lake: See the Hike 85 trailhead.
Echo Summit: See the Hike 89 trailhead.

**Introduction**   In his *Roughing It* Samuel Clemens (alias Mark Twain) describes his first visit to Lake Tahoe: "The lake burst upon us—a noble sheet of blue water lifted six thousand three hundred feet above the level of the sea, and walled in by a rim of snow-clad mountain peaks that towered aloft full three thousand feet higher still! It was a vast oval, and one would have to use up eighty or a hundred good miles in traveling around it. As it lay there with the shadows of the mountains brilliantly photographed upon its still surface I thought it must surely be the fairest picture the whole earth affords."

Today, the lake isn't the pristine beauty of Clemens' time, for high-rise casino complexes reflect in its not-so-clear water while haze permeates the basin's air. Still, the lake does command a lot of admiration. You can appreciate the lake's size and beauty by getting lofty, spectacular views of it from Mt. Tallac, Jobs Sister or Snow Valley Peak. Other peaks on or near the Tahoe Basin rim add to the variety of views. But if you'd hike from one rim viewpoint to the next, you'd have a panoply of views—and that is the idea behind the Tahoe Rim Trail.

Perhaps a number of people thought of this rational route, but no one did anything about it until 1980. Late in that year Glenn Hampton, Recreation Officer of the Lake Tahoe Basin Management Unit, proposed that a trail might be built around the rim of Lake Tahoe. He suggested that this could be accomplished by constructing new trails to connect with the existing National Forest and State Park trail systems. To test the appeal of the idea he introduced it to a cross-section of outdoor and recreation people: an outdoor writer, a college professor engaged in recreation research, members of outdoor clubs and trails conferences, and public officials on the local and state levels. The response from all was enthusiastic, leading him to further explore the idea in a report *The Rim Trail: A Hiking Adventure.*

In the introduction to this report he asks the reader to imagine a trail that winds completely around perhaps the most spectacular lake in the United States. As you hike along this lengthy loop trail you meander through areas rich in Basque history, where some of the West's first Basque sheepherders roamed through mountain meadows over 100 years ago with their flocks. You wade through waist-high grass and groves of aspens, through magnificent stands of red fir and Jeffrey pine, and stop to drink from cool mountain streams, sweet to the taste. The trail wanders through old Washoe Indian hunting grounds and along vanished game trails as well as trails made by early settlers fresh from obtaining their provisions from Nevada's first settlement at Genoa. You may wander high above mysterious places with names like Hell Hole, with its many small pools and water-saturated ground that shakes, rolls and sways. And often you are able to view the highest and largest subalpine lake in North America, Lake Tahoe. You travel through six counties, three National Forests, and two states, and two weeks later, you're back where you started.

**Building the Tahoe Rim Trail**   *You* can make the dream of the Tahoe Rim Trail come true by being a part of the trail's development. You can give money, tools or material, lend equipment or, more important, give a part of you. Contribute to the planning, construction and maintenance of one of the most spectacular trails in the United States. Gifts will be used for acquisition, planning and construction of the Tahoe Rim Trail, feeder trails, trailheads, educational interpretive centers, rest areas, overlooks, picnic areas and campsites.

Projects are carried forward by local fundraising committees made up of volunteers who serve because of their concern for the Tahoe Rim Trail Project. Volunteers will be needed to assist with trail planning, construction and maintenance, legal and administrative practices, publicity, fund raising and membership drives.

You or your friends can get involved in this all-volunteer (no tax dollars) project by assisting in the analysis and planning of a mile or more of a specific stretch of trail. The contribution might consist of historical, archeological, natural-features and wildlife research, engineering and design work and any plan preparation necessary.

If you don't have special design skills but have a strong back, you're even more desirable. It is one thing to design a trail and its sundry features, but it's another thing to get the necessary volunteers to build it. You can assist in the construction of, say, a mile or more of trail. The contribution might consist of shovel-and-pick work, construction of a small bridge or rock wall, operation of trail-building machinery, or donation of materials and/or equipment. You can construct a complete trailhead, a comfort station, a picnic site, a campsite, a trail marker, an interpretive sign, or a display case at an interpretive overlook. Finally, after the trail and its accouterments are completed, there comes the never-ending task of maintaining them, which too often is a thankless though necessary chore.

To get involved in the Tahoe Rim Trail Project write to the Tahoe Rim Trail Association, P.O. Box 10156, South Lake Tahoe, CA 95731.

**Description**   Once the Tahoe Rim Trail is completed it will be accessible from at least nine main trailheads and perhaps from two dozen other trailheads and feeder trails. Until then you should not attempt the entire route, although in 1983 a group of twenty-seven equestrians, under the leadership of George Cardinet, Jr., successfully circumnavigated the rim. Before doing so, they first scouted the route to see what they were up against in terms of terrain, logistics and private property.

For the backpacker, only the private property is the *real* problem, since the terrain is usually quite easy, even when cross-country, and one need not go out of the way to resupply. Starting counterclockwise from Highway 207's Daggett Pass environs, you can reach Tahoe City in 5-7 days, resupply there, reach Echo Lake Resort or Little Norway in 5 more days, resupply at either, then conclude your hike in another 4-5 days. But I must stress that at present private property will impair, if not totally defeat, your efforts. For about half of the route I have purposely not included the necessary maps since this would only encourage trespass, which in turn would anger owners. And this would only make it all the more difficult to secure rights-of-way across some essential properties.

In *The Rim Trail Environmental Assessment* (September 1982) the Forest Service depicts the route on maps, starting at the old Tucker Flat trailhead, along the north edge of Highway 89. This spot, about 1.8 miles west of Luther Pass, is above the west edge of a large, flat meadow which holds Grass Lake. The Forest Service shows the route in a counterclockwise direction and, to be consistent, the author will describe it (in summary form) in this direction.

It is interesting to note that in the environmental assessment the Forest Service had estimated the total length for the loop at 138.9 miles, while the author had estimated it at 173.2 miles. That's quite a discrepancy. When I had determined my route I followed the USFS route

as close as possible, but took into account two main considerations: avoid as much private property as possible, and restrict the trail's grade to a maximum of 10%. It's the latter consideration that greatly increases the length. And, if one designs the trail for a maximum of scenery, water and campsites, then the mileage becomes even longer—in the 180–190 mile range. Since the mileage of unbuilt trail segments is still uncertain at present (early 1987), I'm stating both the original USFS figures and my original figures.

### Highway 89 near Luther Pass
### to
### Highway 207 near Daggett Pass
### (18.6 miles/25.7 miles)

By late 1986 about 7 miles of this section had been built, taking the trail to within a mile of Armstrong Pass. From that pass the segment around Freel Peak will be hard to build, as may be the last 6.7 miles (author's estimate) before Daggett Pass. The route north to Star Lake may be completed in 1988, north to Daggett Pass in 1989. Hikes 100–104 describe the situation as it stood in late 1986.

### Highway 207 near Daggett Pass
### to
### Highway 50 near Spooner Summit
### (11.5 miles/18.1 miles)

A lot of private property lies along the first part of this section. The USFS route plows through it while the author's route deviates to the east, considerably increasing the section's length, but giving you views, water and public land. However, by late 1986 almost 8 miles had been constructed south from Spooner Summit, the trail dying out close to Genoa Peak.

**The Tahoe Rim trail passes by Lake Aloha and the Crystal Range**

## Highway 50 near Spooner Summit
### to
## Highway 431 in Tahoe Meadows
### (18.0 miles/21.5 miles)

Roughly the first 13½ miles will lie mostly or entirely in Lake Tahoe Nevada State Park, with perhaps a small part of this mileage on adjacent public land. Hike 105 describes an existing route to Marlette Lake, which lies near the center of the park, and one to Snow Valley Peak, which stands on adjacent USFS land. North from the park the route is partly across private land—that of Boise Cascade and the Redfield Estate. By late 1986 about 4 miles had been constructed north from Spooner Summit. By late 1987 the trail should reach Snow Valley Peak, if not Marlette Peak.

## Highway 431 in Tahoe Meadows
### to
## Highway 267 at Brockway Summit
### (11.0 miles/17.1 miles)

Existing roads and trails make this section already hikeable, but unfortunately most of the terrain is privately owned. Properly designed, the trail west to Mt. Baldy could be highly scenic, but beyond it views diminish drastically. A temporary route along existing roads and trails is largely viewless. You should avoid this section until a final route is built.

## Highway 267 at Brockway Summit
### to
## Highway 89 in Tahoe City
### (13.0 miles/17.8 miles)

In 1983 you could start southwest from Brockway Summit along Road 16N73, following it all the way to its end, after 12½ miles, from which you could descend another road, first ½ mile west then 2¾ miles southeast, to a junction with Highway 89 just west of the Tahoe City Y. Such a route, while simple to follow with the right set of maps and a trusty compass, is hardly imaginative. It may take a lot of imagination to produce a scenic route, for views—of Lake Tahoe or otherwise—will be few to nonexistent all the way west to Painted Rock. But from there southward a trail along the brink of the Truckee River canyon will offer fair views. By late 1986 several miles of trail had been built toward Painted Rock. To reach the trailhead, drive one block southwest (downstream) from the Tahoe City Y, turn right, and drive 0.2 mile up to the signed trailhead.

## Highway 89 in Tahoe City
### to
## Forest Route 3 at Barker Pass
### (14.3 miles/17.6 miles)

From the city the Tahoe Rim Trail will likely climb west up a ridge that caps the south wall of

**Mt. Rose and Slide Mountain, viewed from Snow Valley Peak**

In the Upper Truckee River basin, the route is currently along the floor, not the rim.

the Truckee River canyon. This ascent, about 2 miles to about the 6950-foot elevation, will surely offer you rewarding views down the canyon and across the lake. The trail then may skirt west through the Page Meadows flatlands, offering water and campsites, then climb to Ward Peak. This may be one of the last segments of trail to be built. However, in the meantime you can take an alternate route. Follow Hike 51's trailhead directions from Tahoe City south to the start of Trail 15N47, then follow the hike's route description up past Stanford Rock to Twin Peaks and the Pacific Crest Trail. On this trail you follow the first part of Hike 51 (in the reverse direction) south to Barker Pass.

### Forest Route 3 at Barker Pass
### to
### Highway 50 at Echo Summit Ski Area
### (36.7 miles/37.9 miles)

In 1983 the author's measured mileage for this section was 34.6 miles. His 37.9 miles goes on the assumption that a particularly distasteful stretch of PCT will be rerouted, this stretch and the proposed replacement both being mentioned in Hike 75. You follow that hike to Middle Velma Lake, then the reverse of the last half of Hike 66 to the northeast corner of Lake Aloha. (This stretch is also mentioned in the last parts of Hikes 77 and 83.) From the lake's corner you take Hike 87 in the reverse direction to Hike 85, and that hike in the reverse direction to the trailhead parking lot *above* Echo Lake Resort. From the east side of this lot the PCT traverses 1.3 miles over to Highway 50, which it crosses 100 yards east of Little Norway. Both Little Norway and Echo Lake Resort have a store and post office, the latter's store catering to backpackers. Across the highway the PCT climbs southeast, paralleling the highway 0.7 mile to the entrance to the Echo Summit Ski Area.

### Highway 50 at Echo Summit Ski Area
### to
### Highway 89 near Luther Pass
### (15.8 miles/17.5 miles)

Follow Hike 89, which goes 8.3 miles to Showers Lake, then follow the last 2.2 miles of Hike 93 in reverse, to a junction with the Meiss Meadow Trail. On it you head an easy, almost level 2.3 miles north to Round Lake's northeast corner, then backtrack 4.9 miles along Hike 92 to the Big Meadow trailhead, on Highway 89. Currently you have to head 1.7 miles up this highway to reach your starting point at the Tucker Flat trailhead. However, perhaps by 1987 or 1988 you'll hike up a new stretch of trail, which will parallel the highway at a respectable distance.

# Appendix. Scientific Names of the Wildflowers on Plates 1-17.

**Plate 1 (p. 38)**
1 Perideridia parishii
2 Ligusticum grayi
3 Angelica breweri
4 Heracleum lanatum
5 Sphenosciadium capitellatum
6 Cirsium foliosum
7 Antennaria rosea
8 Hieracium albiflorum
9 Chaenactis douglasii

**Plate 2 (p. 39)**
1 Eriogonum nudum
2 Polygonum bistortoides
3 Polygonum phytolaccaefolium
4 Lewisia nevadensis
5 Phlox diffusa
6 Pyrola picta
7 Zigadenus venenosus
8 Veratrum californicum
9 Habenaria dilatata

**Plate 3 (p. 40)**
1 Anaphalis margaritacea
2 Achillea lanulosa
3 Erigeron peregrinus
4 Thalictrum fendleri
5 Caltha howellii
6 Streptanthus tortuosus
7 Pedicularis semibarbata
8 Calochortus leichtlinii
9 Polygonum davisiae

**Plate 4 (p. 41)**
1 Arnica longifolia
2 Arnica mollis
3 Balsamorhiza sagittata
4 Chrysopsis breweri
5 Eriophyllum lanatum
6 Microseris nutans
7 Senecio integerrimus
8 Senecio triangularis
9 Wyethia mollis

**Plate 5 (p. 42)**
1 Sedum obtusatum
2 Brodiaea lutea
3 Potentilla glandulosa
4 Eriogonum umbellatum
5 Verbascum thapsus
6 Mimulus guttatus
7 Viola bakeri
8 Viola purpurea
9 Erysimum perenne

**Plate 6 (p. 43)**
1 Zauschneria californica
2 Castilleja applegatei
3 Penstemon newberryi
4 Lilium parvum
5 Aquilegia formosa
6 Ipomopsis aggregata

7 Cirsium andersonii
8 Pterospora andromedea
9 Sarcodes sanguinea

**Plate 7 (p. 44)**
1 Allium validum
2 Allium campanulatum
3 Agastache urticifolia
4 Dodecatheon alpinum
5 Geranium richardsonii
6 Pedicularis attollens
7 Sidalcea glaucescens
8 Calyptridium umbellatum
9 Epilobium angustifolium

**Plate 8 (p. 45)**
1 Lupinus arbustus
2 Phacelia hydrophylloides
3 Monardella odoratissima
4 Delphinium nuttallianum
5 Delphinium glaucum
6 Aconitum columbianum
7 Hackelia velutina
8 Penstemon heterodoxus
9 Penstemon rydbergii

**Plate 9 (p. 60)**
1 Adenocaulon bicolor
2 Montia perfoliata
3 Heuchera micrantha
4 Calochortus albus
5 Chlorogalum pomeridianum
6 Calochortus monophyllus
7 Iris hartwegii
8 Sedum spathulifolium
9 Dudleya cymosa

**Plate 10 (p. 61)**
1 Silene californica
2 Corallorhiza maculata
3 Pedicularis densiflora
4 Mimulus bifidus
5 Penstemon heterophyllus
6 Mimulus kelloggii
7 Brodiaea elegans
8 Dicentra formosa
9 Asclepias cordifolia

**Plate 11 (p. 85)**
1 Arenaria nuttallii
2 Raillardella argentea
3 Helianthella californica
4 Erythronium purpurascens
5 Chaenactis nevadensis
6 Penstemon deustus
7 Valeriana capitata
8 Primula suffrutescens
9 Polemonium pulcherrimum

**Plate 12 (p. 170)**
1 Viola macloskeyi
2 Apocynum pumilum
3 Phacelia heterophylla

4 Lotus oblongifolius
5 Madia gracilis
6 Solidago canadensis
7 Collomia grandiflora
8 Sidalcea oregana
9 Castilleja miniata

**Plate 13 (p. 205)**
1 Camassia leichtlinii
2 Smilacina racemosa
3 Calochortus minimus
4 Gentiana newberryi
5 Oxyria digyna
6 Hackelia micrantha
7 Pyrola secunda
8 Lupinus polyphyllus
9 Astragalus bolanderi

**Plate 14 (p. 227)**
1 Lewisia triphylla
2 Claytonia lanceolata
3 Dicentra uniflora
4 Saxifraga aprica
5 Ranunculus alismaefolius
6 Sedum rosea
7 Hieracium horridum
8 Crepis acuminata
9 Silene douglasii

**Plate 15 (p. 262)**
1 Senecio canus
2 Polemonium californicum
3 Castilleja nana
4 Mimulus tilingii
5 Mimulus lewisii
6 Penstemon speciosus
7 Linum lewisii
8 Frasera speciosa
9 Mertensia ciliata

**Plate 16 (p. 289)**
1 Phacelia hastata
2 Arabis rectissima
3 Arabis platysperma
4 Orthocarpus copelandii
5 Linanthus nuttallii
6 Leptodactylon pungens
7 Eriogonum incanum
8 Paeonia brownii
9 Lupinus breweri

**Plate 17 (p. 292)**
1 Cryptantha humilis
2 Ipomopsis congesta
3 Phlox covillei
4 Phacelia frigida
5 Haplopappus acaulis
6 Erigeron compositus
7 Senecio fremontii
8 Hulsea algida
9 Penstemon davidsonii

# Recommended Reading and Source Materials

## General

Crippen, J.R., and B.R. Pavelka. 1970. *The Lake Tahoe Basin, California-Nevada.* Washington: U.S. Geological Survey Water-Supply Paper 1972. 56 p.

Darvill, Fred T., Jr., M.D. 1985. *Mountaineering Medicine.* Berkeley: Wilderness Press. 68 p.

Gudde, Erwin G. 1969. *California Place Names.* Berkeley: University of California Press. 416 p.

Schmidt, Adolph, and George Cardinet, Jr. 1980. *California Riding Trails Directory and Manual.* Santa Rosa (CA 95404; 897 3rd Street): California State Horsemen's Association. 168 p.

Smith, Zane G., Jr., and Glenn Hampton. 1982. *The Tahoe Rim Trail Environmental Assessment.* South Lake Tahoe: U.S. Forest Service, Lake Tahoe Basin Management Unit. 75 p.

Winnett, Thomas. 1979. *Backpacking Basics.* Berkeley: Wilderness Press. 132 p.

## History

Egenhoff, Elisabeth L. 1949. *The Elephant As They Saw It; A Collection of Contemporary Pictures and Statements on Gold Mining in California.* Sacramento: California Division of Mines and Geology. 128 p.

Farquhar, Francis P. 1965. *History of the Sierra Nevada.* Berkeley: University of California Press. 262 p.

Jenkins, Olaf P. 1948. *The Mother Lode Country; Geologic Guidebook along Highway 49-Sierran Gold Belt.* Sacramento: California Division of Mines and Geology Bulletin 141. 164 p.

Reid, Robert L., ed. 1983. *A Treasury of the Sierra Nevada.* Berkeley: Wilderness Press. 363 p.

Scott, Edward B. 1957. *The Saga of Lake Tahoe.* Crystal Bay (Lake Tahoe), NV: Sierra-Tahoe Publishing Company. 519 p.

## Biology

Barbour, Michael G., and Jack Major, eds. 1977. *Terrestrial Vegetation of California.* New York: John Wiley & Sons. 1002 p.

Basey, Harold E. 1976. *Discovering Sierra Reptiles and Amphibians.* Yosemite: Yosemite Natural History Association. 50 p.

Crampton, Beecher. 1974. *Grasses in California* (California Natural History Guide 33). Berkeley: University of California Press. 178 p.

Gaines, David. 1977. *Birds of the Yosemite Sierra.* Oakland: Cal-Syl Press. 153 p.

Grater, Russell K., and Tom A. Blaue. 1978. *Discovering Sierra Mammals.* Yosemite: Yosemite Natural History Association. 174 p.

Grillos, Steve J. 1966. *Ferns and Fern Allies of California* (California Natural History Guide 16). Berkeley: University of California Press. 104 p.

Hartesveldt, Richard J., and others. 1975. *The Giant Sequoia of the Sierra Nevada.* Washington: National Park Service. 180 p.

Harvey, H. Thomas, and others. 1980. *Giant Sequoia Ecology: Fire and Reproduction.* Washington: National Park Service Scientific Monograph Series No. 12. 182 p.

Horn, Elizabeth L. 1976. *Wildflowers 3: The Sierra Nevada.* Beaverton, OR: Touchstone Press. 128 p.

Keator, Glenn. 1978. *Pacific Coast Berry Finder.* Berkeley: Nature Study Guild. 62 p.

Munz, Philip A., and David D. Keck. 1968. *A California Flora and Supplement.* Berkeley: University of California Press. 1681 and 224 p.

National Geographic Society. 1983. *Field Guide to the Birds of North America.* Washington: National Geographic Society. 464 p.

Niehaus, Theodore F., and Charles L. Ripper. 1976. *A Field Guide to Pacific States Wildflowers.* Boston: Houghton Mifflin. 432 p.

Peterson, P. Victor, and P. Victor Peterson, Jr. 1975. *Native Trees of the Sierra Nevada* (California Natural History Guide 36). Berkeley: University of California Press. 147 p.

Powell, Jerry A., and Charles L. Hogue. 1979. *California Insects* (California Natural History Guide 44). Berkeley: University of California Press. 388 p.

Smith, Gladys L. 1973. "A Flora of the Tahoe Basin and Neighboring Areas." *The Wasmann Journal of Biology,* v. 31, no. 1, p. 1-231.

———. 1983. "Supplement to a Flora of the Tahoe Basin and Neighboring Areas." *The Wasmann Journal of Biology,* v. 41, no. 1-2, p. 1-46.

Stebbins, Robert C. 1972. *Amphibians and Reptiles of California* (California Natural History Guide 31). Berkeley: University of California Press. 152 p.

Storer, Tracy I., and Robert L. Usinger. 1964. *Sierra Nevada Natural History.* Berkeley: University of California Press. 374 p.

Thomas, John Hunter, and Dennis R. Parnell. 1974. *Native Shrubs of the Sierra Nevada* (California Natural History Guide 34). Berkeley: University of California Press. 127 p.

Watts, Tom. 1973. *Pacific Coast Tree Finder.* Berkeley: Nature Study Guild. 62 p.

Weeden, Norman F. 1986. *A Sierra Nevada Flora.* Berkeley: Wilderness Press. 406 p.

Whitney, Stephen R. 1979. *A Sierra Club Naturalist's Guide to the Sierra Nevada.* San Francisco: Sierra Club Books. 526 p.

# Geology

American Geological Institute. 1976. *Dictionary of Geological Terms.* Garden City, NY: Anchor Books. 472 p.

Bailey, Edgar H., ed. 1966. *Geology of Northern California.* Sacramento: California Division of Mines and Geology Bulletin 190. 508 p.

Birkeland, Peter W. 1964. "Pleistocene Glaciation of the Northern Sierra Nevada, North of Lake Tahoe, California." *Journal of Geology,* v. 72, p. 810-825.

Burnett, John L., and Robert A. Matthews. 1971. "Geology of the Lake Tahoe Basin." *California Geology,* v. 24, no. 7, p. 119-130. Includes geologic map of the basin.

Clark, Lorin D. 1976. *Stratigraphy of the North Half of the Western Sierra Nevada Metamorphic Belt, California.* Washington: U.S. Geological Survey Professional Paper 923. 26 p. plus geologic map.

Curtis, Garniss H. 1954. "Mode of Origin of Pyroclastic Debris in the Mehrten Formation of the Sierra Nevada." *University of California Publications in Geological Sciences,* v. 29, p. 453-501.

Dalrymple, G. Brent. 1964. "Cenozoic Chronology of the Sierra Nevada, California." *University of California Publications in Geological Sciences,* v. 47, p. 1-41.

Dodge, F.C.W., and P.V. Fillo. 1967. *Mineral Resources of the Desolation Primitive Area of the Sierra Nevada, California.* Washington: U.S. Geological Survey Bulletin 1261-A. 27 p. plus geologic map.

Ernst, W.G., ed. 1981. *The Geotectonic Development of California.* Englewood Cliffs: Prentice-Hall. 685 p. (Note: This book's 71-page bibliography is extremely useful to those who wish to explore California's geologic history in depth.)

Evernden, Jack F., and Ronald W. Kistler. 1970. *Chronology of Emplacement of Mesozoic Batho-lithic Complexes in California and Western Nevada.* Washington: U.S. Geological Survey Professional Paper 623. 42 p.

Harwood, David S. 1983. "Stratigraphy of upper Paleozoic volcanic rocks and regional unconformities in part of the northern Sierra terrane, California." *Geological Society of American Bulletin,* v. 94, p. 413-422.

Kachadoorian, Reuben, and others. 1967. *Effects of the Truckee California, Earthquake of September 12, 1966.* Washington: U.S. Geological Survey Circular 537. 14 p.

Mathieson, Scott A. 1981. *Pre- and Post-Sangamon Glacial History of a Portion of Sierra and Plumas Counties, California.* Hayward: California State University, Geological Sciences Department. M.S. Thesis. 258 p.

Nokleberg, Warren J., and Ronald W. Kistler. 1980. *Paleozoic and Mesozoic Deformations in the Central Sierra Nevada, California.* Washington: U.S. Geological Survey Professional Paper 1145. 24 p.

Scott, Kevin M., and George C. Gravlee, Jr. 1968. *Flood Surge on the Rubicon River, California—Hydrology, Hydraulics and Boulder Transport.* Washington: U.S. Geological Survey Professional Paper 422-M. 40 p.

Yeend, Warren E. 1974. *Gold-Bearing Gravel of the Ancestral Yuba River, Sierra Nevada, California.* Washington: U.S. Geological Survey Professional Paper 772. 44 p.

# Geologic Maps

CDM = California Division of Mines and Geology, Sacramento

USGS = U.S. Geological Survey, Government Printing Office, Washington, D.C.

## Scale 1:250,000 (1° × 2°)

*Chico.* 1962. CDM.

*Sacramento.* 1981. CDM.

*Walker Lake.* 1982-83. USGS Map MF-1382.

## Scale 1:62,500

*Fallen Leaf Lake* 15' quadrangle. 2 maps plus 24-page text. 1983. CDM Map Sheet 32.

*Freel Peak* 15' quadrangle. 1983. USGS Map I-1424.

*Freel and Dardanelles Further Planning Areas.* 1981, 1983+. USGS Map MF-1322.

*Granite Chief Wilderness Study Area.* 1981-82. USGS Map MF-1273.

*Raymond Peak Roadless Area, east part.* 1982. 1983+. USGS Map MF-1365.

# Index

Numbers in italics indicate photographs.

# If you enjoyed this book . . .

Discover other **Wilderness Press** books and maps
on Northern California including:

*DESOLATION WILDERNESS AND THE SOUTH LAKE TAHOE
BASIN.* Jeffrey Schaffer

*LASSEN VOLCANIC NATIONAL PARK.* Jeffrey Schaffer

*MARBLE MOUNTAIN WILDERNESS.* David Green

*SIERRA NORTH.* Thomas Winnett and Jason Winnett

*THE TAHOE SIERRA.* Jeffrey Schaffer

*FORKS OF SALMON/SAWYERS BAR* Topographic Map

*UKONOM LAKE/SCOTT BAR* Topographic Map

*THE TRINITY ALPS.* Luther Linkhart

---

Ask for them from your dealer or write to us for a complete catalog.

**WILDERNESS PRESS**
**2440M Bancroft Way**
**Berkeley, CA 94704**

**(415) 843-8080**